North American Adult Educators:

*Phyllis M. Cunningham Archive
of Quintessential Autobiographies
for the Twenty-First Century*

Keith B. Armstrong, Lee W. Nabb, Anthony P. Czech, editors

Discovery Association Publishing House
Chicago, IL

www.discoveryap.com

FIRST EDITION

Copyright © 2007 by

Discovery Association Publishing House
Chicago, IL

Library of Congress Control Number 2006925488

Armstrong, Keith B., Nabb, Lee W., Czech, Anthony P., editors

North American Adult Educators: Phyllis M. Cunningham archive of quintessential autobiographies for the 21st century/ Keith B. Armstrong, Lee W. Nabb, Anthony P. Czech, editors.

p.cm.
ISBN 1-931967091

1. Autobiographies. 2. Adult Education Archive. 3. Phyllis M. Cunningham. 4. Ronald M. Cervero. 5. Sharan B. Merriam.

H|50 = 8%

Table of Contents

Preface
Keith B. Armstrong i

Tribute: Dr. Phyllis M. Cunningham, Spacemaker
Ronald M. Cervero and Sharan B. Merriam iii

Autoblographles
Phyllis M. Cunningham 1

James C. Alexander 11

Mary V. Alfred Ireland 17

Paul Armstrong 23

Ian Baptiste N.C. 29

Gretchen T. Bersch 33

Roger Boshier 39

Marcie Boucouvalas 47

Ralph G. Brockett 53

Shauna Butterwick Ireland 61

Paul Brian Carr 69

Ellen Carusetta 73

Mary Katherine Cooper 77

Patricia Cranton 83

Michael Day 87

M. Gail Derrick 93

Leona M. English Ireland 99

Benjamin Feinstein 103

Tara Fenwick 107

Barbara A. Frey 113

Jeanne d'Arc Gaudet 117

André P. Grace 123

Catherine A. Hansman Ireland, N.C. 129

Tom Heaney 135

John Arthur Henschke 139

Roger Hiemstra 145

Bob Hill 153

E. Paulette Isaac 159

Carol E. Kasworm 165

Kathleen P. King 171

Alan B. Knox..177

Randee Lipson Lawrence 183

Vivian W. Mott 189

Michael Newman 193

Larry Olds..199

Michael K. Ponton 207

Robert C. Preziosi 211

Esther Prins 217

B. Allan Quigley 223

John R. Rachal 229

Kathleen B. Rager 235

Jost Reischmann 241

Jennifer A. Sandlin 249

Vanessa Sheared 255

Joyce Stalker 259

Alan Thomas 267

Susan Ann Timm 275

Kristopher Wells..285

Stephen R. White..291

Miriam Zukas..299

Postscript

Lee W. Nabb..305

Preface

Keith B. Armstrong

Readers of *North American Adult Educators* will note how it exemplifies the potency of community activism and partnership, demonstrated by the fifty contributing adult educators. In the context of this book, partnerships are built on the authors' indomitable commitment to democratic work, and for decades to come, their concerted voices will certainly inform new generations of adult educators. As life is at least a journey through lessons over time, contributors' entries in this book are also a historical record that reveals the connection of their socially conscious *talk* to their *walk* among the students, communities, and programs to which they have given so greatly.

Against refreshing historical backlighting, these adult educators share their memoirs to afford us a glimpse into their personal meaning making—a singularly difficult task for anyone, even for the sake of producing an important adult educational legacy. Nonetheless, each author approached this daunting task in her or his own insightful fashion, thus offering the reader a genuine diversity of human experience and perspective.

From its outset, the mission of the Dr. Phyllis M. Cunningham Archive has been to create a forum where familiar adult educators may help others to understand the significant life experiences that led to their engagement with adult education. To that end, many adult educators have assisted the editors in developing an egalitarian forum in the book. For example, Dr. Susan Imel helped the editors expand diversity through suggesting a broad definition of adult education and encouraging a fresh appreciation for the inclusion of diverse responses. Similarly, when Dr. Quigley and associates of Canada argued in defense of the term "North American" rather than "American" they helped move the editors to greater clarity of thought and purpose and demonstrated anew that adult educators both teach and are taught for the purposes of self and social betterment.

The editors believe readers will feel personally enlightened by the autobiographies collected here, but because the archive is also the gathering of quintessential adult educators nominated by their colleagues and peers from across the United States and Canada, it is equally likely that the archive will enrich overarching notions about contemporary adult education, ones that may inspire progressive research perspectives. For example, the editors immediately recognized in the autobiographies a markedly liberal tenor and voice expressing generative themes of transformational potential.

That potential lends itself (and thus this book) to a plethora of courses in adult education: foundations and history of adult education courses as well as transformational leadership courses, among others. Although the editors avoid grouping the authors' works into preconceived themes and categories, the archive is also a valuable resource for courses seeking to interpret or analyze primary sources.

With the support of Dr. Phyllis M. Cunningham, *North American Adult Educators* is possibly the first contemporary adult education "workshop" of its kind, striving to provide new insights into the nuances of this dynamic field. Modeled after Dr. Cunningham's own presence in her communities and in the classroom, this anthology of adult educators' autobiographies demonstrates a similar tenacity for meaning making, contextual learning, and policy studies. In this volume, quintessential adult educators stand alongside Dr. Cunningham as tall and as strong as their commitment and labor have been hard and long. To these individuals the editors extend their deepest respect and appreciation.

Keith B. Armstrong

Tribute:
Dr. Phyllis M. Cunningham, Spacemaker

Ronald M. Cervero and Sharan B. Merriam

Although the motto on the website of the Dr. Phyllis M. Cunningham Archive is "Equality for All," that is entirely too abstract a concept to adequately define her contributions to the field of adult education and to the people whose lives she has shaped since Pioneer Girls. In her own words, Phyllis gives us a metaphor that is much more connected to the physical world: spacemaker. As she writes in the last sentence of her autobiography, "As a professor in my later years, to help build a program that opened up space for others is my greatest accomplishment, and in doing so, others have been encouraged to be spacemakers as well." It's not that Phyllis is dismissive of concepts, theories, and ideas; in fact, she's always giving her friends and students the writings of theorists unknown to us. It's that she believes these ideas have to be lived "on the ground," in praxis.

As Phyllis recounts in her life story, many of the themes that marked her work as a spacemaker at Northern Illinois University were evident in her previous work settings. She had been a spacemaker in Pioneer Girls to the young women who "came to think of themselves as more than 'just a housewife.'" She was a spacemaker at the Urban Life Center where youth who came to live at the house on the south side of Chicago had their consciousness raised (another spatial metaphor) so that they could see how to live out the professed ideals of Christianity.

Ron Recalls

I came to be part of Phyllis's spacemaking at the City Colleges of Chicago in 1974. She had graduated with her Ph.D. from the University of Chicago in 1973, and I started my degree that September. She came to Bill Griffith's adult education seminar in September 1974 to recruit a graduate student to work on an exciting new program, GED-TV. I could not possibly have known that having Phyllis as the first person I worked for in adult education would turn out to be a life-changing event. We made space together until 1976 when she took a faculty position at NIU and was given responsibility to direct the Adult Education Service Center at a City College campus on Chicago's south side. As always, her spacemaking was very practical as she hired a multiracial staff of women and men. She also was at the forefront of securing funding for community-based literacy programs where so much was happening in the Black and Latino communities. She gave me a chance to be a spacemaker too, when she left the Chicago Center to move full-time to the NIU campus in DeKalb. She was instrumental in hiring me as a faculty member at NIU in 1980 and appointed me to be director of the Chicago Service Center. Over the past 30 years, Phyllis has been a friend and mentor, always providing guidance and inspiration. I hope to be one of those people whom "she has encouraged to be a spacemaker."

Sharan Recalls

One year later, in 1981, I joined the faculty at NIU. At the time, Phyllis was the senior woman in the adult education professorate and she again made space for more women such as myself to join this male-dominated club. Making women in the professorate more visible was a prime motivation behind our competing for the editorship of the 1990 *Handbook of Adult and Continuing Education*. Not since the 1948 edition had there been a woman editor (Mary Ely), and most chapter authors were White males. Phyllis led the way in recruiting chapter authors for our handbook, women and people of color, who represented diverse perspectives.

Phyllis became a mentor to me in my process of becoming more conscious of opening up the field to more diverse and more critical perspectives. Through her I also became more conscious of the political nature of higher education. In my years at NIU from 1981 until 1985, Phyllis was chair of the Adult Education Program. I thoroughly enjoyed faculty meetings, which were laboratories in how to work the system for the benefit of all the stakeholders. I recall one occasion in which getting a particular curriculum change through the departmental curriculum committee was particularly important. Phyllis assigned each one of us to lobby a committee member. My project was to have lunch with a relatively new woman faculty member in Instructional Technology. We became close colleagues after that and we also got the curriculum change!

******

For all of the accolades that Phyllis justly receives as someone totally committed to social justice and "equality for all," she would be the first to warn you not to romanticize her or the work of spacemaking. Only in books, in the realm of ideas, is spacemaking easy. Real-world spacemaking is hard, full of contradictions. There have been many instances, as Phyllis recounts, that some of her best friends have criticized her work as "antirevolutionary and reformist." We have seen members of the Black and Latino communities involved in community-based literacy efforts criticize her efforts, even as she was allied with them in the struggle for equal treatment and funding. We have seen a colleague and friend dismiss her publicly at an Adult Education Research Conference for not "having the right political analysis," even as she applauded her heroic efforts in working in a Black community group's struggle for knowledge and power. Phyllis has always been clear that our lives and praxis as adult educators are full of contradictions. She has never let these contradictions get in the way of being a spacemaker. She sure has had lots of practice working through these contradictions in her own life and work, from her ideals of equality being nurtured in a "staunchly

Republican family" to working with a Christian organization (Pioneer Girls) that was rife with racism and sexism.

In the end, Phyllis would want us to focus on the question: Spacemaking for whom? And it's the practical answer to that question that makes Phyllis's legacy so enduring. She has been a spacemaker for people whose lives have been delimited by unequal relations of power and whose stories have been silenced. Phyllis's most profound legacy is that through her mentoring and support, "others have been encouraged to be spacemakers as well."

Phyllis M. Cunningham

Roots

My mother, in exasperation, called me John L. Lewis, and though I was fourteen at the time and living in rural upstate New York, I knew that was not a good name to be called in my highly conservative Republican clan. After all, I had been simply drawing attention to the fact that my foster brothers and sisters and I were being subjected to unfair working arrangements by my mother. This difference in political positioning continued between my parents and me and, though friendly, our starting points in politics became increasingly oppositional.

We had chosen to move to New York State from Maine in 1929. Almost immediately we were faced with the inability to make payments on our farm because of the Wall Street crash. We survived and kept our farm because of the social safety net laid down by the Roosevelt Administration, yet my parents were having none of that liberalism. Their ingrained New England individualism and reliance on local self-help could not stomach policies that paid farmers not to grow crops or paid federal milk subsidies to us so that New Yorkers could pay less to have a quart of milk delivered to their doors. To this day, my family remains staunchly within the embrace of the Republican Party.

My parents were also an important example to me. Their generosity in the midst of poverty, always there for friends and neighbors regardless of social class, provided me with my primary instinct for social justice and equality. Because of the accident of birth, I fell naturally into the role of becoming my father's "right-hand person." It was virtually effortless for me to see myself as an economic producing person, as there was no son. Like my father, I gravitated toward strong positions and speaking forthrightly with candor. My own sense of independence, interwoven with an ability to be frugal for the sake of principles, I attribute to my mother, who remained self-sufficient and active in her community until her final days in her nineties. It was a strong heritage.

I divide my story into two periods: my formation as an educator and my life as an adult educator.

My Formation as an Educator

College

Our family may have been economically poor but we were culturally rich. We knew who we were and our work and reputation defined us. I grew up in a time when women did not usually seek careers. In addition we lived in a community that could be classified as low to moderate income; only two from our high school class of seventeen went to college. As the youngest of six children, I was the first child my parents could afford to send to college. Luckily for me, the only college that would accept me at fifteen years of age was a small women's college of 400 students. Here we women were challenged intellectually with a strong liberal arts curriculum. After graduation, when I moved on to Western Reserve University, as a nursing student with four years of college, I was put in with medical students for the initial science courses. I became acclimated to a rigorous academic curriculum and it has never occurred to me to think that it should be different because I am a woman.

Pioneer Girls

In Cleveland, as a young nurse, I made the first decision that set me on the path toward becoming an adult educator. Though I had done a short stint of visiting nurse work in the center city of Cleveland that required a lot of health teaching, it was my volunteer work in my church with a girl's club called Pioneer Girls that proved to be pivotal. I participated in area leadership training functions, including summer camp counseling activities that quickly escalated into training adult leaders throughout the state as well as directing the Ohio camp during the summer.

Meanwhile, I acquired a master's degree in Administration and at the age of twenty-eight was offered a job directing a hospital. At the same time I was asked to become a field representative for Pioneer Girls. The choice was a momentous one—to stay within the medical profession or to take on a role which promised growth in helping to shape a fledgling organization's development in two ways: first, expansion internationally (my territory would include Ontario and Quebec in addition to Ohio and western New York), and second, helping the organization conceptualize its mission with regard to training of professional and volunteer leaders upon which it depended. At a less conscious level, a profound religious experience was impelling me to take seriously my own professional calling within an environment that I thought fostered taking moral and religious issues seriously.

I took the job with Pioneer Girls and was very successful with the first goal, creating training procedures for field staff, and in three years I was moved to California to inject new energy into an area on the verge of growth. Three years later, the organization tapped me to return to Chicago headquarters to build a National Leadership Training Center.

The years from 1965 to 1973 were among the most formative of my life. I was beginning to discover resources within the field of education that stretched my thinking. I had begun using Malcolm Knowles's book on group dynamics (*Introduction to Group Dynamics*, 1959) as leader training materials and was impacted by an intensive workshop at the National Training Center at Bethel, Maine. I had had no formal courses in education so I started classes at the University of Chicago where I discovered the existence of the field of adult education.

In 1965, I was living in suburbia consumed with my job of raising a half million dollars, planning a permanent adult training facility in the upper peninsula of Michigan, and developing an educational program for training the leaders. Concurrently, during the fall and winter quarters I took classes at the university, where antiwar and civil rights disturbances were brewing. I attended an integrated storefront church in Chicago that was a part of the West Side Christian Parish, an urban church ministry of a half dozen mainline denominations dedicated to maintaining a presence in the city even as their White congregations fled. It was this group of churches that hosted Martin Luther King when he brought his movement to Chicago, creating much political movement on the ground and in the street at this time. This contact with real politics caused the dissolution of the parish. As the denominations told us, "We are about preaching the gospel, not politics in the street." Only two of the churches survived; ours was one of them. We changed from being called Community Presbyterian to Faith Community Church and, now except for one or two Whites, it is a Black congregation. It was a lesson about the institutional church that has remained with me.

When King was assassinated, I don't think I will ever forget the images of Army Jeeps and National Guard troops patrolling our streets on the west side of Chicago where fires raged. I still belong to that congregation, where I have experienced more humanity and Christianity than in any other church I have attended.

University of Chicago

At the University of Chicago, several professors influenced me strongly: Marlene Dixon, who taught social theory, and Richard Flacks, who taught a sociology course on Marxism. They were activist scholars, and both were turned down for tenure despite strong student support for them. Flacks became a victim of violence when a political dissident who disagreed with his point of view entered his office one afternoon and viciously attacked the professor with a hammer, wounding Flacks seriously.

It was a time on campus when it was hard not to be involved, yet some still were not. When I attended a Students for a Democratic Society (SDS) convention in Chicago and was asked to declare my preference for political action, I favored the Worker/Student Alliance. In July of 1969, as Neil Armstrong took his historic walk on the moon, all twenty-plus of our university Adult Education students were huddled in a Hyde Park apartment developing a declaration to the faculty demanding student representation at faculty meetings and a cessation of certain activities considered to be parental rather than collegial. It was the zenith of collective antiestablishment activity for our Adult Education graduate students. But when it came to occupying the administration building, I was the only Adult Education student to go in. So the revolutionary spirit among Adult Education students was only so deep. After all, one could lose one's scholarship.

The university cultivated a deep culture of belonging among Adult Education students. The number of graduates was small and many were well known. At every national Adult Education Association, students and alumni were introduced and visited together over lunch. By the time we graduated, networks had been established, and we knew every graduate and what that person did. So when I walked into the Commission of Professors of Adult Education (CPAE) or the Adult Education Research Conference (AERC), I knew many of the leaders there and they knew me.

Lucy Ann Geiselman and Bill Griffith were the two Adult Education professors who influenced me most at Chicago. Lucy Ann, very intelligent, creative and a closet Marxist, was an exciting programmer in professional continuing education. She ran the Continuing Education Residential Center as well as holding faculty rank. As a Kellogg Residential intern, I worked directly with her my first year as a full-time graduate student. She understood participation as bottom-up education, and we did national welfare programming with maximum feasible participation of the poor and exploration of youth group structures (read "gangs") that became national exemplars.

She also helped each of the five interns do a major conference of their own. Mine, Double Exposure on Race, brought sixty of my White evangelical Christian colleagues to a conference about Blacks, with a Black curriculum, led by Blacks and located on the Black south side of Chicago. The White people were certainly out of their comfort zone. In 1967 this type of conference was unheard of, but Lucy Ann encouraged me to be bold and rely on the process. It was so successful that this type of participatory process-oriented education is what I later tried to provide for graduate students working with me.

Bill Griffith and I had a very strong relationship that may be related more to our common backgrounds than to our similarity in politics, where we were diametrically opposed. It was Bill who informed me that I was an adult educator and from whom I took my first formal course in adult education. We had much in common in terms of values of honesty, integrity, and respect for humanity. We enjoyed working together and complemented each other's talents. Bill and his family became my long-time friends; Bill remained my mentor until his death.

Cyril Houle was at the University of Chicago all the time I was there, but our personalities and politics kept us at a distance. However, when I became an instructor replacing Griffith while he was on a Fulbright, I fell under Mr. Houle's tutelage. He was most gracious and warm towards me, welcoming me to the faculty! "What courses do you want to teach?" "What do you think we should do about this student?" You would think I was a new tenured faculty member. I knew Mr. Houle was doing his professorial apprenticing duty as I knew all University of Chicago graduates should do. These acts are well remembered because they were a part of the culture.

The Urban Life Center

It was in this period that a group of White graduate students and colleagues in a variety of fields came together to develop what became the Urban Life Center. Blacks were mounting a strong critique about who was really the problem in America, and Lerone Bennett (1962) in particular had made it quite clear that he thought it was the Whites. Accordingly, as a committed group of alienated evangelicals, we decided to develop a non-traditional "free university semester in the city" for Christian college youth. We contacted about a dozen such colleges and arranged for them to pay us to provide upper division students experiential education on the south side of Chicago for fifteen hours of college credit awarded by the college.

The students lived communally in a building we rented and were engaged in prison, welfare, art, and community organizations as interns. Students were taught courses by us, by persons on welfare, and by community activists. We enrolled eight to ten students a semester and forty in the January term. Thirty-five years later the program still exists in a modified form. We were able to take these young adults, many of whom had never spoken with a person of color, and invite them to confront their perspective on race and class in relation to their faith. Again, I experienced the power of participatory education in expanding consciousness, as many of these students had transformative experiences and are today working in movements for social justice. I also learned the difficulty of establishing a nongovernmental organization (NGO) that would create permanent social space in civil society.

By this time, I had left Pioneer Girls over the issues of racism and sexism that were deeply embedded in the churches with which we were working. The curriculum of the Leadership Training Center turned out to be too socially relevant for the local churches as leaders returned home prepared to make changes. One of the most contentious issues was the integration of Blacks into the program. The Pioneer Girls Board acquiesced to conservative political pressure from its constituency and retrenched within narrower limits of vision compatible with the largely suburban middle-class population it served. Many of the top talented leaders left. I was angry, for I had given eleven productive years to the organization. Deeper than the anger was my disheartenment. I had hoped that the church, and religious institutions with which it was allied, had within it the moral and spiritual will to pursue a courageous course at a time when the young were asking for radical change. It gave me a valuable experience in understanding the power of structures in our society to perpetuate displaced institutional goals.

Life as an Adult Educator

In 1973 a new phase of my life began: I graduated from the University of Chicago, worked three years in the City Colleges of Chicago, and then became a professor at Northern Illinois University (NIU) where I stayed until I retired in 2002.

Open Learning and the Community

Upon graduation I tried getting a job in the professoriate and was turned down by Illinois, Syracuse, and British Columbia. I ended up taking a job at City Colleges of Chicago in what became the Center for Open Learning. It was here that the community college/public library consortium was developed utilizing video and audio cassettes and where GED/TV, using the Kentucky tapes, had its most successful national program. I see this program as another of my most valuable learning experiences as well as one of the more creative programs I have had a part in developing.

The public television station broadcast the tapes, the fifty-four library branches registered the students and developed reading support lists, and the college provided the study guides through the library and teacher support. We registered 3,255 students in the first round of the program. It was a win-win situation. The TV channel had such good market share they offered to repeat broadcasting free. Our students passed the GED test at the same rate as those students prepared by taking classes (Cervero, 1976). The librarians were happy as we had brought a whole new clientele into the libraries who had never been there before.

Again those adult educators who made GED/TV work were a "band of brothers" because of the intensity of the program and its pace. All were from the University of Chicago: Mike Havercamp, Peter Finestone, Ron Cervero, and I. There was such satisfaction on its completion because we had triumphed over the college bureaucracy, done an end run around the Springfield "no it won't work" vision, and had met with much success, at least in our minds. Yet some of my best friends criticized my work as antirevolutionary and reformist , a criticism that has recurred from time to time over the years.

The time spent in thinking about access to higher education was important in my own formation. The community college was growing at the rate of one per week; its function was not clear and we had just fought the battle over privilege and elitism in higher education. As dean of Open Learning, I was in a similar position with about ten other administrators of the Chicago higher learning institutions starting nontraditional programs to improve access. We had been thrust into positions that we knew little about or where there was very little known about these programs. Five of these administrators were University of Chicago graduates, so we organized ourselves into the Chicago Area Roundtable of Open Learning. We began trading information at monthly meetings and developing patterns of doing things.

I became very interested in the Black and Latino communities and it was at this time that my knowledge and familiarity with the community-based organizations deepened. Those years in the community college, and in striving to develop nontraditional adult programs, were important in giving me experience on the ground in an urban context, something much needed in my next position.

The Ohliger Experience

I had met John Ohliger when I was still a graduate student and he gave me a bibliography on compulsory adult education. That bibliography grew to five linear feet of bibliographies and other papers along with about thirty tapes of "Songs of Social Responsibility" from his radio program. By the time I got to Northern Illinois University, John had moved to Madison, renounced his tenured status at Ohio State University, given up his car for a bicycle, and was working for minimum wage two days a week so he could spend time living. What a man! His organization, Basic Choices, and his newsletter, *Second Thoughts,* were, in my opinion, some of the best material available for discussion in graduate programs. Here was someone who acted on his convictions. Several graduate students (Jack Ross, Dieter Bussigel, Mickey Hellyer, among others) formed a support group for Basic Choices and did what we could to promote the intellectual freedom and critical inquiry championed by John. John and I became the closest of friends, teaching together and organizing with others such organizations as the National Alliance for Voluntary Learning (NAVL). We promoted actions such as those taken at the Boston AEA meeting where we challenged the association on its values and put out a daily newspaper called *Navel Gazing*. We forced the Association to form a task force on voluntary learning (Cunningham & Hawking, 1981). The following year we worked with our friends to put the Association on trial for "negligence regarding the social action focus inherent in the mission and tradition of adult education" (Mezirow, 1991). John was a person to whom I could always turn and from whom I could get a straight answer. He was one of the very few intellectuals we have had in U.S. adult education. I was honored to be the "best person" at his marriage to Chris Wagner.

A Global Perspective

I had never been outside North America when I came to Northern Illinois University. I signed up to go to Finland/USSR with John Niemi in 1978 because I felt so naïve. The following year, Bob Smith and I took a group of students to England and Scotland. Following that trip I was selected to represent the AERC executive at the United Kingdom research association, Standing Conference on University Teaching and Research in the Education of Adults (SCUTREA). Two years later, I secured funding from the Kellogg Foundation to sponsor a trans-Atlantic dialogue between young British and North American professors sponsored by the CPAE/ SCUTREA. This was highly successful and relationships continue today, but I came to see its Eurocentric limitations. About this time, at a Participatory Research conference sponsored by the Lindeman Center, Budd Hall invited me to the International Council for Adult Education (ICAE) General Assembly that was meeting in Paris. This conference changed my Western view to a global view and introduced me to adult educators who have been highly influential in my life: people like Dame Nita Barrow and Pat Ellis (Barbados); Rajesh Tandon(India), Jaya Gajayanake (Sri Lanka); Elsa Lobos(Brazil), Paulo Wangoola (Uganda), Derek Mulenga(Zambia), and Larry Olds from Minnesota. I became active in the ICAE and in 1984 attended the two-week symposium in Shanghai that opened up Chinese adult education to the Western world.

At this time I was chair of our faculty and brought to them the possibility of further internationalizing our program through building on the China opportunity. The faculty was eager for experience abroad and agreed that we would be careful to frame any agreement so that it promoted two-way equal exchanges. And for the next ten years that is what we did. Over twenty-five Chinese students enrolled in our program, several Chinese visiting scholars came to our faculty for several months and seven NIU professors taught for one month in Shanghai. Three NIU books were translated into Chinese.

China: Lessons from Practice was published as a Jossey-Bass source book (Wang et al., 1988) to bring Chinese thought to the West, and three binational research conferences were held. The Chinese experience was a large part of what became a wide recruitment of international students from the global South from twenty-seven different countries. Between 1990 and 2000 there were over 200 doctoral students in the program and eleven percent of them were international students of color (Cunningham& Shim, 2001). Much, if not most, of the recruitment came through contacts with the IACE or with contacts from Wheaton College's (Illinois) Billy Graham Institute missions programs that brought a number of persons from Africa and the Caribbean into their Master of Communications programs. Those with an interest in education for social change were naturally attracted to our doctoral program.

The Chicago/Conscientization Experience

One can trace the development of my critical consciousness from its early beginnings, but it was not until I became involved with Budd Hall, John Ohliger, and especially Marcelo Zwierzynski that I was able to conceptualize and name the oppression that I had seen and experienced many times in my life. Marcelo, an Argentinean political refugee, worked with Tom Heany in the NIU Chicago Lindeman Center. He introduced us to social theorists from both Europe and Latin America. We taught classes together, wrote grants for community-based organizations, and worked with community activists in the areas of popular education, popular culture, and participatory research. There was a group of about two dozen students committed to the concepts of educating for social change.

They demanded changes in the curriculum to neutralize the psychologizing hegemony that permeated it. We were also able to democratize our recruitment and admissions process. We brought the community into the campus and the campus into the community by developing community-based research projects and linking our research and intellectual activity with popular social movement activity.

We could not have done this without our base in Chicago. It was fortuitous that in 1975, Bob Mason made the decision to apply for both Region 1 & 2 Service Centers for training teachers in ABE, GED, and ESL. He was also sensitive to the African Americans in Chicago when they insisted that a center be placed in the city. So for ten years NIU had a funded campus in the very center of Chicago with connections to all the community colleges and public school districts receiving federal adult education funds. Utilizing this base we were able to reach out to community-based programs that did literacy and popular education as well. The Lindeman Center, based in our University Extension, was also operating in Chicago. Collectively we became a force in developing a progressive training program, a popular education curriculum, and an Africentric curriculum.

Then with a new department chair, Glenn Smith, we developed a cohort program that favored recruitment of people of color. In fact, between 1991 and 2000 we graduated 210 doctoral students compared to 130 the previous fifteen years. The percentage of students of color rose from 14% to 42%, with 22% of that latter group being African Americans from the United States (Cunningham & Shim, 2001). NIU began to be cited in national statistics for graduating a large number of African American doctorates. We launched African/Latino research conferences and listed over a dozen of our graduates of color as adult education professors. This was the work of another band that had a profound effect on me: Donna Amstutz, Ian Baptiste, Scipio A.J. Colin III, Bernice Chapman, Suzanne Davenport, Elio DeAruda, Phyllis Ham Garth, Derek Mulenga, Joye Knight, Elizabeth Peterson, Jack Ross, Javier Saracho, Margaret Shaw, Vanessa Sheared, Fred Shied, and Gabriella Stroschen.

Summary

As I think back over my life, I can follow the threads of influence woven first of a mother who embraced friends, neighbors, and foster children regardless of social class or economic circumstances, providing me with my primary instinct for social justice, and second, a father who treated me as a person who would contribute in my own right, fostering my independence and sense of empowerment.

Spending my formative years in a women's college, whose motto was "The first women's college to give a degree equal to that of a man," and then on to nursing, a women's field at that time, I escaped much of the male hegemonic forces experienced by other women my age. I do know that behavior which I define as normal is seen by others as strange for a woman. I have never let this bother me for I feel I have a clear head on the equity issue.

The adult education experiences that I cherish most are those that have brought about some social justice or changed a person in such a way that they are working to bring about social justice. I think of the many women in Pioneer Girls who came to think of themselves as more than "just a housewife." I know that some of them have become agents of change in intransigent local churches. The same can be said of those idealistic youth who studied at the Urban Life Center and opened up their consciousness from the construction of a rigid White evangelicalism that only honors "preaching, not politics." As a professor in my later years, to help build a program that opened up space for others is my greatest accomplishment, and in doing so, others have been encouraged to be spacemakers as well.

References

Bennett, L. (1962). *Before the Mayflower*. Chicago: Johnson Publishing Company.

Cervero, R. (October 1, 1976). GED/TV Final Report. Unpublished report, City Colleges of Chicago.

Cunningham, P., & Hawking, J. (1981). "Review of research on mandatory continuing education." AEA USA Task Force Report on Voluntary Learning. Washington, D.C.: Adult Education Association, 13 21.

Cunningham, P. & Shim, H.S. (2001). "Linking the global South with the South in the NIU Adult Education Graduate Program." Proceedings: African and Latino (a) American Adult Education Research Conference, Chicago, April 21.

Knowles, M. (1959). *Introduction to Group Dynamics*. Chicago: Association Press.

Mezirow, J. (November 15, 1991). Faded visions and fresh commitments: Adult education's social goals. A policy paper prepared for the AAACE <http://www.nl.edu/academics/cas/ace/resources/jackmezirow_insight.cfm>. Retrieved 12/15/05.

Wang, M., et al. (Chinese Eds.) (1988). *China: Lessons from practice*. New Directions in Continuing Education, No. 37. City: Jossey-Bass.

James C. Alexander, Ph.D.
A Charmed Life: An Autobiography

I sometimes think that I have lived a truly charmed life. This is, of course, not to say that there have not been a number of twists and turns in the road that have often thrown me for a loop. I think you will see what I mean on both counts!

A naturally inquisitive child, it seems as if I was always seeking to know or discover something. When quite young, my thoughts often tended towards the philosophical and metaphysical. I also dreamt very big. If you had asked me early on what career I would choose for myself, I could have answered without a moment's hesitation. I wanted to be an astronaut. I had visions of exploring the uncharted regions of space.

Neither Mom nor Dad finished high school. I was my father's last child, a child of his second marriage. Dad was born in 1909; I in 1956. My mom's poor health had seriously detracted from her plans of finishing school. Family problems derailed Dad. When Dad had to go on Social Security in the mid-sixties due to severe respiratory difficulties, it hit our family hard. We had never really arrived at the status of "middle class," and Dad's disability pushed us even further into poverty.

I was around eight or nine years old when my little "problem" began. First, it was just a few annoying noises. It progressed to head jerks, spastic movements, echoing what others or I said—either aloud or subvocally. The year was 1965. No one really understood my behavior. The school dealt with the problem through the judicious application of yelling and punishment. (I often found myself on the business end of the principal's paddle!). Kids mimicked me, and I became a laughing stock. I covered by becoming the class clown. As a teacher of small children and later as a teacher of preservice educators, I have frequently noted that children, for all of their charms, can be terribly cruel. I also note that we may not understand *why* folks act in annoying ways. Simply put, we are quick to judge.

We all must cope in some way. As an adolescent in the late sixties and early seventies, I coped by identifying with the emerging hippy scene in Kansas City. At age fifteen, I completely quit school and moved out of my parents' house. My parents seemed powerless to stop me. Where did I go? Early on, I slept wherever. That often meant such arrangements as sleeping in the display window in one of the shops in the "hippy part of town." I was in the full hippy swing of things with all that entailed. As to my oddities, well, no one seemed to care in this environment.

There is a very real tendency in our day to assign blame to one's parents for everything and anything. This I cannot and will not do. They did the best they could with a child who had become what some might call incorrigible. I certainly do not blame them. Since that time, I have come to view my parents as two folks severely challenged by the circumstances of life. Coping with health and money problems certainly did not help the situation. After all, had anyone taught them what to anticipate? In the final analysis, we each must take life as it comes along. Sometimes it deals us a hand we would rather not take. I currently teach a course at the college dealing with family dynamics. It is so easy to be judgmental. I think it often boils down to the luck of the draw. Parenting education can help. However, kids and parents will always be unpredictable variables when it comes to stating rules for what constitutes good parenting. In addition, at least in the case of my dad, he was playing out the life of someone with a good deal of childhood baggage. Being deserted by his own father, little modeling was available when it came to raising children.

At any rate, a very significant event took place in my life just before I turned seventeen. I encountered the Jesus Movement and had a radical reorientation of views and values. Since that time some thirty years ago, I have often wavered in my faith. At times I have doubted everything I believe. Still, the basic reorientation (perhaps *conversion* is a better word) took. The change remains. It was from this impetus in my life that several changes took place.

First, a friend in the faith recognized that I had a questioning mind. He suggested I could find the answers I sought through formal education. Therefore, I headed for the Kansas City Plaza Library and enrolled in GED classes. It was pretty depressing and embarrassing at my original testing. I seemed to be right where I had left off at school—cruising at a beginning high school level.

However, of course, I was not really the same. I was a changed individual. I was now motivated to learn in a school setting. I wanted more from my life. I wanted answers, and I wanted to discover the questions. It was not easy. I would have given up, if my girlfriend, a freshman in college, had not tutored me. I quit work and went at it all day. In a few months, I passed the GED test.

The other major event was my decision to enroll in college. I started at the community college; I really did need the help offered there. However, after two years, I transferred to Central Missouri State University and finished my course work in elementary education. I student taught first grade. That was pretty unheard of when it came to men in that day. Once again, motivation pushed me on. I came to see that the seeds of my failure were deep rooted in and nurtured when I was a little boy. Seeds of self-doubt were planted. Now I wanted to be a role model. I wanted to help steer others away from that path.

An even better event occurred on 26 February 1977 at 2 p.m., when Ms. Irene Mary Schaeperkoetter became my wife. She was everything I was not: salutatorian of her high school class and college magna cum laude. (I rather graduated mighty darn lucky!) She was brilliant. Her brilliance made me shine. She was (is) the light of my life. Her belief in me helped me learn to believe in myself.

What about the noises, jerks, echoes, and all of that? In 1978, we discovered that I suffer from Tourette's syndrome. That diagnosis might have only served as a kick in the teeth to some. It was a bit of good news for me. Now many pieces of the puzzle fell into place. Also, treatment options (complete with rather unpleasant side effects) were available.

From there, it was on to my early years as an elementary school teacher. After earning a master's degree in reading education and learning disabilities, I became a teacher of those much as I was in my early school years. Some were severely disabled. Others were just *severely labeled*. I could reach out and help because I understood. It takes an understanding teacher to reach those others have written off. I had one thing going for me in this regard: I had a keen sense of who I was and where I came from. It informed all that I did. I knew that nothing succeeds like success.

In 1981, I enrolled in a graduate program in theology. During my seminary years, I ministered at a small church on the eastern plains of Colorado. Upon finishing seminary, I moved on to a full-time parish in Virginia. In the hills of Appalachia, my wife began her work as an adult educator amid much poverty, illiteracy, and hopelessness. She was well aware of my story. I think in some ways it spurred her on. It was also in Virginia that I set up a church-based tutoring program for the local kids who were falling behind and were likely to end up like the adults Irene was working with each day.

Then? Back to teaching! Ever since that time, my life has seemed a patchwork of ministry and teaching, never being able to absent myself very far from either. It often seems to me that one partakes of the essential nature of the other. As I write, I serve as both a professor of education and a minister at a small congregation near the college where I teach. I graduated from seminary as a merit scholar. In all my subsequent theological studies and in my doctoral program in education, I excelled. I think that Irene, the Good Lord, and those around me served as healers.

The lessons of my life burn in my heart every day. When I was working as an adult educator for the Missouri Department of Corrections, I saw myself in my students daily and heard a voice from somewhere within, *"Don't sell them short! Things aren't always what they appear!"* In my work as a professor and a minister (which is certainly work of an educational nature), I am compelled to look beyond what the eyes can see. In the story of the anointing of King David in the Old Testament text, we are told, "God doesn't look at outward appearances. God looks at the heart." I am glad that some folks did not look at the *surface value* of James Alexander. They looked deeper and saw potential to which I was completely oblivious. My best friend, Irene, reminds me every day that people respond to being loved, accepted, and expected to succeed. I know that I needed a hand to get out. I did not need a handout. I needed hands to show me the way out. Everyone needs at least one person who will believe in him or her. Can you and I be that person for others?

I spent a brief time working as an adult educator in the Department of Corrections. I was always astonished at the intelligence and quick grasp of the material exhibited on a daily basis by my students. Since then, I have often wondered if there is not some way for society to reach out and captivate the bright young men I worked with rather than incarcerate them at taxpayers' expense—frequently starting a pattern of repeated incarceration. Thinking of nothing but economics, it would surely be in the best interest of society to spend large sums of money designing systems to address at-risk youth before they are tried, convicted, and incarcerated, often only to refine the tools of criminality.

It seems to me that the answer is not to be found in reducing social services and building more jails. The answers lie in a societal adjustment. Maybe the place to begin is by building on the words of the One who taught us to *love our neighbors as ourselves*. That injunction is found repeatedly in all of the great religions of the world. Perhaps it is time for us to listen.

I cringe when I read news concerning the reduction in actual percent of funds spent to offer Pell Grants to the poor. It comes down to this for me: I am a product of these so-called *failed* social programs. Some would say that society made a good investment in helping me and others like me pay for higher education. It saved me from a life of aimlessness and allowed me to contribute to society.

In 1991, I returned to public school and taught in inner city Kansas City. Frequently the inner city community is sorely misunderstood and misrepresented in American thinking. Parents of inner city children care deeply about the future of their children. There is a cycle of poverty and lack of formal education that is perpetuated by default. Like any default "program," a knowledgeable individual can change the way that the "software" works. I do not know much about computers. I turn mine on and hope it works. I find myself at the mercy of the thing. My oldest son is a computer science graduate and a systems analyst for a good-sized software design company. He does not accept the default settings that come on his computer as he removes it from the box. He sets things up the way he wants them to function.

I do not deny teaching in the inner city can be pretty draining. After moving from the neighborhood as a child, I had an extremely difficult experience teaching in that environment. After I time, I left. I had given all that I had to give at the time. I thought it would be a cakewalk, my positive hopes seeing me through. I felt a bit like someone deserting a sinking ship. A crucial need I detected early on was the need for colleagues who are interested in education more than commiseration. Inner city teaching is not for everyone. There should be no guilt associated with the realization that one's gifts are better used somewhere else. On the other hand, we must not leave the inner city to the forces of mediocrity. The inner city folks deserve better. A multifaceted approach is needed, combining reforms in early childhood, elementary, secondary, adult, and higher education. Educators must learn to see the other as a part of the same team.

There is a need for a massive invasion of the little corners of society that we would rather not think about. What is needed is a highly trained committed corps of teachers, social workers, ministers and ministries, and volunteers to work to change societal structures and offer a way out for those who will take it. We need to refuse the default way things tend to go. The answer is likely not in more tests, as offered in *No Child Left Behind*. I have written elsewhere about the need to restructure our educational system to adopt a mastery approach, over and against a competitive, high-stakes testing approach (Alexander, 2002).

I was awarded a Ph.D. in elementary education, reading, and educational psychology in 1995. With that, a new chapter began in my life. I had developed a rather severe case of rheumatoid arthritis, and we all (family, friends, physicians) wondered if I might need to stop working altogether. Thank heavens, as well as good medical care, patient employers, and an understanding family, sixteen years after the fact, I am still quite actively employed. I was always interested in working on a doctorate and teaching college or seminary. The arthritis became the impetus for moving ahead. It seemed as if it might easily become a "now or never" thing. The decision after the decision was which route to travel?

I had a very keen interest in theology and pastoral studies. I had also had some good fortune publishing in that arena. On the other hand, I had a true sense of call to make a difference in the lives of adults and children. I experienced mixed feelings concerning the decision I needed to make. Then, it was clear, education won the day. I matriculated at the University of Arkansas. Since that time, I have been able continue seminary studies, although another seminary degree does not seem to be in my future (I might be fooled!).

I worked as a graduate assistant teaching developmental reading to freshmen. Once again, I was glad that I could relate to the need of being offered a helping hand. I also think that I have a good handle on what developmental students need to gain from developmental studies. Perhaps the greatest need of developmental education students is self-esteem. Most are not thrilled at the prospect of placement in developmental courses (Let us face it; most are there by placement, not choice.) The issue of self-esteem, and sometimes a bit of anger needs addressing. It is here that relationships become all important. Developmental education students, even college students, regardless of age, seek a sense of belonging. In Glasser's choice theory (1986, 1992), it is stressed that we each need at least one person to believe in us and accept us for who we are. We need to be *liked* and *respected* if we are to advance as humans and approach our potential.

In that respect, my work and calling as a minister and a teacher fully intersect. Those who know me can vouch for my tremendous interest in neuroscience and what we might be able to learn about teaching from our study of brain function. I see how some practices clearly follow from what we know about the brain. I also can see how other practices appear to be contraindicated. Still, as many writers have pointed out, we have to watch ourselves and not claim more than we can deliver when it comes to brain-based learning and teaching.

Even though I am fascinated and consider myself a bit of a number cruncher when it comes to research, I am not without concern in this arena. I see a tendency towards *reductionism*. As we learn more about how connections are formed in the brain when learning takes place, and as we press always onward (and rightly so) to seek a scientifically based pedagogy, we have to remember that people are spiritual beings. In this, I am not talking about religion—at least not as commonly understood. I am talking about something much more universal than any religion in particular, and a phenomenon that does not depend on the idea of religion as a construct.

I am speaking of the spiritual nature of people, the meaning with which we endow every aspect of our lives. Life is always giving us messages about who we are, the ultimate meaning of things, our worth, and the importance of others. In this regard, education is a spiritual endeavor. It is people work.

Continuing my work as an educator and a minister, I constantly rediscover everyone has a part of their being crying out to be valued. It is in valuing that we gain the right to teach. It is in valuing that developmental students as well as adult basic education and high school equivalency students discern the worth of the long (often very long) journey they are starting. The same is true of the education majors and psychology majors I deal with on a regular basis. When they sense that I truly care, they also care about things.

They care about their work in and out of class. They care about the material we are dealing with. They care about how what they do or will do affects others: family, friends, and future students. I regularly begin my college classes by saying that we are here to study the reading process or the information-processing model or children's literature. Then, I usually tell them that I am also here to teach them about life. I do not mean preaching on "life." I mean that in everything I do, I hope there is so much respect and empathy and challenge and painful reality and hope that they know what it means to teach from a fully human perspective.

Does all of this sound idealistic? I still teach developmental college literacy from time to time. I still go out in the schools and teach kids a few hours a week. I still come on Sunday morning to hold before my small congregation the example of the Great Teacher. Do I succeed in living up to the picture painted here? Hardly! Nevertheless, it is and must be a very real goal.

I started by saying that I have lived a charmed life. Indeed, I have! I came from an unlikely environment, yet I have degrees in education and theology and more studies besides. In short, I have an education that most folks dream about. I am a teacher and a minister. I can claim a modestly successful publication record. I have managed to deal with two serious illnesses. More friends have surrounded me than I can count and a wife and sons who believe in me. All of this, every bit, has *conspired* to make an educator of me. Moreover, from that, idealistic, mystic, and otherworldly as it sounds, I have learned an important lesson. If the nature of love is faith and hope, the source, the route, and the destination of education for me will always be *love*.

References

Alexander, J. (2002). For what purpose: Some thoughts about grading. *New Horizons in Adult Education*, 16:1. Retrieved 23 August 2005 at http://www.nova.edu/~aed/horizons/volume16no1.pdf.

Glasser, W. (1986). *Control theory in the classroom*. New York: Harper.

Glasser, W. (1992). *The quality school: Managing students without coercion*. New York: Harper.

Mary V. Alfred

My career as an adult educator is what some would call a "chance career" as, I believe, most careers happen. A career that began as an elementary school teacher progressed through elementary administration (though briefly), secondary school teaching, community college teaching and program administration, and has culminated in university adult education. This journey has led me from one end of the spectrum—elementary education—to the other—university adult education. As I reflect on my journey of lifelong learning and teaching, several pivotal moments stand out. However, because of the limitations of this paper, I will highlight just a few, but that in no way diminishes the totality of the life experience.

The Beginnings of a Life Career

My life began on the small Anglophone Caribbean Island of St. Lucia, where I spent the first 24 years before immigrating to the US. My parents welcomed me into the world as the second of three daughters, and although there were five of us in our immediate household—my parents, my sisters, and me—the extended members, drawn from family, church, and community, created a network of supporters who collectively contributed to my development to adulthood.

Born to parents who were sharecroppers, I became aware of the concepts of marginality and outsider-within very early in my development. Although I had not acquired the language to name my location, it was obvious that color and class created social divisions among the populace. While the inhabitants of the island are predominantly of African descent, the varying shades of Blackness, coupled with social class status, created a multi-class culture. Our dark skin tones, together with our status as share croppers, placed us within the lower-class community. Having been cast in the lower-class culture was not problematic for us as certain legacies came with it. Our network of communities instilled in us certain legacies, for example, financial responsibility, pride, honor, honesty, determination, hard work, excellence, and a responsibility for community uplift. For example, in discussions of money in the home, one of my grandmother's favorite sayings was, "Money does not make a man [woman]; it's all about your good name and your honor." Similar life scripts were constant echoes, and they later became road maps that helped guide me through adulthood.

Although racial discrimination was not a factor in our being, color was a determinant in our social location. Senior (1991) speaks to the significance of color in Caribbean identities. She notes, "Notions of color and status are underscored by the perception that the educational system itself still reinforces the European or white bias as the ideal and, up to recently, implicitly or explicitly denigrated the black or African." This denigration of the Black or the African in West Indian communities is the direct result of the legacy of slavery that denigrated Blacks and privileged Whites and a colonial system of education that continued to perpetuate White superiority. After slavery and long after the colonial master had physically exited the islands, their legacies lived on as families continued to transmit the values of the society that emphasized color as a predictor of social class. According to Senior (1991), "The family has been regarded as the main agent for transmitting the values of a society regarding skin color and racial values, especially the mother, since it is the Caribbean female who has in the past carried the burden of moving the family to higher status" (p. 27). As a result of the value West Indians hold for color as a symbol of social status, parents often encouraged their children to marry "light" for the sake of their offspring, meaning that the lighter the color, the less likely one would be subject to color discrimination in schools and the wider society.

Fortunately, education was a stronger predictor of social location than color, and as a result, one of the recurring messages during the early development period was to get an education. My father's constant message to us was, "Get an education if you want to be somebody. Learn the books so you don't have to end up working on somebody's land like me and your mother. Learn the books and get your own land." That message was even more important to those of us with very dark complexion. As Senior (1991) reminds us, "Since education is perceived as an important contributor to upward social mobility, parents of lower socio-economic groups have high aspirations for their children to raise themselves out of poverty-stricken conditions by success in this sphere" (1991, p. 27). My father, a tall man at six foot four inches, functionally illiterate and very proud, was one of those parents whom Senior speaks of. His life's goal was to educate his three daughters so we could rise above color and class discrimination inherent in West Indian societies.

Upon graduating high school in rural St. Lucia at the age of 16, the options available for a professional career were teaching or nursing. My father made the choice for me when he went to our parish priest and requested a teaching position for me. At the time, the public schools were under the jurisdiction of the Catholic Diocese in partnership with the Ministry of Education. After two years of teaching as a probationary assistant teacher, I was awarded a scholarship from the Ministry of Education to attend teachers' college. As one of the three youngest students to attend teachers' college at the time, I graduated at age 20 and became a school principal at 22. I was the youngest person at the time to have been selected by the St. Lucia Ministry of Education to take on the leadership of a school.

Migration, Rupture, and Reconciliation

I left St. Lucia at 24 to join my husband who was then in the United States Army, stationed in Texas. Coming to America was, indeed, a major life-transforming event. I went from someone who was highly visible in my country to one who became totally invisible within American society. With no family, associates, or community affiliations, I began to question my identity in this new life space. In particular, my career as an educator and as a community activist helped define my place, and hence, my identity in the old world. Without these identifiers in the new world, the perception of self and identity were in question.

In my attempt to build a life in the new country, I first sought employment as a public school teacher with the local school district. To my dismay, I was told that I did not have the required qualifications to teach in American schools because my teaching certification was not from a US academic institution. That was a major blow. The question then was, if I could not be a teacher, what other career options were available to me? After all, teaching was one of my defining characteristics. I could not envision myself outside of teaching, and yet, I was faced with what I felt at the time as a life-altering dilemma. In pondering over a resolution, my father's famous words came through very clearly. As he always said, "If you want to be somebody, you must have an education. … You have to learn the books." In my father's view, knowledge was acquired from written texts, and he did not view his indigenous wisdom as avenues for survival. However, Collins (1990) reminds us that "knowledge without wisdom is adequate for the powerful, but wisdom is essential to the survival of the subordinate" (p. 208). My father's wisdom was the cornerstone for his survival as a functionally illiterate adult. Similarly, the lessons learned from such indigenous wisdom helped me reconcile with the struggle for self-definition in a different cultural space.

Armed with some of the ancestral wisdom, I decided to reclaim my positive sense of self and embarked on an educational journey in academic cultures that were quite different from the ones I had experienced in the home country. My first stop on that journey was at the local community college in Texas, where I had taken up residence. I decided to return to college to acquire some vocational skills in office administration. I rationalized that if I could not teach, then I could learn how to type so I could get a job beyond the fast food industry. Fifteen months later, I acquired an associate degree in Applied Science, specializing in office administration. With that degree, I acquired my first job in the United States as an office assistant, at a salary rate of $2.10 an hour. That was in 1979, two years after I made entry into the United States. After three months as an office assistant, I was promoted to an executive secretarial position in the Department of Nursing Education. Working in that environment was a turning point in my career within the host country. Working with the nurse educators, in an environment of teaching and learning, made me realize how much I missed my life as a teacher. Observing their interactions with their adult learners also inspired me to focus on an academic discipline that would prepare me to work with adult learners.

A small college in the community offered a bachelor's degree program in Occupational Education, the closest discipline to adult education I could find in the immediate community. I enrolled in the program, specializing in office administration. Doing secretarial work was not inspiring to me as some of the work was just too mundane. Therefore, I decided that rather than work as a secretary, I could educate others in developing their administrative skills. That would keep me grounded in the profession and fulfill my need to reclaim my role as an educator. Luckily for me, the chair of the department within the community college where I completed my associate degree agreed to have me complete my student teaching in the department. Two years later, I was back in the department, not as a student but as a student teacher.

Upon completion, the department chair offered me a part-time instructional position and one of my prior instructors in the department assisted me in securing another part-time position in community adult education, teaching office occupations skills and adult literacy. I was then on my way to a career in adult education. Less than a year later, I was offered a full-time position with the Department of Office Administration as faculty and coordinator of the newly designed nontraditional programs in office occupations, office information technology, and health information technology. Many of the students were returning adults with little preparation for college-level programs. Many struggled with learning, and instructors also struggled with the traditional approach to teaching under-prepared adult students. My experience with this population highlighted a need for a deeper understanding of how sociocultural contexts can influence teaching and learning.

Five years after getting a graduate degree in Counseling Psychology, I completed my doctoral work in the area of adult education and human resource development leadership because I wanted to expand the practice of teaching to include the scholarship of adult teaching and learning within the context of adult development. I wanted to move beyond the administration of programs to a place that afforded opportunities to construct knowledge about good teaching, particularly as it relates to the facilitation of learning among marginalized populations. As a result, I made a career move to the University of Wisconsin-Milwaukee (UWM) in 1999 and then to FIU in 2004. My life and career experiences, both at home and in the US, have contributed to the scholarship endeavors I have undertaken as an adult education scholar.

The Intersection of Life History, Scholarship, and Practice

My research agenda has focused on learning and development among those the literature has termed "marginalized populations" or underrepresented groups, particularly those of African origins. Part of my research interest has stemmed from my own developmental history and from my work with returning adults at the community college. Although my work has taken several dimensions, I will highlight two significant pieces that have particular meaning for my career as a scholar and practitioner.

As a doctoral student, I became disheartened as I reviewed the literature on Blacks in higher education, and particularly the statistics on Black women in higher education. Not only were the figures dismal, the experiences that were revealed left me with the impression that Black scholars were not finding success in the majority White institutions of higher education. Since I was considering a university faculty career transition, I was interested in finding out what it took for a Black woman to be successful in predominantly White institutions of higher education. Therefore, for my dissertation study, I completed a qualitative study of tenured women at a major university. Again, to my dismay, I found that in 1994—about the time I was conducting the study—there were only five tenured Black women at that university, none from the College of Education. In fact, the College of Education did not have a Black female on the faculty. Moreover, at that time, there were very few tenured Black women in the field of university adult education, nationally. Therefore, the biographical study of these five women explored the learning experiences and the events that contributed to their success in the academy. I approach learning not from a cognitive,but from a more sociocultural perspective.

The ingredients for success for these women were a strong sense of racial and personal identity, a fluid life structure that allowed for navigation among the multiple sociocultural worlds, visibility in the profession through scholarship and service while maintaining visibility within the institution, and mentoring relationships with professors and other significant members of the culture. Their mentoring relationships started in their graduate programs, and to them that was a very significant contributor to their success in the academy. These findings continue to influence my development as a university professor and my approach to teaching and learning.

Continuing my work on adult learning and development of marginalized populations, I next wanted to explore how immigrant women like me learn and development within the context of transnational migration. Since 1965, the immigrant population of people of color has increased to now 75% of the immigrant population. This increase has significant impact on teaching and learning in adult education. With a fellowship grant from the Houle Scholars of Adult Education program, I conducted a study that explored how 15 women from the Anglophone Caribbean experienced learning and self as they transitioned from their home countries to the US. They were asked to explain how they experienced the higher education classroom, to compare the teaching and learning that took place in the two contexts, and share the strategies they used and the changes they made to manage the classroom dynamics. The most significant findings were the adjustment to a less structured teaching environment, the difficulty with constructing knowledge where many were used to banking knowledge in the home country, their sense of invisibility and alienation in and out of the American classroom, and their perception that because they remained silent in the classroom (a cultural practice) professors doubted their knowledge base. They asked not to be called on to speak openly in class, especially as a new student, but to allow them time to find their voices and transition into the milieu of the classroom. Once again, there was that interconnection between this work and my practice to create an environment where students could find their voices to articulate their world views. Understanding immigrant students' experiences can inform how we deliver instruction and facilitate learning.

In summary, the underlying purpose for much of my work is to make visible the life world of those whom the literature classifies as marginalized populations and to make their experiences available for open discourse. I hold the view that the more knowledgeable we become about the "Other" in our midst, we will be encouraged to be more critical about teaching, to continuously reflect on practice, and to take action to create equitable learning environments that foster social justice and an ethic of care.

References

Collins, P. H. (1990). *Black feminist thought: Knowledge, consciousness, and the politics of empowerment.* New York: Routledge.

Senior, O. (1991). *Working miracles: Women's lives in English-speaking Caribbean.* London: Villiers Publications.

Paul Armstrong

In the postwar United Kingdom, a new, supposedly diagnostic, method of selection for the transition from what we call the primary school (ages 8-11) to secondary schools (11-15, later 16) was introduced under the 1944 Education Act. This method of selection was based on research on intelligence carried out by Cyril Burt, in which potential for achievement was seen as innate, yet achievement was related to social class. It was commonly known as the Eleven-plus. On the basis of the result of this test children were allocated, in theory, to one of three types of secondary schools: the grammar, the technical, and the secondary modern. In the postwar expansion, there had been a large build of secondary modern schools and a few technical schools, but mostly the grammar schools were those already in existence. These had existed in England and Wales since the Middle Ages, built for children of the newly emerging commercial classes, providing an education for those who were going to be the capitalists who were to establish trades and industries over the centuries. Most of the grammar schools had been endowed by industrial families and received fees from the parents of other children from these new middle classes. Meanwhile, the so-called public schools, such as Winchester, Harrow, and Eton Colleges, were the preserve of the landed gentry, the nobility that ruled the country, if not the world.

I was born into a working-class family. My father was conscripted into the armed forces shortly after the end of the Second World War, where he was in catering (peeling potatoes apparently), and on completing his period of national service, he became an apprentice tailor. However, on getting married and beginning his family, he decided that he needed to earn more money and went with his elder brother into painting and decorating. He never took any qualifications and for the most part was self-employed. (I can vividly recall those once-a-year tax returns that required the shoebox to come out of the cupboard, stuffed full of scraps of paper, often covered in oil and paint, which provided the basis of the tax return – it was an annual time of stress in our household.)

My mother, by contrast, came from a lower middle-class family. My grandfather was a third-generation watchmaker and ran a family business in the small town in which we lived. I remember quite proudly seeing a photo of him, his father, and his grandfather standing outside their shop in a book on the history of the county in which I was born and spent the first 18 years of my life. My grandfather had a genuine love of books and was surrounded by them, and in his retirement most of his life was spent reading, unless he was in the "club," of which he was president before he died, drinking and smoking, not approved of by his wife. My maternal grandmother had never really worked in the labour market and spent most of her life being a mother and a housewife. They had two daughters, ten years apart, and my own mother was the youngest. She did go to a grammar school for girls but left at an early age to spend a short time in retail before getting married and devoting the next 16 years to having eight babies (I was the second). It was always evident that my mother had the same love of books and reading as her father. We, her children, were introduced to the public library from a very early age (it was free to borrow books) and we were encouraged to read. I am not sure my elder brother was too enthusiastic, but the visits to the library were certainly something I looked forward to on Saturdays during school time, two or three times a week during school holidays.

I went to school just before my fifth birthday. The highlight of my early schooling was coming first in a test out of a class of 48. I was well aware that there were a couple of children in my class who were, it seemed, naturally brilliant (one of whom ended up at Cambridge University, but I don't know what became of him). I had to work hard.

Then, in the fourth and final year at the priamry school, one Friday in February I took the Eleven-plus. I was not aware of the significance of this test or what it really involved, but afterwards I became aware that the results of this test meant that our class would be going different ways after the summer recess. When my parents were told the test results and that I would be attending the local grammar school for boys, there was a mixture of celebration and concern. When an aunt sent me a postal order for £5 (a lot of money in those days) and another gave me a leather satchel, I began to realise that I had achieved something that was not only giving pride to my mother (and possibly my father, but he never showed those kinds of feelings) but to my extended family.

The grammar school was endowed by a wealthy trust who had built their wealth on mercantile trade. The school itself was on the northern side of the river in the town centre. There were just two other children from my primary class transferred to the grammar school that year. The others in my class were fee-paying, of which a large number were residential. (For some reason I used to feel sorry for them, not having a home to go to, even though my house, rented from the council, was overcrowded and on a public housing estate on the southern edge of the town.)

Going to the grammar school gave me my first sense of class consciousness. I was at school with children who came from considerably wealthier families than myself. I was wearing a second-hand school uniform acquired by my mother through the school shop, usually too large to begin with and for a short time fitted me well enough, before being too small for a period. However, the next two of my younger brothers also passed the Eleven-plus and followed me to the same grammar school, wearing my now third- and fourth-hand outgrown uniform. If my mother reads this, she will probably deny that this was ever the case – even though we were not very well off, they did their best for the children, and my father worked long hours to keep our large family above the poverty level.

The class divide in the school was made more obvious when the English teacher (whom I disliked intensely) made reference to "those who live on the other side of the river" in a disparaging way. It took some time before I realised that I was one of those who lived south of the river and became aware that most of the public housing estates in the town were on the south side of the river; virtually all the privately owned housing was on the north side. The town was renowned for its multiculturalism, having attracted a significant number of European émigrés to the town in the postwar period, especially to work in the brickfields and on public transport. I was more aware of class difference than race and ethnicity. I was aware of religious differences because I had to travel to school on a bus that was usually full of children from my area going to the Roman Catholic school on the west of the town.

In retrospect, I realised that there was a degree of labeling going on, which went something like public housing=working class=education failure, and it would have been easy to get drawn into disaffection as one or two of my primary school peers did.

However, I worked hard to stay in the top academic stream. We skipped a year, so I was able to take my examinations a year earlier. Indeed, my first exam I took some 18 months earlier than was expected. Whilst I was never brilliant, I always worked hard enough to get the results I needed to go to university. Although I preferred geography as a subject, my history teacher was encouraging me to study history, and I was offered a conditional place at Swansea University to study history. When my exam results arrived, although I had passed all three A Level subjects that would get me into university, I did least well in history, best in English, with geography in between. It was assumed that I would return to school to retake my examinations and reapply – after all I was a year ahead of where I might have been. Despite my parents' disappointment, I decided I could not go back to the school. In part it was the general culture of the school, but also a particular incident that I took exception to and was in effect expelled from the school, though I would have been reinstated had I gone back to the school and apologised. My crime (the only misdemeanour I ever committed, or at least got caught committing) was to grow a moustache. I had found myself a temporary job after the examinations, as we were free to do, but we had to return to school on the last day of term to say our farewells. I had already had my one-to-one with the head-teacher, who clearly had no idea who I was (that comes of being no good at sport, but at the same time not getting into trouble – I was anonymous) and was about to leave the school for the last time when we were called for the school photograph. The school secretary organising the photo shoot saw my moustache and told me to go home and shave immediately and return for the photo. I had take time off my temporary job to return to school, and rather than going home to shave, I went to work. My parents received a letter stating I would not be permitted back at school until I apologised. They may still be waiting!

By this time – the late 1960s - I was interested in politics, and in particular the idea of political revolution, and overthrowing capitalism. In the last two years at school, a small group of us from school would gather together to read *International Times,* listen to Bob Dylan, and discuss how we would put the world to right. I had also been given Peter Berger's *An Invitation to Sociology* to read by a teacher at school. I had never heard of sociology before and did not appreciate the distinctiveness of Berger's approach at the time, but it made me curious. I left home to go to college in the north of England to train to be a journalist. My parents, particularly my mother, was disappointed that I had not returned to school to reapply to university. My decision to train to be a journalist had been prompted by seeing an advertisement for the pre-entry training programme that more orless guaranteed entry into the world of journalism. During the training, I applied again to university without retaking my examinations and was offered a place to study sociology at the University of York, not far from the city of Sheffield where I completed the journalism training programme, but not without some difficulties. Although I enjoyed playing at being a journalist, I lost patience with the academic side, which seemed to me insufficiently challenging, and as a consequence of being away from home for the first time, being able to make independent decisions, and knowing that I was going to university anyway, I set out to enjoy myself rather than take the course too seriously. However, I failed a Use of English exam, which did not matter too much as I already had a qualification in English, but the realisation of failure was significant. I realised I was not brilliant at academic work and could only succeed through dedication and sheer hard work.

This was to be confirmed when I did get to university. Although I really enjoyed studying sociology, I was never convinced that I had developed what C. Wright Mills called a "sociological imagination." At the end of the three years, it was with some trepidation that I looked at the pass list of the final examination results. I had no real confidence that I would get a degree at all, even though one or two members of the lecturing staff had talked to me about the possibility of doing postgraduate research. I recall reading from the bottom of the list upwards and getting more desperate as I did not see my name, and then I found it at the top of the upper-second class honours, just below the first class (this was purely a matter of alphabetical order and nothing to do with how close or otherwise I came to getting a first class degree.

It had been my intention throughout my undergraduate study to get a job in journalism once I had got my degree, but three years is a long time, and by this time the UK was well into an economic recession; it was proving difficult to find a job in the media – I had seemed to price myself out of the market. Why should they pay me so much as a graduate when they could take on a school leaver as a trainee to do much the same as I would be expected to do and pay them a fraction of the salary?

I was fortunate enough to get a scholarship to study for a master's and then a Ph.D. at Essex University. I was about a month away from completing my Ph.D. and my scholarship was running out, but I needed to get a job. Against the advice of my research supervisor, I obtained a job teaching in a further education college, and so began my teaching career. I learned very quickly that I could not cope with teaching teenage girls who had no interest in the subject, whereas the evening classes with adult learners were a real joy. I also undertook two part-time teaching jobs during my first year, with the Workers Educational Association (WEA) and the Open University. The experience I gained over two years, plus the eventual completion of the Ph.D. earned me my first job in university adult education at the University of Hull.

It was at Hull that I really came of age as an adult educator, taking responsibility for teaching programmes and engaging with research networks, including the Standing Conference on University Teaching and Research in the Education of Adults (SCUTREA), which I first attended in 1979 and have attended every conference since then, giving papers at them all since 1986. Why did it take me seven years to give a paper? I suppose the fact that in those days we did not need to give a paper to attend meant that I was not pressured to do so. But there was something about the conference itself that was quite daunting. SCUTREA was much more formal than it is now. I recall at my first conference, Richard Hoggart, author of *The Uses of Literacy* and a former lecturer in the department in which I worked, was proposed for membership by a colleague from Hull, and his nomination was not supported on the grounds of limited contribution to the study of adult education! SCUTREA was a very influential organisation for me, which is why I have continued to support it for over 25 years. Initially, its value lay in the subject-based interest groups that existed within it rather than the main conference. I came into contact with similarly minded adult educators, including Sallie Westwood, Jane Thompson, Nell Keddie, Peter Jarvis, and Nod Miller. Whilst there was a divide between feminists and Marxists (left-wing women and left-wing men), Nod and I established a good working relationship since the very early days of our participation in SCUTREA. We were very soon joined by Miriam Zukas, with whom I now work. I took over as the SCUTREA representative of the University of Hull in 1980, and since then I have also represented the Universities of London (technically, though in reality only the Faculty of Continuing Education in Birkbeck College as part of the University of London) and now Leeds. I had been an individual member throughout an eight year period when I worked outside the higher education sector in the UK but continued to attend SCUTREA.

I have organised three SCUTREA conferences (Hull 1996, London 1997, and Leeds 2006) and have been on the conference planning group of many more. Between 1992 and 1996, I was the Honorary Secretary with Miriam Zukas as the Honorary Chair and in July 2005 was elected to the Chair. One reason that I have supported SCUTREA so consistently is that it was this organization that gave me my first opportunity to gain experience of international adult education. I was selected to be one of the British adult educators to participate in the Kellogg-funded transatlantic exchange scheme. This brought Gary Conti to Hull in 1984, and I was supported to go to the AAACE in Louisville, followed by short visits to Colorado State University in Fort Collins and the University of Wyoming in Laramie, organised and hosted by Mike Day, a wonderful person whose commitment to the teaching of adults was absolutely outstanding. The transatlantic experience was very important to me because I met many excellent adult educators from different parts of the world whose ideas were fascinating as Britain entered a new era of a market-driven economics that had turned the UK education system into a profit-seeking, entrepreneurial culture from its previous commitment to equal opportunities and social justice. We might have despaired even more had we not had regular opportunities to meet with our international colleagues in order to deepen our understanding of the significance of this shift and to consider strategies for survival. Since 1987 I have attended 12 AERC conferences in the USA and Canada and had the privilege of serving on the AERC Committee for two years in the 1990s. During the same period, the international representation at SCUTREA conferences grew tremendously, and although we occasionally designate SCUTREA conferences as "international," there is a sense in which they have all been international for many years. This has enabled us to escape from pure parochialism to having a deeper understanding of the local and global significance of the role of learning in adults' lives in a variety of settings and cultures.

My career in university adult education has not taken a normal academic trajectory. In total I have worked for 17 years in three universities (Hull: Birkbeck College, London; and currently in Leeds). I have never been promoted within the higher education sector in all this time; in fact, on joining Leeds I had a feeling of being back where I was in 1979 when I first joined Hull. In two transitions, on joining and then leaving Birkbeck College, I realized that there were limitations to learning through experience if that learning was not converted into some substantive and observable achievement, such as promotion or publications. I had returned to higher education with a much richer and varied experience in both terms of teaching and research. Yet, it felt like it was discounted. I knew that the world of university adult education had changed significantly in the time I was away, particularly with the introduction of quality assurance of teaching and learning

and research (through the now infamous Research Assessment Exercise). I have throughout my working life struggled with contradictions, most fiercely experienced, though consistently unresolved, through praxis. I do know, however, that the needs of adult learners will always take precedence over my own professionalism, even at the expense of a conventional career trajectory.

Ian Baptiste

Dr. Baptiste is an Associate Professor of Education and Professor-in-Charge of the Adult Education Program of the Pennsylvania State University. He was born in Trinidad and raised in Grenada (two island nations in the Caribbean). He holds a B.Sc. in Agriculture from the University of the West Indies, Trinidad; a master's degree in Education from Wheaton College, Illinois; and a doctorate in Adult and Continuing Education from Northern Illinois University. After graduating in 1994, he taught at National Louis University (Chicago) for three and a half years and chaired the Department of Adult Education for most of his tenure there. Professor Baptiste joined the Adult Education Program at Penn State in August 1997.

Growing up in rural Grenada, young Ian had no interest in being an educator. He was going to become a physician. Being hospitalized for two long weeks at the age of thirteen cured him of the desire to be a medic—too much blood... and the smell!!! But a career in the sciences still tugged at Ian's heart. So when he applied to college (at the University of the West Indies in 1979) he chose natural sciences as his major. He had decided to become a chemist. A friend, Lisle, who had completed a natural sciences degree and was teaching chemistry at a secondary school in Grenada talked Ian out of a career in chemistry. "In Grenada," Lisle informed Ian in 1979, "teaching is the only career option for a chemistry major; agriculture offers more career opportunities." Since young Ian had no interest in teaching he switched to the College of Agriculture based on his friend's advice.

In the College of Agriculture, Ian majored in food technology and microbiology (intent on staying as close to chemistry as possible) and right out of college landed a job as a research technician in his field of study at the Caribbean Industrial Research Institute (CARIRI), located in St Augustine, Trinidad and Tobago. The year was 1982. Cultivating staphylococcus, salmonella, and e-coli bacteria turned out to be less exciting than Ian had envisioned. So beginning in 1983 (while still working as a research technician) Ian helped to organize the skilled and unskilled workers of CARIRI and those workers took over the reins of CARIRI's in-house trade union (which, up to then, had been dominated by university graduates—mostly masters and Ph.D.s). Ian became chairman of the trade union and remained in that position until he resigned in 1987 to attend graduate school at Wheaton College. Organizing workers, collective bargaining, helping to increase workers' awareness of their rights and responsibilities proved to be far more intriguing for Ian than donning a white coat and peering through a microscope.

Beginning in the mid-1970s and continuing until 1987, Ian also coordinated youth leadership training and development efforts (as a volunteer) for the youth arm of the Pentecostal Assemblies of the West Indies—a religious organization serving the eastern Caribbean region. Those two experiences (youth leadership training and development and trade unionism) catapulted Ian into education.

When Ian enrolled in the Masters of Education program at Wheaton College in 1987, he had not heard the term "adult education," even though he had been doing adult education for over 17 years. At Wheaton, Ian was introduced to critical pedagogists such as Michael Apple and Paulo Freire and to Phyllis Cunningham, who, at that time, was teaching at Northern Illinois University in DeKalb, Illinois. To say the least, the one-hour drive from Wheaton to DeKalb to meet with Professor Cunningham was worth it. Ian had planned to pursue a Ph.D. in educational policy studies after completing his master's degree. A career in educational policy, he thought, would provide the best opportunity to effect badly needed structural changes in educational systems in the Caribbean—systems that in 1989 were still wedded to human capital theory, to what Freire calls "banking education," and to a colonial legacy of intellectual dependency on Europe and the United States. "*Adopt, wholesale and uncritically, irrelevant ideas from Europe and the United States; pour those uncritical ideas down the heads of unsuspecting school children, and send them out with the misguided notion that their foreign credentials would qualify them to earn a decent living in the Caribbean.*" Such a moribund educational system, Ian believed, needed serious structural transformation. He planned to use a Ph.D. in educational policy studies to help trigger such structural changes.

But alas, Ian was not happy with his research into educational policy studies in the United States. The US educational policy studies programs that he researched were too top-down for him; i.e., the approach was that of academic policy makers creating policies in Ivory Towers and then telling teachers and other educational practitioners what to do. Ian wanted to be part of a process that was more participatory, i.e., policy makers working with grassroots organizations to develop policies in a collaborative way. Moreover, Ian found that US educational policy studies programs focused on *formal* education only (K-12, post-secondary, and higher education). Informal learning and learning in the workplace and community were not part of the equation. Given his interest in lifelong learning, he wanted to focus on both formal and nonformal education. Speaking with Professor Cunningham, Ian came to realize that adult education was a better fit because it examines policies affecting both formal and nonformal education; moreover, it emphasizes a participatory approach to policy development.

Currently, in addition to chairing the Adult Education Program at Penn State, Professor Baptiste teaches graduate courses in adult teaching and learning, community capacity building and qualitative research and conducts research using a variety of qualitative research methods. He has been a committee member on over 50 doctoral dissertations—of which he has chaired over 25. He has published several articles in refereed journals and proceedings.

Professor Baptiste has served on the editorial board of several refereed professional journals (including *Adult Education Quarterly* and *Canadian Journal for the Study of Adult Education*) and each year he reviews journal manuscripts for many more. He has been a member of the Future Directions Committee of the Commission of Professors of Adult Education and has also served on the Steering Committee of the Adult Education Research Conference (AERC). During his tenure on AERC's Steering Committee, Professor Baptiste helped to establish the Cunningham Award for Social Justice, of which he currently serves as an advisory board member.

His current research examines how the production and use of knowledge foster and impede civic engagement and democratic participation—particularly in the context of community organizing and capacity building. Pursuant to this interest, Professor Baptiste has been a participatory research consultant to community-based organizations, governmental and nongovernmental organizations, and community colleges in Chicago, Philadelphia, South Africa, and the Caribbean islands of Grenada and Trinidad.

Much of his current research is conducted under the auspices of CCDRE (Committee for Community-Directed Research and Education), an organization he co-founded with adult education students at Penn State in 1998. Ian currently chairs CCDRE. The goals of the organization are: (1) to improve the civic capacity of Penn State and community organizations with whom CCDRE partners; (2) to provide opportunities for Penn State students, staff and faculty who are interested civic engagement to integrate their teaching, research and service; and (3) to conduct research on the role of service learning in community capacity building.

For the past three years (2002-2005) CCDRE has been partnering with community organizations on the island of Grenada, West Indies, and in Belmont, West Philadelphia. Partnering organizations include community development organizations; community advisory councils; community learning centers; youth and sporting organizations; small business enterprises; small business associations; local schools, churches, and other places of worship. For updates on CCDRE operations visit http://www.publicscholarship.psu.edu/projects/ccdre.htm.

Gretchen T. Bersch

The Dream of Teaching

We are each a product of our experiences, our heritage, our relationships, our learning. As the oldest of six in my own family and for many years another five cousins next door, I had lots of experience with children. By the time I was ten, I knew I wanted to be a teacher. My father was a scientist-inventor and a professional engineer. I helped him in his laboratory for many years, so I grew to love science as well. I learned persistence and hard work as my family homesteaded on an island in Alaska in days without much good equipment or money. My mother, professional architectural and engineering model builder, taught me to be patient, responsible, and adventurous. Once I graduated with my class of 16 from Homer High School, I salmon fished in the summers to earn money for college, and I became a junior high math and science teacher.

The fifth year of teaching, my husband, Peter Bersch, and I had left Alaska to organize a business processing herring roe for the Japanese, so I found myself during the academic year teaching junior high math at Poulsbo, Washington. One day, my principal asked me if I would teach GED at Little Boston Indian Reservation. I did and I loved it. After herring and salmon seasons were over that summer, we moved to Kaltag, an Athabascan Indian Village on the Yukon River in Alaska's Interior. The population: 232, including us. Peter was the coordinator of a self-help housing program where 2/3 of the families in the village worked together to build themselves new houses. From my Athabascan women friends, I learned how to set a fish net under the ice on the frozen Yukon River and how to sew a good pair of mukluks to keep my feet warm at 50 below. In January, I was supposed to go to an adult education training session, but for three weeks the temperature never got warmer than 45 below zero; no bush planes flew, no mail or supplies came, and eventually, I unpacked and didn't go.

Anchorage Community College hired me as a writer/researcher for an adult basic education project. My job was to write culturally relevant books and materials for rural adults and to teach village teachers how to teach adults. I worked for this project for a decade, first from Kaltag, followed by living in Goodnews Bay, a Yupik Eskimo village on the Bering Sea. Then we moved back to Anchorage and I worked from there, teaching ABE teachers from villages with names like Chuathbaluk, Savoonga, Koyukuk, Shaktoolik, and dozens of others. I loved this work, and the friendships I made over ten years were very special. It was an adventure coordinating a statewide GED by TV program when Alaska still had four time zones and satellite television was just being built in rural Alaska.

Along the way, I met George Aker from Florida State University, a kind and wonderful teacher who worked all over the world. After ten years of work in the villages, I decided I should have some formal training in adult education, so I began what were to be many years of commuting from Alaska to Tallahassee to do graduate work in adult education. George Aker had an overflowing love for humanity and a gift for teaching and mentoring that changed my life.

There were tremendous changes during that time—my mentor George Aker died in a car accident in the wilds of Panama; I became a single mom with 22 apartments and huge debts as the Alaskan economy tanked. Our rural project was deleted. The community colleges were absorbed into the university and suddenly I was a faculty member of University of Alaska-Anchorage, teaching beginning algebra to terrified adults. On all fronts there were crises. So, it took a little longer to finish the degree. I started my doctorate when my daughter was nine; I finished when she was 18. She said, "Mom, you've been working on that degree all my life."

So that is how I got into the field and stayed. I've had various visions/dreams over more than three decades of teaching adults.

The Dream of Creating an Outstanding Adult Education Graduate Program

I was asked by UAA to create and coordinate a master's program in 1990 and it has been a great success. We dreamed of building a community of scholars. I've chaired more than 150 thesis committees with some wonderful research, each one completely different, providing me with vast learning opportunities. Once they finished, the graduates were such a strong group that they created the UAA Adult Education Alumni Association. Several years ago, they requested space, raised substantial funds for, and established the Adult Education Reading Room in the newly remodeled Consortium Library. I was deeply honored in fall 2004 when they named the collection for me.

In my teaching, I think that being learner centered is critical. I assume that people are naturally good and that all are capable of learning and growth. Each person is a puzzle to learn how and in what ways I can unlock more potential or motivation. Process is a potent teaching tool and as important as content. It is about giving up your power, building collaboration, helping each learner find his or her own ability and passion.

The Dream of Establishing a Center for Learning on Yukon Island

For thirty years I wanted to build a unique and wonderful center for learning at my family's homestead across Kachemak Bay from Homer on Yukon Island and to bring national and international scholars to teach there. We cleared the spot on a bluff overlooking the bay in 1975-76. I began the construction of the center in 1994 and finally I am nearly finished, but I have hosted adult education scholars every summer since 1992 as well as various scientific, humanities, and other retreats over the years. What a marvelous opportunity for our graduate students to have studied with the best of the best and a precious opportunity for me to get to know those scholars on a personal level.

There is something quite magical about learning in a place so close to nature. Ages of indigenous people lived on the island; our family has hosted University of Alaska archaeological work. In addition to adult education courses, I have enjoyed hosting writing retreats, geology explorations, marine biology and botany field trips, Tai Chi/Qi Gong retreats, and others. And then, of course, there are times of fun and leisure. For more than 25 years our Abbott family has held a 4th of July celebration. About 80 of our friends come—kids, tents, sleeping bags, food—for a three- or four-day campout. There are games, sandcastle building, music making, beach fires and collaborative living. Each summer my book club comes for a weekend on the island, four couples and me, who have been meeting monthly for 19 years. And my annual grandchildren, godchildren, and their siblings for Gretchen's Kid Weekend, with learning as varied as wilderness taught by my ER nurse sister Becky; archaeological learning from brother Findlay; and all manner of crafts, nature identification, boat picnics, berry picking and hiking.

The Dream of Working Internationally

My grandmother, Mildred Towne Powell, was a remarkable stateswoman. She graduated from Smith College in 1908 and came west with her husband, who died rather young, leaving her with three children. She ran for office and was elected in 1935 to the Seattle City Council and served as the only woman for twenty years. In 1955, she was invited to join a world statesman peacemaking journey to 28 countries in Asia and the Middle East, so she resigned from the city council to do this. She continued to be involved internationally for many years. From her I have my middle name, her love of international work, and I hope some of her leadership skills.

Colleagues and I have been heavily involved in work in the Russian Far East and the creation of and ongoing partnership with the Northern International University in Magadan. Russia and Alaska have long history together as less than 140 years ago Alaska was purchased from Russia. Once in the 1970s when I was flying to teach in Wales, a village on the Alaskan coast close to Russia, our small bush plane became lost. We feared we might be shot down if we strayed over the line dividing Russia and Alaska. This experience made the opening of the Iron Curtain between us in 1988 a miracle.

I began to host university colleagues from Russia in 1989; by 1991, I traveled to Magadan for the first of my annual three-week trips. Magadan, sister city to Anchorage, was the place of Stalin's terrible camps and millions died there. While the camps are gone, life in Russia for my friends and colleagues is very difficult. We worked together to create an international university, student and faculty exchanges, and many joint projects. Two of my UAA adult education graduate students have done their practica in Magadan, teaching language students in the English Kaffedra [Department]. I've also worked with two women's centers, a baby orphanage, and others. In the late 1990s, I won several teaching prizes in Alaska, so I took some of the money and established an annual outstanding teacher of the year prize at the university in Magadan. The deans nominate faculty, a committee selects the person to be honored. It has been a great honor to go there every year, organize a reception, and present the award.

It was a pleasure for several years to chair the international preconference that was part of the American Association of Adult and Continuing Education conference. It was a thrill to be invited to be one of the U.S. representatives to the 5th UNESCO Conference on Adult Education/Adult Learning. I continue to be involved internationally, traveling in the past several years to Abu Dhabi/Dubai, Malaysia, and other places.

The Dream of Interviewing/Filming Noted Adult Education Scholars

I had the idea to do this when I was first a graduate student at Florida State University in 1981. I have worked on it from 1992 to the present, creating a series called Conversations on Lifelong Learning, interviewing scholars who are recognized nationally and internationally. I hope this will be one of my lasting contributions to the field and I can see it will keep me busy for many years to come. At the time of this writing, I have filmed 55 people and only completed less than one third, so I have enough editing and production to keep me busy for some time. While I have not had much institutional support of any kind, I love this project. Hearing people's stories is fascinating, rather like the idea behind this book. And it has made the literature written by these scholars come alive for my students and me.

The Blessing of Family and Friends

I feel fortunate to have had a close extended family and have drawn great strength from each member. My father taught me to believe anything is possible. He died at 52, when some of my five siblings were still young. His gravestone on Yukon Island reads, "William F. Abbott, a creative and enthusiastic scientist who loved his family." Until our mother, Alice, died in 2000, every week for years and years, we all gathered for Friday night at Mom's—her children, their attachments, grandkids in a lively group. It is a marvel to me how she taught us to be close and at the same time independent. We range from pacifist to militaristic preferences—all opinions were discussed and authors valued. She's buried on Yukon Island, overlooking the homestead house and the bay; her carved granite stone reads, "A woman of wisdom and adventure who was the center of our lives."

A great blessing came into my life when my daughter Jennifer found my son, Chris, the child I birthed in the 1960s as a junior in college, when social pressures were strong against being an unmarried mother, not only against the mother but the child, so I chose to give him up for adoption. An agonizing decision, but one that taught me sensitivity to and tolerance of others. Chris is a scientist-inventor and registered engineer, just like my father was. We've become great friends and his two daughters call me Grandma.

Over many years, I was mentored by my friend Audrey, who was teaching adults in Alaska by the late 1920s and encouraged and inspired me. I felt incredibly grateful for the support of family and friends when I spent a summer undergoing breast cancer surgery and radiation treatments and a subsequent complete recovery.

Now and the Future

I would say I have always been an optimist, an energetic leader, and a dedicated teacher. What a pleasure to teach for the whole of my adult life. I have loved this work. I'm pleased to have received among my honors the UAA Outstanding Teacher of the Year, the Northwest Adult Educator of the Year, the Alaska Professor of the Year from the Carnegie Institute, the Edith Bullock Prize for Excellence, the title Honorary Professor from the

Northern International University in Russia, and the great honor of being invited to be part of this book.

While I officially retired in 1997, until 2005 I was still teaching graduate adult education courses and advising thesis students as an "adjunct professor emerita." After this year, I expect to be minimally involved with the UAA adult education program and to explore new directions that are beginning to open. I will finally finish my Learning Center on Yukon Island and expand the programs. I know I will continue to be involved internationally. I am leaving myself open to discovering new and different ways to contribute to the field.

Roger Boshier

Mediocrity and Violence

Hastings Boys' High School on the east coast of New Zealand's North Island built a reputation for mediocrity and violence. I was only one of several Boshiers who endured lazy teaching and, by the time I got out of there in 1959, had little respect for education and educators. Hence, it was probably a mistake to go to Teachers' College in Wellington where I was soon swept along in the protest against the Vietnam War.

My father was once a signwriter and I knew how to make protest banners that looked good in newspapers and television. I could not resist the chance to address protest rallies and became vice-president of the Committee on Vietnam. The president was Teachers' College lecturer Barry Mitcalfe. Most of what I know about organization (otherwise known as program planning) was learned from Mitcalfe. He was a genius at getting Communists to work with Quakers, unionists to cooperate with students, nurses with teachers, and so on. In Wellington, our committee mounted a determined (and mostly successful) attempt to keep New Zealand troops out of the Vietnam quagmire.

Gun in the Back

We had to educate the populace in order to keep New Zealand troops out of the Vietnam mess. Hence, Mitcalfe, myself, and others wrote and published a serious (often high-brow and detailed) pamphlets and booklets explaining both sides of the conflict. We were left-activist protesters spending hard-earned funds debunking the fiction of the "domino theory" and other untenable arguments for fighting peasants in Asia.

The most dangerous point in this process occurred when Vice President Hubert Humphrey visited Wellington. I shook his hand and had a brief conversation during a morning encounter outside Parliament and, in the afternoon, was felled by a gun-toting CIA or FBI agent outside the U.S. ambassador's house in Wellington. New Zealand police didn't carry firearms. So when the evening newspaper showed the American agent sticking a gun into the junior lecturer from the university it caused a big stir.

Mitcalfe believed the average New Zealander wanted to give the Vietnamese a "fair go" and most were appalled by pictures of napalm pouring down onto women and children. Prime Minister Keith Holyoake was known to walk to work and Mitcalfe would sometimes fall in beside him on the trot down Molesworth Street.

"Mr. Prime Minister, what have the Vietnamese done to us? We should be giving them a fair go," he'd say.

Today some people think "Kiwi Keith" (Holyoake) minimized the NZ involvement in Vietnam. Others claim he was in bed with LBJ and the US administration. Mitcalfe tried to appeal to his "kiwi-bloke" side. After the Holyoake government fell, I joined Mitcalfe, trade unionist Toby Hill and others in a delegation to meet Norman Kirk, a larger-than-life boiler maker who had risen to the apex of the Labour Party and was now Prime Minister of New Zealand. We were all Labour Party members. I was president of the fairly famous Farm Road Branch.

The plan was to get Kirk to commit to a withdrawal date and I was happy to leave the talking to Mitcalfe. His arguments appealed to egalitarianism, the need to have cordial relations with neighbours, the special obligations of small countries, and the way American media spread myths about the domino theory. It was adult education at the highest levels of New Zealand politics.

Soon thereafter Mitcalfe and I (along with thousands of others) lobbied Kirk to dispatch a New Zealand frigate to exercise our rights to navigate in international waters in the French nuclear "blast zone" off Mururoa atoll near Tahiti. Much to our astonishment, he sent a frigate and, as such, made a significant contribution to worldwide attempts to end nuclear testing. *Boy Roel: Voyage to Nowhere* was our book about the antinuclear protests. What we learned opposing the Vietnam War played out beautifully when our efforts, and those of others, compelled the French to stop testing in the atmosphere.

I was also involved in attempts to stop taking all-White (i.e., with no Maori players) rugby teams to South Africa. I was arrested and thrown into the ablution block under the grandstand at Athletic Park after running onto the field during the All-Black trials. I landed on a concrete floor alongside notorious Wellington Trotskyites. But I was never charged and still don't have a criminal record.

Each of these protests involved large doses of adult education (directed at ourselves, politicians, and the public). But, being a protester was a full-time job and my Ph.D. languished. Ethnopsychologist Ernest Beaglehole was the supervisor but died before I got finished. I changed topics, built the Education Participation Scale, and made what airmen call a hard landing. Unlike the other Ph.D. candidate in psychology, I somehow satisfied Marie Jahoda, president of the British Psychological Society. The study wasn't great. Moreover, with an *n* of over 4,000 cases, it was too ambitious. But nobody told me to stop.

Small Detour

The Victoria University of Wellington Psychology Department and the Wellington Teachers' College were both staffed with stimulating left academics and, bit by bit, my aversion to education was being eroded. I am forever grateful to Anton Vogt who ordered me to go to university and John Adcock who applauded my very-public political activities, and protected me from administrators who heard there was "commie propaganda" in the Psychology Department. Adcock also taught me the difference between a correlation and an eigenvalue. I also met my lifelong friend, Dave Harré, who was the psychology technician and would later make films in China and author the Moeawatea heritage-conservation adult education process for marginalized youth.

In 1971 I moved to the University of Auckland and had an office next to Rangi Walker, a leading Maori scholar and activist. In 1974 I was contracted to accept an appointment with Cyril Houle and Bill Griffith at the University of Chicago. But, at the anticipated departure time, Mitcalfe and the fishing vessel Boy Roel were lost somewhere between New Zealand and Mururoa. I was frantically pressuring the government into mounting a search and trying to discover if kiwi protesters had been captured by the French Navy. Eventually, Mitcalfe and the crew turned up in Rarotonga.

Quite by chance, I met a recent Chicago adult education graduate in an Auckland street and was persuaded that Cy Houle, Bill Griffith, and Roger Boshier would not be paddling in the same canoe. While they strutted in three-piece suits, I shuffled around in shorts and sandals. Soon thereafter Coolie Verner arrived; we walked around an Auckland marina and he said I should go to Vancouver. There are mountains and boats in Vancouver. Nudge, nudge! Wink, wink! Canada. Not the U.S. I think he also liked my politics.

I landed in Vancouver August 28th, 1974. Nixon had just resigned because of Watergate. Colleagues were formal and some were religious. This didn't feel right. But I liked Verner's scholarly attitude, the money was good, and there was a nude beach under our office. Adrian Blunt showed me the factor analysis program at the computer centre. I joined Greenpeace (Vancouver) but there were too many big egos. They didn't have a Mitcalfe. Verner was revising the Adult Education curriculum and, as a result, I learned a bit about what he called "the discipline and the field."

Like Verner, the UBC president at that time was gay and single. He preferred to live downtown – not in a university mansion with enormous gardens. Hence, Coolie grabbed the president's house for what was then the Department of Adult Education. Verner had a Jensen-Healey sports car and, during the summer would drive to Cambridge, Massachusetts, and loiter in secondhand bookstores. In this way be built up a worthwhile collection of books on adult education. After he died, his collection anchored the Coolie Verner Memorial Reading Room.

At the 1975 Adult Education Research Conference in St. Louis, Bill Griffith and other panelists were talking about Title I of this and that. It meant nothing to me. Across the road at the airport were fighter aircraft recently returned from Vietnam. I was cavorting with the enemy and surprised they had let me in. Bill Griffith was probably still annoyed by the fact I'd ditched his job offer and went to Vancouver. But Griffith had the last laugh. After the Chicago program folded, he came to Vancouver.

UBC eventually got a new president who fancied the mansion in the gardens. Hence, the Adult Education Research Centre was ejected. They tried to put us in the bleak Faculty of Education Building but Verner arranged a move to a fraternity house on Toronto Road. It was here Paulo Freire later sat in an office four feet across the hall from my 70-square-foot rathole. I was his minder and, when he grew tired of visitors, he gave me a prearranged signal which meant, "Let's get the hell out of here, go to the beach or get some fish and chips." Paulo practiced what he preached. Walked the talk. And liked red wine.

We all produced an enormous amount of research from the ratholes on Toronto Road. Not long after moving there, we heard terminals could connect us to the far-off computer centre. I was one of the first UBC faculty members to get a Bitnet (later Internet) address. At a meeting to decide whether the student workroom should get a computer terminal, Jim Thornton wondered what it would be used for and who would supervise it when students wanted to use it on a Sunday." Jim was not the only pedant around. In another famous encounter I reproached Tom Sork for suggesting we would all one day have a "mini" or small computer on our desks. Why, when there was a big rip-snorting mainframe in another part of the campus? Sork had a Kaypro – one of the earliest "personal" computers. I've apologized to him numerous times but still feel like a goat.

We had plenty of students and, until the 1980s, were on track to establish adult education as a viable graduate program within the university. For nearly a decade about a quarter of all papers presented at AERC were from UBC faculty and students. Many thesis projects and faculty projects arose from AERC road trips during which Dan Pratt would try to tune the car radio to Mozart and I'd change it to the Beach Boys.

I was shocked when my two-year appointment was renewed for two and then another two years. I had to burn bridges back to New Zealand and seriously contemplate the meaning of Canada. Mercifully, I fell into the arms of the beautiful and charming Ingrid Pipke. Second, I joined (and later ran as an electoral candidate for) the New Democratic Party, and third, at the urging of Adrian Blunt, I got a boat and explored the Gulf Islands. In 1986 I laid down a deposit of $4,000 and bought my own island. Today I live on solar power and reach the Internet through a clunky Motorola bagphone.

Creeping Managerialism

In the 1980s universities were restructuring. Verner's dream was ebbing. The Adult Education Research Centre sign was removed and we were forced into bed with Higher Education and Educational Administration. To this day, I cannot detect any communalities that link these fields. Educational Administration didn't have the culture of research so carefully nurtured by Verner. The Department of Administrative, Adult and Higher Education staggered forward until the next round of restructuring. This time we landed in a unit with a remarkable title – the Department of Educational Studies! I voted against all these realignments but was widely regarded as obdurate. Not a team player.

Certain colleagues were tired of the Adult Education espirit de corps, lobbying concerning Verner's collection, and the alleged special status of the field. Certain Adult Education professors sat on their hands when it was clear we were being set up for a fall. New-generation "leaders" and the "transition team" ensured half the Adult Education faculty were in one building and the other half in the other. It was a divide and conquer regime executed in the name of interdisciplinarity and partnerships. It worked. Today, the Adult Education group is testy and fractured.

Throughout the 1980s I was director of the UBC Adult Education diploma programs in Hong Kong and Singapore. When Lim Hoy Pick, the National University of Singapore director of Extramural Studies, tried to get a security clearance for Ingrid and myself, hers was received within the hour. Mine was stalled. New Zealand has a security-sharing agreement with Singapore and my file suggested I had fallen off the earth in 1974. Eventually Singapore authorities decided I wasn't about to topple their government and issued the clearance. By that time we were back in Canada.

In 1984 Ingrid Pipke, James Boshier (my youngest son), and I went to Shanghai. This trip launched a lifelong fascination with China, which in the 1990s opened access to the highest levels of the Communist Party and, as such, an insider perspective on the 21st century 61 learning-city initiative. I also taught in Taiwan.

Ingrid Pipke ran courses for Singapore police who adored the beautiful Canadian. In Shanghai we met comrades who had fought in the anti-Japanese and wars of liberation only to later endure the excesses of the Cultural Revolution and cult of Mao. At the dawn of the 21st century, Yan Huang and I went to China to see them and produced a nifty reflection on the 1984 Shanghai symposium for *Convergence*.

As a youthful adult educator I was taken with UNESCO's 1972 Faure Report. Being scarred by formal education and not having met a teacher I admired, I identified with the notion of foregrounding informal and nonformal settings for learning. Recent research has focused on "farm-gate" (or self-educated) intellectuals. My favourite is three-time America's Cup winner Tom Schnackenberg. What he says about learning doesn't have much to do with educational leadership, formal education, benchmarks, best practices, or schools.

From 1986 onwards I sat on an 8-acre island with no electricity but, through a solar setup, listening to VHF radio. There were maydays and people drowning within sight of my dock, so I bought a pair of salvage boats and got into the marine rescue business. What I saw was a fertile arena for adult education research. As well as involving high drama and life-and-death situations, preventing incidents involves familiar problems for adult educators – participation (or lack thereof), culture, gender, a population that hates school and won't attend classes. Over the years, I've tried to figure out how to build a culture of safety amongst commercial fishermen.

In 1989 the International Development Research Centre in Ottawa asked me to lead an international workshop designed to build a research agenda concerning HIV/AIDS. I was deeply moved by what I saw there and for the next five years did research and wrote about this challenge to adult education theory. I still wonder why young professors are pontificating about spirituality and critical reflection when people were (and still are) dying of AIDS?

Collapse of Consensus

When I reached Vancouver in 1974 there was a consensus concerning what Verner called the fundamental concepts of adult education. Some people wrongly dismissed his work on methods, techniques, and devices as illiberal and wrong-headed. The same people blamed Malcolm Knowles for being a psychologist and not a sociologist. However, the Marxist know-it-alls were wrong and all graduate students should know about earlier attempts to conceptualize adult education and characteristics of the adult learner. Verner had been chair of the Adult Education Association (USA) Committee on Academic Freedom, erected as an adult education bulwark against McCarthyism. In 1976 I co-taught a course with Knowles at Concordia University.

These days, whatever consensus we once had has been eroded by lazy "research," disdain for theory, and the hegemony of critique. Postmodern and critical perspectives offer incentives for clobbering the "founding fathers" (who get slammed for not being mothers) without producing alternatives. Publicly yearning for the halcyon years and getting back to fundamental concepts is usually dismissed as unrealistic or outmoded.

As part of the UBC ADED412 distance course I got access to a television studio and made a 22-program interview series with adult education illuminaries. Students are always keen to see Jack Mezirow and Steve Brookfield. But my favourite is the 53-minute interview wherein Majid Rahnema provides a behind-the-scenes look at processes used to build the Faure report. I have another interview where, instead of going for fish and chips, Paulo Freire and I sat down and talked in UBC's Nitobe Garden. I also have two long audiotaped interviews with Malcolm Knowles recorded in a Montreal hotel room. Like Verner, Knowles liked whisky and the interview was improved because of it.

Ingrid Pipke and I more or less organized the 1980 Adult Education Research Conference in Vancouver and my foothold in Canada depended to a large extent on her. Hence, I (and many others) were devastated when a rock fell from a speeding truck and took away part of her face. Ingrid died in awful circumstances. I am now able to drive past the place where it happened without having a panic attack. It was Ingrid who first took me to the island I now own, so she is there in spirit – along with her friend and my student, Gayle McGee, who died at age 39 of a diabetic condition.

After New Zealand won the America's Cup in 1995 (and successfully defended it in 2000) I felt this contest had more to do with program planning and learning for extraordinary projects than sailmaking or rigs. I decided to find out how extraordinary (and high-achieving) New Zealanders go about learning. Sir Edmund Hillary was the obvious starting place, but since Everest, the uneducated Peter Jackson (*Lord of the Rings*, *King Kong*) and Tom Schnackenberg (America's Cup sailing) and many others have profoundly shaken up the idea that formal education leads to "excellence." Schnackenberg came to Vancouver and out to the island. During the 2003 Cup defence, as part of my fieldwork, I inveigled my way onto a race committee boat. Extraordinary projects are the ultimate test of theory concerning adult learning and education. Significantly, Schnackenberg (and Dennis Conner), Peter Jackson, and many others tend to talk the same language as Verner and Knowles.

September 11th, 2001

After September 11th, 2001, I was appalled by the absence of discussion concerning the root causes of terrorism and, with a contingent of Brits, Kiwis, and Aussies, walked out of an AERC symposium where people were asked to get into groups and "discuss where you were on September 11th, 2001." I am concerned by the current preoccupation with "spirituality" in adult education and absence of research. I taught a research course in the Royal Roads University Masters in Human Security and Peacebuilding program. As a result, I was in daily contact with students deep in the Baghdad green zone or others protecting themselves from Israeli aggression in Ramallah on the West Bank in Palestine. This program has problems, but I learned a lot and admired the spirit of the students.

Personal Politics of Writing

I have my own way of working and am particular about writing and editing. I had earlier tried writing articles with others but found them difficult. They likely regarded me as rude, irreverent, demanding, and never satisfied. Hence, I nearly fell over when I met Yan

Huang and, without trying, got into a productive writerly relationship. Hence, in the last five years I've probably coauthored more articles than in all the years between 1968 and 2001.

Yan is from Guandong province and, in the many articles we've written about the Chinese learning initiative, she corrects my mistakes, fills out the background, and insists on changing the order. She has a fine-tooth comb like no other and a well-tuned hyperbole and exaggeration detector. I once sat with her in a hot pool and talked for several hours about Chairman Mao as lifelong learner. She likes "the freedom" of Vancouver and is a fast learner. She understands software and tries to teach me. In 2005 we co-taught an adult education graduate course at East China Normal (a key university) and did four (what I consider creative and, for China, daring) research projects.

Half Dead or Fully Alive

By more or less jettisoning psychology in favour of adult education I have met and worked with extraordinary people and acquired an insider view concerning the politics of academic adult education. I believe the New Zealand tendency to figure things out for oneself, along with knowing and working with people like Verner, Knowles, and Freire, slightly dampened my tendency to be overbearing and opinionated. The work Yan Huang and I are doing in China has the potential to be revolutionary. I also hope that, because of my efforts, certain fishermen who would otherwise be dead are today alive. As well, there are lost divers and recreational boaters walking around because I adore theory and am fully alive during searches for people lost overboard or otherwise in distress. Bank robbers also feel like this. Finding distressed mariners is a deeply theoretical problem but also an adrenalin rush. It also helps to have pumps that start on the first pull.

I have always galloped out of town just before floods take out the bridge. I left New Zealand before the worst neoliberal excesses of the 1980s and reached Vancouver for the halcyon years in adult education at UBC. I participated in the birth of the Internet and, from a base in western Canada, went to every continent except Africa. Retirement beckons and this might be a good time to go.

A cloud hovers over academic adult education. Everywhere governments are extolling the virtues of learning and promoting a "knowledge-based" future. Hence, adult education should be at centre stage. Yet, in university faculties of education, adult education programs languish, disappear, or are too easily forgotten. Sometimes this is because of jealousy and personal acrimony (we've had both at UBC). Other times it is because of uncritical commitments to schooling. I've annoyed several deans by "inadvertently" calling our outfit a faculty of schooling.

Maybe I should have stayed in psychology or, like relatives (including my daughter), become a lawyer. Or follow my sons into filmmaking. Today, the need for adult learning and education pervades every social issue. Adults are not just kids in long pants. Although there have been big challenges, adult education was worth the effort. As Maori adult educator Rangi Walker used to say, "Ka whawhai tonu mātou!" Building adult education is a struggle without end.

Marcie Boucouvalas

Career trajectories are fascinating phenomena, especially in this richly diverse field of adult education and learning, a field dedicated not just to the development of individuals but equally geared to the development of the contexts in which adults are unfolding: relationships, groups (professional, racial, ethnic, etc.), organizations, communities, nations, and the globe or planet. For that reason we find adult educators "growing" self and others in a spectrum of venues in society-at-large, and my own career actually reflects that diversity of context over the past 35+ years, as will be evident later. Each of us writing in ths volume has been asked to reflect upon and share some insights about our own pathways, about what has influenced us, including shedding light on historical links that may otherwise go unknown or unheard except perhaps in impromptu conversations. What a fascinating idea! Unfortunately, space constraints preclude "telling the whole story" of all those colleagues, friends, family members, and kindred spirits, having graced our lives' path, who so deeply influence us; but they know who they are. One who may not yet understand how much she has taught me about life's delicate and often precarious balance is my daughter Anastasia (Stacie), a point of light in the next generation as she begins the young adult journey.

So many factors influence us, from our early years onward, but I will spare you the details of my formative years, although I must say that the experience of growing up Greek American in a Boston suburb did influence me in many ways: from the loving warmth of my immediate and extended family and the joys, retrospectively speaking, of having learned about and lived in more than one culture simultaneously (that is, well before its contemporary recognized value) to the pain of seeing my mother wash the physical and emotional wounds of my bleeding sister who had been chased home from school and had tacks stuck in her back because she was Greek. At 3-4 years old that scenario, I believe, forged a commitment within me to the plight of those far more oppressed than I. Although very minor in comparison to the conditions of humanity around the world, addressing the larger "suffering" of humankind and better understanding the aspects of the human phenomenon that fuel the behavior of the perpetrators are important matters which I have always seen as an integral part of the adult education map. Of course, I had also learned hope via education since the school principal heeded my parents' concern and afforded learning to the school about the contributions of the Greeks to civilization and thereafter about the contributions of different cultures to America. My father had come to the USA when his father, who had run for mayor and lost by one vote, decided America was probably a better democracy than Greece, and my mother was the oldest child of parents who were married in Greece. All were avid readers, what we might today call renaissance people. So I grew up surrounded by all sorts of books in many areas of interest (both Greek and English) and of course a strong emphasis on the value of education for all, as well as learning both for the sake of learning itself and for practical value.

The year 2005 marks my 25th anniversary in the professoriate, but I had embraced the identity of adult educator over a decade prior. Fresh out of college, equipped with a double major in psychology and sociology and good research preparation, I was hired as a member of the research staff at the Postgraduate Medical Institute, the educational arm of the Massachusetts Medical Society at that time. I joined an ongoing project researching community general hospitals in New England, investigating the venue as a viable context for the continuous learning of physicians. An important task was to help directors of medical education become "adult educators." The era was the late 1960s, early 1970s. Beyond the analysis of data, I expressed interest in learning more about how workshops were designed and the different learning design formats. The director was most accommodating and suggested that I go over to Boston University (BU) and take a course from a fellow named Malcolm Knowles. The Institute, in fact, would help sponsor me and I could bring the learning back to the Institute.

So, on a cold Boston wintry night in January (they called it "spring" semester) I trudged to the university after work. Traveling high up in a building of the university overlooking the Boston skyline, I entered a room where all the chairs were arranged in a circle—concentric circles that is—because there were what seemed to be 75 matriculants in this class entitled Design and Administration of Adult Education Programs. I sat near the door for an escape if necessary. Clearly these individuals were older than I. As we introduced ourselves I learned that these seasoned professionals had purposely come from geographically diverse regions to study with a professor and respected practitioner and administrator of whom I was not even previously aware. Moreover, most were pursuing doctorate degrees and I did not even have my master's degree at that point. What experiences are you bringing, we were asked. Experiences were resources for learning I was to later learn, recognition of which was equally important in according respect due the adult as a learner. As the rounds progressed, the richness of the room became evident and a learning climate and environment like I had never experienced enveloped me. Still, what am I bringing, how can I contribute, were questions that plagued me as I planned my potential escape. Surprisingly, my young professional status was valued in that I was just beginning a career in this field. Some lamented that they had not discovered the field much earlier. What a bonus, they convinced me, that I was able early on to fuse study and practice. Malcolm, as I gradually became comfortable calling him, stayed later talking with me about the depth and breadth of what was a global movement and re-emphasized the value that I would bring to the field by the time I was 50 or so, should I decide to pursue study in this arena. Most "students" at that time came to the field in midlife. I stayed, not only in that class where we field tested the Modern Practice of Adult Education, but joined the master's program with Malcolm as advisor and chair of my thesis, a valued interaction which continued until his passing in November 1997. I subsequently learned about andragogy not just as method, but to me it was clearly a way of Being, an integral part of which was the cultivation of an adult-adult relationship in learning endeavors. The approach was geared not just to those already adults but as a process to work with maturing learners and to help learners become more "mature," responsible, and increasingly and incrementally less dependent upon the educator. What an integrated bonus it all was indeed for my studies and everyday professional practice to reinforce and inform one another—although not without its challenges in juggling, time management, etc. This early experience helped immensely in subsequent work settings, especially in working with graduate students over the past 25 years. From BU I have also retained some lifelong professional colleagues such as John Henschke, Leo Johnson, and Beverly Cassara, with whom I continue to collaborate.

Moving on from Boston to South Carolina and work with the rural poor (preceded previously by work with the urban poor in Boston during my college years) and then with the criminal a justice system (including HRD-related functions), and also with telephone intervention counseling during those years, I began to see the similarity across contexts in working with adults as learners—a large part of which was affording choice where choice was possible. Again, I learned a new culture. Actually, it was a two-fold benefit: the corrections culture along with Southern culture, with all the adaptations that entailed as a "Yankee" and female in those years—especially before the Fair Credit Act of 1974. I was being well prepared for the international work that commenced and continued in the 1980s, 1990s, and of course the 2000s. I was a bit feisty in those years and learned both from my Southern colleagues, both male and female, and later in my doctoral program from my Asian female colleagues (Thailand and Sri Lanka) a different meaning of "assertive" professional. Rather than the American rendition, I learned how they worked within systems for change, often being able to transcend (not suppress) their own egos to the larger task. Of course, these were selected females and not everyone felt so empowered. The experience of their endearing friendships and colleagueships continue to incubate over the years and is currently fueling some writing I am undertaking regarding a different meaning of "power."

When I had indeed become ready to return to a university to pursue a Ph.D. degree, with Malcolm's assistance I narrowed it down to four schools and feel grateful for the growth that resulted by exposure to individuals at all four venues: Len Nadler at George Washington University, Alex Charters at Syracuse University, and both Cy Houle and Bill Griffith at University of Chicago. Even though I did not choose to matriculate in those programs, good colleagueship continued. I eventually decided upon Florida State University after interviewing with George Aker, who would become my advisor (along with Charlie Jones, co-advising, and on faculty Charles Adair, Roy Ingham, Irwin Jahns, and Wayne Schroeder). These were the mid to late 70s when FSU had a huge cross-section of international students who were in positions of leadership in their respective countries. The theme I had learned earlier of rich experiential resources rang loud and rang clear. I was being educated for a global world. I formed so very many meaningful colleagues and friendships that are unfortunately too numerous to mention. These interactions first catalyzed, among other things, the research and publications I would begin on adult education in Greece (during the late 1970s), the study of which continues to this day. Examples include Ratana Poompaisal (Thailand), Dulcy Windsor (Sri Lanka), and Americans such as Lorraine Zinn, my roommate for a while, and others.

It was during the mid-1970s that I also became active in the adult education professional association, influenced by both Yvonne Rappaport and Beverly Cassara, who drew
me into the Commission of the Status of Women and also welcomed me to International
Associates and the Coalition of Adult Education (now Lifelong Learning) Organizations,
where Alex Charters was also a catalyst. Later I became active with Adult Psychology and
with Ron Gross and the Conference Report Team. My first national conference was in 1975
in Salt Lake City and I have not missed one since. One of the first sessions I attended was
run by Alan Knox, who immediately drew me and my experience into the discussion as I
was working in the criminal justice system (corrections) at that time. Hmm. He is practicing andragogy, I thought, but in retrospect, perhaps he was just being Alan.

My doctoral years witnessed the fruition and convergence of many streams of personal and professional interest in my opportunity to analyze lifelong learning and transpersonal psychology as two complementary movements reflecting and contributing to societal
transformation. It took years, as I knew it would, to complete that inquiry, but it continues
to be a lifelong quest. My committee was most accommodating and gave me the freedom
to pursue my vision, a gift for which I will forever be grateful. I knew I was in a position
such that I would need to be comfortable "going where there was no path and leaving a
trail," as a poster hanging above my desk for inspiration suggested. I discovered who I was;
exploring the unknown was what motivated me most. I started gravitating toward visionary
literature while simultaneously working in grounded reality. Roby (J.R.) Kidd's occasional
paper, "Education for Being, Becoming, Belonging," and his proposal of a depth dimension
to lifelong learning became an inspiration for me. George Aker urged me to contact his
colleague Kidd (at the Ontario Institute for Studies in Education), which initiated a letter-
writing exchange with him until his death on 21 March 1982. He implored me to follow
my "passion" with regard to my proposed dissertation, which he saw as a most worthwhile
inquiry, and offered as well the caveat about the way of pioneers. Others may not understand but I was to let my inner voice guide me, so to speak. I did and was transformed in the
process. Decades later, I continue to return to that "center" within me as a way of knowing
and have not been disappointed. Another person (now retired from OISE) whom I hold in
high regard and who has been an avid and vocal supporter of my transpersonal vision and
writings (explained below) is Allen Tough, fellow patron of the World Future Society and
fellow traveler in exploring the extended trajectories of the human phenomenon. His lucid
voice figured prominently in my promotion and tenure decisions. This sentiment is not just
of the political layers but of a kindred spirit who deeply understood, understands, and is
committed to the future of humanity.

Joining the faculty at Virginia Tech's graduate center in 1980 afforded the opportunity to pursue two lines of inquiry already begun: adult education in Greece and the
transpersonal movement. With regard to the latter, I was invited as a field editor to the
Journal of Transpersonal Psychology in 1981 and selected as editor in 2001. The transpersonal refers to (a) transpersonal experiences: consciousness expanding beyond ordinary
time and space, including all the levels, states, and structures of consciousness that offer
different ways of knowing, and (b) transpersonal developmental potential inherent in humanity, an identity beyond the small separate self sense and beyond a motivation that re-
volves primarily around one's ego. Emphasis of this area of study and practice is not solely

on the individual, but equally concentrated on the macro context of relationships, groups, organization, society-at-large, and the planet.

Prior to my academic interests in this terrain, as a youth I seem to have had access to many levels and states of consciousness in learning as well as musings and insights about the human condition. Of course at night, like others, I had my dreams about the future and other symbolic experiences. One "dream" was the distinct experience of lifting off the ground and flying, remembering what it was like to lift above my own niche and see the greater whole of which all our niches are part. I was neither sleep deprived nor hallucinating. It was a world that I visited at night, which afforded me a broader perspective during the day. I was dubbed one with a good imagination, but I knew it was more than that and that there was much more to our levels, states, and structures of consciousness that related to our learning—how we know what we know. I gradually stopped talking about it and heeded the advice of my undergraduate professor of experimental psychology, Dr. Robert Goodale, to whom I will always be grateful. He emphasized to me that I must first demonstrate that I was proficient in what I would now call mainstream matters so that I would have credibility and that others might be able to hear my "different" ideas.

Then (much later) came the Academy of Consciousness Studies at Princeton University in 1994, which was the brainchild of Robert Jahns and Brenda Dunne. About 35 of us from different disciplines (and from around the world) were competitively selected to gather together in learning and exploring consciousness. What a treasure trove of kindred spirits it was, what a model in listening to and learning from other disciplinary perspectives. I felt I had come home. Participants in the Princeton program knew there was more to our consciousness than our educational systems address, were not about to give up that vision, and were engaged in rigorous research that they shared. That experience profoundly influenced me and still supports and reinforces my deep conviction of the role that the field of adult learning/education has the potential of playing in that vein. We cannot afford not to address and understand our consciousness. With the risk of sounding melodramatic, the future of the human species depends upon moving beyond development of a purely autonomous nature to better understanding and nourishing the complementary developmental trajectory of homonomy (the meaning derived in life by being and feeling parts of greater wholes, ranging from immediate group reference to embracing an identity as a planetary species). Also, in an unfortunately deleterious rendition, our consciousness is amenable to manipulation in a myriad of subtle ways. Mind control is more than a myth.

This opportunity and experience came at a fortuitous time since I had begun intense study of the then-emerging research on the adult brain during the 1980s, complemented by study of the wisdom literature. The streams of literature began to further coalesce and converge for me under the more unifying theme of consciousness studies.

With regard to my continuing research on Greece from 1980 to the present, I initially had the direct benefit of intense learning from an original: Petros Kehayiopoulos, director of adult education in the country, from the latter 1940s to the early 1980s. He afforded insights as well as use of his personal library. I also have in my possession copies of proceedings from the early years of the modern adult education movement in Greece which I must archive because I may have the only copy of some. Kehayiopoulos was held in high regard by the UNESCO consultants to Greece in the 1960s. One such individual was Edwin Townsend-

Coles who invited me to his place in Oxford, England, to offer input and to encourage me to research and write, as no one had as yet told the comprehensive Greek story in writing. I am grateful for their graciousness and that of numerous notables in Greece who gave generously of their time and energy and influenced my thinking. Examples include Amalia Fleming (wife of Alexander Fleming), who educated me about the woman's movement, and of course Magda Trantallidi, who has been head of International Cooperation for the Ministry of Education for decades. The longevity of my research (ca.1979/80-present) spans a number of changes in political party governance across the years, but during the change of government in the early 1980s it was George Papandreou despite his busyness who took the most interest in supporting my efforts and in fact reviewed a copy of my book prior to publication as a quality check (along with an earlier review by Kehayiopoulos). I learned and continue to learn much about separating the political layer from the academic trek, as well as about taking in feedback and suggestions but maintaining responsibility for one's claims.

I continue to pursue international interests, and am grateful for the numerous opportunities over the years to represent the USA at international assemblies including both the International Council for Adult Education and UNESCO, but I want to note that it was an early career opportunity (four years into the professoriate) that launched me permanently into the global arena. The year was 1984 and six of us were chosen to become exchange professors to England with our counterparts in the UK coming to our universities. This Kellogg-sponsored feat was the innovation of Phyllis Cunningham and others here in the USA, facilitated by Gerald Normie in the UK. Not only did the experience forge lifelong colleagueships (my exchange counterpart was Athalinda McIntosh, with whom I continue to dialogue, and another round of exchanges the following year sent Leni Oglesby to my university), it also emblazoned within me the understanding and continuing recognition that despite purported similarities in language (or not) there are profound differences as well. The aim it seems is to keep mindful of differences in similarities and similarities in differences whenever engaged in international work.

In the short space permitted, these are only a few highlights of the influences on my career path and my involvement with and interest in the past, present, and future of adult learning and education on our planet and its multifaceted role in contributing to the human species.

Ralph G. Brockett
Blazing Trails and Building Bridges

I have long been fascinated with biography. For me, learning from the lives of others has offered insight into the joys and struggles that are a part of human existence. In this brief essay, I share some insight into my own story as an adult educator.

The metaphor "blazing trails and building bridges" came to me early in my academic life. It serves as a way for me to describe the different roles of scholarship in adult education. Blazing trails centers on creating new knowledge and, ultimately, toward the idea that if the knowledge does not stay ahead of practice, the practice will most likely stagnate. Likewise, building bridges is essential to adult education. Building bridges involves making connections with others, searching for common ground, and striving to create a practice that gives voice to all and emphasizes the myriad ways through which it is possible to push back knowledge boundaries. The more open adult educators are to building bridges, the more there is to be gained. Thus, the themes of "blazing trails" and "building bridges" have served as guideposts for my teaching, research, writing, and service over the years.

Early Years

I was born in Toledo, Ohio, in 1954 and grew up in a working-class community. My father, who had left school in the 9th grade to go to work, was a WWII Army veteran who later became self-employed delivering building supplies. He died at age 36, after a long illness. I was six years old and my sister, Pat, was 13. My mother, who had graduated from the same high school as my sister and me, worked in retail for many years and eventually retired as the payroll manager for a nursing facility. There were some hard times, emotionally and financially, but I have mostly positive memories of my childhood. My mother was very supportive and involved in our lives and, despite working full time, provided us a good home life for my sister and me.

I attended Toledo Public Schools where, through the 8th grade, I was an above-average student. Early on, I found that I enjoyed writing and decided that I would like to become a journalist. During these years, I liked playing sports but quickly realized that my athletic skills were limited and my talents lay elsewhere.

High school was a time of adjustment. Unfortunately, I struggled academically and, eventually, lost interest in most classes. Socially, I felt awkward and did not "fit in" very well, which made the transition even more difficult. I clearly fit the description of an "under-achiever." Yet, during these years, I was in fact a very active learner, with particular interest in learning about the social, political, and cultural issues of the late 1960s and early 1970s. At the same time, I also participated in Junior Achievement, and as a company "president" for two years, began to develop leadership skills that would serve me well in my personal and professional life as an adult. In fact, years later when beginning my research in the area of self-directed learning, I would trace this interest back to my high school years as an active learner who was nonetheless an academic underachiever.

Finding My Voice

I entered the University of Toledo in fall 1972 as a psychology major. The freedom of college life was very appealing, though I was an average student for my first two years. However, as I began to find my way as an adult, I showed much improvement during the last two years. During part of my time as an undergraduate, I had the opportunity to work in a community center providing recreation programs for young people in a low-income community. During this time, my commitment to social change, which had begun to develop during my high school years, solidified as I saw first-hand the immediate and long-term impact of poverty on the lives of the families in this community. During my junior year I became interested in gerontology. Here, again, I saw an opportunity to work toward helping people who were often disenfranchised.

I received my B.A. in 1976 and had applied to several graduate programs in industrial psychology, without success. However, I was encouraged by two of my undergraduate professors to apply to a master's program at Toledo and was accepted into the program in Guidance and Counseling, where I was able to tailor my program to focus on counseling older adults. This turned out to be a year of self-discovery and personal growth. I wrote a final project on counseling middle-aged and older adults, which helped me to pull my interests together in a capstone experience. It was during this year that I was first introduced to adult education through an introductory graduate course.

During my five years at the University of Toledo, I was fortunate to have many supportive professors. Three in particular stood out as having had a major influence on my early academic life: Dr. Robert Burns in psychology, Dr. Seamus Metress in anthropology, and Dr. Newton Rochte in adult/higher education. In different ways, each of these professors taught me valuable lessons that I would carry with me throughout my own life as a professor.

In January 1978, shortly after completing my M.Ed. degree, I went to work for the State University of New York at Albany (SUNY). There I joined a project providing staff development for personnel in county welfare departments across New York State. My main role was writing instructional materials. For me, this first professional position offered the excitement and challenge of taking a step into practice, as well as frustration and disappointment resulting from my inexperience and naiveté about organizational politics. I realized that my heart and my skills were focused more on the academic side of adult education and decided to return to graduate school with the goal of eventually becoming university professor. I was accepted into the Ph.D. program in Adult Education at Syracuse University for the fall of 1979 and was offered an assistantship.

The Path to the Professorate

August 1979 was a pivotal time. During that month, I was married, my wife and I both resigned our jobs and moved to Syracuse, and I began the doctoral program. Although I had only been away from school for two years, it took a little time to adjust again to the life of a student. Before long, though, I knew I was where I wanted to be.

I knew from the moment I arrived in Syracuse that I wanted to study self-directed adult learning, particularly in relation to older adults. Upon reflection, my interest in self-direction can probably be traced to three experiences. First, my years as a high school "underachiever" were juxtaposed with a curiosity and enthusiasm for learning about many things, most of which happened to be outside of the high school curriculum. Second, throughout my undergraduate and master's programs, I was enamored with the ideas of humanistic psychologists such as Carl Rogers and Abraham Maslow, who emphasized a positive view of human nature, unlimited human potential, and a goal of helping people strive toward self-actualization. Third, through my work developing instructional materials at SUNY/Albany, it became apparent that in many instances, conducting large-scale training programs was not practical. Instead, it seemed to me that these institutions would benefit from an approach where materials were shared as resources for independent learning, determined in large part by specific needs of each individual practitioner, with the staff development coordinator serving as a facilitator of the learning process. Each of these factors contributed to my desire to better understand the nature of self-directed learning and its potential for improving the education of adults.

Early in my doctoral studies, two books played a crucial role in helping shape my commitment to the study of self-directed learning: *The Adults' Learning Projects* (1971; 1979) by Allen Tough and Malcolm Knowles's *Self-Directed Learning* (1975). These books reinforced my belief that self-planned or self-directed learning could play an important role in helping people fulfill their potential. In fact, upon reflection, Tough's metaphor of adult learning as an iceberg, where the vast majority of learning lies beneath the visible surface, is perhaps the single research finding that has most shaped my own scholarship over the years. For me, the mystery of what takes place below the surface has intrigued and guided my own scholarship ever since.

There are times in life, too, when things just seem to come together and the door to new possibilities opens. Such was the case for me when Dr. Roger Hiemstra joined the faculty as professor and coordinator of Adult Education in fall 1980. I served as Roger's graduate assistant, and we quickly developed a good working relationship. Most important, Roger's research interests were parallel to mine: self-directed learning and older adults. Knowing that my goal was to seek a faculty position upon graduation, Roger helped me gain experience by inviting me to coteach a course on educational gerontology, introducing me to prospective employers and inviting me to do some professional writing with him.

I completed my Ph.D. in September 1982 and was offered a nontenure-track position as assistant professor at Syracuse, helping to coordinate a "weekend scholar" degree program that Roger had created. I loved working with the weekend students. They were enthusiastic and, fortunately, were very patient with and supportive of their young, inexperienced professor. I quickly learned lessons about humility and respect for learners' experience – lessons that remain central to my teaching philosophy today.

During this first year as a professor, my daughter, Megan, was born. Roger and his family were at the hospital the very next day and were among the first people to hold Megan. Becoming a father was a time of great joy, but it was also one of the major adjustments I have had to make in my adult life.

I was on faculty at Syracuse for two years. Being in a nontenure-track position, I knew that I would eventually have to leave. This was very difficult because I loved Syracuse and felt very connected to Roger and Burt Sisco, who had joined the faculty that year. However, in 1984, I accepted a tenure-track position as assistant professor of Adult Education at Montana State University in Bozeman. In Montana, I found a place of great natural beauty juxtaposed against geographic isolation and chronic fiscal problems. It was a very productive time for me, however, and I had the chance to work with some excellent graduate students.

Shortly after arriving in Montana, I was invited to edit a volume of original readings on ethics in adult education. Though my background in this area was limited, I was intrigued by the opportunity to work on such a project. When the original proposal for the book did not materialize, I chose to search for another publisher and, in 1988, *Ethical Issues in Adult Education* was published by Teachers College Press. For me, this book was significant for two reasons: first, it helped fill a void in the literature and stimulate dialogue on an overlooked aspect of practice and second, I was grateful for the willingness of many leading scholars in the field to contribute chapters to the book.

In 1986, MSU was awarded a grant from the W.K. Kellogg Foundation to establish a Center for Adult Learning Research. We hired two senior-level professors, offered doctoral and postdoctoral fellowships, and funded an array of research projects. During my time at Montana State, I began to participate in leadership roles in professional associations. As a member of the Commission of Professors of Adult Education (CPAE) Executive Committee, I was actively involved in planning the 1986 and 1987 CPAE conferences. All in all, my time in Montana was significant because it was when I began to lay the groundwork for my future teaching and scholarship.

Opportunity, Disillusionment, Transition, and Renewal

In 1988, after four years at Montana State, I moved to my current position at the University of Tennessee in Knoxville. I joined a program with a rich history and plenty of opportunity to help shape the future. Just prior to my arrival in Knoxville, I had been appointed editor-in-chief of *New Directions for Adult and Continuing Education* and was elected to a term on the board of the American Association for Adult and Continuing Education. These opportunities came at an important time and served to reaffirm that I was beginning to establish myself in the field. The editorship of New Directions was especially significant because it allowed me to help shape directions for the literature of the field and to build bridges by identifying prospective issue editors and chapter authors and by connecting with other educators and new areas of practice.

For the most part, my time at Tennessee has been rewarding. Like most universities, we have undergone several restructurings and fiscal crises, which have sometimes been difficult and discouraging. In the end, however, what has mattered most is that I have worked with some wonderful students and faculty in an environment that has afforded me freedom, flexibility, and support to pursue my teaching and scholarship interests. Overall, I have very good feelings about my years at Tennessee.

During the 1990s, however, I found myself entering a period of questioning assumptions I held regarding the adult education field. For many years, I had been committed to strengthening professional adult education – not through certification, requirements, or codes, but rather through demonstrating how adult education is vital to our society and that there is a need for professionals unified in their commitment to promoting learning opportunities for adults on a large scale throughout society. However, two key events led to a shift in my position. First, in the early 1990s, the graduate program at Syracuse was closed. Throughout the 1980s, the Syracuse program grew to the point of being one of the preeminent graduate programs in North America. But a restructuring led to closure of several programs, including Adult Education. As a graduate and former faculty member of the program with strong ties to the people, especially Roger Hiemstra, I was deeply disheartened by how vulnerable the program was in spite of its growth and a large grant from the Kellogg Foundation only a few years earlier.

A second factor contributing to my disillusionment had to do with what seemed to me to be a more confrontational attitude among adult education scholars. One of the core values I hold as an adult educator is a deep commitment to what I describe as "the free exchange of ideas." This exchange, which is a cornerstone of what I try to achieve in the classroom, is based on encouraging learners to share different viewpoints, which can then be subjected to critical analysis. Through dialogue, points of dispute are brought to the surface, but this is done in a way that shows respect and support for class members, even though their positions may be in dispute. To me, this reflects the notion of building bridges in order to ensure that all people have a place at the adult education table.

Regarding what seemed to me to be a shifting attitude, I applauded the increasing emphasis on looking at the field through a critical lens, framed in discourse from a socio-political foundation. However, it seemed to me that over time much of this dialogue took on a confrontational and even self-righteous tone that sought to silence certain perspectives while defining those holding such views as "enemies." Thus, in some circles, those adult educators concerned with focusing on human growth and psychological dimensions of adulthood, as well as those educators working in settings such as human resource development and the military, which did not fall within the prevailing definition of "critical," were devalued and sometimes attacked in certain circles within the academic field. With my commitment to searching for common ground and for building bridges, this climate was very disheartening. I found myself disenchanted because while social change, equality, and justice are central to what I value about adult education, I was dismayed by the negative tone of this discourse. I believe that this confrontational approach has done much harm to the scholarly community in adult education as it drove away many long-time scholars who came to believe they no longer have a voice and discouraged many potential scholars who became confused and intimidated by the tone of such discourse.

During these years, as I began to question some of my earlier beliefs about professional adult education, I nonetheless remained involved in different activities. These included serving for two years as Chair of the Commission of Professors of Adult Education and helping to host the 1994 Adult Education Research Conference in Knoxville. The latter was particularly memorable because it offered an opportunity for our students to play key leadership roles in bringing the conference to fruition.

Another important opportunity arose in late 1994, when Sharan Merriam invited me to co-author an introductory adult education text. I was thrilled to accept this chance to work with Sharan. This book became an ideal forum in which to put in writing many of the ideas I had been studying and teaching about for years, particularly on the history and professionalization of the field. Writing the book also gave me a chance to put some of the factors contributing to my disenchantment into a broader perspective and, ultimately, helped me make some decisions about where to focus my own scholarship in the coming years. *The Profession and Practice of Adult Education: An Introduction* was published in fall 1996 and was a bright spot at an otherwise difficult time for me.

At about the same time, I found myself in the midst of a personal transition. Triggered by the onset of Type II diabetes, I began asking many questions commonly associated with midlife transition. Over the years, my wife and I had grown in different directions and we divorced in early 1997. For the next several years, I went through many ups and downs. I enjoyed spending time with Megan, and we had the chance to take trips together on different occasions. Then, in the fall of 2000, I met my future wife, Mary, a social studies teacher. We found a special connection and commitment and were married in July 2002. Feeling that I have come full circle through my personal transition, I have found much happiness in my life these past few years. Mary has been at the heart of this happiness.

In my professional life, I began taking stock of how and where I wanted to put my energy. This led to one of the most rewarding opportunities of my academic life. When Roger and I had our book, *Self-Direction in Adult Learning: Perspectives on Theory, Research, and Practice,* published in 1991, I thought that I had made as much of a contribution to self-directed learning as I could. However, several presentations at the International Self-Directed Learning Symposium and a second book, edited with Roger, *Overcoming Resistance to Self-Direction in Adult Learning* (Jossey-Bass, 1994) convinced me that there was still much I wanted to accomplish in this area.

Over the next several years, I continued to write and present about SDL and chaired two dissertations on the topic. In late 1997, a milestone opportunity presented itself when I was faced with a very heavy doctoral advising load, including several students who were searching for a dissertation topic. I invited my doctoral advisees to an informal meeting to explore creating a dissertation support group. Several people were interested and we eventually began to meet and discuss different research ideas. Eventually, group members expressed an interest in undertaking some sort of collaborative research project. Out of this emerged a content analysis study on the literature of self-directed learning found in 18 mainstream adult education periodicals during the period of 1980-2000. Our presentation of this research was well received and was subsequently published in ERIC. Since then, this group has continued to do research and make contributions through presentations, papers, and doctoral dissertations. Seven group members completed dissertations on SDL between 2001 and 2005. In addition, by the end of 2005, group members had contributed close to 10 publications and 20 presentations in a five-year period. This group remains active, with several new members as well as several of our graduates who have chosen to remain involved with the group. Working with this group has re-energized my commitment to self-directed learning, and I now expect to continue my work in this area for the remainder of my professional life.

There is one other area in which I have worked to make an ongoing contribution. After the ethics book was published in 1988, I found myself being invited to give presentations or to lead workshops related to ethics and to serve as a guest presenter via teleconference or in a visiting faculty position at several different universities. Over the years, these presentations helped push me to rethink and expand my earlier ideas about ethics. In talking with Roger, who had contributed a key chapter in the 1988 book, we agreed that it was time to take another look at ethics. We began writing a new book on ethics. Because of various commitments and changes in our lives, the book took longer to write than anticipated. However, this additional time allowed us to study the topic further, resulting in a more comprehensive book than what was originally proposed. *Toward Ethical Practice* was published by Krieger in 2004 and represents over 40 years of combined thinking about a topic that has often been underemphasized.

Taking Stock and Looking Ahead

As a way of closing this essay, I would like to look back over my past to identify some of the highlights of my professional life. Then I would like to offer a closing comment about what I envision for the future of adult education. Several highlights of my professional life are discussed below.

First, I have had the opportunity to travel, meet others, and share my work widely. While most of my travel has been in the U.S., I recently traveled to Denmark on two occasions, where I served as a visiting lecturer at the Danish University of Education in Copenhagen.

Second, I have been able to fulfill my lifelong dream of being a writer, albeit in a different context from my childhood ambition to become a journalist. As I near my 100th publication, I find myself still energized by the desire to contribute to the professional literature. Along with this, I have valued my opportunities to serve as editor and editorial board member for several adult education publications.

Third, many teachers have touched my life over the years from elementary school through doctoral study. I especially value the long-term personal and professional relationship I have had with my very best teacher, graduate advisor, mentor, collaborator, and friend – Roger Hiemstra.

Fourth, I have received three honors that have meant a great deal to me: the Cyril Houle Award for Outstanding Literature in Adult Education, the Malcolm Knowles Memorial Self-Directed Learning Award, and induction into the International Adult and Continuing Education Hall of Fame.

Fifth, I have worked to reconcile much of my disillusionment with certain aspects of the professional adult education field by recognizing that regardless of the direction the field takes, the need for educators committed to working with adult learners will continue. What matters most to me at this point in my life is to serve adult learners as best as I can, by building continuously on the knowledge and skills that have guided me for more than a quarter century.

Finally, I have valued the opportunity to work with many excellent student colleagues at three different universities. I have learned much from them and hope that I have been able to "repay" in some way the many teachers who have inspired and encouraged me over the years by touching their lives in some small way.

In trying to envision the future of adult education, I really have no way of knowing what directions the scholarship will take. What I do know is that it is important for people to have a sense of what matters to them and to move their scholarship forward, regardless of whether it falls within prevailing trends and theoretical frameworks. This is how it is possible to blaze trails into new territory. Yet we cannot afford to isolate ourselves simply because we may be disheartened by the ideas and approaches of scholars who seek to dominate the discourse through confrontation and intimidation. There are enough unanswered questions relative to adult education that it will take many lifetimes in order to get answers. There is a place at the table for all of us. It is my hope to continue pursuing ideas that have intrigued me for my entire adult life, and even earlier. There are new trails to blaze, new bridges to build. In my quest to help adult learners reach their fullest potential, I hope that I can serve learners and in some small way touch their lives and, in doing so, make a small contribution to helping create a better society for all.

Shauna Butterwick

The journey of identifying adult education as my major area of practice and a key part of my identity has, like many of my adult education colleagues, been circuitous. Reflecting back on this path I see that my gender, class and cultural heritage, parents' educational experiences, high school political activities, education and work experiences, and involvement in advocacy organizations, particularly feminist coalitions, are all important touch points that have shaped my identity and practice as an adult educator. I have not always named my professional identity this way, but now it feels familiar and welcoming. About 20 years ago I began graduate school at the University of British Columbia. That master's program proved to be a kind of homecoming experience; here I was discovering a history, a body of theory and writings, well-known figures and leaders and a vast collection of grassroots educators (who often did not make it into the official history, many of them women) that were all part of this phenomenon called adult education. I also met and took a course from Paulo Freire. Let me map out some of these touch points, beginning with my family, my first and probably most significant educational environment.

I was part of the post-World War baby boom generation, born in 1950 to parents of English and Scottish ancestry; that rather privileged ancestry and the hopeful culture of the times have profoundly shaped my worldview. My mother was born into a working-class family in Scotland in a small town not far from Glasgow, one of three children. She came to Canada when she was 10 years old and did not finish school, and that fact haunted her for the rest of her life. Her father, a rather fierce Scottish patriarch, regarded her struggles with grade-nine math as evidence that it was time for her to leave school and find work. She took secretarial training and worked for years in that role before marrying my father in her mid-thirties. Although she had left formal education as an adolescent, my mother was an actively engaged learner all her life. She was an autodidact, an avid reader who became a writer of short stories and poems. My father was born in Calgary and came from a middle-class professional family. His dad was a family physician during a time when there was no public health insurance and most of his practice involved working with poor families, so he earned a modest income giving care out of his home-based office. Following high school my father attended teacher training for one year at the local college, which was then called "normal" school. After that he worked in a one-room schoolhouse for several years during the Depression. We still have a picture of one of his classes: 12 students, no more than two per grade, standing in front of a tiny building in the middle of the prairie grass, many bare-footed and poorly dressed. In the summer he took some university courses at the University of Alberta in Edmonton, hoping to eventually, one summer at a time, complete a university degree. My father left his teaching position and worked for a brief time as a labourer in the oil fields and then, with his father's encouragement, turned his sights to law. There was no university in Calgary and no local law school nor money to go elsewhere to study. What was available, however, was an apprenticeship program, where my father worked for a tiny wage for five years in a local legal office, studying the same texts and writing the same yearly exams as the university-based students. Like my mother, he regretted not having the opportunity to complete his university degree, and like my mother, he was an avid learner, a student of life who continued to study law on his own for the remainder of his professional life.

Thus I grew up in a context where books, education, and lifelong learning were central. And, not surprisingly, completing a university degree was regarded as something I would, of course, do. Much to my parents' dismay, I resisted this destiny, regarding universities as not about the real world. I'm not sure where I developed that sentiment, as I completed all the required high school courses that one needed to enter university and I recall enjoying school. I was also active in the student council, learning some early lessons about sexism when I ran for school president only to be told I should shift my sights to being student council secretary. Perhaps my resistant-to-university stance was partly informed by the fact that my parents' access to postsecondary education had been thwarted; it was also likely to be the typical adolescent resistance to any pathway that had been preordained by one's parents. So what was I to do having finished school? I had been working since I was sixteen in a department store and knew that retail sales at $1.25 per hour would not provide a living wage. And so, with a desire for work that was real, that would give me mobile skills, I entered a three-year hospital-based nursing program in Calgary, Alberta.

In the nursing program, we were required to live in residence, which became another significant context of my learning, and the relationships developed there with my classmates have endured for over 30 years. Nurses' training in the late 1960s and early 1970s still had remnants of its military history with relationships organized on clear hierarchical lines and charges of insubordination were not uncommon if one did not obey those in higher positions of authority (I had a few of those charges on my file). As student nurses, we paid little tuition, contributing to the costs of our education and room and board by working as relief staff every summer. I don't think I was very happy these three years; I resisted the top-down order, the institutional culture, and subordinate status of nurses, especially student nurses. In my family, however, one never quit what one started, and I think this kept me in the program. In hindsight, I see now that it was a thoroughgoing education that prepared me for just about anything that could happen in a hospital and later in life; long after I'd left the practice of nursing, it proved central to my role as an advocate for both of my aging and ill parents.

After receiving my nursing diploma, I worked for about six years in my training hospital on a variety of wards. A couple of years after graduation, I saved my pennies and took one year off to travel, spending most of the time in Africa—a mind-altering journey that illuminated for me the profound disparities between North and South and the generosity of people who had little to give. I also undertook intensive meditation training and brought this practice into my work with patients. When I returned to work at my training hospital, I covered for the patient teaching nurse while she was on an extended leave. I remember feeling like I'd found a space inside the hierarchized institutional structure of the hospital that suited my interests and visions of what nursing could be. Here I had my own office and classroom space where groups of patients and their families came to learn how to cope with their new diagnoses of diabetes and cancer. I also did a lot of one-to-one teaching, traveling to every ward. In this space, education and learning, most of it for adults, was at the centre of my practice. I learned to be a facilitator, a kind of educational broker, bringing knowledge of medicine and health to individuals so they could take charge of their health. As a bedside nurse, I was often frustrated with how patients were left in the dark and not included in decision making. In this position, this was actually the goal and it was liberating for me. The role of broker, bringing people together and providing information to people to help them solve their problems, is a position that I continue to occupy.

After moving to Vancouver, I returned to bedside nursing as that was the only kind of position I could find with my nursing diploma. Other positions were only available for those with a degree, so having resisted this destination for almost ten years, I entered university. In that program, two years of credit were given for my three-year nursing diploma and years of work. Here I joined a group of returning RNs (we called ourselves "the retreads") who became an important community of solidarity. While our nursing experience and previous education was given some credit at entry to the program, this experience was often ignored and dismissed in the curriculum. Nursing theory, they told us, was to be our salvation. Perhaps there was some important knowledge to be gained, but the group I affiliated with strongly resisted this orientation. Here was another moment in my journey where I came to appreciate the experience of adult learners returning to education (somewhat reluctantly, forced by economics and credentialism). My orientation to learning was again quite pragmatic. I noted a palpable difference between the younger students and our "retread" gang; for us, this was an expensive endeavor and one we were going to maximize. We were a noisy group, challenging theories that bore no relation to our lived experience, complaining about poor instruction and generally holding the program accountable to delivering what we needed. I must say that there were instructors who were remarkable, who did acknowledge our experience and developed curriculum grounded in that recognition and respect. In their eyes, we had something to contribute. Indeed, we could even be teachers, and the others in the class, including the instructors, would be learners. I did not name this experience as dialogical learning at the time, but in retrospect, I see that this is what it was. I also think my going to university later in life has made me mindful of those students I now work with who are engaged with their learning in the midst of complex family, community and work responsibilities. They, like me, demand quality and relevant curriculum and access to the full range of resources.

When I finished my nursing degree I worked for five years as community health nurse (CHN) involved in organizing and delivering educational activities across the life span and in community clinics, schools, and social housing projects. In schools, I worked with teachers and children, teaching various health-related topics and managing school health programs, including a brief stint as a sexual health educator. This was an exhilarating time where I daily reached the limits of my knowledge, and so on-the-job training was a necessity. This work required a great deal of planning of programs, community building, and adult education (although I did not use that term then). It was here that I became aware of the importance of on-the-job learning, community-based practice, and the breadth of learning activities that exist beyond formalized programs and institutions. It was also a very challenging time as I encountered the limits of my abilities and that of a health system that did not seem equipped, or interested, in addressing poverty, child abuse, domestic violence, and racism against newly arrived immigrants. My social justice sensibilities were sharpened as well. I observed with dismay the lack of respect for women's, especially poor single mothers, caring responsibilities and prejudice against people of color. It was here that I also began to take very seriously the limiting and enabling role of institutional and state policy on women's lives.

At this point, I had been working as a nurse for almost 14 years (including my various training periods) and I was burnt out and wanting to make a career shift. Newly divorced, and much to the shock of my family and friends, I quit my community health job. I worked for a brief time with the local school board running fitness classes for teachers and I also started volunteering at a women's centre where I obtained my Peer Counseling Certificate. At the centre, I ran career and health-related workshops, consciousness-raising groups, and offered career counseling services. I loved it. These experiences sparked my desire to improve my educational planning and instructing skills and it also fueled an intense interest in women's access to education and good jobs. With some hesitation, given my earlier experience with university, I took several different graduate courses as an unclassified student. Having heard of the adult education program from one of my retread nursing friends, one of the courses I took was an introduction to the field taught by the effervescent Paz Buttedahl. Paz actively recruited me into the master's program which I began in July 1984, where I had the privilege of taking my first course from Paulo Freire. Paz, who was from Chile and had many contacts in Latin America and knew Freire, had worked her magic and brought Paulo to UBC. His name had been one of the many I'd encountered in the introductory course, but I had not read any of his books.

When I began my master's, my mother had become seriously ill, so my attention was elsewhere and I was somewhat oblivious to the frenzy of activity surrounding Freire's presence at UBC. My memory of that summer was visiting my mother in hospital then cycling to UBC and then going back to the hospital on my way home, sitting beside her bed reading the assigned books and articles. I was not very patient with any theoretical discussion, nor was I partial to engaging with abstract ideas. My mother's illness was at the front of my consciousness and I challenged Freire on many occasions to bring his ideas down to the ground and to include gender in his analysis. He responded to me with great gentleness and respect and I quickly came to see that his ideas were firmly rooted in his heart as much as his mind. Even though we were talking about education for critical consciousness and liberatory curriculum grounded in the lived reality of disenfranchised Brazilians, his ideas and quality of engagement helped me to cope with my mother's illness. I wrote my final class essay for Freire about my mother, as I could think of nothing else at the time, and he responded with great thoughtfulness and empathy. He was a fabulous educator (as well as theorist); he was attuned to what was alive in people, a key aspect of being an effective adult educator.

As I observed the large role that Freire's ideas played in the global community called adult education, I noted that little was known or acknowledged about a feminist social revolution taking place in North America. This desire to bring into the adult education arena the important role of consciousness-raising groups as the educational foundation of the women's movement led me to my MA research (1987), which was a comparative analysis of feminist notions of consciousness raising and Freire's notion of conscientization. Having great respect for Freire's ideas, I also wanted to challenge adult educators in North America who seemed oblivious to what was happening in their own local context. I have continued to be curious, at times very frustrated, by the way in which feminist thought which has contributed enormously to understanding how we think about emancipatory and transformational learning is pushed to the margins of adult education or seen as somehow a completely separate field of studies. My commitment to the educational project of women's movements was informed by my engagement with feminist and adult education advocacy organizations, most of them concerned with women's access to and the funding for high-quality employment-related training. While completing my master's degree, I was bitten by the research bug. Again, I felt that my skills and knowledge would only take me so far and so I entered a doctoral program. At this point, my father, immensely proud but a little curious, pointed out to me the declaration I had made at the tender age of 17, that university was not about the real world. I had come to see that theory and scholarly ideas did have a role to play in changing relations of inequality, although the academy also created barriers to bringing this kind of activist orientation to research and teaching.

My connection with women's advocacy organizations led to the focus of my doctoral research (1988-1992) which, informed by various feminist theories of the state, investigated federally funded re-entry programs for women. Some members of my supervisory committee were concerned that my feminist politics were detracting from my doctoral studies. I had been involved with a national protest of funding cuts to women's centres, an enormous learning experience that piqued my interest and appreciation for the central role played by adult education, particularly popular education, in progressive social movements. In response to my committee's concerns, I argued that my activism actually strengthened the validity and rigor of my research; it offered an arena of practice where my ideas and analysis were tested and refined. Women's job training programs and the policy context were at the centre of much of the work undertaken by a national feminist coalition I was working with. My doctoral research helped me to make sense of the problems and the process of politicizing women's needs. Feminist theory figured prominently, particularly the work of Dorothy Smith and Nancy Fraser and others, who focused their analysis on women's lived experiences and the role of state policy. I wrote my dissertation following the traditional structure. It was unlikely that women's advocacy grassroots organizations would be reading it, but I was committed to making my work meaningful to more than the academy and to giving back to the community. And so I secured funding and helped to create two editions of "The Back to School Survival Guide for Women," a booklet based on women's stories which mapped out the various routes and entry points for women to return to learning.

There were other important learning experiences during my graduate training. In response to a lack of feminist theory courses, I joined together with other graduate students to create our own curriculum, copying articles and meeting regularly to discuss them. In 1988, I participated in an intensive residential training program at the Summer Institute for Gender and Development in Halifax, Nova Scotia. This program was a partnership between a Canadian international development agency and several Halifax universities. Here I met women from around the world all working in some development capacity. Also attending that institute were several Aboriginal women from Canada. These women regularly challenged the Eurocentric curriculum and the problematic assumptions (about the "First" and "Third" worlds) underpinning notions of development. Although I had read about colonial and cultural studies, this program was where I really learned through the experience of others. It was also here that I came to more deeply understand the longstanding colonial and racist practices inflicted on First Nations people by the Canadian government and other agencies and how as a descendent of a White settler society I embodied that legacy. I had another opportunity to view adult education from an international perspective in 1990 when I attended, as a representative of a national women's organization, the Fourth World Assembly of the International Council of Adult Education (ICAE) held in Bangkok, Thailand. Part of that gathering of more that 600 delegates from around the world involved what was called "solidarity visits." Before the official conference started, I traveled with a group of other conference attendees to several small villages in what is known as the Golden Triangle, learning from local villagers about their adult education and community development activities and the struggle they faced in relation to the drug trade, addiction, and government regulations which constructed them, because they were not literate in Thai nor considered economically stable, as noncitizens. At that international meeting, my education continued through the women's program of ICAE, which brought to the conference local and national women's groups who were working to free women and their children from the sex trade industry. I visited cooperatives where women were making various crafts, earning decent wages and living in secure environments. Here again, I was reminded of the interconnection between adult education and community development and of the power of popular education.

After completing my doctorate in 1993, I had many jobs as what I came to call a "just-in-time knowledge worker." I was a part-time instructor, research coordinator, educational consultant, and faculty development educator. In the latter job, I discovered that all that I had learned about the principles and politics of adult learning were relevant to the services and workshops we created for faculty, helping them in their work as educators, curriculum developers and educational leaders. In 1997 I acquired my current tenure-track position in the Adult Education program in the Department of Educational Studies at UBC. Here I teach not only in that program area, but also in educational leadership, social justice and teacher education, feminist theory, and research methodology. In that faculty position, I have continued to conduct research on women's learning experiences and have engaged with several community-based and action-oriented projects and have worked to build partnerships between universities and communities. One of my projects involved popular theatre, which has fueled a strong interest in the power of the expressive arts as a research, social justice and community-building tool. I now have tenure and, as of

2004, have taken on yet another new role, that of graduate advisor in our department which has multiple graduate programs and more than 420 graduate students. In that position, I have again undertaken much on-the-job learning, regularly coming into contact with my limited knowledge. This position, like the work I undertook in faculty development, has also afforded me yet another new view of the university. Here, as with other academic roles, I bring my commitment to building community, creating learning opportunities outside of the traditional formal classroom structure, and acting as an educational broker. I am mindful of students' multiple roles as they attempt to maximize, much like I did years ago, their graduate educational experiences.

Reflecting back I see some threads weaving their way through my development as an adult educator. In my nursing, community-based, feminist advocacy and academic experiences I value learning experiences that are often not on the radar, the teaching-learning dialogic relationship and the importance of using my privileged position in the academy to create space for learning that matters. It is difficult at times to bring the principles of adult education, respect for the learner's experience and desires, into the sometimes rigid walls of the university, but the walls are not permanent and there are cracks in the mortar where the light comes in. I try (and often fail) to stay tuned to what is alive in my colleagues and my students as the beginning and end point for our educational relationships. So much to my surprise and that of my parents, my third (or is it fourth?) and likely final career will be as an academic. If my mother were alive, she would be look at me with those agate blue eyes and wonder, "Just what does she think she's doing!"

Paul Brian Carr

First, I must state that I am astonished and humbled to be included in this text. To be considered for such a publication; and among some of the truly gifted educators of our time, is awe-inspiring for me. I am truly grateful to my peers, friends and colleagues who recommended me for inclusion in this text.

Early Recollections of Learning

I have been a curious person as long as I can remember. I recall sitting in kindergarten and elementary school classes daydreaming about possible connections and solutions to some of the more basic questions associated with just about any topic. I would sit in class and drift away from the lectures that prompted one to learn the correct answers to specified questions and think about such intriguing anecdotes as to how the lead got into the middle of my big yellow pencil. I would also ponder the rationale for being constantly reprimanded for asking questions and talking to my classmates about what we were learning. My teachers appeared to be constantly annoyed with my questions regarding why things were related in such a manner – I learned very early that for one to survive the S-minus (less than satisfactory) grades on report cards one must develop an accomplished memory and not ask too many questions. I also realized that I could ask my grandmothers (Granny and Nana) any question at all without them becoming annoyed with me.

My grandmother, who lived across the street, was always available for my questions and curiosity – Granny was a proponent of learning who most always sent me to a dictionary, thesaurus, or encyclopedia and helped me to research the question I posed to her. She would always read the words to me as I would follow her finger under the text – in essence we would look up the information together. She would also read the children's book, *The Little Engine That Could,* to me very often; and in a similar manner. As I became a reader I felt an increasing power associated with the freedom of learning what I wanted to learn and not depending upon the answers of others, which increasingly annoyed some of my teachers later in school. I recall feeling an immense sense of curiosity and efficacy associated with books, learning, and writing.

Middle School, High School, and Dropping Out

As I progressed through to middle school, I became very bored with the pace and the topics of study; it appeared as though we were learning only the perspectives of teachers about subjects that had little or no bearing upon what really mattered. I had the feeling that thinking and learning were far too important to be discounted during the academic discourse. I was interested in the overall courses of study, but the learning endeavor offered little room for thinking and curiosity – we needed to learn the right answers according to someone else. As my educational experience progressed I kept thinking, writing, and asking questions; I recall carrying a thesaurus around with me and utilizing new words whenever I could. I remember being preoccupied with institutions of higher learning such as Harvard University and Oxford – I even wore clothes that I associated with the Ivy League institutions such as plaid jackets, white buck shoes, bow ties and khaki pants.

When I made it to high school I was very interested in English, writing, art, and music – I was also interested in activities such as surfing, skateboarding and trying to be cool. In retrospect, the students who were labeled as being smart were not very cool. I believe this played a profound role in my decision to quit high school before completing the eleventh grade. After quitting high school I began a full-time job changing light bulbs in traffic signals and assisting in basic traffic engineering activities – this was a job my father arranged for me hoping I would return to school. He was a local traffic engineer who thought the type of work would encourage me to return to school. However, I loved the job and the people with whom I worked; I stayed with the same municipal employer for over ten years.

As the years progressed I was able to move into more demanding positions that not only required a high school diploma but some college coursework – no one ever asked if I had finished high school; and I was able to learn what I needed to learn in a relatively self-directed manner. I did however learn that the so-called college guys I worked for were not any smarter than I was – actually many of my co-workers (who were not college graduates) appeared to be smarter than our bosses. I did become increasingly annoyed with people whom I viewed as being pretty much the same as me making more money and having a better life than me due to my lack of education. I became interested in college (and education) based upon what I later learned to be a construct called vicarious reward (Bandura, 1997).

I quit my job and started thinking about possible careers such as real estate, insurance, and investing due to their limitless potential for income. I also found it attractive that several of the most successful individuals I met had also quit high school. I dabbled in various businesses until I began reading some of the books I had enjoyed while in school; I read some of the classics as well as biographies of successful and brilliant individuals. I was learning and thinking again and I very much enjoyed the freedom and power I gained from conversations with my grandmother that I instantly recalled. I was learning simply for the sake of learning – it felt wonderful again.

Dropping Back In

I began to think about attending the local community college and taking some courses – I was constantly faced with making self-efficacy assessments regarding my fit for such an endeavor, however. I finally gained the courage needed to visit Tidewater Community College and make an appointment with a counselor. I felt a great sense of relief when the counselor entered the room for our appointment – he had been a friend of mine from my high school days. He did a wonderful job of validating my quest for attending college by saying it was never too late for one to begin college matriculation. He also reminded me that I needed a high school diploma or a GED.

I reluctantly went to the local adult learning center in an effort to learn about the GED test. A friendly lady welcomed me and asked if I was there for the test. I replied that I came to get some information about the test. She then informed me the test began in about ten minutes and to sign in. I followed her instructions and sat for the GED test; just like that. I felt the test was relatively easy and I really enjoyed the stressors associated with actually sitting for the exam as well as the writing aspects. I very much enjoyed the endeavor. I learned in a couple of weeks that I had passed the GED test on a fall day in 1990.

When I learned that I successfully negotiated the GED test I called my friend at Tidewater Community College who was very happy for me. He arranged a meeting for me to discuss the upcoming spring semester with him and to register for classes. I began my first day of college in January 1991 with a spattering of English, general education, math, and philosophy courses. I loved the courses as well as the professors – they actually elicited my participation in class, which was vastly different than my earlier experiences in schools. I began to feel the freedom and fondness for learning I had once felt as a child – college was wonderful.

After two years of successful matriculation at Tidewater Community College I applied to a small, private liberal arts college (Virginia Wesleyan College) that was highly rated as being an excellent four-year institution. I was accepted and began studying all of the subjects that had interested me all of my life. Virginia Wesleyan was an outstanding institution; the professors were able to stretch me as a student but they did not lecture and test for the right answers – they were collective proponents of learning and thinking. I completed my studies at Virginia Wesleyan College in May 1995 when I earned a Bachelor of Arts in English with minors in Art and Religious Studies.

I then applied to several institutions for graduate studies where I was accepted at all of them. I ultimately chose a master's degree program in Human Resource Development at the George Washington University (GWU). GW proved to be an exceptional institution with a relevant and very interesting program of study. I cannot name all of the outstanding professors I met during my matriculation who made a profound difference in my life – I was learning that making a difference in the lives of others was an additional benefit associated with the learning endeavor. I had the fortune of taking several classes with Dr. Sharon Confessore who first introduced me to the freedom of self-directed learning in a formal learning environment. She also introduced me to her husband, Dr. Gary Confessore, who ultimately turned out to be my mentor, dissertation director and academic father – he was the director of the Higher Education Administration Doctoral Program at GWU. I completed the program in September 1996 with a master's degree in Education and Human Development - the very next day I began the doctoral program in Higher Education Administration under the guidance of Dr. Gary Confessore.

The doctoral program was an intense and invigorating endeavor that allowed me to actually become a doctor instead of getting a doctorate. Gary Confessore treated me as a colleague instead of a student during the entire course of study; I later came to think of this privilege as a method of contributing to the common learning. Learning, and the facilitation thereof, had changed me and the way I viewed learning – my grandmother and Gary had a great deal in common because they both knew when to spark my desire to learn and stay out of my way during the process.

The Privilege of the Professoriate

I am now a professor in a Ph.D. program in organizational leadership and human resource development. Thus far I have held teaching positions at several top-tier institutions at the baccalaureate master's and doctoral levels. I am very interested in learning and the facilitation thereof from an autonomous learning posture – in essence, I am interested in creating environments that may act as a catalyst for learning and thinking. I am also interested in creating similar environments that I experienced during my college and university matriculation where learning is a paramount consideration, not lecturing and testing for the correct answers.

I consider it a privilege to be in a position where I can possibly influence the self-regulation of others in a formal learning setting while sparking the conative factors of desire, initiative, resourcefulness, and persistence requisite for an accomplished autonomous learner. In essence, my doctoral students have the opportunity to essentially become doctors instead of simply getting a doctor's degree and thereby influence others. Learning and thinking are constructs that afford one the opportunity to be free, curious and deliberate throughout their lives. Being a professor also affords one the opportunity of commingling texts and other materials in order to promote thinking and learning. One of my doctoral-level courses features two required readings that have vastly impacted my life – *Self-Efficacy: The Exercise of Control* and *The Little Engine that Could*. These two texts provide unstinted opportunities for thinking, learning and other caveats associated with self-efficacy.

I constantly remind students that I am a new doctor (and professor) and I hope that I will continue to act as a new professor as long as I am afforded the privilege of being in this position. I also reveal that I am a high school dropout who dropped back in and chose to stay – and to think it all began with a children's book that read: "I think I can…I think I can…I think I can."

References

Bandura, A. (1997). *Self-efficacy: The exercise of control.* New York, NY: W. H. Freeman and Company.

Piper, Watty (1976). *The little engine that could.* New York, NY: Platt & Monk.

Ellen Carusetta, Ph.D.

Adult educators like metaphors and as I began to think about writing this piece, I tried to think of an appropriate metaphor. I know it is a metaphor of journey but I am not sure what kind of journey. I hope that through my writing, it will emerge.

I began my professional career as a social worker. In the early 70s and coming from an Italian-Canadian family, career choices were limited. I could be a teacher or a nurse. I don't relate well to large groups of young children or sight of blood. So, what else could I do with my life? I was supposed to work until I was ready to marry and have children – after all, that is what was expected of women in my family.

My parents, especially my father, wanted me to go to university. I would be the first in my family on my father's side to do so. The idea of moving away from home and being on my own was enough to have me agree. I found myself drawn to sociology and psychology courses and realized that I would like to work with people, so social work seemed like a good avenue.

My first position was in the welfare system as a case worker. While I enjoyed the challenge and pace of the work, I realized that I had very little to do with actually helping people. I also found I had little respect for the welfare system. It was fraught with rules and regulations I found degrading and demeaning to the people we were supposed to be helping. I did my best to challenge the rules but with little success. One case I remember in particular was a family where the husband stayed home and the wife went out to work. Her income was low enough to make the family eligible for an income supplement. However, the regulations did not acknowledge the woman as the head of the household and her income was considered in a category which made them ineligible for assistance. This regulation has since been changed but at the time I was frustrated by my inability to help this family.

I left the welfare work for a position in Big Sisters with teenage girls who had outgrown their "big sisters" but still wanted a connection. The support group I ran opened my eyes to the life of these girls and made me realize how little I knew about their world. It was the first time I remember being challenged to look at my assumptions about the world and realize that I lived a privileged life that restricted my ability to truly relate to these girls. For example, I could not understand why these girls thought it perfectly appropriate to have a child so they could be independent and collect welfare. My assumptions had led me to think that everyone wanted at least a life like mine.

From Big Sisters I moved to a position in a YWCA program called Fit for Life. Here I ran a life skills group for low-income women to help them look at their lives and see where they were headed. It was my first real teaching position. I can look back now and see that I naturally worked as a facilitator. We planned the course together, and I planned small group work, simulations, and field trips. We watched movies and we talked. I learned as much from these women as they did from me. I truly enjoyed this time of my life.

Our funding was cut and the program at the YWCA ended. I found myself at a crossroads. I decided that if I liked teaching I should find out more about it. I was accepted into the Master of Education program at Brock University and I found where I wanted to be when I grew up. I look back now and realize that I was the "typical" adult learner; I encountered many of the barriers and motivators that adult learners face.

My barriers, while not financial, were situational. I had a family that thought it was "interesting" that I wanted to go to school and did not mind as long as it did not interefere in their lives. However, the biggest barrier for me was dispositional – I was unsure of my abilities. I was 38 years old and had not been in school for 16 years. I remember clearly saying to one of my professors when I handed in my first paper: "You know, I haven't written anything but a letter in a very long time." He just smiled at me. If I had a dollar for every time I have heard that very same line since then, I could retire.

It was during this period that I met Patricia Cranton. She taught me my first adult education course using a text written by Dorothy MacKeracher. Sitting in a circle discussing the readings, I quickly grew to appreciate her quiet, composed teaching style. Once, when no one would offer to be a part of a role play and I reticently put up my hand, she quietly said to me, "You do not have to do this." I had a choice and she knew how uncomfortable I was. I was amazed at how perceptive she was. Patricia became my mentor, my thesis advisor, and subsequently my friend. She has been a part of my journey ever since. I learned from her the importance of connecting with learners, not just "teaching" them.

When I began my doctoral work at the Ontario Institute for Studies in Education, I felt even more the challenges that faced me. As the mother of two young boys, I felt guilty driving to Toronto for classes two and three times a week. My husband was not sure what I was doing but reluctantly supported me. I found my friends were leaving me behind. I made new friends and found a support system in my graduate student colleagues. Many of these are still good friends today. There was a process of transformation happening and I do not think I understood it at the time.

What I did begin to understand is who I was as a person and where I wanted to go with my life. I enjoyed the teaching/learning process. Along with my doctoral work, I took part-time work in the Brock University Teaching and Learning Centre where I was able to work with Patricia Cranton again. The area of faculty development and improvement in the teaching learning process became my passions.

One day a job posting passed by my desk. It was perfect for me except that it was at the University of New Brunswick (UNB). Patricia encouraged me to apply for it. She said the application process would do me good. Neither of us dreamt it would be offered to me.

I came for an interview and met, among others, Dorothy MacKeracher who ran the adult education program at UNB. I was completely intimidated. This was the person whose work introduced me to adult education. What could I possibly offer to a program that she ran?

In July 1993, I was hired and here I remain. I began working in the undergraduate adult education area, mainly organizing a program for the New Brunswick Community College instructors. I loved the work and the freedom to explore and learn that an academic position afforded me. In 2000, Dorothy MacKeracher retired and, working with Liz Burge, I took on responsibility for the graduate program in adult education.

During these years I learned a number of important lessons. Dorothy taught me my favourite: to ask forgiveness instead of permission. I learned to take risks on my students' behalf. I learned many ways to work around the system. I also learned that when asked, if I offered good logical reasons for the things I did, I could usually have them sanctioned.

Adult education is viewed as a poor cousin in the Faculty of Education. Because we are seen as somewhat peripheral we find ourselves being able to do things that might be more stringently scrutinized in other areas. For example, we were the first to offer credit for prior learning in our undergraduate program. It was years before the rest of the university caught up to us.

Since writing my dissertation I have done little research on my own. I much prefer the collaborative process – whether it is with graduate students or Patricia Cranton who has been my coresearcher in much of my research. I love exploring the tensions of the teaching-learning process. At the present time we are looking at the concept of authentic teaching.

Our work on authenticity has given me pause to look at my own life. In my early years at UNB, my first marriage failed. I realize now that in my first marriage I was completely inauthentic. I could not carry my working life into my home life. I look back now and realize how important it is to me to feel like my life is seamless – that I do not have to live in compartments. I have thoroughly enjoyed having my sons here and able to drop in to my office – to meet my students and to have a sense of what I "do for a living." My husband works in the same field so we can have long discussions around our work and we can present at conferences together. The people in my life understand that my work is important to me and is a part of who I am.

Having attained tenure, I feel free to do more of what I want in my work rather than what I need to succeed. I define success differently. I work in committees that can make a difference in the teaching/learning process. I no longer worry about doing too much teaching and not enough research. I have recently agreed to take on the duties of associate dean as I feel the need to give back to a place that has given me so much.

This is where I now find myself as an adult educator. My journey metaphor found me near the end of my writing. As a child, I would go to an amusement park that had a funhouse of mirrors. I would travel through the mazes, in and out of the light, to come upon one oddly shaped mirror after another. These mirrors distorted my image in all kinds of ways and I really had to look at myself in each one. I think I am still in this fun house but the mirrors are not so distorting and the journey continues to be fun. I look forward to the next glimpse of who I am.

Mary Katherine Cooper, Ph.D.

Becoming an adult educator, as with so many others, came later in life for me. It was not until I was in my forties that I even became aware that there was an academic field called Adult Education. My journey for some meaning to my life consisted of many false starts and disappointments. Born a year after the Second World War, I was part of a generation who saw many changes and went in search of themselves and a better world.

False Starts and Expectations

With family that came out of two world wars and the Great Depression, it was expected that I would find a "good job", with benefits, and marry, thus ensuring fiscal stability. If there was a possibility of attending college, it was to get a better class of husband. Based on society's expectations, there were three options for a woman: secretary, nurse, or teacher. I did not type well, couldn't see being a nurse, and although I loved playing school, didn't really want to be a teacher. This was during a time when my college education would have been paid for if I went into K-12 teaching. Having good grades, I was accepted at Iowa State University in the Food Science emphasis of the College of Home Economics. This course seemed to be far away from societal expectations while still being considered acceptable. Although still extremely immature, I left home for the college experience. This was more to leave home than anything else. While a degree from this program would have ensured employment at corporations such as General Mills and Pillsbury (both in my home city), I could not deal with the freedom of college life. I became ill, missed the boyfriend back home, and dropped out.

This started a decade of holding menial clerical and food service jobs while in a frantic search for a husband. After being engaged a number of times, I realized that I was not ready for marriage. I sought out short-term routes of education and training, but could not seem to find a place that felt right for me. Holding a job with good benefits that I disliked only exacerbated what I came to find out was clinical depression. I always seemed to be out of step with the mainstream and found most educational systems too restrictive. A multisided peg trying to fit in to someone else's round hole. At some point I realized that I needed further education to open up more options and was encouraged to go back to college.

Vocation

Still unaware of adult education, I decided to embark on a health management course of study. Since there was no undergraduate degree that matched this goal, and I am a firm believer in a liberal arts approach to learning, I located an option that would allow me to combine core business management and public health within a liberal arts degree option, a Bachelor of Individualized Studies (BIS). I was beginning to see ways in which one could adjust existing systems in order to personalize a course of study. With this degree, I moved into the healthcare sector. While working for a major healthcare provider, I was recruited into nursing education in order to provide educational program planning. The director, who recruited me, held a Ph.D. from the University of Minnesota, specializing in Adult Education. Through her I became aware of the field and individuals such as Knowles (1970, 1980). Still pursuing education in Health and Human Services Administration, now at the master's level, I began to see that much of my past experiences placed me into the category of the nontraditional learner. Adult education is about the nontraditional learner. As I privately researched what adult education was about, I realized that this was a viable alternative to the way I had previously been educated. I discovered a concept that spoke to the way in which I approached life, especially in the realm of teaching and learning, that of *andragogy*.

I was in my mid-forties when I decided that I wished to pursue a doctorate in Adult Education. When accepted at the University of Minnesota in the doctor of philosophy program, I found that I had come home. Adult education gave a theoretical foundation to my life experiences. I found that I fit the profile of the adult learner in all of the aspects. In fact, rather than being unusual, my experience was similar to other adults. My dissertation research supported this (Cooper, 1999). As I pursued my studies, I became aware that I had a true calling. The education career that I had avoided most of my life was based on a pre-scriptive system that had little to do with how I best learned. In the doctoral program, I had professors that truly modeled adult learning theory and began to treat me with respect and as a colleague. I was fortunate in being able to teach graduate and advanced undergraduate students before obtaining my Ph.D. This had been unheard of in the Adult Education program previously. As both teacher and learner I developed a philosophy of adult education that was based on sound learning theory, my experience, and a love of learning.

Philosophy

My philosophy of teaching can best be understood by considering the advising and mentoring of the adult learner. Since most of what I teach relates to my philosophy of teaching, I am in the position of attempting with each class to practice what I preach about teaching and learning. I seek through each class in adult education to apply the assumptions of the centuries-old concept of andragogy, the art and science of helping adults learn. Based on this tradition, I believe that learning is fundamentally a process of personal transformation that affects not only the learners but also the ways in which they relate what they learn to teaching, learning and self-discovery. I cannot be in a classroom without further developing as a human being. As teacher and learner, for me life is a journey of discovery.

Research in andragogy, transformative learning, and other adult learning theories has shown that adults have the capacity to be *self-directed*. This does not mean that the learners are on their own, rather that they be encouraged to take responsibility for their learning experience. As a learner, I realize that my self-direction was often what got me into trouble in the prescriptive system of my youth. As an adult educator, I see my role as being one of a guide to encourage a more active role on the part of the student in designing the means to reach educational objectives. In addition to being the content expert, I consider myself to be a resource facilitator. That is to be a guide to a broader, multidisciplinary research base.

A second concept of andragogy is that the adult brings a *wealth of experience* to the learning situation. When teaching and advising, this diversity of experience brings a richness to every teaching and learning experience. Building upon these experiences, much like in social constructivism, critical thinking is encouraged using both theoretical knowledge provided through the classes and personal experience. Research in the learning sciences has shown that individuals construct new understandings based on the interaction of their previous understandings and their experience of the world. Through class discussion and decisions in activities and design projects, I encourage students, through modeling and responding to their comments and ideas, to value and critically consider their experiences and assumptions. My goal throughout all these processes is to encourage experimentation, creativity, and to challenge the learners to go beyond the course information.

Third, the adult learner has a *need to know how things relate to their life and work*. This was especially true for me as a student. Most undergraduate degree programs did not provide what I felt I needed to learn. Until I found the option of designing my own degree program, I felt distanced and frustrated. Therefore, as an instructor, within each class setting, I require in addition to theoretical competency both a personal assessment and an examination of current practice. Since I began teaching at the university level, I have seen many of the course projects applied to work settings, locally and nationally, by the working adults who are also my students. This is related to another concept that adults are *intrinsically motivated*. As much as wanting another credential for work advancement, in the sharing of experience I see and encourage new ways of viewing the world. As the learners discuss, share and present, I encourage alternate ways of approaching any situation. It has become apparent that the need for personal development is often of primary importance to the learner.

At the core of these assumptions is the need for *environments conducive to lifelong learning*. In my teaching I provide this type of environment by modeling a respect for a diversity of opinion and experience. Within course parameters, I also encourage projects that hold personal or practical meaning for the learner. By providing flexibility in methods of exploration, the students feel free to take risks not normally considered previously. Although demanding rigorous scholarship, I encourage new approaches by using the concept of *mastery learning*. Within the allotted time frame of the course, feedback and formative evaluation are used.

Finally, research has shown that learning involves the development of both conceptual and practical knowledge. Since adult students need to see a connection between what they are learning and real-world applications, I have students read, produce, and share practical projects, as well as create individual presentations about concepts and participate in the collaborative construction of theoretical models. In these processes, I play the role of gathering and organizing stories and concepts, and in dialogue, highlighting the positive and refining that which needs improvement. I believe that education is, by nature, developmental. Therefore, in each teaching and learning environment, personal, theoretical and practical applications are required. Synthesis of all three through *critical thinking* is encouraged with the ultimate goal being that of transformation. *Transformative learning* is the objective of all of my teaching and advising.

My research agenda focuses on developing a greater understanding of environments conducive to lifelong learning. My research consequently focuses on developing a greater understanding of instructional and developmental inquiry learning in formal and informal educational contexts. My research is in the area of study referred to as the learning sciences, or studies of educational practice. I utilize a combination of developmental and socio-cultural theory, combined with interpretive research methodology, to inquire into the science of helping adults learn. Specifically, I study how learners and teachers or adult facilitators in educational contexts develop personally and professionally and which practices can assist them in their educational journey. I have researched more holistic aspects of instruction, beginning with an anthropological examination of the learning strategies conducive to group formation in *Play as a Component of the Adult Educational Experience.* Realizing the developmental aspects of education, and examining my philosophy of teaching and learning, I became aware of the necessity of inquiry into philosophy and its impact on learning environments and wrote *The Politics of Humanism: Defining Your Educational Philosophy.* Realizing that the experience of graduate study was more complex than I first thought, through interpretive inquiry I sought to determine what factors contributed to the graduate experience. My dissertation, *The Return to Academics: The Experience of the Older Graduate Student,* helped me to gain perspective on the learning experience for adults. Since this population had not been examined in this way prior to my dissertation, this work has been cited in multiple dissertations, both for the themes that emerged and for the phenomenological research paradigm.

Further Research

My research projects involve the award-winning adult education program at the UM-St. Louis College of Education, for which I have acted as coordinator of the online degree program. In considering the research on environments for lifelong learning, multiple delivery methods are considered optimal. Therefore, when the dean of the College of Education and the director of the Teaching and Learning Center wished the Adult Education master's to be delivered online, I worked to accommodate them and our learners. A study of the first summer of offering courses through MyGateway was written and presented to the Continuing Education Association. That study, *Investigating the Experience of On-line Learning: The Formulation of a Comprehensive Evaluation Plan,* began an inquiry into teaching and learning via the web. I have written and presented a number of works providing phenomenological snapshots into the experience. I gathered data across two years for an ethnographic examination of online teaching and learning.

At the same time, I worked to expand the program by developing 15 new courses to accommodate the topics required to have a thorough understanding of adult education and research. This has involved extensive study into distance education which can be said to be a practical application of adult learning principles.

Andragogy is related directly to the in-class and online teaching and learning experience. Popularized in the 1960s by Malcolm S. Knowles, andragogy has been debated in the U.S. since that time. However, what is known about the concept in the U.S. is limited. With my colleague, Dr. John Henschke, an international and historical inquiry was begun in 2001. Starting with 13 foundational works in English, our research continues. At the point when 18 foundational works were identified, we were invited to publish in the only journal devoted to andragogy, *Andragoske studije,* or *Studies in Andragogy.* It was published as *Andragogija, osnove teorije, istrazivanja i prakticnog povezivanja.* Our research continues in order to assist adult educators and learners to gain a deeper understanding. The most recent iteration of this research involves over 100 works (2005).

Conclusion—So Far

As one of my colleagues replies when asked if they are a lifelong learner, "I am not one yet." Wherever I go and whatever I do for the rest of my life, it will be about environments of respect, diversity, and above all learning throughout life. I will continue to assist adults to learn and grow and to learn and grow myself. I intend to do this by continuing to be active in organizations such as the American Association of Adult Education (AAACE), the Commission of Professors of Adult Education (CPAE), the Commission on International Adult Education (CIAE), Midwest Research-to-Practice, and other adult education organizations.

References

Cooper, M. K. (1999). *The return to academics: The experience of the older graduate student.* Doctoral dissertation, University of Minnesota.

Cooper, M. K., & Henschke, J. A. (2001). Andragogija, osnove teorije, istrazivanja i prakticnog povezivanja. (translation from English by Kristinka Ovesni). *Andragoske Studije,* 8(1-2).

Cooper, M., & J. Henschke. (2005). "Additional thinking about andragogy: The international foundation for its research, theory and practice linkage in adult education and human resource development – an update." In *Proceedings of the Commission on International Adult Education (CIAE) Pre-Conference of the American Association for Adult and Continuing Education (AAACE).* St. Louis, MO: University of Missouri.

Knowles, M. S. (1970, 1980). *The modern practice of adult education: Andragogy /Pedagogy.* New York: Cambridge Book Company.

Patricia Cranton
A Circuitous Journey

In the 1960s in Western Canada, there was a severe teacher shortage, especially in the remote rural areas of Alberta and Saskatchewan. Rural school districts, in an attempt to recruit teachers, would pay the tuition and some expenses for young people to go to university for the two years required to become a certified teacher on the condition that they returned to that school district to teach. I grew up in a community that placed far greater value on the calluses on a person's hands from hard work than it did on education. I also grew up in a community that wasn't especially well-suited to farming (it was dry, and the soil was sandy and quickly eroded in the prairie winds). We were poor. I was desperate to go to university, and the local school district's offer was the only way I could get there.

I worked at night (in a drapery factory, a pool hall, a telephone company, a drive-in restaurant, and when I was old enough, a bar) to save the money to pay back that school board so that I would not have to teach. My student teaching experience was the worst experience in my young life. I hated telling people not all that much younger than I, and in some cases, the same age as I (high school students, and I was 18), what to do. "Discipline," according to my advisory teacher, was my fatal weakness. I would never be able to "manage" a class.

Ten years later, I completed my Ph.D. in measurement, evaluation, and computer applications. I loved being a student and loved learning, and so I had just gone on doing both, but now that was finished. Teaching university would surely be much better than teaching high school; I applied for jobs. McGill University's Centre for Learning and Development (a faculty development service) was preparing to design a course and faculty evaluation system to be used across the university. This time, the mid to late 1970s, was the hayday of student ratings of instruction. Every university was inventing such systems and hundreds of people dedicated their research to analyzing the numbers in ways that showed the great usefulness of student ratings. McGill's Centre was struck by the "measurement and evaluation" in my Ph.D. studies and hired me. I did not know what faculty development was; I had never thought twice about student ratings of instruction; I had never taught. But there I was. Almost 27 and with no experience and responsible for the McGill Course and Faculty Evaluation System. It's a good thing I loved learning, and it is an especially good thing that I had the opportunity to work with Janet Donald, George Geis, Bruce Shore, and Glenn

Cartwright in those early years. They were my friends and mentors—they involved me in their research, taught me about faculty development, worked with me as I learned to be a faculty developer, and invited me into their homes and lives.

We were all cross-appointed to the Department of Educational Psychology and Counselling as our academic home, and it was there I learned to teach. I still wonder about the experiences of the students in those first courses I taught. I did not dare ask for feedback, me, the designer of the evaluation system. My first course was General Methods in Special Education. It was for practicing teachers, working toward a certificate in special education. The person who assigned me to that course must have been seeking revenge on someone, but I was too young and inexperienced to even know that I should have objected. The course was held in a school way out somewhere in an English-speaking part of Montreal. I took a city bus to get there. I bought and read the textbook one chapter ahead of the good and patient teachers who came to meet with me one evening a week. I did not have "discipline" problems, but that's about all I can say. Introduction to Educational Psychology was a little better. At least the students were younger than I was (first-year education students), but there were so many of them (more than 100), and I really did not know what to do with them, nor did I know much about the topics.

By the time I left McGill University ten years later and entered for the first time into the realm of adult education, I had grown to love teaching. My students worked in groups, they participated in the decision making for the courses, and I was far more at ease facilitating than professing. I was ready to leave Quebec, which had become somewhat uncomfortable for a unilingual Anglophone in those days (and all of my attempts to learn French had failed). A position was advertised in adult education at Brock University in Ontario. There was a colleague down the hall from me who was in adult education, so I went and asked him what I should read to get an overview of the field. He lent me Darkenwald and Merriam's book, *Foundations of Adult Education,* and a book by Jarvis, the title of which I no longer recall. Armed with the knowledge from these books and with the belief that faculty development was, after all, adult learning, I went to my interview, and then a few months later, to my first position in adult education. I was assigned three graduate courses per semester—Introduction to Adult Education, Techniques and Methods in Adult Education, and Introduction to Research Methods. Except for research methods, I was back to reading just ahead of the students, but by this time I was a good teacher and took advantage of my novice status to become a co-learner with my groups.

At McGill, it was my colleagues who helped me grow and learn; at Brock it was my students. I was as often in the graduate student office or the computer lab as I was in my own office. We debated, discussed, argued, exchanged ideas and readings, and worked to figure out what we were doing. Many of the students from those years went on to doctoral studies in higher and adult education and many of them remain my friends and colleagues today—Ellen Carusetta, Janice Clark, Valerie Grabove, Tony DiPetta, Tiiu Strauss, Phyllis Stanley, and Susan Wilcox, to name just a few of them.

The year that I moved to Brock University, 1986, Stephen Brookfield's book, *Understanding and Facilitating Adult Learning,* was published, and I was hooked. I read that book as though it was a mystery novel, staying up late and picking it up again first thing in the morning. (I still respond to Brookfield's books in this way; how I wish I could write like that!) I had found my place. I wrote my first book in adult education, *Planning Instruction for Adult Learners,* and shortly after that, my second, *Working with Adult Learners.* When Jack Mezirow's *Transformative Dimensions of Adult Learning* was published in 1991, I was immediately intrigued. I and my students held long and sometimes heated discussions on topics that seem silly to me now. How many meaning schemes are in a meaning perspective, we wondered, and just how many meaning perspectives can a person have?

By this time, I had initiated and was directing Brock University's Instructional Development Office, so I had the opportunity (and some meagre funds) to invite Jack Mezirow to speak to our faculty. The true motive was to meet him and to talk with him in our graduate student group—to find the "answers" to our questions. Jack Mezirow's book, his visit to our university, and now his continuing presence as a colleague and friend changed my life as an adult educator. When he came to visit—it might have been 1992 or 1993—I was preparing a proposal to write a book on transformative learning. Jack gently responded to the foolish, urgent questions we all had ("Who knows?" he would say, "I certainly don't"), but in spite of this, he encouraged me in my plans to write about transformative learning. I thought of this when, at the recent Sixth International Conference on Transformative Learning (Vlosak, Kielbaso, & Raford, 2005), John Dirkx named me as one of the foundational contributors to transformative learning theory. I remembered that evening more than a dozen years before—I think we were driving back from some dinner with Jack and a group of students—when I mentioned to Jack that I wanted to write something that followed his 1991 book with an emphasis on application. I hope I have been able to support others in turn, in the way that Jack supported me then.

My interest in transformative learning did not wane with time. I went on to combine my work in faculty development with transformative learning theory, proposing that faculty development could be and perhaps should be transformative in nature. In the mid 1990s, I started to pay attention to those people who suggested that more intuitive and extrarational understandings of transformation were needed. I was editing a New Directions volume on transformative learning, and I invited John Dirkx to contribute a chapter. That chapter (Dirkx, 1997), followed by others of John's publications, led me to begin an important expansion of my own thinking about transformative learning.

Now, I need to go back and pick up another thread. In those early exhilarating years at Brock University, in the late 1980's, I became interested in Carl Jung's work through the back door of psychological type. A colleague and later good friend, Robert Knoop, came to my office one day and handed me a Myers-Briggs Type Indicator to fill out. He told me how he used psychological type theory in his teaching, and he invited me to join him in a project to develop an alternative to the MBTI. This work engaged us for several years.

When I first encountered John Dirkx's work, I knew little of Jung outside of psychological type, but I quickly became intrigued with individuation, projection, the shadow, archetypes, and the animus and anima. I had previously proposed that psychological type preferences would influence the way people experienced transformative learning, but now I made small forays into linking transformative learning to individuation.

At the Fifth International Conference on Transformative Learning (Wiessner, Meyer, Pfhal, & Neaman, ,2003), I was almost struck speechless by John's presence in a discussion group I was leading following one of my sessions. The discussion was on the Jungian psychology and transformative learning, and there was John, who knew so much more than I about this topic. I think I made some embarrassing remark about his presence. Since then, I have been honored to have the opportunity to correspond with John and eventually collaborate with him. His thinking has had and continues to have a profound impact on mine. At the Sixth International Conference on Transformative Learning (Vlosak, Kielbaso, & Raford, 2005), when I facilitated a dialogue between John Dirkx and Jack Mezirow in a plenary session, I felt the great joy of seeing two parts of my life being represented and integrated. I have come to see that transformative learning is *both* rational and extrarational, and I can no longer imagine how I could have thought otherwise. Nevertheless, I did get a shock when Ed Taylor (2005), who is now a colleague of mine at Penn State University, listed me as a part of the "psychoanalytical" stream of writers on transformative learning.

Only yesterday I was 12 years old and riding my palomino horse, Toby, bareback and with only a halter across the dusty, dry prairie to bring in the cows. Today, nearly 45 years later, I am writing about my place in adult education and my contributions to the field. How did I get here from there? As Jack Mezirow might say, "who knows? I certainly don't."

References

Dirkx, J. (1997). Nurturing soul in adult education. In P. Cranton (Ed.), *Transformative learning in action: Insights from practice*. New Directions for Adult and Continuing Education, no. 74. San Francisco: Jossey-Bass.

Taylor, E. (2005). Making meaning of the varied and contested perspectives of transformative learning theory. In D. Vlosak, G. Kielbaso, & J. Raford (Eds.), *Appreciating the best of what is: Envisioning what could be*. Proceedings of the Sixth International Conference on Transformative Learning. East Lansing, MI: Michigan State University and Grand Rapids Community College.

Vlosak, D., Kielbaso, G., & Raford, J. (Eds.). (2005). *Appreciating the best of what is: Envisioning what could be*. Proceedings of the Sixth International Conference on Transformative Learning. East Lansing, MI: Michigan State University and Grand Rapids Community College.

Wiessner, C. A., Meyer, S. R., Pfhal, N., & Neaman, P. (Eds.). (2003). *Transformative learning in action: Building bridges across contexts and disciplines*. Proceedings of the Fifth International Conference on Transformative Learning. Teachers College, Columbia University.

Michael Day
Shaping a Career in Adult Education

When I consider the central ideas, people, and places that helped shape my career in adult education many things come to mind. Highlights would include my work with the University of Maryland's overseas undergraduate program during the early 1970s, my selection as a Kellogg Scholar in 1984 to participate in their first exchange program between North American and United Kingdom professors of adult education, my 1988 sabbatical leave to investigate distance education as conducted by the Open University at Milton Keynes, UK, and my early 1990s work with the Wyoming Adult Education Social Theatre Company. But, given space limitations, what follows generally focuses on my stay at the University of Wyoming and the two events that probably shaped my approach to adult education more than all the rest: graduate work at the University of Michigan and experiencing the University of Wyoming Mountain Folk School.

In 1982 I was hired by the College of Education at the University of Wyoming to guide their adult education graduate program. Graduate study in adult education began at UW in the early 1950s (initially called the Department of Adult Education Instruction), but in 1981 the department was eliminated and the program moved to the Department of Educational Administration. Faculty in my new host department could not have been more gracious. For the next three years I was the only adult education faculty member, but supportive individuals, in and outside the department, surrounded me. Twenty-three years have passed and Wyoming has become home. The adult education graduate program at UW thrives (three adult education faculty and over fifty graduate students) and there are still lots of interesting projects to complete.

UW hired me, I believe, because of my training as a generalist. For that I have faculty at the University of Michigan to thank. During the late 1970s U of MI was one of the premier adult education graduate programs in the United States. I did not realize how prestigious a place it was until I arrived in the fall of 1977. Up to that point it was more the university itself that was promoted and colleagues knew little about graduate study in the field of adult education or even if such a field actually existed. Let me back up.

From 1971 to 1977, I lived in Wiesbaden, West Germany. While there I completed my bachelor's degree through the European Division of the University of Maryland -- in a few fields of study, the university provided undergraduate courses and bachelor's degrees to members of the U.S. military, support personnel, and their families. After graduation, I was hired by U of MD to coordinate a fairly large adult education enterprise in Wiesbaden. It was during this time the world of adult education emerged as a viable field for graduate study and I began considering returning to the U.S. to pursue graduate study. Many U of MD instructors were familiar with the University of Michigan and encouraged me to apply there. I did and was accepted.

When we arrived in Ann Arbor in the fall of 1977, neither my wife nor I knew much about the university, its adult education graduate program, or living in the Midwest. With few resources, little debt, simple living arrangements, and an adventurous spirit, this soon became the best of times. Able to pursue studies full time I submersed myself in what the program, university and community had to offer. At that time the minimum coursework requirement for the PhD in Education at U of MI was sixty credit hours of course work beyond the bachelor's degree: twenty credit hours in the field of study, an additional twenty credit hours in education foundation and support courses, and twenty credit hours in coursework outside education. Because of transfer credit, I only needed to complete twenty additional credit hours from the School of Education and twenty credit hours outside the school. I chose courses from the History of Art Department to fulfill the out-of-school requirement. My preparation as an adult education generalist received a major boost from this decision.

In my first semester at U of MI, the national Adult Education Association held its annual fall meeting in Detroit, just a forty-minute drive from Ann Arbor. I volunteered to assist with the conference. In doing so, I experienced firsthand some of the personalities who studied, promoted, and challenged adult education beliefs and practice. I also witnessed the respect shown U of MI faculty, especially toward professor emeritus Howard Yale McClusky. (Each semester Howard still taught a course at U of MI and I enrolled in whatever he offered.) As a postconference event, U of MI faculty organized a small select gathering of leaders in the adult education field on the Ann Arbor campus. Again, I was fortunate to attend and help record these sessions. By the end of my first semester in Michigan I had personally met some of the major U.S. leaders in the field, including Cy Houle, Malcolm Knowles, and Alan Knox, as well as numerous international leaders such as John Lowe. I learned an actual field of adult education study existed, it was wrestling with numerous issues, and U of MI faculty had much to offer. Over the next few years I had the opportunity to meet and attend sessions with Paulo Freire, John Ohliger, Phyllis Cunningham, Bonaro Overstreet, Jonathan Kozol, Sharan Merriam, Michael Collins, and many others. Like a sponge, I recorded both visually and on audiocassette many of these encounters. To highlight the dynamism of the field, these materials were also shared with my Laramie students, as was the suggestion that perhaps one of the most recent dramatic movements in education was the adult education movement. In Ann Arbor, I also learned adult education had an interesting past.

This awareness led to one of the more memorable experiences I had at U of MI, an experience that greatly influenced my classroom approach to adult education in Laramie. In the summer of 1979, a group of graduate students approached Department Head Larry Berlin with a request. Having sampled a bit of history in a general adult education survey course, and somewhat fascinated by the evolution of adult education practice, we asked for an opportunity to more thoroughly study the roots of our new discipline. No course existed, therefore no academic credit could be offered, but Larry suggested we form a discussion group. Provided group members took the sessions seriously, read the assigned readings, and actively participated in discussions, Larry would lead the group. We agreed; books were chosen and ordered. Initially, we met for two hours twice a month, usually in Larry's home. These discussions continued well after I finished my degree two years later.

By the time the book discussions began, my adult education horizons had expanded dramatically. I experienced firsthand a seemingly dynamic field of study made up of colorful, approachable and interesting personalities. Supplementing these experiences was exposure to a new literature and research, to contemporary issues in need of attention, and to a seemingly endless assortment of adult education agencies and opportunities. My previous experience with adult education at the University of Maryland seemed a small piece in an ever-expanding tapestry. In addition, my studies in the History of Art Department were leading me toward a dissertation topic and perhaps a career within museum adult education. Then the book discussions started.

Under Larry's tutelage, and along side a seemingly insatiable group of graduate students, new ideas unfolded. A variety of U.S. classics were examined through the lens of adult education. I recall reading works clearly related to adult education theory and practice, such as *The Autobiography of Benjamin Franklin*, *The Chautauqua Movement* by John Vincent, *Hull House* by Jane Addams, and Eduard Lindeman's *The Meaning of Adult Education*. We also read works seemingly less focused on adult education such as, *The Federalist Papers*, and De Tocqueville's *Democracy in America*. We also read John Dewey. These were lively conversations punctuated by examination of our nation's brief history and discourse about the purpose and significance of adult education. I left these discussions with great respect for both the progressive and liberal values that helped guide the adult education movement in the U.S. during the 1920s.

The general effect of the discussion group experience on shaping my adult education career was significant. First, I changed my dissertation topic from museum adult education to a content analysis of the *Journal of Adult Education*. The journal, published by the American Association for Adult Education (AAAE), can be viewed as the mouthpiece of the early U.S. adult education movement. I also changed career aspirations. I now desired to share with graduate students in a university environment my enthusiasm for the underpinnings of current adult education practice. The University of Wyoming provided me the opportunity to do just that.

Since leaving Ann Arbor and our discussion group, I have been caught in a bit of a time warp. Both colleagues and students kid me about my reverence and admiration for John Dewey. I introduced two new courses at UW directly shaped by participation in the U of MI book discussion group: a teaching adults course that applies themes and values shaped during the first few decades of the twentieth century (with a modern twist) and a foundation course titled The American Adult Education Movement. In both courses students read, discuss, and apply Deweyan concepts, but in the Movement course students also read and discuss works selected by Larry Berlin nearly twenty-five years ago. Integrated into these courses are connections to other disciplines such as history, philosophy, psychology, sociology and art. Throughout these courses, as well as others, discussion often returns to values: to the ultimate purpose and significance of adult education practice.

What are some of these values? As noted above, today these values might be viewed as progressive or liberal; they seemed to seep through the pores of early members of the AAAE such as Dorothy Canfield Fisher, Eduard Lindeman, Alvin Johnson, and Everett Dean Martin. Though these individuals might differ as to the social or individual focus of adult education, they seemed to agree that it was serious work, undertaken to add meaning to life and/or to challenge and change social restraints and relationships. Often both intrinsically and extrinsically worthwhile, such education takes vision, effort, commitment and discipline.

Though I learned much from current and popular adult education theorists, such as Malcolm Knowles, K. Patricia Cross, Paulo Freire and Jack Mezirow, it was from Dewey I learned the most valuable lesson regarding teaching adult learners. Dewey cautions that three outcomes can occur when students (adults as well as children) undertake a learning objective, and two of them are not good: 1) the past experience of students is successfully linked to new concepts, ideas, or ways of performing and growth occurs, expanding possibilities for future learning; 2) the past experience of students remains unconnected to the new learning objective resulting in no consequence; 3) the intersection of old experiences and new learning results in feelings of inadequacy that restrict and limit future learning. This lesson continues to guide my teaching, reminding me of the seriousness of my role as an adult educator. To minimize restricting possibilities for future learning, I am constantly challenged to build constructively upon the previous experience of students, their understandings as well as their behaviors.

Throughout the 1980s and into the 1990s the pedagogic values I learned in Ann Arbor served me well as an adult educator. I found in the values of early members of the AAAE, in the adult education literature discussed with Larry, and in Dewey's work the foundation for contemporary themes such as critical theory, perspective transformation, and issues of diversity, access and voice. But something was missing.

In the mid=1980s, providing both friendship and much needed support, Burt Sisco joined the UW faculty. During his stay at UW, Burt implemented a program I still strive to maintain: the UW Folk School in the Mountains. Burt shared my interest in the roots of adult education practice. He was especially interested in the 19th-century Danish Folk School Movement as well as twentieth-century programs in the U.S., such as The Highlander Center, that shared similar characteristics. Burt came to me with a request in 1992 to organize a folk school type of experience in the mountains above Centennial, WY, a thirty-minute drive from Laramie. He suggested we encourage our graduate students to organize a weeklong program during the summer. They did. Since then, for the most part, the program has been offered each year. Joining thirty participants the first year, I found something I had not expected.

The University of Wyoming possesses a rather rustic residence complex situated in the Medicine Bow National Forest; it is made up of a number of cabins, a bathhouse, and a main lodge. For nearly ten years, this is where the folk school was located. Generally the programs have a strong relationship-building agenda to the topic as well as amongst graduate students and faculty. Sprinkled with numerous references to social change, the program's focus the first year was the environment. Gradually, throughout the week, a kinship with nature evolved, resulting in a deepening regard for the natural world. I was awestruck by the beauty, diversity, complexity, drama and grandeur of the setting surrounding the residential program. I began taking nature seriously and behaved more humbly toward it.

I also realized something was missing from my preparation as an adult educator. The field of adult education seemed rather silent about connections between human beings and other species. Both the progressive and liberal values I adopted in Ann Arbor were products of a mindset focused primarily on the relationship between individuals and society. Missing was the acknowledgment of coexistence with other species. The place of human beings within nature was something I did not take away from previous studies. Increasingly, it is the interdependent connection human beings have to the natural world that occupies my attention. Humility, death, birth, struggle and courage are lessons the natural world shares with those willing to observe. We have the ability and resources to be good stewards of nature but sometimes lack opportunities to fully experience and appreciate nature.

By the end of the 1990s, I was spending more and more time in and near wilderness areas. I hiked and backpacked extensively. I began reading new authors: Aldo Leopold, Roderick Nash, E. O. Wilson, John Muir and Henry David Thoreau. My writings and presentations began incorporating rationales and tools for strengthening bonds with nature. The Mountain Folk School was moved to Yellowstone National Park and the program was redesigned to provide closer connections to wildlife and the natural landscape. I also became a more serious photographer of nature. All in all, I have become a nature enthusiast who can think of no better medium for conducting serious adult education than with nature as guide and constant companion.

M. Gail Derrick, Ed.D.

Specific events and circumstances have a definitive impact upon the life course of an individual and can be influential factors in the choices and decisions that are made throughout the lifespan. These powerful motivators and elements serve as instrumental determinates of future choices and courses of action, and may or may not be readily apparent or even understood by the individual given the circumstances. These factors and circumstances are influential on how one develops and views learning not only at distinct points but also throughout life. My purpose is to share how certain events and specific influences have played a significant role in my life and learning journey to adult educator. The three major points I want to emphasize and discuss are centered on culture, efficacy, and curiosity. The relationship of these areas is within the context of learning. The significance of culture, the activating events that enhance efficacy towards learning, and the role and impact of curiosity are factors to consider for those in the field of adult education. These three areas had exerted a strong influence on how I learn and view learning in general. The opportunity to reflect upon how these circumstances frame what has motivated me to engage and participate in lifelong learning has been insightful and hopefully will provide the reader with ideas for future research in the field of adult learning.

The major topic within the realm of cultural influences is the notion of one's social position within the larger cultural context. The questions that arise are: How does one participate and interact within the boundaries of their culture? In addition, how cognizant are we of the influence of the norms and mores of our cultural background as we progress through stages of development? In particular with learning-- do we understand the influence of culture upon our own personal development and do we appreciate and understand cultural aspects in others? The rules, both explicit and implicit, associated with cultural patterns bind one to certain behaviors. It can be challenging to break away from deeply ingrained customs and rituals in order to move forward to another stage of life development. These passages evolve over time and have common threads and themes with those of the same generation with similar cultural influences.

There has been a renewed interest in the role of culture and learning that I have found interesting for the K-12 educational setting. Questions such as, how does culture affect learning and what does it mean to be culturally aware, mandate many of our educational priorities as a result of the disparity in achievement for diverse groups of populations. We are a much more diverse society than ever before with different languages, cultures, values, and beliefs. This was not as true for those of us who grew up in the 1950's in a conservative, Southern homogeneous background, specifically Columbia, South Carolina.

The period appeared to reflect a time in which roles (mother, father, male, female) where clearly defined. In some aspects, the Leave It to Beaver television show did portray a real way of life. Of course, the lens was that of a child; however, Dick, Jane, and Sally were symbols that represented everything that was good and safe. You could leave your door unlocked, children did take the bus to go to the movies uptown, and one had more freedom than children today will ever experience.

However, it was not a Shangri-La, and challenges and differences existed just as crucial and important as those we face today. The differences were more in line with economic status and wealth, which is still a dividing line for many current social issues. The community was an extended neighborhood with similar beliefs and values that stressed family and church with very established rules of conduct and behavior. You were taught to be polite and respectful to others, a graciousness still evident today when I travel back to the area. Of course, there was another side to this idyllic time-- limitations and frailties existed, I just did not know that until I became older.

My mother was a single working mother with a sixth-grade education and we were poor. I did not comprehend the significance of that fact at the time and it had little impact upon me until I became aware of the relationship of power and influence with money and wealth. I realized the very first day of seventh grade that those big houses we saw on our Sunday drives throughout Columbia—well, these kids actually lived in them. I instantly understood the relationship of money to power and status and I remember being rather surprised by the idea .This dividing line became more obvious as I moved into high school. I noticed and observed the differences but was never as concerned as some of my friends. I think I was always assured of my self-worth and value despite the lack of monetary resources. I never defined who I was and continue to be by money or external or material objects. In hindsight, I believe I had developed a more resilient attitude than most children my age due to a family structure that emphasized the person, the individual, over anything else. You were valued because you existed. That is not to discount the quest to be in a better or more comfortable circumstance, it was just never the ultimate goal. I believe we see this in many family structures today. The emphasis on student achievement and success use indicators such as socioeconomic status, family structure, and parental involvement. A temporary barrier does not have to become a permanent obstacle to success. All of these areas are important and certainly have been researched for their effectiveness. However, I see and hear many generalizations made as if there is only one way to define parental involvement or that poor families have less aspiration and hope for their children or themselves. We have to be cautious in our interpretation and explanation related to success since it is filtered through our own cultural lens. Limitations can be avenues for success and we should focus on how to develop resilient approaches to life events.

For me, the development of a resilient perspective can be attributed to family and their attitude that I could do anything; you were only limited by yourself and the vast possibilities. We were poor in many respects and the family structure was not the norm for that time. However, we did have a close and large family who supported each other. I can still hear my mother saying, "You can do anything if you just work hard and apply yourself." As I think about this now, I understand the powerful social forces that were integrated into my framework for understanding personal responsibility for myself and for others. This deeply developed attitude and work ethic continues to define what I do in my professional and personal life. I think it is very important in working with adults that you have them think and articulate how certain events and environments had influence over their development. If you were to review the larger social movements of the 1950's one can certainly determine how these events had influence over family structure.

It was not unusual to have a family member or some relative live with us throughout my youth and a few siblings lived at home for extended periods of time. Sometimes this was for a few weeks and sometimes it was for years. Regardless, the house was generally always full. It is interesting that I remember not the overcrowded house with one bathroom, but the Sunday afternoon coffee and cake with lively conversation. I am quite sure that my mother and older brothers and sisters had never heard the term "efficacy" or understood what research has to say about this construct. However, they demonstrated a strong belief in their capacity to effect change in situations and the environment through as strong sense of personal capability. They fostered a strong sense of efficacy in their relationship with me and with each other through their interactions and affirmations of possibilities. This sense of belief in my own ability to effect change and to believe in my own ability has had a lasting influence over the choices I have made. I learned very early to attribute success to hard work and sustained effort and that failure was only an opportunity to try again.

I had another distinct advantage—I was the youngest of seven children. I was and will always be the baby of the family. When I visit my mother who is now 93 years old, I am still introduced as the baby of the family despite the fact that there are only two surviving children both over the age of 50! Some of you will appreciate and understand the real value of this position in a large, Southern family—you were treasured tremendously. This blanket of protection envelopes one with a sense of security and confidence that I believe enabled me to overcome barriers and obstacles. This sense of value was a very strong family bond that made one feel secure and confident; I had a rich environment despite a lack of monetary funds and family wealth. This solution to a lack of monetary wealth was seen through the framework of education and opportunity.

My mother, despite her limited education, always understood the value of education. She understood how education created opportunities for increasing economic security and how it created opportunities for a woman to become independent and self-sufficient. Of course, I think she would have rather not to have been faced with the challenge of being the sole support for seven children with little chance of moving herself out of poverty. What she did know was that her children had a better chance of becoming successful through education. She ultimately bought and paid for her own home, a huge accomplishment for a woman in that era. She valued what this independence represented and was most determined that her children would not be limited by a lack of educational opportunity. The culture of that era offered little real support in terms of equality or equity for women and girls. I think I was most fortunate to have a family that supported and accepted the best that this Southern culture had to offer and yet was light years ahead in their thinking. We were able to live and participate in a culture steeped with tradition and value and yet able to navigate within the limitations constructed by that same culture. As a result of my own experiences, I believe I am in an excellent position to work with adult learners with diverse backgrounds. What appeared to be a limitation became an asset over time. In order to appreciate other diverse cultures I believe you have to understand your own and how it has influenced you over time.

I briefly discussed the role of efficacy in learning. The construct of self-efficacy has seen a tremendous amount of research with multiple areas of focus during the past decade. I am very interested in the relationship of self-efficacy with autonomous learning or more commonly referred to as self-directed learning. Within the construct of autonomous learning, my colleagues and I have hypothesized the role of self-efficacy as a mediating force for the development of autonomous learning characteristics. I believe that everyone can identify significant leaning events that affect one's self-efficacy—either positively or negatively. I believe these events have the potential to set in motion certain beliefs and attitudes towards learning. I ask my doctoral students in one of their adult learning courses to identify and discuss a significant learning event. Most all can do so and most all report these events generally occurred between the ages of 9 to 13. Many of these events were the result of coincidence or chance and had a lifelong impact upon the learner. I would say, however, that opportunities could only be viewed as an opportunity once the individual has interacted with that opportunity. In other words, you may not be able to ascertain an opportunity or a choice even exists.

When I was around 10 years of age, I discovered the joy of reading to learn. I spent one summer reading every book that my local school library had on certain topics. That summer my small neighborhood elementary school decided to open the library one day per week so the local children would have the opportunity to read over the summer. I do not remember reading as a passion until that summer. I took advantage of that opportunity and started to read. What I discovered was that I could read and learn anything that I wanted to learn about or had an interest. I could do this independent of a teacher or the formal classroom setting. I decided I wanted to learn about archeology and studied everything I could about Egypt and the pyramids, and so began a life journey of adventure and inquisitiveness. For me, this was a profound way to think about education and I remember being taken aback at this idea. I could go learn anything at anytime without actually being in school— what a novel idea. I was good at going to school and the process of schooling but more importantly I learned I did not need someone to teach me everything; I could teach myself. My love of reading and learning has carried with me over the world and through many situations. What this opportunity did was present an event that had lasting influence over my learning and the possibilities related to learning. Both formal and informal learning situations are opportunities to learn collaboratively and/or independently: you can do both or either with or without a teacher; the process is the same. If you want to learn anything, you can create the opportunity. This way of thinking becomes a way of life; you do not sit there and wait for someone to tell you the answer. You have the desire, resourcefulness, initiative, and persistence to engage in learning to your own level of personal satisfaction.

Knowing that I could learn about anything not only enhanced my efficacy towards learning it also motivated me to learn about things that aroused my curiosity in many areas and topics. While the topics and contents have changed over the years, the driving curiosity has not. This is a strong motivational force for learning both in my professional work and areas that are just interesting to me. In retrospect, that single event of taking advantage of a reading program one summer so long ago coupled with a belief about learning and a questioning mind all intersected at a fortuitous moment and ultimately set the course of a lifelong journey. While the circumstances occurred by chance, I believe we have the opportunity to structure learning for others to deliberately include components that change the way we view and organize learning. I believe that curiosity is strongly overlooked in the field of adult learning and perhaps learning in general. We recognize the importance and value but do little to foster a curious and inquisitive mind.

As we work with adults and those adults who work with children we should consider ways to develop the lifelong independent learner. Lifelong learning is a national goal for many countries including the United States and developing nations. We understand how participation in learning improves the quality and satisfaction of life for the individual and the larger social setting and provides economic capital and cultural wealth. More importantly, I think it has the potential to change the way we view and understand the teaching and learning process. These events altered my capacity to participate and engage in dialogue and work with others in understanding the dimensions associated with adult learning theory. The forces that set me on a life course (cultural background, self-efficacy, and curiosity) continue to be driving motivational factors even today. I believe these are common factors in diverse individuals with different circumstances, and yet we display a shared set of attitudes and values towards learning. As we continue to work and research the factors associated with adult learning theory and development, opportunities exist to further refine and explain the relationship and importance of culture, efficacy, and curiosity with learning.

Leona M. English
The Sea's Strong Voice

Here the tides flow,
And here they ebb;
Not with that dull, unsinewed tread of waters
….But with a lusty stroke of life
Pounding at stubborn gates….
Leap under throb of pulse and nerve,
And teach the sea's strong voice
To learn the harmonies of new floods (E.J. Pratt, Newfoundland)

Newfoundland poet E. J. Pratt captured in these lines about our home province the essence of Newfoundland people and how the weather and the elements have worked to shape and mold and influence us as people, resilient, strong and yet subject to the unknown vagaries of the universe. This love of language, bred to the bone in my family, has nurtured and sustained me for as long as I can remember. This poem in particular serves as a reminder of the way in which people born on an island in the North Atlantic have had to encounter, embrace and conflict with the sea. Pratt's facility with language is a model hard to follow but its ever-relevant message is a touchstone for me and one that carries me forward and back in a steady rocking motion in my adult education life. It is a poignant reminder of the ways in which culture and tradition shape and are shaped by us as individuals.

I was born on November 10, 1963, into a large Roman Catholic family in Branch, a coastal community in Newfoundland, the most easterly province in Canada. My parents, Leo and Mary Anne English, owned and operated a local grocery and hardware business. My siblings and I worked in the family business, learning a lot about hard work, social justice, and good relations with neighbors, all the while surrounded by family, love of school and a love of music, dance, and poetry, though we were more likely to call the latter recitations than poetry. Though my parents are now deceased, I go back every summer for a few weeks to renew acquaintances and spend time on the veranda of our family home. The poem "Newfoundland" is a constant reminder to me of roots and of the love of language and learning that have shaped my life and my vocation in adult education over this past number of years. As Celts and diehard Irish (albeit 5th generation) we continue to know the importance of words to convey our thoughts and to change the world and ourselves. And, our fights as people have been many—whether it be resisting our colonial status, or fighting for ownership of our fishing grounds, or rights to royalties from oil exploration.

My undergraduate education was at Memorial University of Newfoundland, our only university, which is located in the city of St. John's. I majored in English, Religious Studies and Education graduating with a BA and BEd in 1984. This was a huge university compared to my high school size of 150 students. I followed my graduation with several years of teaching high school students in a rural community where I developed teaching skills that have served me well to this day. Kids, like adults, want their classes to be relevant and connected to their everyday life and to be respected as learners. Those students taught me about connecting with them as people, being passionate about my work, and having fun while I was doing it. They knew well the economic hardships of rural living and of an economy based on natural resources such as the fishery and yet they showed dedication and a commitment to improving their community's odds. These themes are as present to me now as they ever were.

When the opportunity arose, I went to study for a Master of Religious Education degree in a school of theology at the University of Toronto, a natural progression from teaching in a Roman Catholic school and wanting to move into a leadership position. Here is where I learned to think critically about the economy, education, institutions and the role of women. This may well have been the most exciting learning experience of my life, an academic nirvana in the sense that it allowed me to continue the conjoint studies I had begun earlier in religion and education and to learn to question and to challenge long held notions and beliefs. My classmates and I were studying fulltime and deeply committed to excellence and to critical thinking, and in the case of most of them, questioning the role of women in institutions such as schools and churches. This was an intergenerational experience and an interdisciplinary one in which my experience as a learner and as an adult (a young one, aged 23) actually counted.

One of my most distinct memories was of the first term paper I was assigned to write. The directions were to theorize and to incorporate my own experience into the theorization—dumbfounded, I muddled through it, resisting line by line the "public" revelation of my own ideas and the use of the once-forbidden "I." Slowly I was coming to understand the importance of my own experience in the learning process.

Following completion of this degree, I returned to Newfoundland to take up an administrative job directing religious education curriculum and doing continuing professional education with teachers, school board personnel, parents, and administrators across the province's districts and schools. Writing reports, running pilot projects and organizing conferences were skills that I honed that I have drawn on time and again. I learned also the practical skills of facilitation, needs assessment and evaluation, which were a daily part of my administrative tasks. Most importantly, however, I learned about power and influence and the interesting and intriguing ways in which they intersect to affect our thinking and efficacy in our jobs. There were more questions than answers in that continuing professional education position.

I took an academic leave from this position to start my doctorate at Columbia University in New York City. Although I was registered in the Philosophy and Social Sciences Department, I kept finding my way into other departments to take courses in adult education and curriculum. I completed my Doctorate in Education (in religion and education, in 1994) with a committee comprised of scholars from four different departments. This interdisciplinarity and interest in a pastiche of courses has become a trademark of my scholarly career, though it was never quite intentional. While I enjoyed the courses at Columbia and the affiliated studies at Union Theological Seminary, which was across the street, the best part of my doctoral school experience was the variety of students and interests, and of course, the absolutely magnificent libraries that Columbia and New York City provided.

In 1996 I came to St. Francis Xavier University in Antigonish, Nova Scotia, brimming with ideas to pursue, papers I wanted to write, and research projects that were literally calling my name. Along with learning academic culture, I learned to write and to do research that is of interest to me and which helps me live my own questions of justice and meaning. I have found an intellectual home with the colleagues in my department and a way to do my work that allows me to be healthy and which involves participation in women's causes and justice activities, which are integral to life in rural Nova Scotia. My intellectual interests continue to range from Foucault to epistemology to women's issues, and my fascination remains with language and its possibilities, regardless of the topic or the immediate goals of the research. Now at the midpoint of my academic career as I look simultaneously forward and backward, I find that I still listen to the "sea's strong voice," and am shaped by its call to rigor, steadfastness and the rhythms of the universe.

Dr. Benjamin Feinstein
A Lifelong Search

Being of Jewish descent, I was raised in the traditions of my ancestors. My parents divorced when I was 8 years old, and my mother came out as a lesbian. As a teen, I grew up spending summers with her living on women's land in the mountains outside of Santa Fe, New Mexico. I spent the rest of the year living with my father and going to school in Springfield, Ohio. I was exposed to many cultures through these experiences. In New Mexico, I was introduced to Native American (Tewa / Pueblo) culture, Hispanic culture, and Mestizo culture. In Ohio, I lived in an urban location and was a part of the local African-American culture. In addition, I was exposed to the socio-economic stratification present between the inner city and the suburbs. The tensions and inequities that existed in Springfield set me on an ongoing search for social justice and critical multiculturalism; this search was continually fueled and informed through my growing experiences.

I left Springfield in 1988 to attend Bowling Green State University, where I majored in chemistry and biology. I was quite active as an undergraduate in a myriad of activities, including serving as a science tutor/mentor for both the Study Skills Lab and the Athletic Department. Serving in this capacity gave me my first taste of adult education, as I tutored and mentored students of all ages. I was also employed my senior year as an undergraduate teaching assistant in General Chemistry. I enjoyed teaching at this level immensely. This was the beginning of my love affair with teaching undergraduate science, a love affair that has continued to this very day.

I left Ohio in 1993, after spending three summers working with urban Detroit kids at YMCA Camp Nissokone. I moved to one of the most vibrantly multicultural places on the planet: Honolulu, Hawai'i. I initially moved there to pursue a master's degree in pharmacology at the University of Hawai'i, but very shortly after arriving, I switched my major to education. I began to teach Biology and General Science at a public high school in Honolulu, where I had classrooms full of teenagers from all over Asia and the Pacific. I was also hired by the university as a teaching assistant in the Department of Physics and Astronomy. As a graduate T.A., I learned much from my colleagues about the difference between dealing with teens and dealing with adults. It was at this point that I began to develop my methodologies as an adult educator.

While in Hawai'i, I continued my personal investigation of issues of social justice, observing what the tourism industry and the military had done to the people and environment. I met many Hawaiian people and had the opportunity to interact with them on several different levels. My interest in Native cultures was expanded, as my knowledge expanded. I, of course, placed this new knowledge immediately in the context of critical multiculturalism and did not see it as a possible academic pursuit at that time. It was not until I returned to the Islands after having lived and studied in New Mexico that I realized the possibility of entering this field as an investigator and scholar. I left Hawai'i with my master's degree in Education, knowing full well I would be back sometime soon.

I went back to Ohio to reconnect with my family and re-group. Shortly after, I traveled to Honduras, Guatemala, and El Salvador, where I volunteered my services in a medical clinic as the Health Education Curriculum Coordinator. The majority of my time was spent teaching, working with, and caring for adults. While there, I learned much from the other translators, many of whom lived in the place we were staying. They introduced me to their own culture, along with the Garifuna culture and the Native American Moskito People. In Central America, my compassion for humanity expanded exponentially. Working in the conditions I worked in with the amazing people I worked with really opened my eyes in many different ways. I saw the world in a completely different light after that experience. Again, my framework for social justice and critical multiculturalism shifted and expanded.

I left Central America and returned to graduate school, working on my Ph.D. in Education at the University of New Mexico. Several key elements came to fruition for me in Albuquerque. I continued teaching in the sciences at Albuquerque TVI (community college), and I had the opportunity to work with the faculty at UNM.

At TVI, my methodologies became sharper. My classroom was shifted from one of straight lecture and discomfort to one of exploration, group communication, and laughter. I redefined myself as an adult educator, gaining proficiency both in my subject area and in the arena of interaction and support to people of all ages and walks of life. I was no longer a boring instructor hired to fill a 100-level space. I was empowered to feel comfortable creating my own environment of inquiry and learning. My experiences at TVI solidified my love for teaching adults.

My graduate work at UNM altered my entire concept of academe. Previously, I saw teacher education as a series of boring and required hoops to jump through. It was not until I began my work at UNM that I understood that it was possible to incorporate several areas of interest into one main investigation. The catalyst for this shift came through my initial coursework and subsequent relationship with Dr. Gregory Cajete, the Head of Native American Studies. Indigenous issues have been a personal interest of mine since I was a teenager and had been continually up until this point. However, it was not until I worked with Greg that I actually began to gain a multifaceted understanding of the issues. Through two of his classes (Native Art and Native Science) and numerous discussions, I began to understand contemporary issues and began to read contemporary authors like Deloria, Churchill, LaDuke, Kay-Trask, Giroux, Freire, Ross, Davis, Guevara, Cajete, Chomsky, Foucault, and West. Through Native American Studies, I was able to place a discipline to my philosophical stance: Critical Multiculturalism. I was a voracious reader and began to ingest as much material in the discipline as I could. It was also through these studies that my passion for social justice began to evolve from gut anger into intellectual expression. My interest led me to a survey of material, but I still lacked focus. Greg was an excellent guide and continues to be a friend and colleague.

My graduate work at UNM was cut short by the birth of Solomon, my first son. We moved to Ohio for a year to get organized, and at the end of the year returned to Hawai'i, where I finished my Ph.D. at the University of Hawai'i-Manoa. I spent two years immersed in the Native Hawaiian culture creating and facilitating a course on Hawaiian Traditional Environmental Knowledge. Through this experience, which was an integral part of my dissertation, I gained a much clearer focus about issues of critical multiculturalism, social justice and equity, prostitution of cultures, and anti-bias discourse. I was lucky enough to be able to learn from many local experts in a variety of traditional and contemporary fields, including Pauline Chinn, Neil Pateman, Will McClatchey, Sam Gon III, Lilikala Kame'eleihiwa, Winston Kong, Kawaikapu'okalani Hewett, and the legendary Haunani Kay-Trask.

While working on my Ph.D., I was an adjunct instructor at Hawai'i Pacific University, where I continued to teach the sciences. At HPU, I had students from all over the world. My experiences at HPU helped me to become a more effective educator through learning how to communicate with people that do not necessarily have a strong grasp of the language of instruction. It was also there that I ran the course on Hawaiian Traditional Environmental Knowledge. I am grateful to HPU for affording me the opportunity to teach such a cutting-edge course as an adjunct.

Upon completion of my Ph.D., we returned to Ohio, where I currently reside. I took a full-time position at South High School, where I am a science teacher and the International Baccalaureate (IB) program coordinator. I have been working diligently for the last four years on incorporating and infusing critical theory and issues of social responsibility into a standards-driven curriculum. South is an urban school in a Title-I district, a district in the midst of fiscal emergency and under the control of a state-appointed Oversight Committee. The position I now hold is incredibly challenging.

In addition to teaching at South, I am an adjunct instructor in Nursing at Clark State Community College, where I teach Anatomy and Physiology. I am also an adjunct professor in the Master's of Education Program at Wittenberg University. My love for adult education continues in numerous fields, including the sciences, education, and nursing.

In closing, my praxis is one founded in critical multiculturalism and issues of equity. Through my experiences working with international and indigenous communities, I have gained a sense of our interconnectedness and mutual responsibility for our planet, and for one another. My practice is one that aims to facilitate collaborative exploration of these crucial issues.

Throughout my professional career, it has been my privilege to work with adults. I am continually inspired by my students, many of whom have made difficult decisions and personal sacrifices, returning to school to provide a better life for themselves and their families. It is my sincere hope to be able to infuse them with a sense of lifelong learning and the knowledge that our time together has been my honor.

Tara Fenwick
It's About the People

I found myself directing my first adult choir at South United Church at the age of 15. Having grown up taking music lessons in a modest suburb of London, Ontario, I was now proudly launching my work career earning $30 a month as the church organist, choir director, youth music leader, pianist and violinist for church socials, and general jill-of-all-music provider. I didn't know how little I knew, so I was blissfully unencumbered by anxiety or what I learned later to call "imposter syndrome." And of all the mistakes I made and the patient people who helped me through the job, the ones I remember most clearly today were the good folks of the adult choir. Perhaps it is not well known how much pedagogy is involved in directing a choir. I certainly didn't know, at the time. Week after week I stood at the piano pounding out notes to teach these poor souls their respective parts, exhorting them to sing louder, to sing in tune, to sing better (pedagogical techniques I must have abstracted from my own piano training at the hands of one particularly unhappy nun.) Then one day Bettyann took me aside. She was almost in tears. "You know," she said, "I think we could learn how to sing better. But we're all sort of paralyzed trying to do these tough songs. I just don't think I can continue." Wow. Here I'd been preening myself on doing what I had assumed was fantastic work, bestowing beautiful music upon this tiny congregation, when I'd actually been traumatizing these learners. Maybe we all have a powerful memory of having our youthful arrogance poked right to its core – that was mine. I had for the first time realized that for me, it was not about the product, it was about the people. And in particular, it was about people learning – not just to sing, but to work together as a community.

As it turned out Bettyann did not quit; in fact she and Carline and Mike and some others in the choir helped me find ways to experiment with music education. In the years to come I learned to use vocal games, breathing exercises, dramatic movement and imagery with choirs – but always to play with song and to focus on people's engagement, not their performance. Something special happens through music in building a community. Singing is one of the more inclusive forms of musical participation, requiring no special equipment, environment, or able-ness (deaf choirs are common). It is holistic, uniting breath, vibration, language and synchronous connection with others. In singing with a group, people – including those insisting that they cannot sing—learn to reclaim their own voices, to express their own sounds, in defiance of mass-produced commercial music. They also learn to listen. And so do I. When I think back on the shiny moments of my adult life, they often are about adult "non"-singers who found themselves bellowing out their hearts in waves of sound, gloriously free and completely immersed with one another in those thrilling movements of ensemble singing.

So I became a teacher. But not of music. I kept music for joy, in an ill-founded notion I held at the time that paid work and joyful vocation were separate. When I graduated in the late 1970s there were few teaching jobs, so I was lucky to get my post teaching English literature and drama in a small country school in Alberta. To earn a little extra money I agreed to teach adult night classes in the next town, for the fall term – and then for the winter term, and then for the next year. And before I knew it, I was not only an adult educator, but I looked forward to those classes above all other work.

My job was to teach adults the English matriculation courses they needed to complete their high school diploma. Most had lived in rural Alberta all their lives. Some had not had school opportunity beyond grade 9 and had stayed on the farm, some had left school to work the oil rigs in Alberta's 1970s boom, some had become teen mothers. Some struggled with English. All were facing what then seemed to me an impossible journey: completing, on a one-course-at-a-time basis, up to eight courses to finish high school, then entering some two- or four-year postsecondary program to obtain certification for occupations ranging from nursing assistant to certified management accountant. I was struck by the clear and compelling dreams these adult learners had created for themselves. Many had resolved to become a carpenter or an interior designer. They could picture this work; it fuelled their energy and their hope—sometimes over years, as I watched them completing their required high school English courses. Perhaps more than anything, I was amazed at the courage and grit of adults confronting perpetual difficulty to participate in education. Ginny had been sneaking out of the house to come to class, using as her excuses a variety of neighbourly errands. We found out only because one morning her husband roared into the school, banging on walls and yelling for the principal, demanding to know how long she had been enrolled and insisting that she be removed from all future classes. Jamal worked three low-paying jobs to support his large family, leaving our class at 9 to catch a couple hours' sleep before his night shift began. Helen was a low-income single mother with Crohn's disease who struggled to keep up with the work when she was too ill to make it to class. Mike's struggle was alienation; he was the only one of all his friends and family trying to finish school, and when they taunted him to give up and come out to the bar, he found himself sliding back to beliefs that at 30 he was beyond rescue from the oil rigs. And these learners did not just show up to class. They engaged with the literature in ways that I had never experienced with high school students. I don't think I will ever forget Ginny, in one discussion of *Grapes of Wrath*, looking up at the group to say that she knew exactly why Ruth gave her breast to the old man and proceeded to tell us about poverty. Or Mike staying after class once to say, holding his school-issue copy of *To Kill a Mockingbird* taped together so many times the pages barely held together, "It feels so good to ... to think again."

It is relationships with these sorts of students that I think commits someone to adult education. My commitment came with two realizations. The first, at the risk of sounding maudlin, was that when one has the privilege to see this sort of everyday human courage up close, one can only try to become worthy of it. The second was the power of dialogue and the powerful learning that can occur when people are allowed to gather around good stories to talk about their lives. Perhaps the only outstanding part of these tales, which every adult educator can tell, is the fact that every adult educator can, has always, and will continue to tell dozens of these sorts of tales. People of limited means confront oppressive workloads, marginalization and family resistance to do something as simple as reading and talking about literature together, to complete an education which institutions have defined in ways that thoroughly suit institutional needs.

And it was with this recognition that I realized I needed to study adult education further. Surely there were ways to change a system that forced these adults to struggle along one course at a time, in topics ranging from present participles to functional algebra that seemed to me completely irrelevant to the postsecondary certificates they needed to pursue their dream jobs. The curriculum and materials often presented to these adult learners was directly derived from programs designed for teenagers and taught by teachers like me who thought we just had to repeat at night the lessons we gave during the day to rooms packed with ball-caps and bubblegum. Some texts for these adults were particularly appalling in my view: developed for "reluctant readers" in high school, the literature consisted of quick stories and dumbed-down opinions about fast cars, fashion, and horror movies.

So, I entered graduate education with high hopes of changing the provision of adult basic education, becoming, perhaps, a curriculum developer or at least an activist for better approaches. In graduate courses and readings, I encountered those in Canada who would become my heroes of adult education. Gordon Selman, who is known as a Canadian pioneer of adult education for his extensive books building our Canadian history and foundations of adult education. Mary Norton, who has been working through community participatory initiatives to transform literacy education in Alberta. James Draper, a teacher par excellence who fought for adult education in the academy and made a special, vibrant space for international students. Don Chapman, a champion for grassroots adult education who introduced me to Freire's writing. Shahrzad Mojab, who continues to fight for women's equity and security around the world with boundless energy. Budd Hall, the great international popular educator whose talks inspired me to think beyond schooling to fight for democracy and social justice through adult education. And along the way, I became most interested in the education of adult educators.

Around this time I was invited to travel to China with a project to develop educators in Hebei province. The project ended up lasting five years and involved several trips to China; myself and my partner along with two graduate students typically worked with groups 200-300 in size in what sometimes seemed like fruitless attempts to create participatory, dialogic learning environments. As anyone does who has the opportunity to work in large international projects, I learned much about patience with complexity and contradictory agendas, about my own cultural myopia, and about the bewildering generosity and optimism of people who appear to have little except barriers and persecution. Among the moving encounters I had with these amazing people, one in particular I treasure. At one of the mass teacher institutes we held, a young woman came flying straight towards me as the hundreds streamed out of sweltering rooms on a lunch break. The English name she insisted we call her was, aptly, Sunny. Sunny was 19 years old and taught school in three

QUINTESSENTIAL AUTOBIOGRAPHIES FOR THE 21ST CENTURY

villages among which she travelled everyday by bicycle even in the harsh winter. Sunny usually declined to speak directly to those of us facilitating the institute despite our efforts to appear friendly and unintimidating; we were after all native English speakers and foreign experts to boot, as the Chinese guides kept loudly reminding the teachers. But on this occasion Sunny faced me head on. She grasped both my wrists, hard, and looked straight into my eyes. Before I could speak or even laugh, she said urgently, "Do you dream?" "Of course," I replied, thinking she was trying out vocabulary about sleep. 'No!' she shook her head, and said again, squeezing my wrists hard, "Do you dream? I have dream," she went on. "I dream to be teacher for teachers, like you. But how? I have job named for me. I have family. They want me do my job, get married. How do you dream?" I remember looking at Sunny blankly. What indeed was my dream? And how dare I dream when I could so easily have everything that she so desperately longed for? Everything I knew about gendered work, about the problems of international development, about the continuing struggles of teachers around the world, converged in the pleading face of Sunny. And I had nothing to offer her.

Back in Alberta, to help put me through graduate school I taught night courses again, but this time with people who wanted to become adult educators. The program was a Certificate of Adult and Continuing Education (CACE), and the participants were community workers, tradespeople, health care employees and government staff who all found themselves falling into or pushed against jobs to teach others. The time was the early 1990s in Alberta, a period of drastic job-slashing piloted by lean-and-mean mantras. In fact many of the CACE participants had been downsized and had dreams of turning their crash into a christening: a new life, helping others through education. At the time I had been starry-eyed myself with the new literature about "learning organizations." I was thinking that the question was not so much how to educate adult educators, but how to turn work environments into inclusive educational milieus—democratic sites of learning through participation in work activity. However the people—mostly women—whom I met in my four years facilitating courses for CACE opened a new world for me of brutal corporate pressures and persecutions. "Learn or die" had become the hymn of human resource salvation. A few CACE students opened entry for me to their organizations which were implementing learning organization principles, and there I saw firsthand how stirring grassroots ideals could be distorted into top-down tools of surveillance, discipline and deception. This led me to start writing critically about the learning organization and the more manipulative practices of human resource development. I also become committed to exploring notions of workplace democracy and learning through work as a way to approach the ideals of adult education: equitable access to learning opportunity, critical awareness of economic structures, and collective participation to bring about sustainable lives and work that people dreamed of having. Especially people like Sunny. This became my dream.

I have been particularly lucky in having wise guides to help me navigate academic adult education. Butch Wilson at Cornell University encouraged me to keep writing about power and learning in the workplace when I was ready to leave academia because I couldn't find a job. John Dirkx at University of Michigan showed me how to write about soul as well as science and to examine the psycho-sociodynamics as well as the politics of workplace learning. Valerie-Lee Chapman, one of the most creative educators I ever met, opened for me a new way to understand and write about embodiment in learning. Richard Edwards at Stirling University taught me about precise writing, actor network theory and about how to laugh at oneself while remaining deadly serious about one's purpose. Miriam Zukas is a model of academic leadership, showing how one balances rigorous standards with caring and thoughtful relationships. And Sue Scott at University of Alberta was a constant model of putting one's students before everything else, of always stopping to ask about every project or academic commitment: What am I accomplishing, really, for adult education if I do this?

So what keeps me excited about adult education are the people. Between my Canadian heroes and ancestors, the many guides who've helped me, and my current network of passionate colleagues around the world, I've found people who move in solidarity to confront the daunting challenges of neoliberalism and globalized capitalism. I still love to lead choirs and make music. But I've found joy in my work as an adult educator, too. And as long as workplaces continue to be targets for state learning policy, sites of worker oppression and sacrifice, as well as openings for genuine democratic learning and social responsibility, I will continue to focus my efforts in research and teaching upon questions around learning in work. The people, the adult learners, whom ultimately we all serve are worth everything we can give.

Barbara A. Frey, D.Ed.
Life as a Series of Teachable Moments

It seems as though I entered the classroom at age five and never left. The primary difference between now and then is that the chairs are larger and I'm usually on the opposite side of the desk. As an adult educator, instructional designer, high school teacher, and former administrator, I have more than twenty-five years of experience in the field of education. My background includes curriculum development and teaching in public, private, and higher education institutions.

I grew up in a home where learning was a way of life. My father's passion was visiting historic places and national parks, and my mother enjoyed touring factories to see how products were made. Consequently, most of our family vacations involved visiting Ford, Quaker Oats, Kellogg's, Heinz, and Oscar Meyer factories or touring parks like Grand Canyon, Yellowstone, Yosemite, and Mount Rushmore. With such a stimulating background, I surprised no one when I attended college as an education major.

Just like Mr. Kotter in the old television show *Welcome Back, Kotter*, my teaching career began at my high school alma mater, Highlands High School in southwestern Pennsylvania where my former teachers became my colleagues. Observing my teaching role models as peers left a lasting impression. In fact, two of them became my most valued mentors – they shared lesson plans, learning activities, and enthusiasm; they coached me in the critical classroom management skills necessary for school teachers. I came to associate student learning with effective planning and meticulous organization.

Attending graduate school at the University of Pittsburgh, I focused on teaching effectiveness and subsequently became interested in the "new" concept of student-centered teaching and learning. Upon completion of my Master of Education degree, I married, relocated, and accepted a position with Kings River Community College in Reedley, California. I taught textiles and merchandising courses. Since California had an open enrollment policy, I realized more than ever it was necessary to plan for students with diverse backgrounds, learning styles, and levels of aptitude. In general, community colleges take great pride in quality teaching and Kings River was no exception. After teaching high school students, this world of higher education with more mature learners and an extensive network of resources seemed like teacher paradise.

After four years in California, my husband and I returned to Pittsburgh to start our family, and I accepted a position at the Art Institutes International where I became interested in faculty development. Although most instructors had devoted years to developing specialized knowledge and skills, this expertise did not always translate to effective course design and teaching. Lacking formal study in teaching methodology and communication, the majority of instructors developed their teaching skills through trial and error. When I was promoted to department director, I had the opportunity to plan and implement faculty development initiatives. Because I had to justify the expense of these programs, I scrambled to demonstrate their effectiveness. Unfortunately, the available literature offered little support, yet faculty gave positive feedback on the programs.

My interest in faculty development and adult learning led me back to school at Pennsylvania State University's Department of Adult Education, Instructional Systems, and Workforce Education. Attending Penn State required a three-hour commute, but the highly regarded program made it worth the time and effort. While a doctoral student, I took advantage of numerous internship and consulting opportunities to apply my instructional design and teaching skills. For example, I designed and conducted training programs at J.C. Penney, Calgon Corporation, Education Management Corporation, Laban Trainings, and Ketron Corporation. In addition, I participated on a team that designed three major training programs for the United States Army Security Assistance Command with the Department of Defense. Based on my consulting experiences, I developed numerous publications and presentations.

After completing my doctoral course work, I accepted an offer from the Adult Education program (in the Department of Learning and Performance Systems) to teach graduate courses in human resource development at the McKeesport campus of Penn State. I still teach adult and distance education courses at Penn State as an adjunct assistant professor. Several years ago the Adult Education master's degree program moved online as a part of the Penn State World Campus. I facilitate my web-based course at home from a desktop computer. As I develop online teaching skills, it has been valuable to be a participant in many high-quality faculty development initiatives at Penn State. Whether it's online or face-to-face, teaching challenges me to keep up with the literature in the field of education, to engage in meaningful classroom discourse, and to use new teaching strategies and technology. Teaching adults is rich and fulfilling because of the knowledge and experience adults bring to the classroom. I have taught students with careers serving in the military, developing communication technology, manufacturing steel, and training in all areas of healthcare.

I completed my dissertation in 1998. My topic was the evaluation of a faculty development program in Western Pennsylvania community colleges. The study was a quasi-experimental research design that monitored student achievement and satisfaction before and after the intervention of presentation skills training for ten female instructors. The training was individualized, with participants receiving quantitative feedback on their volume, rate of speech, variation in pitch, number of fillers, and wait or pause time after asking discussion questions. SoundEdit 16® software was used to quantify these qualities from audio tapes. Overall, the results noted no significant difference in student satisfaction or achievement following the faculty training. However, one sub-group of learners ages 18-25 reported a significant increase in their course satisfaction. There was also a qualitative focus group aspect to my study. Instructors who participated in the workshop reported positive reactions to training because of the individualized data and higher levels of confidence in their presentation skills. They also noted that it required concentration not to return to their old patterns of speaking. Perhaps more important than the details of my research, were the opportunities it has provided. My dissertation served as my calling card and opened doors in training and faculty development in higher education.

In my current position as a Senior Instructional Designer at the Center for Instructional Development & Distance Education (CIDDE) with the University of Pittsburgh (http://www.pitt.edu/~ciddeweb/), I work with faculty to design, develop, and assess their teaching and instructional materials. For major learning or course development projects, I am project manager working with a very talented and creative team including an editor, production specialist, graphic designer, and instructional technologist. Also, I provide training in instructional design for faculty teaching hybrid and distance education courses. I collaborate with CIDDE staff on many interesting projects.

Since it is the "need to know" that brings most faculty members to CIDDE, they expect to be accepted, respected, and supported with accurate, timely, and practical information in a professional environment. While I make recommendations in course design and teaching strategies, the final decision is always with the course instructor. As a constructivist, I believe in a framework where learners (faculty) construct meaning to interpret and direct their ideas and activities. I devote a significant amount of hard work, time, and expertise to earning the trust of faculty. Many of my recent professional presentations and publications have been collaborative efforts with University of Pittsburgh and Penn State University faculty.

My current research examines the design, facilitation, and assessment of online asynchronous discussions. Personally, I find Web-based discussions somewhat unwieldy and seek more effective strategies for concise, connected, and comprehensive dialogues. While the goals of discussion forums vary, I am most interested in promoting critical thinking to enhance deep learning. The saying, "A picture is worth a thousand words," holds true for understanding the complex linear list of postings which represents the multilayered dynamics of an online discussion. Visualizing the discussion threads allows me to efficiently examine interaction by students, chronological order, levels of responses, or levels of thinking according to Bloom's taxonomy.

Being an adult educator, instructional designer, assistant professor, and scholar demands a commitment to lifelong learning. Learning is not my job; it is my way of life. Family and friends often find me reading journal articles on the treadmill or listening to conference audio files in the car. Technology broadens my ability to access desktop professional development with interactive television presentations, eb-based discussions, online conferences, and cell phone conference calls. In particular, I am interested in teaching and learning in adulthood, and the use of instructional technology to enhance learning.

With a little bit of luck, I will continue to hop from one side of the desk to the other for a few more decades of teachable moments. Toggling between the roles of instructor and learner keeps life rich and fulfilling. Along with a loving and supportive network of family and friends, knowledge is the power that energizes my life.

Dr. Jeanne d'Arc Gaudet
From "Dropout" to Doctorate Thanks to Adult Education

Family and Social Context

I was born in a small fishing village on the Atlantic coast of Canada. My family consisted of my parents, two sisters and nine brothers. Because I was the second-born in the family, I had to assume many responsibilities early on, such as caring for my younger brothers and sisters and helping with the household chores. The family economy was modest, since my father was a fish merchant and my mother worked at home. However, my parents valued learning and they encouraged us to pursue our education, even though they were aware that they didn't have the necessary funds to pay for a postsecondary education for all of us. In the 1960s, if we wanted to continue our training after secondary school, and we didn't have the financial means to do so, we could obtain a government loan, but even that was not enough to cover all of the costs without some help from family. In addition, people from my village who wanted to go to college or university had to move to an urban center, which meant even more expense.

The challenge was greater for girls because the social and family expectations were different based on the role they were supposed to play in society. In other words, post-secondary studies were reserved for the boys, and any girls who dared to dream about this could expect many obstacles. Like other girls of my age, I had internalized the message that advanced education wasn't for me. However, I heard a little voice inside me that said that maybe I had what it took to succeed. At the end of high school, I had to choose to further my education or find work, and for financial reasons I chose the job market.

Dropping Out and Dropping In . . . .

After graduating, I left my home looking for work. I got a job as an accounts clerk in a large clothing store. Since I had never had a paying job, I assumed that minimum wage would be enough to satisfy my modest needs. I also had been led to believe that "Prince Charming" would free me from the necessity of having to support myself, as was the custom at the time. It didn't take long for me to realize that the work that I was doing was boring and unstimulating, and my paycheck was barely enough to feed and clothe me. I realized that going back to school was a possible solution; at the same time, I was becoming more confident in my own abilities and potential.

Since I still didn't have the money to pay for a return to school, my father agreed to give me a small loan, and I enrolled full time in a ten-month secretarial program. I was convinced that a college diploma would give me access to a greater choice of jobs and considerably improve my personal and financial situation. Diploma in hand, I landed a position in an insurance company, and this time I really thought that I had reached the pinnacle of my education for the rest of my life.

Shortly after getting my new job, I met the man who would become my husband. It was still an age when it was expected that young women would marry and become mothers. However, my idea of the role of a woman in society and in married life had changed considerably, and there was no question of giving up my financial autonomy, for a number of reasons. At the same time, my work as a secretary was not bringing me much satisfaction, and I still felt that I had the potential to do better; routine tasks, which were undervalued and unappreciated, didn't appeal to me. I decided to make an appointment with an employment counselor to help me explore other careers. It just so happened that, on that particular day, the employment center in my area had learned that the colleges were looking for people in my field who would be interested in teacher training for one year. Their goal, of course, was to eventually have us teach in the community colleges. This was in the early 1970s, and the colleges had just developed secretarial programs and were recruiting specialists from the workforce to teach in these programs. I had more than five years experience in this field, so I quit my job to enroll in the teacher training program. In order to attract candidates for this program, the Minister granted unemployment benefits for the duration of the training. I successfully completed my training, and I received my diploma and my teaching license from the Minister of Education.

The Adventure Continues . . . .

At the age of 28, I finally reached the point of starting my university studies. I now realized that it was important to continue my education in order to increase my chances of getting more satisfactory, better paying employment. Since I would receive my teaching diploma at the same time that the University of Moncton was opening a Faculty of Education, I decided to enroll with the intention of finishing my teaching degree in a year at the most. However, in order to do this, I had to present my academic record and life and work experiences to the personnel of the education faculty. After a discussion with the dean, my experience and education were examined to see how much could be accepted towards my diploma. More than two years were recognized as valid credit, and I was able to complete my diploma in two semesters of full-time courses, with some supplementary credits earned through continuing education at the same university. I got my diploma at 29 after completing the requirements of the program. From this point, I began a long relationship with adult education.

Obtaining my first degree reinforced the idea that I was capable of higher learning and encouraged me to go a little further in the adventure. I had always believed, especially since graduating from high school, that university was inaccessible. This first degree confirmed that I had the intellectual and cognitive potential as well as the skills required to further my studies. I also noticed that the more I studied, the more I developed a passion for knowledge, so I decided to enroll in the Bachelor of Education program. This required that I finish another year of courses by means of an adult education program while working as a teacher. I registered in my first evening course during the fall semester and subsequent sessions. After one year of studies, I got my Bachelor of Education and Teaching Certificate III from the Minister of Education. Since I had begun the habit of taking one or two courses each semester, I continued to accumulate the courses necessary for my third bachelor's degree, this time in arts.

After obtaining three undergraduate degrees, the time had come for a new experience, so I enrolled in the Master of Education program, which was offered through continuing education also. I had good results in my first course, and the program allowed me to focus my learning on the field of research. It took two years of night, weekend and summer courses to fulfill the requirements of the master's program, and I obtained my degree in 1980. This diploma opened more opportunities for employment, and I took a full-time job with the university the same year. At that time it was not necessary to have a doctorate to teach in a satellite campus of the university.

Several years later, the University of Moncton granted me a six years leave of absence so that I could fill a deputy minister's position with the provincial government. In order to fulfill my duties better, I decided to pursue a master's degree in public administration, and once again I was able to do so through continuing education. I successfully completed the requirements of this program. At the end of my leave, I was supposed to resume my position as a university professor, but since I had been working outside of the field of education for five years, I decided to pursue my education, this time in a doctorate program at another university. It took about two years to complete my training, and I returned to the university with a doctorate to teach in the Faculty of Education. In addition to teaching both undergraduate and graduate students and being very involved in research, I now direct the research studies at the faculty and supervise the research projects of many students in the master's and doctorate programs.

Introspection and Reflection

Several persons and events contributed to my professional success. My goal here is not to describe everything which occurred on my path to postsecondary studies. However, I feel I can give some insight into the importance of the role we play in influencing people who are in danger of giving up on their studies or those who need extra help to return to academic learning. In the following section, I will present three themes that I feel are essential in the integration or reintegration into education: 1) dreaming and making the dream a reality; 2) understanding, empathizing and mind opening; and 3) validating prior learning, and experience and recognizing the institutional responsibilities.

Dreaming and Making the Dream Come True

Dreaming is an essential condition to the success of projects! When I was young, I realized that it was alright to dream. I remember times when I allowed myself to build images and scenarios in my head, imagining they were real. Now I realize that all of the dreams I had in my life created mental schematics or a form of internal programming that became guides which, sooner or later, directed my actions. For example, when I was young, as I have already mentioned, I had internalized the message that university studies weren't accessible to me. I still allowed myself to dream that it was possible for me to hold a top-level position in a business somewhere. Even if I did not believe that the dream would become a reality, just the fact that I could aspire to such a goal made an impression in my mind.

I sincerely believe that dreaming gives us the ability to organize our environment in an unconscious manner and leads us to attain our goals when the right conditions fall into place. I think that educators should introduce activities into their teaching that allow students to create scenarios and dreams. It might seem like a waste of time, but isn't it possible that such small, harmless activities could make a difference in young people's lives? I found out over time that learning is not a linear process and that all previous knowledge (life experience and education) that we accumulate prepares us for making decisions throughout our lives. If I had one primary rule to apply in education, it would be to encourage the dream; in other words, for example, invite young people to picture themselves in the far future, successful in what they hope to accomplish. These little steps form a solid base that leads them to achieve one success after another, and eventually to see their dreams become a reality.

Understanding, Empathizing and Mind Opening

In my view, people who help students return to school should have exceptional qualities. Studies in adult learning and cognitive sciences give us a better understanding of the particular needs of adult learners, which are different from those of young people who have never had an interruption in their education. As already mentioned, learning is not a phenomenon which starts at kindergarten and ends with high school or post-secondary studies. It is a process which begins from birth, or, according to some authors, from conception.

The cumulate of experiences that we gain from our families, from school or from society in general contributes to each new lesson, because we are constantly making links to our prior learning. Each individual is unique and has a particular learning style which involves her or his culture, her or his values, her or his beliefs and her or his way of thinking. Adult learners return to education with a diverse baggage of experiences and the people who have the job of evaluating this baggage or helping with career orientation must be flexible and understanding of these new learners. Each person must be treated with respect and dealt with as an individual. We have to create a winning atmosphere to assure professional success for these newcomers to the education system. One way to assure success is to choose people with open minds capable of evaluating a learner's prior experiences and education with flexibility. Often we hear the adult learners comment that the persons who are responsible for evaluating the files, particularly in the universities, are too rigid in their interpretations. In their opinions, many people still have the impression that anything learned outside the university milieu (non-academic learning) can't be recognized as a prerequisite for university admission. In order to evaluate these returning students fairly, it seems to me that the job ought to be entrusted to people who believe that relevant life experience and/or academic history can and must be recognized by the institution.

I was lucky enough to meet people who had confidence in me and who applied the policy fairly. Each time that I left my studies and then wanted to reintegrate into the education system, I was treated justly, but most of all with an open mind. I could immerse myself in either full-time or part-time studies and achieve the personal and professional goals that I had set for myself. The continuing education or adult education services in the schools must become leaders developing innovative policies for validating experience and prior education.

Validating Academic and Life Experiences and Institutional Responsibilities

In my opinion, certain conditions have to be in place when validating prior work and life experiences. On one hand, we need training for the students who want to have their dossiers evaluated, and, on the other hand, there must be training given to the people who evaluate the student files. The learners have to find out how to present their portfolios well. If the goal is to receive credit for prior learning, then the students have to present the proof of this learning. The dossier should contain the necessary documents, and the learner must have the ability to present and demonstrate this proof. The schools or institutions have the responsibility of making the tools available to the adult students for presenting their documentation well. Furthermore, it is important to create teams of evaluators who are capable of judging the dossiers accurately and as equitably as possible. These professionals should have special qualities to allow them to work with open minds and to think from the adult education perspective. Often the people who want to continue their education are faced with too many obstacles, and after several attempts to have their experiences recognized and validated, they become discouraged with the long process and abandon their dream.

Conclusion

In my particular case, I can confirm that I am where I am today thanks to many people in positions of authority who played a key role. Some of them were exemplary role models, and others facilitated my entry into the institutions of higher learning that I attended during the course of my studies. The continuing education and adult learning services helped me to realize my dreams and enrich my knowledge throughout my life. As I have often told my students, learning is a project for life; since the world is changing rapidly, we have to keep up-to-date in our careers and professions. One way to do this is to increase and improve our knowledge through continuing education. In conclusion, I challenge those who think that a college or university education is not for them to reprogram that little voice in their heads to say, "I have what it takes to continue my education, and I have the right to fulfill my dreams."

André P. Grace

I began doctoral studies in adult education in the fall of 1993 at Dalhousie University, Halifax, Nova Scotia, Canada. Like so many other academic adult educators, my journey to our field of study and practice was a circuitous one. I had been a schoolteacher for fifteen years, and during the last few years of that period I had been involved in a school-restructuring project with my school board. This work involved considerable time engaging in teacher development. It was stimulating work that immersed me in literature about how adults learn. I was particularly drawn to academic adult educators like K. Patricia Cross and Stephen D. Brookfield, both of whom attended to the social elements of adult learning and the matters of circumstance and disposition that can impact adult learning in individual and institutional contexts. I found new energy in this work. I was excited to learn and work with teachers as adult learners who wanted to learn, too. Drawn to the challenges and opportunities of adult education as a social learning project, the next step for me became doctoral studies in critical adult education.

However, I was certainly a neophyte when it came to studies in social theory. My undergraduate degree had involved a major in biology and a minor in chemistry. My master's degree in educational administration had been a rather instrumental learning experience that focused on clinical supervision of educational personnel. As I began to read the work of my supervisor, Michael R. Welton, during my first year of studies, I struggled with his Habermasian-influenced critical writing about adult education and society. Still I was drawn to what he wrote. When I had met with him the previous spring before I started my doctoral studies, I discussed my interest in learning for adults and its transfer. He had been kind to me, the instrumentalist who had so much to learn about matters of context (social, cultural, historical, political, and economic), disposition (attitudes, values, and beliefs), and relationship (including the sociocultural mediation of relations including gender, gender identity, sexual orientation, race, ethnicity, class, age, and ability). My first year with Michael and another mentor and friend, Donovan Plumb, became an immersion in critical social theory. I worked through the lineage of critical theorists from the early days of the Frankfurt School and on to Herbert Marcuse and Jürgen Habermas. There were also readings in classical social theory, and many readings by academics in adult education and other fields of study and disciplines who framed their research and practice from critical perspectives. I read criticalists including Ben Agger, Stanley Aronowitz, Michael Collins,

QUINTESSENTIAL AUTOBIOGRAPHIES FOR THE 21ST CENTURY

Phyllis Cunningham, Nancy Fraser, Anthony Giddens, Mechthild Hart, Axel Honneth, Jack Mezirow, and Sherman Stanage.

Of course, working with Michael I also became immersed in studies of the foundations of adult education as a field of study and practice. In particular, I had opportunities to study the international history of adult education. I was drawn to the writings of Eduard Lindeman, who cast true adult education as social education. His work helped me to intersect my interest in critical social theory with my interest in field foundations. Working in this intersection, I focused on adult education as a community-based and critically oriented enterprise that genuinely emphasized the social when it focused on ethical practices and the critical ideals of modernity: democracy, freedom, and social justice. I also discovered the work of two other field philosophers who deeply impacted my thinking about the nature and meaning of an inclusive social: John Walker Powell and Paul Bergevin. As my doctoral studies progressed—I received my Ph. D. in 1997—I immersed myself in the history of the emergence of North American academic adult education. I first studied the period between the end of World War II and the World Oil Crisis in 1973. Then I expanded my study to look at the 20th century as a whole. I discovered the rich and passionate writing of Robert J. Blakely, John Ohliger, Sumner N. Rosen, and others devoted to social education, especially in forms that reached disenfranchised citizens. I read the work of Myles Horton and visited the Highlander Research and Education Center in Knoxville, Tennessee. I also read archival materials written by Jimmy Tompkins, and I read the work of Moses Coady and others who had captured the social spirit of the Antigonish Movement in their writings.

I found this work inspiring. Still, I felt I had discovered a very White and masculinized field that had left certain people out. As a gay man I found that exclusionary history lived in the present in sites like the Adult Education Research Conference (AERC), where one of my queer mentors and good friends, Robert (Bob) J. Hill, had struggled to find space and place for lesbian, gay, bisexual, trans-identified, and queer (LGBTQ) field members. In what became a wonderful example of engaging in transgressive public pedagogy against the cultural grains of heterosexism and homophobia, Bob had initiated the LGBTQ and Allies Caucus in 1993 at the 34th annual AERC held at the Pennsylvania State University. I first met Bob in 1994 and have been part of that caucus ever since. I have witnessed various hurtful moments of exclusion over the years, and Bob has shared many stories of his own struggles with me.

The moments of marginalization around different relationships of power in the history of our field of study and practice have bothered me, but, more importantly, they have left me with impassioned rage to work for social and cultural change in our field and beyond. Obviously, we can preach the importance of adult education as social education, but, if we do not live out principles of inclusion in terms of access and accommodation in our field, then adult education will have little impact in engendering change in culture and society. It is this belief that has influenced my own emergence as a theorist, researcher, and practitioner engaged in service to the community. These days I read widely, and, as a theorist, I am drawn to a multiperspective theoretical discourse invigorated by the tangents and tensions I discover that make me think deeply about words, worlds, and my understanding of them.

124

My passion for and valuing of multiperspective theory were significantly nurtured during my postdoctoral studies (1998-1999) with Henry A. Giroux, then Waterbury Chair Professor of Education and Cultural Studies at the Pennsylvania State University. While I am certainly mindful of the feminist critiques of his work, Henry's groundbreaking work in critical pedagogy remains a vital political and educational project that urges continued deliberation about the parameters and possibilities of critical social education. Henry expanded these parameters and possibilities by bringing postmodernism, poststructuralism, cultural studies, and other theoretical discourses to bear on his understanding of critical pedagogy. Like Henry, my own work keeps critical theory and its focus on ethics and justice at the heart of what I do as I search other theories for pieces missing or underdeveloped in critical theorizing.

In an earnest way in the early 1990s, we witnessed the emergence of multiperspective theorizing that brought competing theories into dialectical intersections in order to explore their possible alignments, oppositions, and tensions. Multiperspective theorizing variously juxtaposes these competing theories. In my own work, I am often drawn to particular aspects of particular theories amid the ensuing tensions and the need to problematize juxtapositions. I turn to critical theory to explore its emphases on the political ideals of modernity, the importance of the historical context in constructing the social, and the value of ethics, especially as a public practice shaped outside an individual's moral beliefs. I draw on postmodernism to understand and critique understandings of identity and difference and its emphasis on relationships of power. I turn to poststructuralism to engage the notion of the multiple subject who can be privileged in some ways and subjugated in others, and to grapple with language and meaning (in text and subtext) in relation to power manipulation. I take up feminist discourses to investigate notions of connection, collaboration, and relationship; to understand how individuals are positioned in the world; and to study how to ground vision and purpose in a political project. All of these theories can be construed in the plural. My engagement with multiperspective theory also takes me into spaces where I explore postcolonialism, which focuses on interrogating canons and exposing privilege and exclusion. I turn to cultural studies to study the effects of culture and power on language and relationships of power. I look at Indigenous research paradigms to gain new insights into the importance of holistic research that focuses on the researcher, the research participants as coresearchers, and the environment as a source of energy and gifts. This turn also emphasizes the importance of critiquing the limits of Western research and research protocol when working in an Indigenous context. Perhaps my greatest passion, though, is my work with LGBTQ theories from the earlier liberatory forms emerging from late-1960s gay liberation to the contemporary queer forms heavily influenced by poststructuralism. Here I am reminded of my most important political and pedagogical project: to fight heterosexism and homophobia where they exist in education, culture and society.

Multiperspective theorizing frames and nurtures my work as a teacher-educator and researcher in the Department of Educational Policy Studies at the University of Alberta. This is where I have worked since July 1, 1999. Effective July 1, 2006, I will be a full professor. I direct Agape, which is a focus group I set up in my Faculty of Education to consider issues in relation to sex, sexual, and gender differences in education and culture. Agape is designed to meet the needs of LGBTQ and allied undergraduate and graduate students, faculty, and staff. I teach education courses primarily focused on inclusive educational policy and practice at the undergraduate and graduate levels. In terms of research, I recently completed a national study of personal, ethical, legal, legislative, and educational policy factors impacting the welfare and work of LGBTQ teachers in Canadian schools. In a new national study I am examining the impact of educational interests groups on the personal and professional well-being of LGBTQ teachers. The Social Sciences and Humanities Research Council of Canada has funded both national research projects. As well, my research in educational policy studies focuses on comparative studies of policies and practices shaping lifelong learning in OECD (Organization for Economic Cooperation and Development) countries. I am particularly interested in what constitutes a critical social practice of lifelong learning, given the chameleonic nature of the term over time and tides. In my community work, I direct an arts-based informal education project for LGBTQ youth, which is funded by Public Safety and Emergency Preparedness, Canada's Community Mobilization Program. This cultural education project focuses on youth leadership and resilience as well as building community awareness and support.

I would like to think that much of the sum of who I am is captured in the statement of my Philosophy of Teaching. I started teaching in 1977. I have been a classroom teacher of junior and senior high-school students, a science department head, a vice-principal, a school-restructuring facilitator teaching teachers with a school board, a curriculum consultant with a provincial department of education, a community educator in informal and nonformal contexts, and an academic adult educator. I have learned much in my collective practice in these roles, which is fortified by my studies in cultural studies and the field of education. These lived-and-learned experiences inform the philosophy that guides my teaching practice. Key principles of this philosophy include:

Principle 1: Education is a political engagement that must be honed as an inclusive practice guided by an ethic of mutual respect. This principle is expressed in the following Equity and Respect Statement that I include in the opening to my course syllabi: In my educational practice I work to live out an ethic of mutual respect. I am committed to using inclusive language to create a classroom atmosphere in which students' experiences and views are treated with respect and value in relation to their gender, gender identity, racial background, sexual orientation, ethnic background, age, ability, and other relationships of power. This reflects my commitment to provide an environment of equality and respect for all people within the university community, and to educate faculty, staff, and students in developing teaching and learning contexts that are welcoming to all.

Principle 2: Teaching has to focus on the mutuality of theory and practice, which is a core tenet of critical pedagogy. As an educator, it is vital that I provide students with resources to assist them as they engage the difficult language and concepts often embodied in theory. Students have to be assisted to overcome their frequent fear of theory that, if left unchecked, can lead to unhealthy anti-intellectualism.

Principle 3: Teaching in education has to address interdisciplinary and intradisciplinary concerns. From an interdisciplinary perspective, a teacher-educator should turn to history, social philosophy, and other disciplinary perspectives to engage the complexity of the topic at hand. In contemporary times this focus has to be expanded to explore post-foundational concerns with subjectivity, the problematization of identities, and the intricacies of the culture-language-power nexus. In the process, tensions between foundational and postfoundational perspectives need to be confronted. This also requires that we address the limits of particular perspectives. From an intradisciplinary perspective, we need to teach in ways that show linkages across public (K-12), adult, and higher education. In an era when neoliberalized forms of lifelong learning, which are impacted by globalization, the privatization of learning, and a melding of the social and the economic, are ascendant, it is imperative that we focus on the discipline and field as the sum of their constituents.

Principle 4: In terms of classroom dynamics, the teaching-learning interaction has to be staged as a critically reflective and deliberative engagement in which the teacher-educator and students focus on issues not personalities. In focusing on issues, they explore the contexts, dispositions, and relationships of power that shape issues as complex and multifaceted.

Principle 5: Since the mid-1990s, the OECD has promoted the idea of lifelong learning for all. From my perspective, contemporary forms of lifelong learning have to be holistic, addressing the instrumental, social, and cultural needs of learners across life, learning, and work. This belief, coupled with my beliefs about inclusion, the mutuality of theory and practice, the need to teach from multiple perspectives, and the importance of deliberation, informs the tenets I use to guide a critical social practice of lifelong learning in my work with students in adult education and teacher education. Central to this practice is helping students to shape roles as responsive and responsible citizen learner-workers. What it means to be a citizen and how the citizen is located in culture and society are at the heart of this political and pedagogical work. Here it is important to inform students that deliberating matters of being and location (becoming and belonging) is often fraught with conflict and risks. Nevertheless, students need to understand that communicative learning is a vital engagement because it keeps diversity and the impact of the culture-language-power nexus upfront in the pedagogical process.

Who am I now? These days I think of myself as a critical social educator who shapes and expands his theorizing, research, and practice by reading and critiquing a range of social and cultural theories. I have a deep interest in educational policy development, and I believe good policy provides both the protection and basis for good practice. As a gay academic working in the intersection of the moral and the political on LGBTQ issues in education, I have found this to be the case. I also believe that I function best as an educator when I engage opportunities to work across public (K-12), adult, and higher education. This may be a product of my lived professional history. However, I do see the need to work in the intersections. I believe that these dynamics are required, for example, for any of us involved in contemporary engagements with lifelong learning. As a notion and a modus operandi, lifelong learning, often presented in an ahistorical manner, has permeated policy and practice across all sectors of education. For adult educators to feel that lifelong learning is their domain or to be preoccupied with the notion that lifelong learning is usurping the role of adult education is to limit opportunities to see the porosity of all sectors of education to the effects of such cultural change forces. I am conscious of this in my national and international service work as I deliberate with colleagues variously positioned in the larger field of education. As the President of the Canadian Association for the Study of Adult Education (elected position, 2005-2008), an elected member of the four-person national

Steering Committee for the U.S. Adult Education Research Conference (2004-2006), and an invited member of the International Advisory Committee on Lifelong Learning, Central Queensland University, Australia (2003-2006), I know there is much work to do to achieve lifelong learning for all across age, class, and other relationships of power.

met NC + Ireland

Catherine A. Hansman

My interests and advocacy for adult learners in higher education grew out of my own experiences as an adult learner. I was the second oldest of five children in a career military family; both of my parents had college degrees, and it was an expectation in my family that all children would attend and graduate from higher education. However these high expectations did not match the family financial realities to support our collective higher educational endeavors, so I left home at the age of 17, worked various blue- and pink-collar low-wage jobs, and supported myself while I earned my undergraduate degree in music. I received my master's and doctoral degrees as a middle-class working adult, wife, mother, and later, single parent of growing children. I recognize the incredible combination of privilege and hard work integrated with luck that contributed to my "success" as an adult learner and to my current career. In recognizing this, however, I also acknowledge that many adult learners, no matter how hard they work, do not have the advantages, family support, good fortunes, right (read "light") skin color, ethnicity, social class, and/or whatever combination of these things is necessary to help them participate in educational opportunities. Despite the myths of achievement through hard work which are perpetuated in popular culture, it has become more and more difficult for many adult learners to gain access to education. I like to think that in my work in a professional graduate program preparing adult educators to work in the field, I help my students analyze inequities in order that we may address some of the issues that create boundaries and borders for adult learners.

Like most of us who become adult educators, I did not grow up with a burning desire to become adult educator. Instead, as most adult educators confess, I entered the field through a back door. However, I was an adult educator and doing the work of an adult educator before I knew what the term meant. On my way to my current position as an Associate Professor of Adult Learning and Development, I have worked in many aspects of education that at the time I was engaged in these activities I did not necessarily consider myself an adult educator. These areas were music education (teaching music lessons to blind adults and band and orchestra in parochial schools), software analysis and training (training military and civilian personnel on an early desktop system similar to Windows), planning training programs for the military (developing computer applications and training users on them), developmental writing (teaching writing to adults starting or returning to college), and training adults in public schools (planning parent education meetings, teaching preschool). But probably the deepest influence on my life, particularly my early life, and my developing worldview was my parents and our life as a military family during the Vietnam War era.

Through the Past Darkly: From the Outside Looking In

My father was a career Air Force Officer, so we moved every one to three years throughout my childhood. In fact, by the time I entered high school, I had attended seven different schools. The difficult part of moving around so much is that I always felt like an outsider—by the time I felt comfortable in a place, we moved again. However, there were definite advantages to growing up as a military brat. I saw a good deal of the different regions of the United States (Massachusetts, Louisiana, Mississippi, Missouri, North Carolina, Texas, Michigan, Ohio) as well as Europe. We spent three years living in Germany in the mid-sixties, a time when Germany was still recovering from World War II. My family observed the many struggles of a nation trying to regain its standing in the world. We also learned that some people never recovered from the war and were unwilling to let old resentments and bigotry die. This notion became reality to me and my family when a swastika was painted on the front door to our quarters one night while we slept, and although I was too young to fully understand the significance of that action, I understood the hatred felt by the person who drew this symbol.

My parents made sure that we traveled widely, and this was particularly true during our time in Europe. We spent one summer traveling throughout Europe – Germany, France, Switzerland, Spain, and Austria. I saw many beautiful sights and understood much more about the world than I had before we lived in Europe, gaining an appreciation for those different than myself and my narrow life. But our trip to Berlin affected me the most of all our travels. Since Germany in the mid-sixties was a divided country, on our way to West Berlin our train had to pass through East Germany and East Berlin. The train stopped at a checkpoint, and through the train window we could see soldiers in long dark coats goose-stepping with guns in the train courtyard. My father, a home movie aficionado, took pictures of this with his Super 8 camera. He stopped, however, when a contingent of three soldiers, carrying loaded rifles, came on the train and demanded our passports. After looking at my father's passport and discovering that he was an American military officer, they took the camera and (more frightening for us), him away for questioning. When my father finally returned, the film had been taken from the camera, but he was safe.

As memorable as the train incident was in engraving on me the ease at which human rights can be taken away, the next two events on this trip were even more significant to my growing understanding of bigotry and hatred and how they shape actions within a complex world. The first was our visit to the Berlin Wall. I noticed the many wreaths that were hung on and placed on the ground by the wall, positioned by friends and relatives of those who died trying to escape from East Berlin and to freedom. It made quite an impression on me, as did the wall itself, which was made up of old bricks and boards and dilapidated buildings, complete with cruel looking broken glass and barbed wire on the top of the wall. When we looked over the wall from Checkpoint Charlie we couldn't help but notice the contrast of East Berlin with West Berlin – the East side had few people on the streets, hardly any automobiles, and was very run-down looking. It was quite distinct with West Berlin, which was bustling with activity and people on the streets, seemingly enjoying life.

But it was the next event on this trip intensely changed my understanding of the world and the ways which intolerance, racism, exclusion and inhumanity lead to war, death, and destruction. My parents took us to a concentration camp. Although I knew of the Nazis and their role in WWII, I had not known up until this time of the ways in which they deprived millions of people their lives. There were bloodstains on the walls of the buildings left standing at the camp, a pile of rocks placed for the lost lives, and a silent flame burning in memoriam for all the lost souls. I will never forget the profound sadness and stillness at this site – I carry it with me always. I left Germany later that year a nine-year-old child, but with the seeds of understanding the world in more critical ways.

When we returned from Europe, I felt that I was different from other kids my age. I had seen more of the world and had a diverse understanding of it that for me was hard to communicate to others. Compounding this situation is that we moved twice more in the next four years, all within the Midwest section of the United States, and after those moves, my father was given orders to go to Southeast Asia for a year. While he was gone, we moved to live with my grandparents in St. Louis. My mother told us kids never to tell anyone that my father was in the Air Force or that he was involved in the Vietnam War. The anti-war movement was in full swing by then (he left the week after the Kent State shootings), and she was afraid that we would be ostracized or worse if anyone in civilian life knew we were associated with the military. When my father returned from the war, luckily unharmed (although he died in his fifties from what we think was a war-related cancer), we were stationed to Wright-Patterson AFB near Dayton, Ohio, the closest thing I have to calling someplace a hometown. My father's last job in the Air Force was as Associate Dean of Continuing Education at the Air Force Institute of Technology. At the time he was doing this work, I did not understand the terms "continuing education" or "adult education," although he did, and he planned programs that encompassed many of the good planning practices (i.e., Cervero & Wilson, 1994, 2005; Cafarella, 2002) we adult education faculty like to espouse in our program planning classes. So I like to think that he was my family's first "official" adult educator – like me, entering the field through the back door.

Fast Forward: Border Crossing

What I learned as a child affects me now as I work with adult learners. I have always felt that adult learners may be outsiders and must cross borders—sometimes covertly— in order to receive the education they deserve. I did my own border crossing as an adult student – first in the conservatory of music, where I received my undergraduate degree while working to support myself, then as a wife, mother, and later single mother of small children earning my master's and doctoral degrees. I have crossed many borders in my career as an adult educator, sometimes easily with the way illuminated by others and sometimes covertly, when the gatekeepers have not been looking. Although women have made great advances in their careers and education, we still are perceived in many areas as second-class citizens. This became very apparent to me when I was a doctoral student in a higher education administration class. I had written a paper on women's leadership style, critiquing historical leadership theories that we were studying from a critical feminist viewpoint.

When I presented this paper in class, my professor (a White male nearing retirement) made no comment on my presentation or paper; however, his body language clearly showed his displeasure. In an informal setting a few weeks later, he stated that he did not feel women or minorities belonged in positions of power in higher education, and he wasn't even sure that they should be professors. He did not return my written research report on women and leadership that semester, but sent it back to me in the mail over a year after the course ended. Although he had given me the grade of "A" for the course, it was obvious that he had not even bothered to read or comment on my work – he had made no marks on the paper. In essence, he was "silencing" me and other women and minorities in our program.

I learned from that experience the subtle (and not so subtle) ways that persons who may be other – due to race, class, gender, religion, sexuality, ability – may be kept outside and not allowed to cross the border to education or employment. However, the rest of my doctoral program helped me to gain and use my voice. My major professor, Dr. Arthur Wilson (now at Cornell), opened the door to the field of adult education in higher education for me, and I gratefully walked through it. I owe much to him and others in the field who have knowingly or unknowingly mentored me: Gretchen Bertsch, Carolyn Clark, Ron Cervero, Brad Courtenay, Carol Kasworm, Sharan Merriam, Susan Imel, and Amy Rose are but a few in a long list of extremely supportive colleagues. Through my participation in the Commission of Professors of Adult Education (CPAE), the Women Professors of Adult Education retreats, and the Houle Scholars Program, I have had much opportunity to travel, learn, and gain much from other adult educators.

Mentors Lighting the Way

As a woman working in the fields of, first, technology then later higher education, I have faced my share of difficulties and barriers. Mentoring has been a research area I have explored, and I have approached the topic from a critical perspective, trying to elucidate the power relationships and barriers that may prevent adult learners from participating in helpful mentoring relationships. However, I have been extraordinarily lucky in my life and adult education career with receiving help and support from caring mentors. These people have been unfailingly kind with both their time and advice as I have faced challenges and struggles, both personal and professional, within my life. Daloz (1999) writes that mentors illuminate the path for their protégés, and I am grateful to the many people who have shone their light on my path to help me learn.

I see my role as an adult educator, teaching in a higher education academic setting, as somewhat similar to what Daloz describes. My early life and my later experiences have taught me that the playing field for adult learners is usually not level, and as an adult educator who teaches in higher education, it is my job to help my students think critically about these inequities in order to address and change them. Adult learners are many times outsiders looking in, hoping to gain access to educational opportunities. I endeavor to help provide light to the paths of others and hold the doors open so that adult learners may also cross boundaries and barriers to education and lifelong learning. I have crossed my share of borders – both openly and covertly – and it is my turn to help negotiate the way for others.

References

Caffarella, R. (2002). *Planning Programs for Adult Learners* (2nd ed.). San Francisco: Jossey-Bass.

Cervero, R.M., & Wilson, A.L. (1994). *Planning responsibly for adult education: A guide to negotiating power and interests.* San Francisco: Jossey-Bass.

Cervero, R.M., & Wilson, A.L. (in press). *Working the planning table: Negotiating democratically for adult, continuing, and workplace education.* San Francisco: Jossey Bass.

Daloz, L. A. (1999). *Mentor: Guiding the journey of adult learners.* San Francisco: Jossey-Bass.

Tom Heaney

When I think of myself as an adult educator I think foremost of my collaborations with low-income and mostly African American and Latino communities in Chicago, linking learning with local initiatives to claim power over decisions affecting day-to-day lives. This work, grounded in political analysis and action, has been reinforced by being shared with others in the academy. I joined the faculty at National-Louis University in the fall of 1993, previously having been employed at Northern Illinois University for sixteen years both as faculty for Graduate Studies in Adult and Continuing Education and as founding director of the Lindeman Center in Chicago.

Who am I? I was born in 1937, raised on Chicago's west side—a fourth-generation American far removed from Ireland's movement for a unified republic but with strong family ties to one of two Chicago behemoths with Irish roots: the Roman Catholic Church (the other being the Regular Democratic Organization). Despite my mother's three brothers who all became priests and the Catholic Church's quiet alliance with City Hall, my young adulthood was more strongly influenced by growing unrest and rebellion within both political and ecclesiastical establishments.

I was always something of a rebel—expecting, demanding, that my voice be heard. As a child I believed that differences could be resolved by reasonable arguments and generally talked my way out of most boyhood fights. Words, then and now, were for me the weapon of choice. But I learned from childhood skirmishes that, if I was to claim a voice in decisions that affected me, then I also had to work to protect that right for everyone. My concern for voice became a passion for democracy.

It was in my mid-twenties that I joined Chicago's independent political movement—an underfunded and disorganized David against Goliath—that challenged the nation's largest and last political machine. Reminiscences of the 1968 Democratic Convention have recently brought to mind the many failed attempts to dislodge Richard J. Daley, culminating in a short-lived (literally) victory by Harold Washington. On the edges, but nonetheless a participant in all of these events, I found it insufficient to merely theorize about power and privilege. It was necessary to risk action—to walk the talk.

My rebellion against the Church took a more circuitous route, tempered by promises of reform under the Second Vatican Council and by the persuasive good humor and generosity of my three priestly uncles. Deciding to work for change within, I entered the seminary, where I organized an underground theological publication highlighting many of the Council's theologians who were already challenging the male hierarchy and its theological elitism. I also organized a "free university" in the underground heat tunnels of the seminary, which pursued themes ignored in the formal, highly doctrinaire curriculum. I later learned that these revolutionary activities were actually "adult education."

I was ordained a priest in 1963 and assigned to a university parish in Hyde Park. Because of my reputation from the seminary underground, I was recruited by the Catholic Adult Education Center, a lay-run, city-wide and progressive organization, and asked to develop an "experimental theology" program with courses being offered in Catholic colleges and universities in the Chicago area. Building on "Death of God" theology and situation ethics in the U.S. and Liberation Theology in Latin America, the "experiment" emphasized the social and political implications of religious beliefs and made explicit connections with the intensifying Civil Rights and Anti-Vietnam War movements.

My own commitments were forged in both of these social movements, as I became an active participant in demonstrations, joined the board of the Catholic Interracial Council, traveled to Selma and Montgomery, walked with Martin Luther King in Marquette Park, was jailed, and experienced firsthand the tremendous educational power of collective, reflective and democratic action in bringing about social change. When I began my formal study of adult education at Union Institute in the late '70s, I relearned what I had already experienced: that the history of adult education in the United States is closely linked with the history of social movements.

In 1969, John Cardinal Cody took over the Catholic Archdiocese of Chicago. High on his agenda was the imposition of clerical control over all lay-run organizations. The Catholic Adult Education Center, for which I now worked full time, possessed significant assets due largely to its expansion into film production. Anticipating a take-over, the CAEC board formed a new organization, the InterMedia Foundation, to which it transferred its holdings before they could be claimed by the Archdiocese.

My role in orchestrating the escape of the CAEC from the clutches of the Archbishop did not ingratiate me with him, nor did it make it likely that I would enjoy favorable appointments within the Archdiocese. I left ministry in 1971 and joined the Center for Continuing Education at Loop College, one of the City Colleges of Chicago. There, as an associate of Aimee Horton, I learned for the first time how to develop education *with* rather than *for* people.

Aimee was married to the late Myles Horton, founder and then director of the Highlander Center in Tennessee—a keystone of adult education history in the United States, having linked adult education with movements for social change in the South for over sixty years. From Aimee and Myles I learned to build education around the real-life concerns of community—problems which people sought to solve by organizing themselves to effect change.

Those years at the City Colleges were a watershed. I learned to harness the power of my rebellious idealism and my visions of democratic movements for change, to bring these to bear on a city deeply scarred by division of race and class. In this, my mentors were Myles and Paulo Freire.

Paulo Freire was a Brazilian exile who had demonstrated that peasants could quickly learn to read and write when literacy was linked with political action, such as land reform or the organization of cooperatives. At the time, Freire was at Harvard University, but I first encountered his writings not in an academic journal, but through "grassroots" organizers in a Chicago *barrio*. Freire's difficult and profoundly challenging book on adult education, *Pedagogy of the Oppressed*, had become the bible of "grassroots" educators long before academics recognized its seminal importance. My teachers during these critical years were all, in fact, people of the community—people "without portfolio" or academic credentials. My understanding of the field in which I work comes from them.

In 1976, I left the City Colleges and joined the faculty at Northern Illinois University to develop a center for community-based education—a center that later came to be called the Lindeman Center (after Eduard Lindeman, one of the early founders of the adult education movement in the United States). The Lindeman Center worked with low-income, mostly minority communities in Chicago, assisting in the design and carrying out of education and research that supported local agendas for social change. Through the Center, resources of area colleges and universities were applied to projects controlled by the local community.

I completed my doctoral studies in adult education at Union—my dissertation committee including Aimee Horton, John Ohliger, and Ira Shor. I subsequently received an appointment as graduate faculty in the Department of Adult and Continuing Education at NIU, retaining my role as director of the Lindeman Center.

My practice as an adult educator continues to emphasize groups and communities facing the combined oppressions of racism, gender discrimination and poverty—groups with a considerable investment in social, economic and political change. While my work with the urban poor does not always directly parallel the work of my students in academia, it nonetheless enables me to help the latter uncover the strengths and contradictions underlying their own practice and awaken in them a sense of vision and social purpose, no matter what venues they choose in which to pursue their careers. The roots of my practice are firmly grounded in the traditions and social philosophy of women and men who founded the adult education movement in the United States. I bring to my students these traditions and this social philosophy as a lived experience.

What values underlie my practice? I bring to my work over thirty years' experience as an adult educator seeking to inform his work with a commitment to social justice and democratic social change. Adult education is a field of practice, not a discipline—which is to say that adult education has not required or attempted to create its own unique principles and strategies for systematic investigation and research. The study of adult education borrows its research methodologies from disciplines, primarily the social sciences. However, adult education remains first and foremost a field of practice. There are fields of study—law, for example—in which one can teach without practicing. Adult education is not such a field.

As an educator and as a researcher, I combine my practice in community with a discipline grounded in critical theory and emphasizing "problematization"—a term frequently used in the discourse of Paulo Freire to emphasize a prior need for problem-posing before problem-solving. The frustration frequently encountered in the practice of adult education (as in life) is derived, in part, from the relentless pursuit of solutions to the wrong questions. I attempt to emphasize in educational work a critical approach to the analysis of day-to-day experience and practice—an approach that, to the extent that I succeed, can reveal hidden assumptions and to reassess the adult education enterprise in its social and historical context.

The aim of adult education, thus conceived, is to build democracy—to enhance the capacity of adults to reasonably and interdependently construct meaning in their day-to-day lives and to both envision and create social order locally and globally. Adult education is democratic in both its process and its product. That is, it respects the rights of everyone to both learn and teach with the ultimate aim of producing a convivial society of lifelong learners whose self-interest is increasingly strengthened and shaped by the interests of all.

What am I becoming? I am strengthened in my conviction that "adult education" is not about schooling for adults. It is not about adapting adults to the demands of the workplace. It is about the facilitation of learning leading to informed participation in democracy, whether at home, in a factory or business, or in civic society.

The role of faculty—my current role—is to infuse the curriculum with this realization by modeling democratic practice in the classroom through which learners develop a sense of mission, of social purpose, a sense of "adult education as vocation."

As faculty, I am the bearer of this philosophical and ethical vision of the field of adult education. It is a vision shared with many of my colleagues, both inside and outside the academy. It is also a vision consistent with the social commitments resonating in the historical foundations of the field. I bring this vision to my students without intending to silence them or to diminish the authenticity of their voice. Thus I hope to encourage respectful debate through which all of us both teach and learn.

John Arthur Henschke, Ed. D.

I heard someone say it is an inescapable fact that many ordinary people who are not themselves very great nevertheless are used by a great idea. I found myself ultimately moving past my reluctance and then taking responsibility for allowing myself to be used by the idea expressed through the word *andragogy – the art and science of helping adults learn.*

Sources That Molded My Life

To me it is a great idea whose time has come, whose hour has struck. It has taken hold of me and used me in molding my life and shaping what I have done in educating adults and helping them learn. Some major elements of andragogy that I include follow.

Central Ideas

First, the potential and ability to learn is in the very nature and personal structure of the adult human being. The propensity, ability, and desire for learning, along with willingness to learn, is there within and is central.

Second, Knowles (1970, 1980) outlined the assumptions and processes of andragogy which I enact and adapt in my adult learning ventures. Assumptions are: The desire, potential, willingness, and ability for self-directedness in learning; the learner's experience is a resource for their own and others' learning; developmental tasks of social roles are crucial in activating the need and readiness for learning; learners need a situation-centered and problem-centered orientation to learning; motivation of an adult's learning is more internal than external; and learners need a reason that makes sense to them as to why they should learn something. Processes are: Preparation, a climate conducive to learning, mutual planning, self-diagnosis of learning needs, dynamic design of a pattern of activities, active involvement in carrying forward the activities, and evaluation or rediagnosis of their learning needs.

Third, the more and better the interaction in a learning experience among the various elements of that setting, the greater the learning is likely to be. Teachers and learners are in a cooperative venture to help the learning take place. Both need to be proactively involved in making that happen. The teacher and learners also involve material resources in some beneficial way to enhance but not be a barrier to the learning.

Fourth, my andragogical conception of preparing educators of adults (which I have used with educational programs in the USA and in many other countries around the world) needs to include at least the following five building blocks: Beliefs and notions about adults as learners, perceptions concerning the qualities of effective teachers, phases and sequences of the learning process, teaching tips and learning techniques, and implementing the prepared plan (Henschke, 1987).

Fifth, in my perception, the adult educator (andragogue) needs additionally to exemplify trust in the potential, ability, desire and willingness of learners to understand and make the right choices in learning. The dimensions of trust at least include: Purposefully communicating to learners that they are each uniquely important; believing learners know what their goals, dreams and realities are like; expressing confidence that learners will develop the skills they need; prizing the learners to learn what is needed; feeling learners' need to be aware of and communicate their thoughts and feelings; enabling learners to evaluate their own progress in learning; hearing learners indicate what their learning needs are; engaging learners in clarifying their own aspirations; developing a supportive relationship with learners; experiencing unconditional positive regard for learners; and respecting the dignity and integrity of learners (Henschke, 1998).

Sixth, my interest in andragogy has taken me into a cooperative research venture (Cooper & Henschke, 2005) to contribute toward expanding and providing a scientific foundation for it as an academic discipline and field of study. Thus far six elements have been identified in this continuing research: Evolution of the term "andragogy"; historical antecedents shaping the concept of andragogy; comparison of the American and European understandings of andragogy; popularizing of the American concept of andragogy; practical applications of andragogy; and theory, research and definition of andragogy.

Seventh, my andragogy website (http://www.umsl.edu/~henschke/) includes an extensive section on andragogical papers, my published articles in which most of them are infused with andragogy, an interactive cultural coloring book, my vita, and proceedings from the first andragogy seminar I conducted at the University of Missouri-St. Louis.

Eighth, I paraphrased a poem by Frost (1995) to depict how andragogy has captivated me:

Andragogy belonged to me before I belonged to Andragogy.
Andragogy was my longing desire in living, teaching and learning
        for a few decades
Before I was her educator. Andragogy was mine
In undergraduate school, in graduate school, in theological
        seminary, in clinical training, in parish ministry, in doctoral
        studies, in university faculty, in consulting with various
        organizations throughout society,
But I belonged to Pedagogy, still captive,
Possessing what I still was unpossessed by,
Possessed by what I now no more possessed.
Something I was withholding made me weak
Until I found it was myself
I was withholding from the dynamic, vibrant idea of Andragogy,

And forthwith found new educational and living possibilities
   in surrender.
Such as I was I gave myself outright
(The deed of gift was many deeds of dialoguing with others about
   Andragogy)
To Andragogy vaguely realizing a new idea embodying teaching,
   learning, and living
But still unstoried, artless, unenhanced,
Such as Andragogy was, such as she will become.

People

The people that have most influenced the molding of my life in general are my parents and extended family. Their beliefs were foundational to me. Nevertheless, ultimately my own beliefs were adapted freely by me and within the situation of my own personal life. My family and I lived in a small rural community. However, we went to church in a town other than where we lived; I went to junior high and high school in a different community; and I worked in banking outside the community where we lived. Thus, relating to multiple contexts allowed me to develop independence in my way of thinking and expression.

When I went into higher education—undergraduate school and graduate school—entering my professional life brought with it freedom and understanding of how to interact with various people and thinking with which I came in contact. A professor in theological seminary, Arnold Schultz, was one I could interact with quite lucidly and I developed my biblical perspectives from his being willing to support my own critical thinking. Malcolm S. Knowles, my first adult educator to work with in depth, introduced me to andragogy and exemplified congruence in theory and practice that made sense to me. What he said and did as a person and an adult educator were consistent. He modeled for me the art and science of helping adults learn, and I bought it hook, line and sinker. Eduard C. Lindeman, through his book *The Meaning of Adult Education,* provided an inspirational vision of the field of adult education. Wendell Smith, a colleague at the University of Missouri, introduced me to adult education in the university and strongly supported my energies in the adult education field. Marcie Boucouvalas and Leo Johnson are my Boston University classmates with whom I have worked in the research and practice of professionally implementing the concept of andragogy in many contexts.

Jost Reischmann, Chair of Andragogy at the University of Bamberg, Germany, has been a close friend and sounding board in my pursuit of the study of andragogy. His website (http://www.andragogy.net) has been very beneficial in continual updating of Andragogical and other adult education activities internationally. Mary Cooper, with whom I have pursued the andragogy research, taught me just about everything I know and practice regarding the expanding internet technology relating to implementing our online master's degree at the University of Missouri-St. Louis. When I teach courses online, I still call upon her for help when I get stuck or some new angle on learning technology shows up. Paulette Isaac-Savage is our adult education professor who has expanded the dimension of our degree programs in the direction of minorities, especially African-American, including drawing many of them into our program.

Places

I have been with the University of Missouri as a faculty member for 35 years at the time of this writing. I have had the excitement of working and teaching in adult education at other locations in the USA and in 13 other countries: Brazil, People's Republic of China, South Africa, Thailand, Hong Kong, Slovenia, Germany, United Kingdom, Egypt, Jordan, Cyprus, Canada, and Australia. I have worked with adult educators and adult learners from a total of 74 countries. I participated in the UNESCO Institute of Education (UIE) 1997 World Conference (Confintea V) in Hamburg, Germany, where there were 1,600 adult educators attending from 160 nations. All of these experiences have influenced me profoundly. The main thing I have garnered from this is that adults learn quite the same everywhere around the world. The only difference I detect and have observed is how their learning relates to their context.

How I Came to Adult Education

I have had two major calls upon my life – my first life call into the Christian Ministry, and the second life call into Adult Education. The foundation of my perception of this is found in the Bible, which I believe and have applied personally to my life: Psalm 32: 8 "I [God] will instruct you and teach you in the way that you should go; I will guide you with my eye upon you." I was raised in a Christian home environment with my parents and my two sisters – Joyce and Doris. All of my extended family were (and I currently am) very devout believers and practice our personal faith. We also were involved in a church (Baptist) that was very strong in the idea of the individual person being born again and baptized at the age of what was called accountability – meaning that to become a Christian believer was a matter of a personal choice made freely at an age when one understood what that involves. I became a believer and was baptized by immersion at the age of five and one-half. Incidentally, my decision to become a *Christian* and having a personal relationship with my Lord and Savior, Jesus Christ, has stayed with me all the subsequent years of my life. However, I have matured, as the years progressed, in my understanding of what that means and how I live my beliefs throughout my daily walk in life.

My father and mother told me that before I was born they prayed to the Lord and dedicated me to the Lord for His Service. It is interesting what influence one's background has on the course of one's life. This same Christian environment in which I was raised emphasized that if one entered into the ministry it was as a result of a personal call from the Lord Jesus Christ. I experienced the first call from the Lord upon my life which was into the Christian ministry in 1949. I subsequently spent nine years in university and seminary academic programs preparing myself to fulfill that call to be a minister. I was duly ordained as a minister in 1954. I met my wife, Carol, during my seminary years, and we were married in June 1958. I was a minister/pastor in local Baptist and Disciples of Christ Churches for 30 years full or part time.

In 1967, I experienced the second call from the Lord upon my life, which was ulti- mately to bring me into the field of adult education. I then spent six years completing my Doctor of Education academic work in preparation for my career in adult education. My wife, Carol, and our three daughters, Connie, Deanna, and Wendy, were with me and very supportive in this process of preparation. Although not an adult educator, Carol has also been my best friend, most enthusiastic booster, supporter and encourager in my ministerial and adult education years. At this writing in 2005, I have been a full-time faculty member at the University of Missouri for 35 years – a continuing education specialist and an associate professor of Adult Education. During some of those years, I was also doing part-time pastoral ministry. I thoroughly enjoy my work with adult learners and am exhilarated by the new research findings in which my students and I are constantly involved.

I do not seek to promote my personal Christian beliefs with the students and others with whom I work, but those and my perceptions about the field of adult education are a part of who I am. I will share my beliefs when asked because I am not ashamed of being a person of strong faith and commitment.

What I Gained from Adult Education

I gained a sense of an identity of myself as a professional adult educator (andragogue). I found an important purpose for spending my time and energy in the field of adult education. This also gave direction for my life and the development of integrity for my contribution to others and the society. I have also gained excitement and a real zest for my chosen life aims. The wealth of learning for me as a lifelong learner is priceless. I have received recognition from my educational peers and colleagues and have been honored with various awards for working in the adult education field. Some of them are: Founder's Award, Missouri Valley Adult Education Association, 1995; University of Missouri-St. Louis Chancellor's Award for Excellence to an Academic Non-Regular, 1997; University of Missouri-St. Louis School of Education Alumni Chapter Distinguished Faculty Award, 1997; Induction into the International Adult and Continuing Education Hall of Fame, 1998; Epsilon Sigma Phi Distinguished Service Award for the State of Missouri, National Extension Honorary Fraternity, 2003; Dean's Award for Lifetime of Service to Education, College of Education, University of Missouri-St. Louis, 2004; Malcolm S. Knowles Award for Excellence in Adult Education Program Leadership to the Adult Education Graduate Program at the University of Missouri-St. Louis, American Association for Adult and Continuing Education, 2004; Outstanding Service Medallion Award, American Association for Adult and Continuing Education, 2005.

What Kept Me Firmly Planted in Adult Education

I have stayed firmly planted in adult education because of my enjoyment, the support of my wife and family, freedom to work in the way I see fit, institutional backing, fruitful interaction with adult education colleagues, and international work – finding out that learners are learners and their learning process is very similar no matter where in the world is their background. I have worked with adult learners in 13 countries and from a total of 74 countries. It is part of my purpose in life and one of the calls upon my life. It is an exciting field of study in which to be. I have been delighted to see numerous people graduated from our adult education master's, Ed. D., and Ph. D. academic programs. They have flourished in their professional careers, and that helps to spur me to continue in adult education.

I have sought to contribute to our field of adult education and have been involved as an officer in various adult education organizations: President of the American Association for Adult and Continuing Education (AAACE); Director of the Commission on International

Adult Education (CIAE) of AAACE; President of the Missouri Valley Adult Education Association (MVAEA); President of the Missouri, USA / Para, Brazil (MO/PA) Partners of the Americas; Historian of the Missouri Association for Adult Continuing and Community Education (MAACCE); and Chair of the St. Louis, MO, Adult Education Council (AEC/STL). I have not found a field of study that would command my energies or is as interesting to me as adult education. My professional growth, maturing, development, and learning needs have been met and are very satisfying in adult education. I also have been able to support my family in this professional career. I receive a great delight in working in this field as I keep growing, developing, learning, maturing and eagerly moving toward a bright future. I invite others to join in this exciting and adventurous adult education field.

References

Cooper, M., J. Henschke. (2005). Additional thinking about andragogy: The international foundation for its research, theory and practice linkage in adult education and human resource development – an update. In *Proceedings of the Commission on International Adult Education (CIAE) Pre-Conference of the American Association for Adult and Continuing Education (AAACE).* (pp.). St. Louis, MO: University of Missouri.

Frost, Robert. (1995). Our gift outright. In *Collected poems, prose, and plays.* New York: Henry Holt and Co.

Henschke, J. (1987). Training teachers of adults. In C. Klevins (Ed.), *Materials and methods of adult and continuing education* (4th ed., 414-422) Los Angeles, CA: Klevens Publications in Adult and Continuing Education.

Henschke, J. (1998). Modeling the preparation of adult educators. *Adult Learning,* 9(3), 12-14.

Henschke, J. (2005). Andragogy Website: Available at http://www.umsl.edu/~henschke/

Knowles, M. S. (1970, 1980). *The modern practice of adult education: Andragogy /Pedagogy.* New York: Cambridge Book Company.

Roger Hiemstra
An Adult Educator from Kalamazoo

The Formative Years

I was born in 1938 in Plainwell, Michigan, a town north of Kalamazoo. Both of my parents were born in the area and raised on family farms. Stopping school after the 8th grade, my father earned a living off the farm hauling milk from farmers to a dairy. At 20 he met my mother, aged 18, picking up milk at her father's farm and they were married the next year.

Aspects of agriculture were an important part of life from birth through my first 25 years. Dad hauled milk, delivered livestock to markets for other farmers, and farmed, too, during those years. We lived on a small farm near Kalamazoo. I and two brothers and three sisters (one sister was actually a cousin who lived with us from age eight after her parents died) often believed he kept a few cows and other animals to generate enough work to keep us busy and out of trouble. Mom was mainly a stay-at-home mother, other than occasional house cleaning and wall papering she did for neighbors. She planted a large garden each year, another ploy to keep us kids occupied, and to supplement our food needs as money was often in short supply.

Because she was home every day and I was the first born, Mom read to me often. She was a high school graduate and helped me become an early reader with a veracious appetite for learning. I also did very well in school. Attending a one-room country school through the 6th grade, I was lucky to have teachers committed to helping kids achieve as much as they could.

From the 7th grade on I rode a bus to Otsego, eight miles to the north. As a mill town of 2,000 people on the Kalamazoo River, employment in the paper industry was a common occupation. Adjusting to a bigger school took awhile, but my elementary school successes helped me maintain good grades all the way through high school. I graduated in 1956, fifth out of a class of 102, and one of only a handful who began college that next fall.

As mentioned earlier, agriculture was an important part of my formative years. This included participation in the local 4-H club where activities with dairy animals and gardening were the norm. Involvement with 4-H and various related leadership experiences were important to my development. Such opportunities, involvement with a few sports in high school, and participating in music activities resulted in an 18-year-old ready for college.

The Launching Years

Because financial support from my parents was not possible, I began college at Western Michigan University in Kalamazoo. I lived at home and had a part-time busboy job at a hotel. Having excelled at algebra and geometry in high school, I began by declaring a major in math but soon discovered that it was a tough area. I limped through my freshman year with average grades and I certainly had no clear occupation goals in mind.

I had begun going "steady" my senior year with a neighbor girl. We continued dating throughout my freshman year at Western, and then when she graduated from high school that spring, she decided to move to California to be near her older sister. I decided to move to California, too. We both began attending Pasadena City College. Having few finances, I had various part-time jobs. Needing to work several hours each week, I struggled to keep up with my studies. I continued having difficulties with math and soon dropped it as a major. In essence, I was floundering and still had no real career goals. The girl of my life and I soon discovered that we had differing life goals and stopped dating late that first fall. I finished my sophomore year and achieved the Associate Arts degree but graduated in May 1958 with only average grades.

Knowing I needed to work for awhile to derive some clear goals, I found a job with the Douglas Aircraft Company in Santa Monica and moved there soon after graduation. I worked initially with data processing activities for a division that was focusing on military missiles. Relatively quickly, I was promoted to being a computer operator. I also began learning how to program computers thus starting a long love affair with computers.

I only worked there about 6 months and became homesick for Michigan and family. I moved back to Kalamazoo in time for Christmas and soon obtained a job with the Brunswick Company working in an entry-level management position dealing with customer complaints. After several months I got the itch to return to college and began at Michigan State University in the fall of 1959 as an undeclared major.

I did not do well there academically and still had no clear occupational goals. In the early spring of 1960 I read about the Naval Aviation Cadet program. I had never thought too seriously about becoming a pilot, but the idea of flying and becoming a naval officer was appealing in figuring out what to do with my life. Thus, I went through the application and testing procedures, was accepted, and began the program in Pensacola, Florida, April 1960.

I enjoyed the basic training and soloed in a couple of different planes. I especially enjoyed learning various acrobatic flying techniques. Unfortunately, as I was nearing the end of my initial training period, I began having headaches after staring at the instruments for very long. After going through a series of tests, it was determined that I needed glasses to correct my vision to 20/20. I was disappointed to subsequently learn that then the Navy was not accepting pilots who needed glasses. One option was to continue training as a navigator, also an officer training program, and finish out a five-year commitment on active duty. I chose another option, converting to a non-officer status with only a two-year commitment on active duty.

Thus, in the early fall of 1960 I became an enlisted man with the grade rate of E-2 and was assigned to the USS Randolph, an aircraft carrier stationed out of Norfolk, Virginia. After arriving there and they learned that I had attended college and could type, I became a yeoman doing secretarial and clerical work in one of the many ship's offices. We generally were two weeks out at sea on maneuvers in the Atlantic and two weeks back in port. I was promoted to a rate of E-3 in March of 1961.

It was an interesting tour of duty. As a country we still were nervous about Russian interventions in the Atlantic Ocean and we were becoming engaged in the space race. During the time I was at sea we constantly practiced against attacks by Russian naval vessels, sat in Cuba's Guantanamo Bay as part of a task force ready to support the Bay of Pigs invasion on April 17, 1961 (that support was called off the night before), sat off the Dominican Republic coast for a week after the May 30, 1961, assassination of dictator Rafael Trujillo, picked up astronaut Gus Grissom after his suborbital trip on July 21, 1961, collided with a Liberian oil tanker, Atlantic Viscountess, and fought resulting fires on October 16, 1961, and picked up Enos the chimpanzee who was launched into two full orbits on November 29, 1961.

Even though it involved exciting times, I knew that a naval career was not for me. I applied for and received an early discharge to attend college and reinstatement at Michigan State that December. After the discharge activities, I was happy to begin life's next chapter.

Looking at Adult Education as a Profession

I re-entered Michigan State in the winter of 1962. During my final months in the Navy I had been thinking about what to do professionally. I realized how important my agricultural connections and association with the Cooperative Extension's 4-H programs had been and began considering a county extension agent career. Thus, I described this desire to an academic advisor the first time I was back on campus. He helped me map out a course of study and I declared as an agricultural economics major with a study emphasis in rural sociology. I also obtained a part-time job on campus as a computer programmer and operator.

Having a clear career goal and the accumulation of life experiences during the previous six years had matured me in many ways. Finally, I knew what I wanted to do and be. Therefore, I found that going to classes was a real joy. I also landed a summer job in 1963 as a 4-H agent in Kent County, Michigan. That very positive experience cemented my career decision. I obtained such a high grade point average during the last two years that my overall average, even with those dismal first attempts, wound up a solid B+.

I graduated with a B.S. in agricultural economics in May 1964 and began an earnest search for a county extension position during that following summer while continuing to work with the computer job. I was invited to an interview at Iowa State University in the late summer, subsequently accepted a position there, and after an initial training period started as an extension agent in Kossuth County in the northern part of the state with a focus on 4-H.

I certainly enjoyed my experiences there, had excellent colleagues with whom to work, and began to add some innovative 4-H programs. Although I gained satisfaction from working with youth, I found my most enjoyable times involved working with the volunteer adult leaders. I seemed to have a knack for setting adults at ease and helping them pick up new skills they could then use with their 4-H club members. This success became noticed by people in the State Extension Office and within a year I was being asked to design volunteer leader training materials for use throughout the state.

I decided to begin a master's degree at Iowa State in the fall of 1966 with a major in Extension Education, the forerunner there of what later became Adult Education. I also obtained a part-time position in the state 4-H office developing training materials for volunteer 4-H leaders. My awareness of what adult education as a profession really was expanded during that first term. Having several excellent professors helped to expand my awareness of adult education as both a career and a profession. I obtained a 4.0 GPA during the year-long master's degree and wrote a thesis on the roles, attitudes, and desired characteristics of 4-H volunteer leaders. My thesis chair encouraged me to apply for a Mott Foundation Fellowship and entrance into the Ph.D. program in Adult Education at the University of Michigan. He thought that with a doctoral degree I could return to Iowa and obtain a good position at the state extension level.

I completed the application, was accepted into the doctoral program, and awarded a good fellowship. However, about the same time all of this was happening I met Janet Wemer at a recreation training workshop. It truly was love at first sight (at least on my part—it took some convincing for her to feel the same way), and knowing that I wanted to make this a permanent deal, I was not sure about a move back to Michigan. Fortunately, University of Michigan's Professor Howard McClusky, who turned out to be my main mentor and a fantastic role model, saw something in me and my application and called me one night from Ann Arbor. After a long conversation he convinced me that the program at Michigan would be in my best interest.

In essence, everything came together and I arrived in Flint, Michigan, in August 1967 to begin my Mott Foundation internship activities. I drove to Ann Arbor three to four times weekly, too, that year for a full course load. I enjoyed most of my professors there, but especially came to appreciate Howard McClusky as a masterful teacher. Initially, I still planned to return to Iowa after the degree if a state-level cooperative extension position was available. However, after only a few weeks of exposure to Howard and seeing his grace, dignity, and skill as a professor, I began to think that the professoriate was a better career route for me. I was enjoying all my research-related courses and experiences, too, so a "fit" seemed to be developing.

Janet came to visit me that first December and I asked her to marry me. She accepted and we began making plans for a June 1968, wedding in Iowa soon after she graduated. Several great intern experiences in Flint with their community school programs, a new appreciation for the relationship between adult education and a community's development potential, much enjoyment with my graduate experiences, and a growing admiration for the impact Howard had on the adult education profession throughout the U.S. helped the time until June pass quickly.

After the wedding we settled into a married-student apartment in Ann Arbor. Janet got a job teaching home economics at the nearby Willow Run High School in Ypsilanti and I started a graduate assistantship in the Adult Education Department. I continued to enjoy my graduate experiences and began the process of developing a dissertation proposal.

The next fall, 1969, Janet started a master's degree in Child and Family Studies at Eastern Michigan University in Ypsilanti and also did considerable substitute teaching throughout that school year. I undertook a part-time job as the Ann Arbor Program Coordinator for the University Center for Adult Education located at Wayne State University in Detroit. The Center offered non-credit university-level courses in various locations. This was a wonderful experience in a university's continuing education program. I also continued as a part-time graduate assistant with the Adult Education Department.

As I had completed my graduate courses, all available spare time that academic year was devoted to the dissertation. As I neared the spring term of 1970, Howard helped round out my higher education experience in preparation for becoming a professor. He arranged for me to have a paid teaching experience with him. We co-taught a graduate course on the future of adult education. This opportunity to become acquainted with a new subject, prepare for and present on the topic, read student papers, and go through the process of determining grades was so important. Here was an experience with Howard for which I was eternally grateful and I later provided many similar opportunities to my own students desiring professorial roles.

I began the search for a teaching position during the early spring of 1970 by applying to several universities. Two institutions, the University of Nebraska and Texas A & M, asked me to come for an interview. I eventually accepted an offer to begin in the fall as an Assistant Professor of Adult Education at the University of Nebraska. I finished the dissertation during the summer and we moved to Lincoln in late August.

A Professor at Last!

I spent six very fulfilling years at the University of Nebraska. During that time Janet worked for awhile with the Nebraska Cooperative Extension Service and then taught sewing to adults in evening courses. We bought our first home; our two children, Nancy and David, were born; and we became actively involved in the Unitarian church.

Research and subsequent scholarship came fairly easy for me. After a couple of successes in having articles published my first year, an editor from Professional Educators Publications asked me to write a couple of books (see Hiemstra, 2005, for a complete resume). My scholarly successes were part of the reasons I was promoted to associate professor with tenure and full professor during my six years at the university.

Although I was finding success with scholarship, I was not pleased with myself as a teacher. That initial teaching experience with Howard certainly helped, but after a few semesters I realized that I could become much better. Two things happened in 1972 that helped me change my approach to teaching and the primary focus of my research. I heard Allen Tough give a conference presentation on his work with adults' learning projects (Tough, 1971). Then Malcolm Knowles came to our campus and talked about his work with andragogy (Knowles, 1970). I subsequently read both books and began using an andragogical approach as an instructor and initiated what has been more than three decades of research on self-directed learning.

In the spring of 1976 I applied for and obtained a position at Iowa State University as Department Chair of Adult Education. Although it was tough to leave Lincoln, we were glad to be back in Ames. I had four good years there honing my teaching and scholarly skills and obtaining invaluable experiences as an administrator.

We did not have intentions of leaving Iowa, as most of Janet's family lived nearby. However, in the spring of 1980 I was asked to apply for a research position at Syracuse University. One of the graduate students there who served as a support person during my interview was Ralph Brockett. This initial opportunity for us to meet was the start of many collegial years together. I obtained the position and we moved to Syracuse in August where I began as a research professor and chair of the Adult Education Department.

A task I undertook immediately was to rebuild a program that had diminished in numbers of students and faculty. I conceived and developed a weekend scholar program that began in 1982 and ran for several years with master's degree programs offered in Buffalo, Rochester, Syracuse, Utica, and Watertown. This and other efforts resulted in many new students at both the master's and doctoral levels and several new faculty. Among the new professors was Ralph Brockett. I had served as Ralph's advisor and dissertation chair. His joining the faculty for two years enabled us to begin some joint scholarship activities and develop several publications over the years. Brockett and Hiemstra (1991, 2004) and Hiemstra and Brockett (1994) are among them.

One of the resources that attracted me to Syracuse University was a large English language adult education archival collection. In 1985 I developed a multimillion dollar proposal for enhanced use of the archives through computer technology that was funded by the Kellogg Foundation. Over seven years a large group of faculty, staff members, and graduate students carried out various activities related to the archives, web technology, and a promotion of adult education historical research (Hiemstra, 2005).

Unfortunately, the university experienced financial difficulties in the late '80s and early 90s. Several academic units were closed, the Adult Education Department among them. This resulted in the faculty leaving over a several-year process, except me because I had tenure. My role was to facilitate as many of the matriculated students as possible as they rushed to complete their graduate degrees. In 1993 I was assigned to the Instructional Development, Design, and Evaluation Department where I taught for three years. In 1996 I accepted an early retirement program offered to various faculty by the university and left with a faculty emeritus status.

In 1997 I accepted a part-time faculty position at Elmira College, Elmira, New York, as Professor and Program Chair of Adult Education. I carried out various administrative and instructional activities and established an online version of the master's degree program. This was a great culminating experience to my faculty career as I was able to work with many wonderful faculty and students. I completed my involvement with the college during the summer of 2005.

Reflections

Janet and I have lived in Syracuse longer than any other place. We have sunk our roots deep in this community. She taught for a few years at Cazenovia College, worked on a research project at Syracuse University, and had a ten-year career as a conference planner for Laubach Literacy. Our children completed most of their public school education here and now are launched in life after good college degrees. We have both kept active in the May Memorial Unitarian Universalist Church.

The time in Syracuse, our years together in other communities, my life growing up in Michigan, and my journey to becoming an adult educator have been fulfilling. I continue to keep busy volunteering, writing, and traveling and plan to do so for many years to come. As I look back on all of this, here are those professional highlights that stand out in my mind:

- I have served as a teacher and advisor to hundreds of adult education graduate students and it has been very satisfying.

- I have carried out an ambitious research and scholarship program over the past nearly four decades that has resulted in a number of publications and much gratification.

- I have been fortunate to have had several interesting international experiences in Canada, Columbia, England, Indonesia, Ireland, Jamaica, the Netherlands, Switzerland, and Tanzania.

- I have received three honors that have meant a great deal, including a teaching award from Elmira College, induction into the International Adult and Continuing Education Hall of Fame, and the Malcolm Knowles Memorial Self-Directed Learning Award.

- I have developed and maintain a huge web page that serves as a resource for adult educators around the world (Hiemstra, 2005).

Like many people, I came to the adult education field via a circuitous route, yet, it has been a most rewarding career. Being able to help adults learn is very worthwhile and serving as a professor means that I have helped many others develop skills to also serve adults. For a farm kid who grew up in Kalamazoo, Michigan, the journey has been excellent and I look forward to traveling many more paths.

References

Brockett, R. G., & Hiemstra, R. (2004). *Toward ethical practice*. Malabar, FL: Krieger Publishing.

Brockett, R. G., & Hiemstra, R. (1991). *Self-direction in adult learning*. New York: Routledge.

Hiemstra, R. (2005). *Roger Hiemstra's web page*. Available at http://www-distance.syr.edu/

Hiemstra, R., & Brockett, R. G. (Eds.). (1994). *Overcoming resistance to self-direction in adult learning*. New Directions for Adult and Continuing Education, No. 64. San Francisco: Jossey-Bass.

Knowles, M. S. (1970). *The modern practice of adult education*. New York: Association Press.

Tough, A. (1971). *The adult's learning projects*. Toronto: Ontario Institute for Studies in Education.

Bob Hill
Breaking Open Our Times (and Other Liberatory Acts)

Delicious Ambiguity

There is a New Age greeting card that quotes Gildna Radner, the actress and comedienne who died of ovarian cancer, as saying, "Some stories don't have a clear beginning, middle, and end. Life is about not knowing, it's about having to change, taking the moment and making the best of it, without knowing what's going to happen next….Delicious ambiguity" (quotablecards, n.d.). This card describes much of my life—seizing the moment and doing with it what I can, hoping for certain results, but knowing that outcomes are often beyond my charge. Yes, delicious ambiguity in results but lucidity in purpose.

My journey into adult education has been like that—in some ways there is no clear beginning, middle, or *specific* ending point in sight. I can, however, identify significant moments, ideas, people, places and events in this sojourn. For instance, the first time I was formally introduced to the idea of "adult education" was in 1989. I was teaching environmental biology at a satellite campus of Penn State University (PSU). Casualized workers were required to attend a preservice session about "non-traditional" students who were showing up more frequently in the undergraduate classroom. The presenter was Jovita Ross-Gordon. As I recall, she briefly highlighted the history and philosophy of the field. At one point she presented a typology that described notions such as "liberal," "behaviorist," "progressive," "humanistic," and "radical" approaches to adult education. The latter immediately caught my attention: *through education*, people were *intentionally* implementing a transformative social, political, and economic agenda. I was amazed! The concept of social change was not new to me; I was a child of the 1960s, and had been actively engaged in many social movements—Peace/anti-Viet Nam War actions, the Civil Rights struggle, and the first Earth Day. I had been captured by the spirit of the Second Vatican Council (1962-1965) and the Social Justice Encyclicals of the Roman Catholic Church. Through my faith life, I needed no convincing that human rights were central to building a new world order, but faith and civil society were two distinct realms. As a member of the Catholic Foreign Mission Society (Maryknoll) for several years (1985-1989), the tenets of liberation theology, and the "preferential option for the poor" had become a lived reality. After all, if the mother of God conjured up such revolutionary notions as "the mighty will be pulled down from their thrones" and the "lowly will be lifted up" (see Luke 1: 46-55), who was I to contest this? Looking back, I see that Jovita's presentation was a tipping point in my life. Radical adult education offered a way to unite my faith-filled commitment to humankind within an academic discourse. I didn't act on this awareness immediately but went on to teach at PSU for several years thereafter.

In the early 1990s, my life was filled with restlessness (a feeling not uncommon to me). I had opened a homeless shelter for women and children with a small team of activists, and I assisted in opening a soup kitchen. Because of hard work, knowledge gained through a bachelor's degree program in biology, and two master's degrees (botany and environmental ethics/theology) I was able to have a successful career with a state (Pennsylvania) environmental agency. This ultimately led to my appointments as the State Botanist, the State Biodiversity Coordinator, and the Chief of Ecological Services. Yet, I was mildly troubled by feelings of "academic incompleteness" because of having forsaken a doctoral program (all but dissertation) in biology at City University of New York and the NY Botanical Gardens in 1978. I felt unfulfilled in my dream of focusing my intellectual life and earning a doctorate. After some deliberation, I decided to apply to the Adult Education doctoral program at Penn State.

Accepted into the program, I was welcomed into the lives and work of adult educators who profoundly influenced my intellectual development and who encouraged my interest in radical adult education. They included Fred Scheid (my major professor), Daniele Flannery, Allan Quigley, and other academics who eventually served on my doctoral dissertation committee, Barry Kanpol and Henry Giroux. Each in her/his own manner shaped me in ways probably still unknown to them. Additionally, I was taught by Peter Cookson the value of trusting in others by his belief in me at a particularly contentious time in the program.

While working on my dissertation, *Growing Grassroots: Environmental Conflict, Adult Education and the Quest for Cultural Authority*, I was deeply impacted by a group of (mostly) women community leaders who had formed an environmental organization, the Palmerton Citizens for a Clean Environment. Informal adult educators, they live in the Blue Mountains of northern Appalachia. Their home is an area contaminated by toxic metals for more than a century. They are brave "organic intellectuals" in the cast of Gramsci. Within everyday life they engaged in ideological-cultural struggle against a powerful industrial elite who were joined by a complicitous State apparatus. Burke (1999) reminds us, "Each social group that comes into existence creates within itself [a stratum] of intellectuals that gives it meaning, that helps to bind it together and helps it function" (¶ 17). Such was the group who allowed me to enter their world for my dissertation research. I learned many things from them and their leader, Louise Calvin, including how to identify and subvert, through education, the processes of socialization that in everyday life lead people to be cowed and subordinated by dominant, repressive authorities.

Risk Taking on a Long Strange Trip

The lyricist for the Grateful Dead, Robert Hunter, penned some verses for which the musical group is perhaps best known. A verse, arguably containing one of the most famous lines in rock and roll (Dodd, 2003), has been a theme in my life. It exclaims, "Sometimes the light's all shining on me/Other times I can barely see/Lately it occurs to me/*what a long strange trip it's been.*" This has been the leitmotiv of my journey. Proclivities, interests, actions, and happenstance in this long strange life have taken me to 32 countries as a missionary, gay activist, environmental biologist, botanist, seeker of social justice, and revolutionary—a scoundrel and reprobate to some, an honorable and competent person to others. Part of this trip has been to dare, to risk, to open myself to vulnerability. My life flows on the line of T. S. Eliot: "Only those who risk going too far can possibly find out how far they can go."

As a queer anti-oppression researcher and educator, risk is central to my life. It appears in my writings when I advocate for activism as the practice of adult education; public policy; international adult education; environmental adult education; lesbian, gay, bisexual, transgender and queer (LGBTQ) issues in education; and queer theory. Embracing risk opens up the possibility to engage with marginalized and oppressed populations, like sex-workers, sexual minorities, self-identified radical environmentalists, people of color, activist women and other trouble-makers (Don't you love the bumper sticker that proclaims, "Well behaved women rarely make history"?). My teaching, research and practice—tightly defined around social policy in several distinct areas, such as sexual orientation and gender identity rights; the impacts of globalization, new social movements, and democracy on lifelong learning; environmental adult education; and learning for social transformation and sustainable development—stem from a pedagogy of risk and possibility. A little outrage goes a long way!

Adult Education: The Call to Resist Silence

In 1963, in his letter from the Birmingham jail, civil rights activist Dr. Martin Luther King, Jr., warned that people will have to repent not merely for the hateful words and behaviors of wrongdoers, but also for the appalling silence of the good people. My work in adult education is a call to resist silence. To be a warrior for social change means first of all, as Woody Allen would say, "showing up," that is, being present. As an out gay man, I understand that there is a pedagogical component to "presence." In my gay work, this is expressed in the language of the everyday as "queering space." Silence is not an option. If identities are grounded in "category membership," as I believe, it is essential to establish an identifiable "we/us." This was articulated in the revolutionary cry of the 1970s, "We're here, we're queer, get used to it!" Visibility helps to drive social change; however, it is not an easy task since we swim in an ocean of heteronormativity (the "heterosexual presumption") that permeates U.S. (and most global) societies. Perhaps most pernicious is the heteronormativity that occurs at the microlevel in the *everyday talk-in-interaction* that transpires in most settings. This talk-in-interaction is powerful since language directs how and what we think and therefore reinforces repression. On the other hand, interjecting queer talk-in-interaction in the everyday disrupts this. I often find support from women—especially third-wave and (so-called) Third World women—who understand life at the margins. We work together for folks who are disenfranchised because of sexual orientation or gender identity, helping sexual minorities to claim a history and a self—free to be, to become, to belong, and to act.

Adult Education as Space Travel

Many supportive adult and community educators have paved the way for me to travel into various spaces to engage in liberatory adult education at the national and international levels. Attempting to name them all risks revealing how short memory can be, but surely the list ought to include Joyce Stalker, Michael Law, Roger Boshier, Stephen Brookfield, Libby Tisdell, Ron Cervero, and Juanita Johnson Bailey, among many others. These adult educators actively supported my queer scholarship more than a decade ago when such erudition was not fashionable (it has since, happily, come in vogue in some quarters of the field). Written works by Frank Youngman, Budd Hall, Michael Newman, Ian Baptiste, André Grace, and Tara Fenwick have positively affected my thinking, teaching, research, and praxis in different and profound ways. When I proposed the first symposium on LGBTQ issues in adult education (Taboo Terrain) in 1998, André Grace, Kathleen Edwards, Brenda and Wanda Henson, and Ed Taylor came forward with me to queer the 39th Annual Adult Education Research Conference at San Antonio, TX.

The single most influential person in my adult education life has been Phyllis Cunningham due in part to her unflagging revolutionary commitment to social transformation. I was honored to chair the Phyllis Cunningham Social Justice Award Selection Committee for the Annual Adult Education Research Conference (AERC) from 1997 to 2001. I have a large poster on my office door for all visitors to read. It exclaims some of my favorite lines, penned by Phyllis (1991):

> Twenty years ago most of us non-traditional educators were trying to reform the university. This is not my goal today. I operate within the university to make ideological space for students and me to do our intellectual work. First we must cease being keepers of the gate and become keepers of the dream....It's about changing the cold ivy walls into a welcoming structure with relevant curricula for culturally diverse groups....We should put [our] privilege on the table as well.

My vocation has been to join the "space makers" in the field, to carve out and travel in an ideological space where we put into practice a comprehensive vision of justice. This is revolutionary pedagogical work. The results of my efforts to fashion this space for voice and praxis are various. It has meant developing ground-breaking courses such as Gay & Lesbian Studies in Adult Education; Queer & Gender Theories in Adult Education; Lesbian, Gay, Bisexual, Transgender, and Queer Issues in Organizational Settings, including in K-12 schooling; and innovative workshops such as Developing Queer Cultural Competence.

Space travel has led me to coordinate the first policy statement to include sexual minority rights in an International Council for Adult Education (ICAE) declaration (at the 6th World Assembly, Jamaica, 2001, the process of which was subsequently published in *Convergence*). Likewise, in 2003 at the UNESCO-sponsored CONFINTEA V midterm evaluation in Thailand, I drafted language and coordinated support for the first gay and lesbian antidiscrimination policy statement to appear in a UNESCO document on lifelong learning (published as point 3, p. 19, in the UNESCO report, "Recommitting to Adult Education and Learning," 2003). These actions were necessary since the CONFINTEA V meeting in Hamburg in 1997 called for governments to adapt to the realities of a host of marginalized peoples, but sexual orientation and gender identity were not part of these realities.

Adult Education: Breaking Open Our Times

Liberatory space is a spiritual space. Sr. Joan Chittister, Benedictine nun and activist, reminds us, "The function of spirituality is not to protect us from our times. The function of spirituality is to enable us to leaven our times; to stretch our times, to bless our times, to break open our own times (2001, ¶ 10)." Although liberatory space includes a queer dimension, leavening our times is of course larger than LGBTQ concerns. Liberatory space is about mobilizing people to take control of their lives. Beyond sexual minority rights, my interests are centered on improving the quality of life for communities experiencing environmental problems, women, and other marginalized populations, through education for better governance, democratic participation and decision making, knowledge construction, capacity building, and empowerment. I work in these areas with nongovernment organizations (NGOs) to help to integrate the work of horizontal networks into the processes of international, intergovernmental organizations (IGOs) on the complex global scene. Thus, I employ locally situated, information-based advocacy with, e.g., the UNESCO Institute for Education and other IGOs. My position as Acting Vice President for North America on the ICAE Executive Council facilitates this. Additionally, I have 17 years of policy experience in government outside of the academy that has prepared me for my academic, interdisciplinary, international social policy work in adult education.

Whither (Wither) Peace

Breaking open our times means resurrecting the questions that Phyllis Cunningham raised in 1991 on the role of adult educators in promoting peace education. Leavening our times means engaging in education toward a culture of peace. Peace adult education recognizes that if we want peace, we must work for justice. It requires asking such questions as why the American Association for Adult and Continuing Education (AAACE) has a Commission on Military Education and Training but none for Peace Education? Why, in the U.S., are there several state-funded War Colleges but not a single government-operated Peace College. Once when I raised this question in class, a former military student responded that peace courses *are* taught at War Colleges. I wondered out loud, "Would the world be in a better place if the situation was the other way: war was a course at Peace Colleges, rather than peace a course at War Colleges?" Peace and justice learning involve being challenged to think critically and to broadly explore issues of fundamental contemporary significance, including those related to conflicts and injustice in and by the U.S.

This was poignantly shown on a recent evening when a news banner flashed across the TV screen announcing that an important Al Qaeda operative, Abu Hamza Rabia, was dead. Debate on the cause centered on whether he had been caught in a deliberate aerial assassination by a U.S. remote-controlled drone missile or he died in an explosion during bomb-making activities. Missing in the presentation was the point that a month earlier his wife and children, as well as several others, were killed in a U.S.-inspired attack (euphemistically termed "collateral damage") mounted against him. Carried out with no trial and no jury, such extrajudicial killings are a tragedy to democracy and to the kind of world we democratic educators strive to build. To understand behavior such as this, one only has to look to U.S. support of Israel, where Israeli occupation forces (IOFs) have conducted 177 extrajudicial murders (assassinations). Because of these and other egregious acts performed under the pretext of security, we are losing more than the idea of global democracy—we are losing what it means to be human. Such events remind me why I have a history of engagement in peace (and antiwar) activities as the practice of adult education. Since the 1960s I have participated in them, including civil disobedience as a member of the swords into plowshares social movement.

Seeing the Moon When It Is Full

Lord Dunsany wrote that there are some qualities in us that come from yearnings deep within. They are akin to the urge that brings up a worm in an Irish bog to see the moon when it is full. For liberatory adult educators, such deep yearnings are a supplication.

Undoubtedly the urge for human rights has many roots in me, not the least of which are growing up gay in a homophobic society, a child of a working-class railroader father and a poor but proud Appalachian mother. As for the earthworm in the bog, there is something magical and mysterious surrounding these yearnings. For me, it's about finding a heart and cracking it open to the world. It's about dancing and singing and celebrating. It's about making space for radical happiness. It's remembering the lines offered by Emma Goldmann, "If I can't dance to it, it's not my revolution." Adult educators who engage in ideological space making—and those who travel in these spaces—would do well to commit this maxim to memory. Although we live and work in disciplinary locations, adult education can be a means, in a grace-filled way, to transform the places we inhabit. As the World Social Forum watchwords so simply and playfully put it, "UM OutrO muNDO é POssÍveL" (ANnOther woRLD is POssIbLe)—one in which adult education has a vital role. In these oppressive times of neoliberalism and globalization, U.S. Empire and Pax Americana, the Bush doctrine of preemptive war against *potential* enemies, state-sanctioned kidnapping (called extraordinary renditions), state-sponsored torture, and the loss of human rights— the message that another world is possible is truly revolutionary.

References

Burke, B. (1999). *infed*. antonio gramsci. Retrieved August 26, 2005, from http://www.infed.org/thinkers/et-gram.htm

Chittister, J. (2001). Spirituality and contemporary culture II. Retrieved September 4, 2005, from https://www.tcpc.org/resources/articles/spirituality_and_contemporary.htm

Cunningham, P. M. (1991, September). What's the role of adult educators? *Adult Learning, 3*(1), 15-16, 27.

Dodd, D. (2003, September 8). The annotated "Truckin." Retrieved August 19, 2005, from http://arts.ucsc.edu/gdead/agdl/truckin.html#trip

Quotablecards. (n.d.). Retrieved September 9, 2005, from www.quotablecards.com

T. S. Eliot quotes. Retrieved September 9, 2005, from http://en.thinkexistcom/quotes/t.s._eliot/

E. Paulette Isaac, Ed.D.

As a military dependent, I was blessed with the opportunity to travel to many places and meet some interesting people along the way. Relocating every two years became commonplace for me. As such, I gained an early appreciation for different cultures. As the oldest child, I can remember my parents teaching me to be independent at a young age. This sense of independency would prove to be invaluable later in life. My parents provided me with a strong foundation. Among other things, they taught me the importance of valuing family and respecting myself and others, regardless of their lot in life. My parents also instilled in me characteristics such as honesty and loyalty, and they demonstrated the value of hard work.

Like my mother, I have a humanistic quality. It has manifested itself in many ways. In particular it shows with my love for older people, which I inherited from my mother. Even today, I would rather spend time with an older adult than a peer. I have always found their stories fascinating. Hearing how my African American elders overcame trials and tribulations served as an inspiration for me to be the best I could be.

Another manifestation of my mother's humanistic nature was her willingness to help others. No matter where we lived, my mother was always busy volunteering at my school and in the community. She, I would later learn, inherited this from her mother. My grandmother was one of the most giving people I ever met. She believed in giving of her time and talents. And, while she did not have much money, she gave that too. My grandmother took everybody and everyone in. I can remember stopping by her house on different occasions to see that she had taken in another cat or dog. Or, some "unknown" relative or stranger had temporarily moved in. My grandmother lived the Christian tenet of loving thy neighbor as thyself. Being named after her is a special honor and one I do not take lightly. My grandmother was certainly one of the people who shaped my life.

Initial Interest

Like many adult educators, my trajectory into adult education happened serendipitously. After graduating with a B.S.B.A. in personnel management, I went back home to St. Louis to seek employment. It was at this point that I became involved in the community. My initial entrance into volunteerism enabled me to use my dancing skills.

While volunteering as a dance instructor at a local Boys' Club in St. Louis, I organized its first dance recital. I had invited several groups, including the youth group of the

Katherine Dunham Dance Troupe, to participate. However, the lack of support I received from the club was disappointing. I felt my services were not appreciated, so I decided to utilize my skills elsewhere.

Not to be discouraged, I decided to find another way to use my various skills. I found a booklet, which listed several non-profit organizations. While flipping through its pages, I read about the Literacy Council of Greater St. Louis. Part of its philosophy was "a genuine devotion to and concern for students." Its basic goal was to "help adult and teenage non-readers acquire basic literacy skills." This was surprising to me. I didn't realize there were adults who couldn't read. After all, as far as I knew everyone in my family and all the people whose paths I crossed could read. I eagerly attended the tutor training session. Although it was a 12-hour training program, the time I spent in that session would pale in comparison to the love I developed for working with adults. I had no idea my involvement with the Literacy Council would be the beginning of my perpetual love affair with adult education.

My first assignment was with a woman who was in her 50s. She couldn't read, but knew her ABC's. I remember struggling with her. It seemed as though nothing I taught her the session before sank in during the subsequent session. I often wondered if I was doing something wrong. After all, I had been "properly" trained. After several months, she had a breakthrough and each tutoring session was more rewarding for both of us. I can still re-member her excitement (and mine) when she was able to sound out the word "stop" from a stop sign she saw while standing on the corner. She said, "I've been seeing that word for years, but I never knew what it said."

While working with my first learner, I was also assigned to a man around her age. Interestingly, he didn't know his ABC's, but he did know a few sight words such as "the" and "is." I found this fascinating. What was even more fascinating about him was that he owned his own business. He shared with me that his wife assisted him. Working with both of these learners was rewarding. It taught me patience and was a constant reminder of how blessed I was. I believed I was providing each learner with a lifetime gift which was immeasurable.

In addition to my work with the Literacy Council, I volunteered with College for Living, an organization that assisted adults with disabilities. I would eventually become involved with several organizations in the St. Louis area.

While donating my time in the community, I worked as an academic advisor and a student support services counselor, respectively, at the University of Missouri-St. Louis. My initial position enabled me to work with adult learners, many of whom were working full time during the day and attending school in the evening. My subsequent position gave me the opportunity to work with many African American students. I noticed many of them were not adequately prepared to enter the job market. Thus, I founded and became the advisor for the Black Business Students' Association (BBSA) at the university. As part of a national organization, BBSA provided students with an opportunity to meet business professionals, network with recruiters, and it assisted them with their professional develop-ment. Each year, we held an annual banquet which underscored achievements of graduat-ing seniors. The highlight of my relationship with BBSA was learning that some of the graduating seniors obtained employment as a result of the banquet. While I was unable to obtain a job in "corporate America," it felt good to help others to do so. Although I enjoyed my work with the students, I felt there was another calling on my life.

Since the university paid 75% of employees' tuition, I decided to take advantage of it and pursue a master's degree. I learned we had an adult education program. With the volunteer work I was doing, I felt this was the perfect match for me.

In 1988, I enrolled in the adult education program at the University of Missouri-St. Louis. My first class, Foundations of Adult Education, was taught by Dr. John A. Henschke. When I initially met him, I had no idea of the impact he would eventually have on my life. Neither of us had any way of knowing how our initial encounter would bring us full circle. Dr. Henschke had a rather unique way of teaching. It baffled me. Like my other undergraduate professors, I expected him to use the "ever-popular" didactic teaching method. I was prepared to take copious notes and regurgitate what I learned. However, I quickly learned that Dr. Henschke was not your "typical" college professor. As I would later learn, he applied adult education principles he adopted from Malcolm Knowles in and outside of the classroom. I only took two classes from Dr. John Henschke, but he opened my eyes to the field of adult education and I have never looked back. Our student-professor relationship would evolve into much more in the subsequent years. Although I had the practical experience, my enrollment in the adult education program at the University of Missouri-St. Louis would be my springboard into the profession.

I didn't see many opportunities for growth at the university, so I decided I had to move on. As John Henschke tells the story, I told him, "I have to do something with my life." I moved to Atlanta, GA.

The Merger

While living in St. Louis, I attended a Baptist Church. I joined this church because my maternal grandmother was a member there. As required by the Baptist covenant, I had to find another church home when I moved to another city. Hence, when I moved to Atlanta, I transferred my membership to Antioch Baptist Church North, where Rev. Cameron Alexander was pastor. Antioch was the largest church I had ever attended. It was 9,000 strong and growing. There were numerous ministries and auxiliaries. And, while I hadn't given it much thought initially, adult education was taking place seven days a week! There was something for everyone there.

As I quickly learned, Antioch, like many churches its size, was able to provide several opportunities for learning and volunteering. This enabled me to be active in the church. During this time, I grew as a Christian. I better understood that servanthood extended beyond the church walls. One of my major volunteer activities came in the way of the Antioch Adult Education Program, which I cofounded. The program was designed to improve the educational skills of adults. We provided one-on-one tutoring, GED assistance, and other educational services. I would eventually volunteer my services for a number of ministries, including Meals-On-Wheels and Project Openhand, an organization that provided meals to people who had AIDS-related illnesses.

Eventually, a friend and I cofounded Adult Planning and Development, Inc., a nonprofit agency which provided educational services to adult learners. When I left Atlanta in 1999, we were providing services to men who were housed in a transitional facility.

Shortly after joining Antioch, I found a job at the Interdenominational Theological Center (ITC), an historically black college and university. While employed at ITC as an alumni coordinator, I had the opportunity to travel to different cities throughout the U.S. and visit many churches. Many of them offered a variety of educational programs. I was impressed to see the impact that churches, led by ITC alumni, had in the community in which they served. They offered an array of services and programs which were not limited to religious education. My experience at ITC along with my work at the church coalesced to serve as the foundation for my interest in adult education within the context of the Black Church.

Educational Background

I continued my master's degree at Georgia State University. After completing it, I was encouraged to further my education. I decided to apply for admission to the University of Georgia's (UGA) Adult Education Program. John Henschke would be one of the individuals to write a recommendation letter on my behalf. I can remember my excitement when I received my letter from Ron Cervero informing me I had been accepted into the program. Based on its reputation, I felt extremely fortunate and proud to be accepted in the Adult Education Program at UGA. To study with the likes of Talmadge Guy, Margaret Holt, and Brad Courtney was a treat! One class that had a major impact on me was Multicultural Issues in Adult Education which was facilitated by Talmadge Guy. While I had already gained an appreciation for people whose cultural backgrounds were different from mine, this class enabled me to apply that appreciation to adult education. To this day, I apply many of the concepts and practices I learned in that class with all the classes I teach.

Initially, I had considered examining literacy in the Black Church as a dissertation topic. However, as I sat in some of my classes and heard that African Americans did not participate in adult education to a great extent, I decided to change. This "belief" contradicted what I saw in my own church and others I had observed. I would eventually examine African Americans motivations for participating in church-based adult education programs. I feel it is my obligation to tell the story of the Black Church and its rich educational history.

Career Highlights

Upon my graduation from UGA, John Henschke asked me if I would consider coming back home (St. Louis) to be a professor of adult education. I immediately jumped on the offer. After all, how often does one get the opportunity to teach in his or her hometown? I have been teaching in the graduate adult education at the University of Missouri-St. Louis (UM-St. Louis) since 1999 and it's been a wonderful experience.

Since my tenure at UM-St. Louis I have worked with many students. As I learned early on as a student, learning is not something that can be placed in a vacuum. Learning should be a positive experience for all learners. However, before any learning can take place, it is important to create an environment that is conducive to learning. This means creating a climate whereby learners' differences and experiences are acknowledged and respected. This, in my opinion, opens the door to learning. I also believe it's important to nurture other aspiring scholars. As such, I encourage my students to become actively involved in adult education conferences by not only attending but presenting as well.

I have been active in the field by serving in a number of capacities. I serve or have served as a member of the Missouri Association for Adult Continuing and Community

Education, Missouri Valley Adult Education Association, American Association for Adult and Continuing Education (AAACE), the Commission of Professors of Adult Education, Religious Education Association and the Association of Professors and Researchers in Religious Education. In addition, I am active with the Midwest Research-to-Practice Conference in Adult, Continuing, and Community Education. I am currently an editor for *Adult Learning*, a publication of AAACE. I serve as an editor for *Education and Urban Society* and *Educational Gerontology*. I continue to volunteer my time with Meals-On-Wheels in St. Louis and as a board member of the Adult Education and Literacy center in St. Louis and the ABE Foundation.

I have had several highlights since I entered the professoriate. During the 2004-2005 academic year, I was promoted to associate professor with tenure. There were many people who nurtured me during the process. By assisting me, they reinforced many of the values my parents instilled in me. Thus, they along with others helped to shape me into the professor I am today. Another highlight was receiving the 2004-2005 Outstanding Faculty Award from the College of Education at UM-St. Louis. This put the icing on the cake of a great year! Having the opportunity to conduct research on Black churches in Cape Town, South Africa, was yet another highlight for me. While I have examined the Black Church in the U.S. extensively (Isaac, 2002, 2005; Isaac, Guy, & Valentine, 2001; Isaac & Rowland, 2002; Isaac-Savage, 2004), the opportunity to travel to South Africa enabled me to examine faith-based adult education from a different cultural lens. The most wonderful thing that happened to me during my tenure at UM-St. Louis was to marry the man of my dreams, Rev. Gerald L. Savage.

Conclusion

While I have only been in the professoriate for a few years, it's been a wonderful experience. I love being an adult educator. From providing a lifetime gift to non-readers to working with adult learners in higher education, I have had the opportunity to work with adults on a number of levels. Adult education is a lifelong journey. I continue to grow and learn not only about the field, but about myself as well. This alone is enough to keep me rooted in the field. There are more stories to tell and more studies to conduct. I hope to be around for a long time to do both.

References

Isaac, E. P. (2005). The future of adult education in the urban African American church. *Education and Urban Society*. 37, 276-291.

Isaac, E. P., Guy, T., & Valentine, T. (2001). Understanding African American adult learners' motivations to learn in church-based adult education. *Adult Education Quarterly*, 52(1), 23-38.

Isaac, P. (Spring 2002). The adult education phase of the African American church revisited. *Christian Education Journal*, 6(1), 7-23.

Isaac, P., & Rowland, M. (2002). Institutional barriers to participation in adult education within religious institutions. *Journal of Research on Christian Education*, 11(2), 101-120.

Isaac-Savage, E. P. (2004). The role of adult education in the African American church: A ministerial perspective. *Perspectives: The New York Journal of Adult Education.* 3(1), 4-16.

Carol E. Kasworm

The longest journey is the journey inwards
Of him who has chosen his destiny,
Who has started upon his quest for the source of his being.
Hammarskjold, 1970, p. 58

Hammarskjold captures the challenge of this chapter. How can I share in a brief sketch the sources that have guided my destiny in the world of adult education? Although there are a myriad of influential people, places, and experiences, I believe that sharing four organizing beliefs will illuminate this journey. These key beliefs include:

- There is nothing as practical as a good theory

- Learning is situated and contextual

- The development of meaningful learning represents co-constructed realities

- To truly understand adult learning and development, one must value and engage in the world of action

These beliefs will illustrate core compass points that have been framed through my consummate curiosity in adult learning, a commitment to adults who desire to purposefully develop their being in the world, as well as a commitment to leadership in formal and informal education as a change agent in services to adults.

Key Beliefs in My Journey as an Adult Educator
There is nothing as practical as a good theory

As a faculty member and a researcher, I start this journey from the valuing of theory, of seeking conceptual understandings of our world of adult learners and adult education. This phrase, "Nothing is as practical as a good theory," is from Lewin, a major researcher and writer in psychology. I valued this stance—that a conceptual frame, a valued theory, is the most practical starting place for action in the world. Having come from a professional practice world into an academic world, I had initially held the common belief of two worlds and two cultures (theory and practice). However, I found that theory frameworks, like windows to the world, gave me freedom to explore, to explain, and to question my practice for enhanced effectiveness. I have become a more effective faculty member, researcher, and academic administrator because my vision for action is solidly anchored in the landscape of theoretical ideas and theories. For me, the capable professional cares about nurturing knowledge, theory, and reflection in action worlds. Thus, I view theory and practice as central to my being and as the metaphoric Yin and Yang of adult education.

My early explorations of how theory informs practice and how practice informs theory were based in collegiate studies of psychology, social psychology, sociology, theology, and higher education. In large part, my undergraduate years in a liberal arts, religious-affiliated environment (Valparaiso University) were a significant crucible that offered support and challenge in these central explorations. This exploration continued through both my master's program in higher education student services (Michigan State University) and my adult education doctoral program at University of Georgia, as well as my concurrent career pursuits in those years. While engaging in academic coursework, I had the opportunity to explore the intellectual places, the leadership forces, and the unsettled middle ground within higher education environments to both impact individual adult learners and societal development. And during these years, I had both intellectual and experiential engagements in the practice worlds of higher education student support services, of adult and continuing education through an outreach and residential university professional education, of ongoing engagement in professional development of staff and related adult professionals, and of bringing deliberative, purposeful, guided change in individuals, groups, and institutional worlds of practice. These early years were also a time of upheaval, a time of significant exploration of beliefs in understanding the world and my place of action in it. During this era of the 1960s and 1970s, I was immersed with a heady agenda of significant questioning and a desire to change the established order for social good. This societal tumult immersed me through a personal loss and ethical concerns in the Vietnam War, through engagements in small-scale projects of institutional integration in relation to the Civil Rights movement, through my administrative facilitation roles as students challenging higher education elitist and segregation policies, and through my personal commitments to the women's movement (which provided voice, complex possibilities for action and power, and the questioning of patriarchal structures in society). Thus, informed action came from the meshing of practical understandings through the framing of theoretical perspectives that defined my world.

Learning Is Situated and Contextual

My second key belief has been expressed in many different forms during my research, but it has been a guiding understanding throughout my career. Early in my research, I drew on the anchoring works of key thinkers in adult education and higher education as they examined adult learners in their varied learning contexts; on theoretical perspectives from psychology and sociology regarding learning, human development, and professional action; on gerontological research of adult development and older adult learning; and on the diverse writings and research in the nascent field of adult higher education. I came to believe that adults were extremely individualistic in their learning engagements (beyond the external boundaries of behaviorist principles); in addition, that instructors, fellow learners, books/technology/other media, and cultural environments were significant influencers in adult learning (beyond the interior boundaries of humanist principles). Of most significance, I came to believe that higher education was a significant crucible in society for adult development and learning beyond the traditional young-adult collegiate student world. During these days of exploration towards committed ideas, I discovered the fascinating possibilities of interplay between adult development, adult learning, diverse programmatic contexts, and societal change; thus varied strands of understanding led to a central belief that learning was contextual and situational.

Through these strands, I have explored the contextual and situated nature of adult learning including the works of Lave, Wenger, contributors to Activity Theory, and other adult learning theorists and researchers. I also have explored the impact of institutional policies, structures, programs, and services for adult learners in varied higher education settings as situated and contextual influences. In specific research and writing projects, the explorations of this belief have taken different foci and forms, to include consideration of adults in varied places and stages of life and learning contexts, elderly adults in literacy programs, adults in residential continuing education, adults in varied higher education contexts (adult degree programs, two- and four-year institutions, as well as other forms of continuing and distance education programs), adult learning in technology, and adult self-directed learning.

As a catalyst for this lifelong exploration, I gained early experiential insights from my work at University of South Florida teaching lower-division social science courses to older and young adults. Because I taught in the late afternoon, these courses had an intergenerational mix of adults with life experiences that offered contextual understandings for learning key introductory concepts. I became fascinated with these older adult learners as they shared their seasoned perspectives, their discourse of intellectual exploration, and their ways of making meaning through their own struggling journeys in higher education. This attraction to the world of adult learners in higher education continued as I took on a leadership role of student services staff and student development at University of Georgia and began my search for a doctoral program. The adult education program at University of Georgia and my position at the Georgia Center for Continuing Education offered a supporting setting with nationally prominent adult and continuing educators. I had the opportunity to pursue intellectual possibilities and a professional practice identity with the support of Dr. Curtis Ulmer, Dr. Gene Johnson, and other key faculty; with very capable doctoral student colleagues; and with the key leaders at the Georgia Center. Situated in an interdisciplinary site for scholarly study of adult and higher education as well as experiential engagement in university continuing education, I had the opportunity to expand my horizons, focusing upon the role and place of higher education as part of a broader mission of lifelong learning and lifespan development.

For me, the attraction to the field of adult education was a fertile arena that did not have status boundaries, discipline silos, or stultifying beliefs regarding where and how learning must occur, who was valued, and who would be served. This field provided me a sense of entitlement to examine the adult learner within the variety of formal education contexts, whether it was in credential environments, continuing education environments, or informal learning transactions. My exploratory interests were also shaped by decades of national experimentation with structures and processes of adult and higher education, the dominant focus on access and egalitarian principles, the beliefs in lifelong learning as a societal agenda, and the excitement of innovative outreach in university continuing education. This belief in learning as situational and contextual has continued up to this present time as a personal journey of learning and development as well as a continuing scholarly exploration of its meanings, shapes, and dimensions in adult learning.

The Development of Meaningful Learning Represents Co-constructed Realities

In my early and middle years of work, it became apparent that many of the key principles and understandings of adult learning and particularly of self-directed learning presumed the ethnocentric notions of self. From my own teaching and working with adults, it became apparent that the complexity of these theories and understandings was not explanatory of the variety of individual adult and group learning responses and non-responses. It was also apparent that the monologue notions of teaching and the solo role of instructor were also insufficient. Thus, through my continued investigations into social constructivism and related theoretical perspectives, I came to believe that each individual developed understandings that were complex co-constructed realities with their learning environment; these realities were ever changing, multisourced, multilayered, and nuanced with specific events and contexts.

This stance was informed through my early and middle adult years when I explored why I saw the world differently from others and had a different set of understandings. I discovered in my explorations of adult learning and, in particular, self-directed learning that the role of cognitive development became a salient and compelling force. In essence, the works of postformal/post-Piagetian researchers led by William Perry and many recent contributors gave me a new sense of "what was meaningful learning" for different individuals, why we held different cognitive realities, and why instructors and facilitators can challenge learners beyond the "information given" (as noted by Bruner). Further, both as a woman and an academic in a professional practice context, I often saw a need to connect theory/research perspectives with a "relational reality" beyond past theories in adult learning. This direction of interest was stimulated by the work of researchers such as Gilligan, Belenky, Clinchy, Goldberger and Tarule and many others engaged in exploring relational connectedness and knowing. I have developed a profound value in the notion of meaning making and its relationships to co-constructed realities, of developmental levels of experience, of cognitive development, and of related understandings of epistemology, ontology, and schemata of knowledge.

As I considered the development of this stance, I believed that I was significantly influenced by my early worldview. I was very focused and held myself responsible for maximizing my talents, my intellect, and my contributions to others in the world. I initially presumed to also "place this set of beliefs" on others whom I supervised in work roles or on learners in instructional transactions. I discovered, with appropriate lack of success, that my sense of assumptions of others and my world beliefs were false. I discovered that I needed to critique my assumptions—that individuals brought their own realities to the interaction of learning and work and thus of subsequent outcomes. Of equal impact to these understandings of co-constructed realities of learning and action was my quest to seek a gendered identity and an intellectual place within an historic, patriarchal academic world. Just as I had placed my values and assumptions on others, so also how could I challenge the values and assumptions of a patriarchal culture placed upon my world as a woman? Thus, this notion of co-constructed realities is still an ongoing challenge of "Who am I?" and "How can I best facilitate and lead others with different life realities?"

To Truly Understand Adult Learning and Development, One Must Value and Engage in the World of Action

I wish to share an analogy for understanding this last belief. Loving the act of gardening, I believe that you need to get your hands dirty in the rich soil; embrace spring and fall planting with gusto; fertilize with care; deal with the pests and the impact of drought, sizzling summers, and freezing cold; and learn to value each plant for its own sense of need and sturdiness, as well as your own limitations as gardener. Although I read gardening books and watch TV gardening shows and discuss various plants and pests with the nursery experts, I have found that my understanding must mesh together the formal understandings with my own tacit learning world of action. Thus, I value reflective understandings of life experiences, of engaging in the application of ideas, and the related insights of the doing. I believe that the world of action is a relational world of friendships, of trust and ambiguities, of power and expertise, of flaws and limitations, and of varied forces in support and in contradiction. For me, this side of my development has been the most compelling and sometimes the most troubling. Although books and writing can speak to the paradoxical nature of this engagement, it is the courage to risk oneself in the act of doing. It is the risk of learning through error, as well as utilizing tested beliefs and assumptions of the past towards future efforts.

Why the commitment to a world of action as someone who lives in the world of research and teaching in academe? And from some of my colleagues—Why do I continue to pursue an academic administrative world beyond the classroom? As with many of my generation, I came from a family who valued education and held a firm belief that quality of life rested in continued learning, personal development, and in "giving back" to society for these gifts. Thus, my early development in Utah as a religious minority (Lutheran) and my career in higher education (Michigan State University, University of South Florida, University of Georgia, University of Texas at Austin, University of Houston-Clear Lake, University of Tennessee-Knoxville, and North Carolina State University) each honed my concerns for serving and enhancing the worlds of the "other" who experienced tacit barriers or explicit messages of exclusion, of being less, of limited life being. I came to value the land-grant tradition, as well as the related missions of the urban university and the community college. I also have continued to value the place of academic programs of adult education in a College of Education. As a faculty member and as an administrator, I found a fertile area of ideas, people, policies, and programs for my engagement at an action level as well as with my own intellectual research and writing. I have been committed to the world of possibilities offered through higher education, a place that seductively offered the most profound gifts of self-enlightenment and development of human capacity to serve the world. Thus, I have truly resonated with Myles Horton's words "We make the road by walking." I truly wanted to offer my gifts through action in the world, to explore these beliefs and commitments through my work in both action leadership and in research and writing and through the much collaboration with individuals who are faculty, staff, and students. Thus, I have continued to pursue academic as well as administrative roles. Further, I continue to pursue leadership roles of service because of this belief in my role as a change agent to enhance the world of adult learners.

Thus, my journey is still unfolding and may hopefully continue to engage you and others in this journey. We do make the road by walking together with our understandings, our research and writings, and with actions in this world of adult learning.

References

Hammarskjold, Dag. (1970). *Markings*. NY: Alfred Knopf.

Kathleen P. King

Innovation and Empowerment—Adult Education, the Cohesive Form

Today: Innovation and empowerment through transformative learning, radical pedagogy, distance education and professional development. Then: Magic through algebra, chemistry, geometry… these were my first loves in the world of learning. To see the order of the numbers, the elements, the equations and, oh, the formulas! To see the way that I could take pencil to paper and make those calculations work out to that answer, it was truly magic to my hungry mind. I was in seventh grade, I had always loved learning, and my mother had frequently taken my books away from me to try to chase me outside to play with the other kids, but it was when I reached these classes that I felt a new dimension of excitement unleash. The power of understanding, the thrill of "seeing" new concepts and ideas; these are the characteristics that math and science represented to me at this point in my life.

Fast forwarding another 10 years or so I will have traversed both a degree and career in science and one in theology (at times concurrently), but I then returned to my science and math "roots" in a very unique way through adult education.

For me, searching out the field of adult education was a critical place to unify my philosophy of life and career and my experiences of the same. At the age of 30, adult education finally began to offer a cohesive form to what had seemed to be such disparate parts. Let me explain.

Many Lives

I have been told I am fortunate, but at times it feels difficult; nonetheless I have what appears to have in a certain way "lived many lives" already. Adult education is a form that embraces those careers accurately and widely.

In the late 1950's I was born in Rhode Island, USA, to parents that were Irish and Italian. To understand that distinction one needs to know that southern New England was particularly ethnic during the 1940s-1980s. My mother was from an entirely Irish family and my father Italian; however, I was decidedly raised to be cognizant that I was *Italian*. My family name is Palombo, which was a very common name in that geographic area but also clearly identified my cultural roots. Additionally, to no surprise, I was raised Catholic and in a family with a working-class culture and perspective. My parents did not complete high school, so my older brother, younger sister and I were first-generation college students within our home.

Our parents highly valued education but honestly did not understand our school work once we passed about 7th grade, because we were enrolled in very good public schools. My mother has a keen and fast mind, but was very ill from my teen years onward. My father is the son of a house painter, who himself was a house painter and became a self-made businessman. That is, he started and ran about four small businesses, most of them centered about house painting, construction, and rentals.

I grew up watching my father run all of these companies from a bar turned into a desk in our family's basement with three stools perched around it and tiny drawers of 5"x7" and 3"x5" index cards that were his files. From this area he did the estimates, billing and payroll. It seemed usual to us to have three businesses run in the basement and a crew of painters showing up every morning at 7am to tromp downstairs. Didn't everybody create their own business and run it on their own? How else would you do it? Wouldn't everybody just create an idea and do whatever was needed to put it into action?

Dad had worked seven days a week between a factory job and starting the painting business, and mom worked at a factory on opposite shifts in the early days of the marriage in order to get things started. Such initiative, schedules, and dedication seemed status quo to the Palombo kids. The first real family vacation when dad was away from his work was when I was 20 years old.

This family history and cultural perspective created some difficult situations as I applied to college and then enrolled at an Ivy League school. In high school I had been the top student and made my way as the "exception" among students whose dads and moms were doctors and lawyers. But suddenly at Brown University I was clearly in a different world, with a culture, language, and experience that I couldn't really grasp. I was sure I was there by error—just like 75% of all freshmen in college today.

Actually, I was in an accelerated academic program to earn a B.A. and M.D. in six years. I had avidly pursued a medical career since I was about 15, living and breathing math and science of all forms. My first job had been as a nurse's aide in a nursing home near our summer home. And I found healthcare tremendously rewarding to work with the elderly and take care of their needs and to understand the medical needs and determine how medical science was going to address those needs.

From 1974 – 1980 I was totally engrossed in the world of healthcare: volunteer work at hospitals, work as nursing home and private duty nurse's aide, operating room technician (aka scrub nurse), laboratory research assistant, and biochemistry major. Then I became involved with an evangelical religious group and adopted a different kind of meaning for my life.

At that point my life took its third major turn (1st the working-class home, 2nd the sciences, 3rd religious education) and I pursued religious studies informally and then formally (a master's degree) to become a religious educator. In 1981, I finished the BA at Brown University; 1983 finished an MA in Missions, and 1983 also was married to a pastor. We then worked with churches in the very rural Northeast for 10 years.

My experiences in religious education are at times difficult to remember, but they are foundational for my adult education experience. It is here that I worked with very little resources, with people from ages 0-100+ and with individuals and large groups. We would come to communities, seek to understand their needs, and design programs that would serve their needs. Rather than some groups that would push an ironclad view, this was much more of a contextualized and compassionate mission.

These factors of compassion, vision, dedication, and initiative had drawn me to the movement. The vast amount and variety of work we did, the numbers of people we worked with, and the changes we saw in people—these are the roots of that transformative learning which has always been my conviction of empowerment within the human life.

The power of learning—the magic of seeing knowledge working in those algebra and chemistry numbers working and feeling my mind come alive! In this work, I was seeing it and helping it happen in the lives of others, just as I had done in the healthcare field. I had assisted people in physical ways; what had attracted me to religious education was drawing alongside and being there to support and empower, now it was more at the core of my efforts, drawing alongside and helping people understand themselves and their worlds.

However, by 1994 this world had seriously unraveled for me. The religious tenets no longer aligned with my convictions and worldview. The conflict that had been rooted within me since adolescence was finally strong enough that I had to step away from this belief system. With the circumstances that closed the 3rd Lifetime for me, adult educators and students of adult education can clearly see why the adult learning theory of transformative learning attracted my interest as I came across it in the next few years (King, 2002, 2003, 2005).

4th Lifetime Dawning

In 1990 my ex-husband, sons and I moved to the Philadelphia area. At this post, he needed a computer and asked me to learn how to "take care of it" because I was good at fixing "things." I refused for a year or two mostly because we were so financially strapped, but finally gave in. I had not used a computer since the late 1970s with keypunch cards; this was now the time of early MS Windows and I was enthralled with DOS and Windows sitting on the desktop with applications running and not having to program them to make them do things!!!! Awesome! No more having to use the old FORTRAN, Basic, and COBOL programming languages I used to have to use! But with the discovery came a startling awakening… another transforming worldview.

I went to visit a nearby two-year college to see how to combine science, math, and computers and they told me about computer-aided design (CAD), which is engineering design via computer. I signed up for a class and by the end of the semester had finished two courses at once. The next semester I was tutoring and taking additional CAD and engineering courses, and by summer I was teaching classes. By the next year I was teaching several computer classes and then hired full time. During the next six years I taught 30 hours in the classroom every week, English, chemistry, computer office applications, engineering, CAD, psychology, anatomy and physiology, and more. It was an open enrollment college and the students were hungry for change in their lives. They were reaching toward education to reach beyond their current life situations. We were not only educators, we were mentors and supporters. This environment resonated with my enduring philosophy of life and my convictions and was again work I "lived for" and could be fully invested in.

The many hours in the classroom were immensely valuable in helping me learn how to teach in a formal classroom. I prepared for hours on end, learned what worked and what didn't, made the mistakes of teaching like I had been taught, failing and picking myself up again. I was totally engrossed in the content and the opportunity. The content was stimulating and unending to me because technology was continuing to change daily and I was teaching these students how to learn this moving target. The students' confidence and lives would rapidly accelerate in new directions as they caught the same excitement.

In 1992 I sought out a doctorate in education program to learn how to teach these learners better, and like many of us, that is when I finally learned that I was an adult educator. What's more, I finally saw how the four lives wove together. Working through the master's in adult education and the doctorate in higher education leadership at Widener University, I not only came to understand the field, theory and research, but I sought to make sense of it for myself as well.

By the time I finished the degree in May 1997 I had left that marriage, accepted an assistant professor in adult education position at Fordham University, and found a new life partner. Life Number 5 was pulling into view.

In 2006, I have now been at Fordham 8 years and with my partner ten years. The "boys" who were born in northern New England are in college; they are men at 19 and 21. My parents are still both living but have been through many illnesses and are no longer together.

Life in 2006 is so very different than in the 1960s, 70s, and even 80s. When my youngest son graduated high school in Georgia last year we traveled there to celebrate and it was quite an odd gathering—today, families are an amazing collection of relationships and everything does not proceed smoothly. And many of us have complex extended family relationships – that is a fact of our world.

Life 5 Phenomenal

Since 1997 I have earned tenure and promotion to full professor, written six books, received over $13 million in grant funding and redesigned and expanded a center at the University. I am working with educators and programs across New York City daily and have had innumerable opportunities to travel across New York State, the country and internationally to share my work and the work of many other adult educators. Most of all I have been able to build these opportunities together to create a place where our team of visionary educators can focus on changing lives and changing learning (http://www.retc.fordham.edu).

Through the directorship at Fordham I have been able to craft the Regional Educational Technology Center (RETC) into a center which focuses on not only professional development services but also undergirds it with *research*. The M.S. in Adult Education and Human Resource Development in the Graduate School of Education at Fordham has been the academic base for this work, and several of our graduates who understand and exemplify the journey of adult learning are now part of the RETC staff.

We have a formative program development model and continually seek creative, innovative, but instructionally sound and significant proposal and program opportunities. We are continually looking for ways that we can serve the community, while also being able to be somewhat self-sustaining within the university itself. I don't know where the distant future will take myself or this educational effort; however, at this point in time we have developed a new model within a traditional university structure. We are agents of change and *transformation*.

On that topic, I have not spoken much about transformative learning in this article; instead, reading my books and articles will provide the detailed academic research, background, and discussion. However I would say that when I came across the theory during study for my second master's degree, I recognized the stories of innumerable people I had worked with in the many different circles of adult education I had worked in my entire adult life. I could see the lives of change and transformation unfolding in front of me, and I knew that what Mezirow had started to unfold had a much further pathway for us as educators and researchers to understand. With my scientific background and broad experience in different formal and informal educational settings, I also wanted to compare transformative learning across many different populations. I wanted to reach deeper into the experiences of adult learners so that the field and the learners could take the fullest advantage of understanding the learning experiences. My transformative learning research has traversed many contexts now, and I do not see a terminating point. This framework has been a rich perspective from which to understand and support adult learners. In a way, as I see it "played out" differently each time, I see that the model itself can be transformed or contextualized.

However, the purpose of all this research and many endeavors, for me, remains supporting learners as they desire to change. The focus is on the learner. Theory, research and practice, we say it so fluidly, but it has great meaning to me because I vigorously seek to apply this theoretical model to research and practice and conversely inform theory with practice and research.

Evolving

What I have purposed to do in this brief article is provide a portion of the personal story behind my academic and vocational interests, pursuits, and commitments. Hopefully knowing a little more about Kathy King, the person, helps to understand those concepts and why I so frequently am eclectic in my models, draw many pieces together, call upon different disciplines, and look at issues and theories from nontraditional perspectives.

Adult education has been a homecoming to me, but I earnestly hope we always keep that door wide open so that we do not closely confine or restrict what it is about. We have to let people of all cultures, views and experiences understand adult education from their contexts and experiences. As we do so we have the opportunity to learn more about it and more about ourselves because of each of them. We have to continue to explore how we can support others and give back again.

Virtually and always evolving,
KPK

References

King, K. P. (2002). *Keeping pace with technology: Educational technology that transforms. Vol. One: The challenge and promise for K-12 educators.* Cresskill, NJ: Hampton Press.

King, K. P. (2003). *Keeping pace with technology: Educational technology that transforms. Vol. Two: The challenge and promise for higher education faculty.* Cresskill, NJ: Hampton Press.

King, K. P. (2005). *Bringing transformative learning to life.* Malabar, FL: Krieger.

Alan B. Knox
FAQ

Over the years, much of my attention has been on future directions for the field of adult and continuing education. I seldom reflect on my own life history. Such reflection has usually been triggered by inquiries from students at graduate programs elsewhere studying about the field. Several times each semester students will ask me about my career and writings, to share with their classmates. They seek information beyond what they can obtain from their library, our departmental website, and Google. Following are their frequently asked questions (FAQ) and my basic responses about my experience and perspectives. I have noted some sources of additional details from other publications.

Q.1 What was your introduction to the field?

As with most of us, I backed into it. My reflections column which concluded the Future Directions special issue of *Adult Learning* (Vol. 13, No. 4, pp. 27-29, distributed August 2004) identified early influences. I taught my first adult education course in 1946. It was an arts and crafts course provided by the YWCA in Albany, New York. Between then and 1953, I taught many part-time courses for people of all ages by school, museum and university providers. During most of that period, my field was art, and adult education was just a place to teach about it.

Q.2 How else has art been part of your life?

I started there and it has been important throughout. I was reading and drawing when I started school at 4. In a rural school with multiple grades in a classroom, teachers allowed me to do artwork to keep busy until I moved on to the next classroom. My experience as an art major in high school and for university bachelor's and master's degrees was supplemented by museum art classes, art contests, teaching and commercial art.

When I accepted a full-time continuing higher education administrative position in 1954, adult continuing education became my vocation and art continued as an avocation. My landscape oil paintings are in collections of family and friends, with occasional shows, including two one-person shows in 2004.

Q.3 Since 1954 what have been your main career roles and influences?

The basic chronology is available in various sources. Included are the UW departmental website http://www.education.wisc.edu/elpa/people/faculty/knox.html; author information in Jossey-Bass books such as *Helping Adults Learn* (1986), *Adult Development and Learning* (1977) and *Strengthening Adult and Continuing Education* (1993); and a biographical sketch in Peters and Jarvis, *Adult Education* (1991, pp. 110-111).

I have been a fortunate beneficiary of societal and educational trends during my career. I and others born during the low birthrate period of the late 20s and early 30s started our careers during the post-World War II period characterized by economic and educational expansion. As the first graduate of the newly established adult education doctoral program at Syracuse University, I joined the relatively few annual graduates of the 16 adult education graduate programs in North America. Concurrent graduate study and work in adult education reinforced a careerlong conviction about praxis between theory and practice.

Serving as administrator of Syracuse University's Adirondack Conference Centers and becoming active in several adult education associations led to invitations to serve as a visiting staff member at the Center for the Study of Liberal Education for Adults and in 1960 as associate director of the Nebraska Center for Continuing Education. My graduate study contributed to such opportunities for scholarship, including initiating the adult education graduate program and related research activities at the University of Nebraska. Similar opportunities led to moves in 1965 to Teachers College, Columbia University; in 1971 to the University of Illinois; and in 1981 to the University of Wisconsin. Throughout the past fifty years, there has been an intertwining of roles as administrator, professor, researcher, association member, and editor that contributed to the specific opportunities that an expanding field made possible.

Q.4 What has been the trend in your scholarly interests?

There has been substantial variety in topics and methods in more than a dozen books and more than a hundred articles and chapters. My perspectives have been enriched from interaction with advisees, colleagues, and authors. After publication of *Adult Development and Learning*, I was pleased to accept Allen Jossey-Bass's invitation to start and edit New Directions for Adult and Continuing Education, which I did for years. My outlook was further enhanced by serving as Jossey-Bass consulting editor for continuing education books and for journals such as *Adult Education Quarterly, Adult Learning*, and *Journal of Continuing Education for the Health Professions*. Assisting authors such as Cy Houle and Sharan Merriam was like taking advanced seminars, replete with new insights and emerging directions.

Within this diverse exposure to the entire field, there has been an evolving trend in my scholarly interests from quantitative to qualitative methods and from personal to societal issues. My early publications address motives and characteristics associated with individual adult participation and persistence in educational activities. This interest merged with a focus on learning style and achievement, including a major experimental study with Sjogren. My reading, editing and teaching about adults as learners at Nebraska, Teachers College and University of Illinois contributed to <u>Adult Development and Learning</u>, which explored both personal and societal influences. Exploration of participation and learning prepared me to delve more deeply into the teaching-learning transaction, such as *Helping Adults Learn*. My administrative experience, combined with collaboration on major qualitative studies, such as the 1975 book, *Last Gamble on Education* (with Mezirow and Darkenwald), further broadened my attention to program development and to institutional and societal influences at the provider agency level, such as *Leadership Strategies for Meeting New Challenges* (1982). Increased association with international students and scholars during the 1980's and 90's contributed to international comparative topics and methods, such as *Strengthening Adult and Continuing Education* (1993). From this field-wide perspective, since then more of my focus has been on future directions. By contrast, a Norwegian colleague noted that the trend in his scholarship has been just the opposite, beginning with more societal and economic dynamics and moving to provider agencies and then individual participation and learning. Each of us came to appreciate essential connections between personal and societal aspects of the field.

Q.5 What about the courses and workshops that you taught?

Especially during periods between major administrative roles, conducting workshops and association activity helped strengthen the praxis between practice and scholarship. Over the years, when teaching courses on all aspects of the field, such praxis has been a major theme, helping students build on their experience and values as they alternate between the realities of professional practice and the insights available from theory and research. All of my teaching is about adult and continuing education, with examples from various segments of the field. Students are helped to adopt at least half of their course experience to fit their background and career directions. In *Enhancing Proficiencies of Continuing Educations* (1979), I outlined desirable areas of mastery, and in recent years I have taught graduate courses on most of these core areas (adult learner, helping adults learn, contextual issues, program development, evaluation, research methods, leadership). My recent course syllabi are on the department website (noted in Q.3 above). In addition, each year I teach an advanced seminar on a specialized topic of current interest to me and advisees.

Q.6 What is your association with students and colleagues?

People attracted to the field are very special, and they have enriched my life. Their role transitions as practitioners, graduate students, and professors help strengthen the entire field and are a major source of the solidarity that exists. Those with an association with graduate study regarding adult and continuing education are aware of the organized knowledge and professional literature of the field, which most of the practitioners in the field are not, in part because most work in the field is on a part-time or short-term basis. Thus, the practitioners, students, and professors with whom I am associated have potential to share their mastery and perspective with many others. I seek to encourage this multiplier effect, especially regarding a fieldwide and future-oriented perspective. However, the transactions are two-way and my perspectives are enhanced. Because most of our students work in the field while they study part time, they serve as junior colleagues and bridges to the field. I am grateful for their many contributions to my field wide perspective, which in turn is my major contribution to them.

Q.7 How did your thoughts about proficiency evolve?

The extreme diversity of theory and practice within the broad field of adult and continuing education is both a strength and a weakness. Collectively we are related to every adult, life role and segment of society. However, fragmentation across the many segments of the field retards our collaboration and impact. For the past three decades, a major quest has been for a set of basic unifying concepts applicable to the teaching-learning transaction in the field generally. The core concept is the combination of knowledge, skills, and attitudes that constitute the capability to perform in any aspect of life. The distinction between current and desired proficiencies helps to relate aspirations, needs, progress, evaluation, and application. Initial mention of a proficiency perspective in articles and chapters as well as courses and workshops drew encouraging responses. This topic is frequently included in FAQ by graduate students. Agreement on such generic components of a rationale for the teaching-learning transaction could contribute to greater cohesion and solidarity in the field generally.

Q.8 How has your career related to the rest of your life?

There is a potential overload with my active and satisfying career, my wife Linda with her career, a large family (we have seven children and more than a dozen grandchildren), and varied leisure activities. We have actively tried to achieve a satisfactory balance and our success has varied. When Linda retired a decade ago, I stopped teaching in the summer and stopped accepting new advisees (the last few are now completing their dissertations). We have enjoyed many forms of outdoor recreation, such as hiking, canoeing, camping and swimming. We share a special fondness for the Adirondacks of northern New York State and similar areas that include lakes and forests. My experience as administrator of the Adirondack Conference Centers, as a Boy Scout and as a Syracuse University Outing Club leader in such locations contributed, and my oil painting of water, rocks, trees and sky reflect my continued fascination with this subject matter. Indoor leisure interests include reading and appreciation of music, theater, and films. When she retired Linda stopped downhill skiing but I continue to do so with friends, children, and grandchildren. During the past decade we built a cabin on a small island in northern Wisconsin which has replaced camping, canoe trips, and backpacking. Although without electricity and phones, this sacred space reflects our conviction that the essence of roughing it is smoothing it, as a result of our construction projects. It is ideal for solitude, wildlife, swimming, sailing and kayaking. We have combined professional and personal travel interests, including one eight-month trip around the world in preparation for the international comparative study of societal influences on adult education that resulted in *Strengthening Adult and Continuing Education* (1993). My painting continues to be an important solitary activity and our leadership in a faith community is a major aspect of our lives and many of our friends are also members.

Q.9 What are major leadership challenges in the field?

In his 1980 book on continuing learning in the professions, Cy Houle discussed more than a dozen features of occupations that deserve attention in the process of professionalization. In recent decades, adult and continuing education has contributed to such professionalization in other occupations but has neglected it for itself. Cy also observed that what the field of adult education can become was a major inspiration, and this prospect continues to inspire me. A fundamental feature of our field is that most of the people working in the field do so on a part-time or short-time basis for pay or as volunteers, focused on their current circumstances and progress. Therefore, leadership depends mainly on initiatives by people with some mastery of basic concepts and literature of the broad field, including past trends and future directions. My mix of administrative and professorial roles has contributed to my appreciation of praxis as a major ingredient of effective leadership.

During the past decade, the W.K. Kellogg Foundation and the University of Georgia conducted the Houle Scholars Program in support of young scholars in the field, for which I have served as external evaluator. During the previous decade we obtained Kellogg Foundation support for two similar national programs, conducted by the University of Wisconsin and patterned on longstanding higher education leadership programs by Kellogg and by the American Council Education.

Local leadership initiatives are also important. During the 1950s as an administrator and recent doctoral graduate at Syracuse, I was serving as chair of the research committees of three of the main associations in the field, each with few committee members interested in research. This led to my founding and chairing what was later named the Adult Education Research Conference, which attracted a critical mass of people prepared to discuss and collaborate on research. During the 1970s, while serving as University of Illinois associate vice chancellor of academic affairs and director of continuing education and public service, we formed the Illinois Council on Continuing Higher Education, which brought together directors from public and private higher education institutions to address planning and policy issues. Today, there are fifty specialized national associations of people who work in various segments of the field. Our Futures web page includes a list of websites for these associations, along with two dozen items on diversity and collaboration. These specialized associations are doing well. The urgent need is for fieldwide leadership characterized by praxis between the action concerns of practitioners and knowledge resources to enhance our contributions to adult learners and to society.

Q.10 Why are you so interested in future directions?

A potential benefit of a grandparent's perspective is firsthand contacts with two or three preceding generations and two or three succeeding generations. This can put in perspective our typical reactive stance regarding the welter of often confusing and upsetting circumstances with which we try to cope. An understanding of larger trends and issues can help us appreciate shared values such as compassion, diversity, interdependence, and collaboration. This is a personal and societal challenge at international, national, and local levels. The total field of adult and continuing education is connected to all adults in all their life roles. The separate segments of the field are each servant to the fragments of our world and lives. Simplistic and polarized personal and societal views undermine shared values which result in conflict instead of cooperation in the world generally. We descend to the lowest denominator instead of a higher denominator of shared values. If adult and continuing education is to become a greater contributor to such shared values, people in the field must increase their attention to shared values and future directions. In recent years, more than a hundred people on the Futures list have been engaged in this effort. The Futures page contains many leads at http://www.aaace.org/futures.

The 2004 keynote to the Midwest Research to Practice Conference discusses ways in which that conference embodies many features essential to desirable future directions as a field for the benefit of adult learners and society.

Conclusion

A central theme over the years has been praxis between proficiency and action. This transactional concept is also important for the future. My experience has been enriched by interaction with dozens of colleagues and close associates, by hundreds of advisees, and by thousands of students and association members. The vitality of the field depends on such collective efforts. The continuing contributions to the field by many people with whom I have been associated is a source of deep satisfaction.

Randee Lipson Lawrence
Dancing on the Edge

My mother used to tell me that I was born independent. I think she was referring to the fact that I insisted on dressing myself at age two and usually made up my own mind about what I wanted to do, which was sometimes in opposition with what she and other authority figures thought I ought to do. Of course this got me into trouble with teachers and employers along the way. At age fifteen I had what I would later refer to as a perspective transformation (Mezirow, 1991). Influenced by the anti-war, civil rights and women's liberation movements of the 1960's I decided that the religion in which I was raised no longer served me. As I began to critically examine the doctrine I had previously taken for granted, I could no long reconcile the teachings with my growing feminist, libratory consciousness. I stopped going to Sunday School much to the consternation of my family. I became an activist while still in high school. I had developed a keen sense of injustice and a desire to right all the wrongs of the world. Rather than accept a world handed down to us, my cohorts and I were determined to change it. We marched in downtown Detroit and in Washington, DC, chanting; "Hell no, we won't go!" and " Give peace a chance." I had no idea then that something called "adult education" could play a role in these and other social movements.

Discovering Educational Alternatives

No one at age five declares, "When I grow up I'm going to be an adult educator." I was no exception. When I was growing up there were few occupational choices open to women, or so I was led to believe. We could be nurses, teachers or secretaries. I was scared of needles and terrible at typing. I liked children, so elementary education made sense. I had this goal in mind throughout high school and college, but I was also becoming influenced by some of the alternative school movements of the times.

My earliest experience with alternative methods of education occurred when I was a senior in high school. It was 1971, Nixon was president, the war in Vietnam was raging and I, like many others of my generation, was searching for a sense of meaning in my life. High school seemed irrelevant and oppressive. On our own we were reading Ivan Illich and Jonathon Kozol and A. S. Neill's *Summerhill*; we knew there had to be a better way. A group of kids got together and proposed a "school within a school" concept where students chose their own curriculum and even some of their own teachers. I became part of a cohort of twenty-five seniors in a program called S.E.E.K., which stood for Student's Experimentation in the Exploration of Knowledge. Our teachers and mentors were parents or other community members, or sometimes each other. During that year I tutored inner-city children, studied French and contemporary social movements ,and was a member of an acting troupe. These activities often lasted until late into the evening. We had discovered collectively that learning didn't have to take place in school.

My high school experience was so invigorating that when I graduated, I looked for alternatives to a traditional college program. I decided on Justin Morrill College (JMC), which was a residential liberal arts college within Michigan State University. At JMC I was part of a cohort of another sort. The residential component meant that many of the classes were held in the dormitory where the majority of the students lived. It was like a big family. We literally ate, slept, worked and played together. A small core of teachers taught the required courses to groups of about twenty to thirty students. There were no grades. Instead, the professors provided written narrative evaluations for each student.

Perhaps the best part of the program was the rich variety of innovative course offerings. These courses were developed by the faculty and changed each term. One of my professors, Betty Dickinson had studied with Fritz Perls in Big Sur, California, and was heavily influenced by gestalt techniques. Her experiential teaching methods had a strong influence on my development as an educator. Looking back, I realize how important it was for me to be connected to a small group of people in the midst of a big impersonal university. I had both classmates and teachers who knew me and cared about my success. College was more than a steppingstone to a career. It was an opportunity to learn about life.

I also volunteered in a "free school" for K-8 students, which was East Lansing's version of Summerhill. The students were not grouped into traditional grades. Instead they were taught what they wanted to learn according to the developmental stage they happened to be at. I was beginning to see that education did not need to follow a traditional school model. During this period I also developed my creative self. My friends and I performed plays in the "theatre of the absurd" genre in our dormitory basement. I studied blues guitar, learned to take photographs and develop them, and also learned to throw pots on a wheel at a local arts collective. While I was immersing myself in all of these creative and innovative endeavors, some rational part of me knew I'd also need skills and credentials to earn a living. While I graduated with a liberal arts degree I also took a dual major in elementary education.

Career Directions

I wonder if any of us actually set goals and objectives and follow a linear path to career development. I certainly did not. I seemed to be guided by the "show up and do the next right thing" philosophy. Ironically I did not teach elementary school. I graduated at a time when there were 100 applicants for every position. My youth and lack of experience did not prove to be an asset. When I failed to secure a full-time teaching job after two years substitute teaching, I took a position in a counseling agency that was short on pay but rich in experience. I decided I liked counseling but really needed a master's degree if I were to pursue it seriously. Consequently, I enrolled in graduate school. My friends wondered about my sanity as I was parenting seven-month-old twins at the time. I think the intellectual stimulation of being back in school actually saved my sanity.

My first job after graduation was as a youth employment counselor for CETA (Comprehensive Employment and Training Act) a government-subsidized jobs program for poverty-level youth ages 16-21. The participants were mostly African American or Latino with a few White kids who were foster children or emancipated minors. Many of the girls already had babies but were completing high school with the help of extended family members. Two of the young people made a particular impression on me. Tracy, age sixteen, was part of the program along with his twin brother and two half-siblings. Tracy's mother, who was mentally ill and a drug addict, was rarely at home. His father had long since left the family. One day I was sitting on the grass outside of our classroom building having lunch when Tracy asked if he could join me. H told me about his life in the housing project and shared his discouragement about ever breaking from the cycle of poverty. My best counselor training had not prepared me to empathize with Tracy's situation. While I had experienced some lean years as a young adult trying to make it, I'd always had a roof over my head and a safe warm place to live. I tried to give Tracy hope but I think I learned far more from him than he learned from me. The myth of meritocracy was insidious.

Mary, age nineteen, was another participant. As an icebreaker in my Job Readiness class I asked the students to write out a card with the answer to the question: If I could be anywhere else right now where would I be? I would then share the responses anonymously and the students would guess who said what. When I came to Mary's card it said, "In the cemetery with my baby girl." I was deeply moved. Of course I did not read this card out loud but later talked with Mary. She'd had an eleven-month-old baby who'd died of SIDS just a week earlier. The baby's father was also a member of the youth program. I couldn't imagine how this young woman in so much pain was able to sit in class. Three months later Mary and I shared a secret. We were both pregnant and both hoped for girls.

My journey through innovations in education next led me to National-Louis University (NLU) where I became a facilitator of learning groups in a program for adults who were returning to school to complete their bachelor's degree. This part-time teaching position allowed me to balance parenting three young children with building my career. Seven years later I became a full-time faculty member at NLU. The strength of this program was the diversity of knowledge and experiences of the students and the multiple opportunities for collaborative learning. Individuals who for a variety of reasons were not successful in their earlier attempts to earn a degree found a renewed sense of confidence and a world of possibilities open to them.

Shortly after my faculty appointment I began a doctorate program in Adult and Continuing Education in order to add a theoretical grounding to what I was learning experientially. I found the program at Northern Illinois University to be a perfect fit. I was able to immediately apply what I was learning in my coursework to my work at NLU. At the same time, I was able to make many contributions to my coursework and fellow students as a result of my teaching. I also discovered a renewed sense of activism; however, through adult education, my activism now was more purposeful and had a focus.

At NIU I had the opportunity to study with such distinguished faculty as Robert Smith, John Niemi and Sherman Stanage (all now deceased). Dr. Stanage introduced me to phenomenology, which greatly influenced how I think about research. Phyllis Cunningham has been a terrific mentor for me. In addition to challenging me to think critically she introduced me to feminist pedagogy and community-based education. She recognized and validated my need to learn experientially and make my own road. She allowed me to substitute assignments to fit my learning needs and let me take the lead with the direction of my dissertation. She sits on my shoulder as I teach and advise doctoral students today.

Educating Educators

For the last ten years I have been teaching master's and doctoral students in the Adult, Continuing and Literacy Education program at National-Louis University. Our doctoral program is cohort-based, collaboratively taught, and has a strong social justice mission. During their program we ask the students to consider three questions: Who am I ? What are my commitments? and Who am I becoming? Since I would not ask my students to do anything I would not do myself (including a 40-foot-high ropes course) I have also considered these questions. I have already addressed who am I; my commitments are described below.

I believe in the freedom and dignity of all human beings to achieve personal and societal transformation through education. These beliefs are manifested in four core philosophical values about education: community, diversity, honoring multiple ways of knowing, and the value of experience in learning.

Community

Learning in community underlies my practice, research and interests. I cannot separate them. What I call my "work" is integrated into all aspects of my lifeworld. I envision the classroom as a community of learners that mirrors society. In most societies we are interdependent upon one another for survival. We have different talents, i.e., healer, mechanic, nurturer, or spiritual advisor, which contribute to the well-being of the group. I believe in the power of the community not only to create a supportive environment for learning but also to provide a context for the co-creation of knowledge. As we contribute ideas, they are given shape and substance as others relate, connect to, challenge and critique them. As we explore ideas through the multiple lenses of various perspectives our understanding is enlarged.

Developing a community of learners, be it in the classroom, workplace or community, means valuing the experience and knowledge of all and creating space for all voices to be heard. I believe that knowledge is socially constructed through participatory means. In order for a community or a learning group to function effectively there needs to be a commitment made to one another and a belief that all contributions have value. Learning to learn communally means reducing dependency on the "experts" and believing in one's self and others. It means extending one's self beyond one's self. This is antithetical to our Western culture with its emphasis on individualism.

I believe strongly in the power of education to create change; however, any lasting change must emerge from the bottom up and must be a shared effort of all involved. This belief is reflected in my teaching as I strive to create environments where students learn from one another and through my research in cohorts, collaborative learning, residential learning and collaborative inquiry process. Although my work has been mainly in higher education, I have also explored ways to build community in nonformal learning contexts.

Diversity

I have learned the most from people who are most different from myself. I have found that when ideas and experiences are viewed from the multiple lenses of a diverse group of participants, understanding is deepened and the potential for knowledge creation is enhanced. As an educator this means giving up some power and temporarily silencing myself at times in order to allow other voices to be heard. I believe in honoring and encouraging multiple perspectives. This means intentionally creating a space for the more marginalized voices to be heard. This sometimes means a deviation from the canon or what we perceive to be the dominant discourse. Honoring diversity often takes the form of selecting literature that represents different realities, providing opportunities for expression that honor diverse learning styles and encouraging group members to contribute from their own experience. Subjective ways of knowing means that there are many ways to view reality. Issues of race, class and gender will arise and they need to be dealt with in ways that do not silence or alienate but increase our understanding and knowledge. I constantly look for ways to infuse multiculturalism content and pedagogy into all courses in the curriculum.

Multiple Ways of Knowing

One of my students has a little box that sits in front of her. When you turn a switch, an increasingly frantic voice calls out, "Excuse me, will you let me out of here!!!!!!!!!" One of my roles as an educator is to help people break out of boxe, which constrain them into believing there is one right way to do things. I believe that teaching and learning are not solely cognitive or rational processes; they have affective, somatic and spiritual dimensions. I encourage students to develop these sides of themselves by incorporating metaphor, storytelling and intuitive knowing into my teaching practice and by allowing for multiple forms of expression of learning, including artistic expression. As a research advisor, I encourage my graduate students to go beyond the boundaries of what they have traditionally understood research methodology to be and consider creative and sometimes radical approaches that utilize multiple ways of knowing. My commitment to honoring and encouraging alternative forms of knowledge construction is reflected in my research, teaching, presentations and papers. I recently edited a book for Jossey-Bass New Directions for Adult Education called *Artistic Ways of Knowing: Expanding Opportunities for Teaching and Learning in Adult Education*, where authors discuss how they incorporate various art forms into their practice.

Experiential Learning

I am committed to valuing the experience of the individual. I have discovered that most people, whether they are graduate students in college or poor people living in housing projects, do not value their experience as a source of knowledge. Years of schooling have taught us to be received knowers or passive learners. We discount our own experience if it contradicts what the experts say. I believe there is a tremendous amount we can learn from our experiences and from the experiences of others when we take the time to examine them.

My mission as an educator, as I see it, is to help people to understand that their experience has value and together we can co-create new knowledge. My job is to draw out these experiences and engage groups in examining, adding on, relating to, challenging and exploring the experiences in deeper ways.

The power of the group is that we don't only have our own experiences to draw upon; we have the experiences of others in the group. Often hearing others' interpretations of our own experiences helps us to understand and learn from them in new ways.

Who Am I Becoming?

The best part of passing the half-century mark in life is the opportunity to look back at the rich variety of one's experience with greater insight and perspective than one might have in his or her 20's. I believe I am becoming more integrated. Parker Palmer (2004) describes this integration as "wholeness" or "living an undivided life" (p.5). I used to wonder what my life would have been like if I were a professional photographer or an actor or an environmentalist. Now I find ways to bring all these different aspects of myself into my work. It feels more authentic. I do not separate my work as an educator from other aspects of my life. All work has to have meaning. I am not altruistic enough to spend my time doing things that do not give my life significance. I am here to learn and grow and, in the process, to help others to learn, grow, and stretch beyond their perceived boundaries. I believe that teaching profoundly affects the lives of individuals and they in turn affect others around them like the concentric circles that radiate when a pebble is thrown into a pond.

References

Mezirow, J. (1991). *Transformative dimensions of adult learning*. San Francisco: Jossey-Bass.

Palmer, P. (2004). *A hidden wholeness: The journey toward an undivided life*. San Francisco: Jossey-Bass.

Vivian W. Mott, Ph.D.
Unlikely Beginnings...

It is both paradox and blessing that to be an adult educator is also to be frequently mis-understood relative to what we actually *do* and exactly how we came to be who we are professionally. It is to our advantage, of course, that our field is broad enough to encompass trainers in business and industry, instructors in literacy programs, higher education faculty and administrators, and medical educators – to name only a few. The breadth of the field and settings of practices, however, can cause difficulty in identifying ourselves profession-ally and creating clear career paths. As a result, among the most often-asked questions of adult educators, particularly faculty, are "How did you get where you are?" or "What did you do before being a professor?" This autobiographical essay is my humble attempt to begin to answer these questions and give honor to a few of my more important teachers and mentors along the way.

Growing up in a large, rural, Southern household full of love, fun, and discipline provided the most consistent experiences for a life of teaching, yet the most unlikely begin-nings for the university position I now hold. Home was a simple, rural, multigenerational household in Appalachia, literally where the corners of Tennessee, Kentucky, and Virginia come together to form the community known as Cumberland Gap. One of my great uncles was fond of bragging that if he had another leg, he could stand in all three states at once and still be on his own land! My mother was the eldest of nine children and I the first grand-child – loved unconditionally, spoiled probably, and definitely held to the highest standards of performance and ethics even in play. I eventually became the first of my large extended family to attend college, let alone graduate.

I lived with teachers around me on a daily basis – uncles who taught me to fish and hunt with a bow and arrow, aunts and a great grandmother who mentored me in domestic chores, my mother who shared her values in our daily living, and even the animals and farm from which I learned lasting lessons of nature. My most significant teachers, however, were maternal grandparents. I return daily it seems to their lessons, support, and admonitions even now.

My earliest memories of learning are framed as a modest farmhouse at the end of the dirt and gravel road – the road simply didn't go any farther than our homestead. The small house and accompanying barns were surrounded by tobacco land where everyone in the family worked hard: wooded glen where my imagination took frequent flight, a small one-room school where some of my earliest lessons were learned communally with cousins and other farm children, and my grandfather's church where lessons both seeped and were shouted into my mind and soul. This scene was for years at least my summer home, where I returned with my family, not for lazy summer days and quiet nights, but for early morning lessons in the fields with my grandfather, or in the farm kitchen with my grandmother or other female mentors, or rich childhood experiences all of which taught resilience and independence, fostered creativity and imagination, and instilled a deep appreciation for nature and intuition. So while the following maxims have been voiced by others before me, these are just three lessons learned and remembered still from these unlikely beginnings.

Life Is Full of Challenge and Promise

Once in the depths of a personal crisis, I returned to that east Tennessee farm one early spring to visit with my grandparents. After a strong and loving hug from my grand-mother and the wiping of my tears with the hem of her apron, she said to me, "Alright, go on out and find your Papaw." She knew his wisdom would help calm me and put my troubles in perspective. As we walked through rows of recently planted corn, he listened to my tale of woe, gently patted my shoulder and gave me his old, worn handkerchief for my tears. Then he kneeled down, scooped up a handful of rich brown soil in his large calloused hands. As he gently uncovered the tender sprout just peeking out from the kernel of yellow corn, he reminded me that the hard, seemingly lifeless seed, properly nourished with rich soil, water, and sunlight, would grow strong and tall, eventually providing food for both family and farm animals before it returned to the soil full circle. "Even in bad years, over-worked and rocky soil, and no encouragement," he said, "this tender young sprout would probably survive, and grow on to be what is in the seed. When conditions are better, when it's nourished with sunlight and life-giving water, the corn will thrive! People are like that; you are like that. Just now, you're tender in a hard spot, but you'll soon move out of it and become strong again." Self-determined, hopeful, and optimistic – these terms defined my grandfather, and these were the early lessons he passed on to me in his support and en-couragement. Now, more than 30 years later, I understand that lesson to be the beginning of the strong humanistic philosophy that would continue to guide my work in adult and continuing education.

All Persons Deserve Respect

For the first dozen years after I learned to talk, I suffered from a terrible lisp and often stuttered when upset, frightened, or angry. Among my family members or even in that one-room country school full of normally mischievous children, these afflictions were of little consequence. I was rarely made to feel self-conscious about it and usually someone would know how to calm me and give me time to speak correctly. Away from that safe-haven, however, in my regular public school, classmates and even an occasional teacher would sneer or laugh as my pronunciation of my grandparents' family name, Smith, came out as a crude expression for a body function. Similarly, although we lived in simple, modest circumstances, I never realized as a child that we were actually quite poor. I had never done without food, never wanted for clothes or toys, and always enjoyed ample affection and support from a huge loving family. Learning about the relative concepts of *rich* and *poor* happened for me during a session with the school social worker and speech therapist. While I remember the speech therapist as a kind and helpful woman, the social worker seemed intent on making us feel not only disadvantaged, but inferior. Her questions of my mother and subsequent explanations about the possible causes for my speech difficulties were harsh and insulting. As my speech worsened during the session due to the strain and embarrassment, my mother's response was gracious but firm that we would "not take part in any remedy that makes us feel less than we are." I eventually learned to control my speech problems – most of the time, at least – but have not forgotten the lesson of affording respect for every person regardless of life circumstances or abilities. As professionals, we must take care not only to respect the dignity and autonomy of all persons but to remember that our words of counsel and teaching are sometimes particularly powerful to those whom we serve.

Schooling vs Learning

I was the first of my family to pursue a college education. College was not an expectation in my culture and environment, and those young girls who did pursue education and jobs outside the home and "off the farm" thought only in terms of nursing or teaching. Even so, my grandparents were proud to tell family and others in their community when – at the age of 35 – I finished my undergraduate degree and remained in school for my master's degree. It took some explaining to help them understand the different academic programs, the varying levels of educational pursuit, and how what I had learned would be used in my small human resources and training business. Later, when I tried to explain to them about my longing for a doctorate, my grandmother's response was, "I thought you had one of those bigger diplomas." Explaining to them that, no, I wouldn't make a lot more money, and yes, I might have to move from Tennessee for work afterward, confounded the matter even further for them. As in many other times and circumstances in my life, my grandfather seemed to understand my need and love for learning and the place where learning and schooling came together. In his typical quiet manner, my grandfather listened carefully and asked a few succinct clarifying questions. Then he pursed his lips and nodded his head in closure, patted my grandmother's hand and said to her, "Vi, she's just making sure she keeps learning so she can help others go on learning; maybe she needs to go away to do that best."

Lessons Recalled

Early in my doctoral program, I knew I was in the right place (at the University of Georgia) when the professors expected my new explorations and learning to be added to, perhaps transform, and deepen what I had already learned in life. None of them approached graduate education from the "vessel" perspective as if my head could somehow be opened, emptied of all that was already there, and filled up again with new knowledge. Rather, they expected that I would not only depend on my prior learning but bring it to our doctoral endeavors so that others could benefit from it as well. I reveled as I was empowered to share lessons from that farm, my childhood, and later professional experience. And I rejoiced in the same support and shared enthusiasm for my broad forays into new topics I'd enjoyed with my family. Now, as I teach the many theories, models, and concepts in the standard graduate course of study for Adult Education, I often think of having learned many of these course concepts much earlier in life. I think of apprenticeships and situated cognition and recall my grandmother's kitchen; when I teach decision-making models, I am reminded of my grandfather's budgeting and resource allocation for spring planting. I understand self-directed learning, life transitions, developmental models, philosophical orientations, and effective instructional strategies all in terms of practical lessons learned long ago in my childhood.

Many years ago in some of my first master's classes and in many leadership and professional development workshops since, I completed a variety of instruments designed to help me formulate my educational philosophy, learn about my own learning and management style, and formalize the instructional strategies I would later use in my own teaching. As I learned to differentiate between what I knew worked well in certain settings with particular content or learners and what I *actually believed* about learning, I've also grown to appreciate how the basics of my values, philosophical position, teaching and leadership styles were actually learned, not in any college classroom, but much earlier – in those early summers and subsequent retreats to my grandparents' farm. With deep respect and appreciation for the models, theories, concepts, and tenets (and authors thereof) we teach in corporate boardrooms, college labs, and university classrooms, for me at least, the foundations of how I teach, what I feel for adult learners, and what I believe about the purpose and value of education were learned much earlier. My beliefs and educational practices were formed and strengthened at the end of that gravel road, surrounding farm, and nearby woods in Tennessee, with my grandfather's spirit whispering reminders as I need them.

Michael Newman

In a recent book I returned to Albert Camus's idea of the absurd. He argues that we long for happiness and reason even when confronted by the "benign indifference of the universe." Absurd though it is, we will spend our lives striving to give purpose to a purposeless existence. Perhaps I can find an explanation of why I find this idea attractive in the beliefs and the lives of my parents.

My father was a Methodist minister and my mother was an atheist. My mother was an educated woman, an early woman graduate from the University of Melbourne in Victoria, Australia. Her mother died in childbirth and her father simply left, so she was effectively orphaned at birth. She was brought up by aunts and, following university, earned her living as a teacher, becoming the principal of a small country school and then the deputy principal of a major school in Sydney. She left all this to marry my father in 1934. She was 35. She predates the feminists of the 1960s but she was her own woman, independent, superbly literate, and an undeniable presence in any gathering. When angered, as she could be by the narrow-minded carryings-on of my father's clerical colleagues, she would range around the house, railing against the inadequacies of others in fluent, colourful, exquisitely phrased invective. My father would sit very still and wait for the storm to abate.

My father was a gentle man, a couple of years younger than my mother. He was born in Sydney, went to the University of Sydney, and then trained for the Methodist ministry. When he married my mother, they went to the UK for two years where he did a post-graduate degree at Oxford. This quietly spoken man returned to Australia to a church in a working-class suburb of Sydney and then to a small country town in northern New South Wales called Tenterfield, where I was born in 1939. My father was a misfit, an educated man unable to engage in small talk in a rural community where everyday chat was everything. He was also a heretic. He saw the bodily resurrection of Christ as symbolically interesting but distinctly unlikely. And he believed in an afterlife where individuals did not maintain their own personal identities but where we would simply experience "a sense of peace." (Of course he kept reasonably quiet about these views until he was well on in life and my sister challenged him to come clean.) When the Japanese entered the Second World War and people in that small country town sought comfort at the Sunday church service, my father told them he was a pacifist.

So I was born to parents whose difference on matters spiritual was mediated by their love for each other and their own uncompromising kinds of integrity.

My father's pacifism meant that he was an embarrassment and the Church managed to find him a post in Tonga Tabu well out of the way in the middle of the Pacific. We went there in 1943, travelling on a cargo boat through waters still occasionally patrolled by Japanese submarines. Tonga for me is a collection of early childhood memories of coral reefs, beaches and coconut trees, of whole communities beating the water with palm fronds and herding thousands of fish inshore, of the Queen of Tonga inviting my mother for tea in her two-storey weatherboard "palace" and dandling me on her knee, of my father sitting at his desk and doing something odd which was described as writing a book (published in London in 1946 and called *Freedom and Control*), of servicemen from passing warships taking tea in our house, and of me running barefoot and starting school, where a couple of years on I was punished for copying the wrong words from the blackboard. No one knew then, least of all me, that I had appalling eyesight.

Back in Australia in the late 1940s my father was sent to another country town called Queanbeyan, where, equipped with spectacles now, I attended primary school, ran with a gang of kids, swam in the river, rode my bike out into the bush, smoked (in retribution for some earlier crime I had committed against him, my brother informed on me) and played cricket in the paddock next to our house. It was in this town that my mates and I would throw stones onto the corrugated iron roofs of the houses and run like buggery when the occupants threw open the flyscreen doors, swearing and waving their fists at our retreating backs.

In 1952 I was sent to boarding school in Sydney and the whole family moved to Sydney a couple of years later. Since then I have lived in Sydney or London or Paris. I have never again lived in the bush and if you sense just the slightest whiff of regret, you may well be right.

I went to the University of Sydney and completed an Arts degree. I drank a lot in the Forest Lodge pub just off the campus. I acted in a swag of plays (and three operettas), sang in the university choir, wrote for and acted in the annual university revue, and wrote for and in my final year co-edited the university student newspaper. It was a wonderful time and I could do all this by not attending lectures. I passed my exams each year (just) by borrowing lecture notes and taking a substance available from a nearby pharmacy (if you asked and paid for it very discreetly) which allowed you to cram for a number of days on very little sleep.

I had worked during one summer vacation as a fruit picker and during another in a factory, riveting handles to saucepans, but my first real job (as they say) was as a journalist with an afternoon newspaper in Sydney. I hated it. Covering the coroner's court and hearing accounts of grubby domestic murders, tragic examples of infanticide, suicides, and stories of the mangled results of car crashes was no fun, and I lasted just one year. But in 1962 (the swinging sixties did not start until at least 1963) it was not the done thing to walk out of a job into nothing, so I said I was leaving the country to go travelling. And I did, with two friends and a car, which we loaded onto a passenger liner, off-loaded at Colombo and then drove (in ever-increasing acrimony) through India, Pakistan, Iran and Turkey to Greece.

I hitchhiked on alone from Athens and arrived in England in mid-1963. I had said I would be away from Australia for no more than eighteen months but I was based in London for nineteen years. Over the next few years I tried my hand at writing (I sold a short story or two and wrote for one of the underground newspapers), acting (I acted in one show, did a very small amount of television work, and played a kind of minor-major role in a feature movie) and movie making (two of us got a grant from the British Film Institute and made a couple of short comedies). None of these activities won me fame and fortune, and to survive I was forced into teaching English as a foreign language in a small private language school in an old Regency house in Kensington.

But hold on! I loved doing this. The students were from the four corners of the globe, some of them studying English for genuine reasons but others having fetched up in the school to avoid work or military service or their country's regime or their partners back home. To me the women in particular were exotic and beautiful. There was an old English pub just along from the school in the kind of street you see in English movies. I did a lot of drinking there with a lot of these exotic and beautiful people and I fell in love with one of them.

At last we come to adult education. Joelle and I got married in Paris in 1968, moving from a posh church to an even posher reception centre. At the time I was not gainfully employed at anything much and I had a feeling this did not look too good in the eyes of my father-in-law, a retired naval officer of a certain ramrod demeanour. Some of my friends who came over from London for the wedding may not have helped the general impression of my worthiness either. One was dressed in a Carnaby Street suit sporting giant lapels and made out of what looked like a horse blanket, and another was wearing (if that is the appropriate word) the most provocative miniskirt on record.

Joelle and I went back to London and I wrote to a large number of institutions listed in a guide to adult classes in inner London, asking for a job teaching English as a foreign language. One of them replied offering me a class called Writing for Pleasure instead, and so I taught my first non-credit evening class for adults, on Tuesdays from 7:00 to 9:00, in the Mary Boon Secondary School in West Kensington, which on the dot of six o'clock each evening (a bit like that pumpkin) turned into a branch of the Addison Adult Education Institute. I was hooked. The people in the class were genuinely interested and genuinely interesting. They took turns reading out what they had written, so in reality we all taught each other. And at ten to eight each evening we would go to the school canteen and queue for a cup of tea along with the teachers and students from classes in keep fit, dressmaking, badminton, cookery, French, cinema, upholstery, know your London, stammering correction and car maintenance!

I got to know the institute's vice-principal and began suggesting courses we might organise, using my friends and contacts from the alternative world in London. Within a year or so my part-time job transmogrified into a full-time one and I was setting up a program of "radical" courses on alternative societies, women's liberation, civil liberties, Black power, serious rock music, welfare rights, science fiction and gay studies.

The gay studies course caused me some strife. Shortly before it was due to begin, the Inner London Education Authority (ILEA) banned it. This was in late 1973. They said it was not their policy to support sectarian organisations. This was patent rubbish, given the kinds of courses I had already set up and given ILEA's support for schools of different denominations across London, and I said so. And when the authorities would not listen I went public, resulting in a story in one of the national newspapers. Needless to say some very senior people were not pleased and I was called into ILEA's massive headquarters on the south side of the Thames and carpeted. Somehow I held on to my job and, to give those very senior people their due, after an official enquiry into "the educational approach to controversial learning situations," which took about eighteen months to complete, I actually did run the course.

My job involved more than setting up "formal" evening courses. Officially I was employed as a community outreach worker and I was required to respond to the adult educational needs of the communities within the Hammersmith and Shepherds Bush area of inner London. To do this I worked with local groups and organisations and set up a range of projects including a parents' and children's arts and crafts workshop, a numeracy surgery, a series of programs for the out of work, English classes in a commercial laundry, and meetings on tenancy legislation for people on the White City Housing Estate. I did this kind of work through most of the 1970s and through most of my own thirties and they were rich, rich years. My institute's patch had Irish, West Indian, West African and Asian communities as well as English people of all but the most exalted social classes. This was a period of social and political change and hectic community action. Joelle and I had our two children and Joelle went into adult education as well, teaching French in a number of adult education institutes, and then teaching the teachers of languages in the adult education service. I wrote about the kind of work I and other adult education outreach workers across London did through the seventies in a booklet called *Adult Education and Community Action*, published in 1975, and in a book called *The Poor Cousin: A Study of Adult Education*, published in 1979.

In 1979 I took up the post of Warden of the Working Men's College, an adult education institution established by the Christian Socialists in 1854. My father was delighted because he had drawn extensively on the Christian Socialists for the book he had written in Tonga! The aim of the Working Men's College (do not worry, women had long been admitted) was to bring a liberal education to "members of the artisan and working classes" and the student body was still a mixture of social classes with prominent silks, civil servants from the Bank of England and people of leisure sitting alongside plasterers, carpenters, people just off the North Sea oil rigs and the seriously unemployed in courses on classical civilisation or the music of Mozart. Over the three and half years I was there I grappled with the daily management problems of this elderly (in adult education terms) institution, set up departments of Irish Studies and of Social and Political Studies, and helped bring the employment practices into the twentieth century. I have written just a little about this period in a book to be published in 2006 called *Teaching Defiance: Stories and Strategies for Activist Educators*.

In 1982 I was invited home to Australia to head up the Workers' Educational Association (WEA) in Sydney. I dragged my French partner and our two inner-London kids with me and we settled in Sydney. But I found myself in the midst of a political struggle for control of the WEA. The faction in command sacked one of my staff and I resisted them. Having chosen sides, I fought. This involved politicking, clandestine meetings in basement bars with a senior public servant, endless lobbying, the orchestration of a Ministerial enquiry into the Association, moves by the other side at WEA Council Meetings for my immediate dismissal, accusations of financial mismanagement, and a lot of stress. I gradually found and built support, and we ousted every single member of the troublesome faction in the Association's annual elections ten months later. However it was like winning the match but being carried from the field unconscious. I was deeply tired and so when I was sure the madness in the organisation had receded and all was back in order, I told the newly elected president that the Association had had five years of my life in one, and I resigned.

I had been supported by some unions in my struggles and a senior official from one of them found me a job with the Australian Trade Union Training Authority (TUTA). From 1984 to 1989 I worked as a national trainer for TUTA. These, too, were very rich years. I was working alongside experienced union campaigners, all of them tough, committed, admirable people. A lot of my work involved designing and conducting residential courses at a purpose-built trade union training college. These were intense affairs, each day starting at 8:30 a.m. and finishing at 9:00 p.m. The training always involved interactive sessions, loads of feisty discussion, and long and often complex structured exercises. Here I could design a scenario that lasted a week or even a fortnight! In everything I have written since, I have drawn upon this experience.

At a meeting of training staff in 1987 I unwisely challenged a policy decision announced by the TUTA Director and from then on my relationship with him was anything but easy. A year or so on a member of staff close to the Director told me my future in TUTA was not secure and with real regret I began looking for another job.

I applied for and won a post at the University of Technology, Sydney (UTS) and I worked there as a senior lecturer in adult education from 1989 until my retirement in late 2001. I designed and taught courses on adult teaching and learning, program development, adult education and social movements, adult education and social action, the theory and practice of Paulo Freire, pedagogy and practice of popular education, and traditions of popular education. In 1996 I was awarded a PhD by publication and from then on also supervised doctoral students. A number of my students were activists, their research was unconventional and challenging, and I was often in awe of them.

In the twelve years at UTS I wrote three books. *The Third Contract: Theory and Practice in Trade Union Training* was published in 1993. It was a kind of thank you note for the years I had worked in the union movement and for the comradeship I had experienced. In that book I began developing ideas about learning in opposition and this led to a book called *Defining the Enemy: Adult Education in Social Action*, published in 1994. In that book I realised I was touching upon questions of choice and morality and this led to a book called *Maeler's Regard: Images of Adult Learning*, published in 1999. On reflection I felt that I had been drifting away from what actually happens in the magical encounter between the learner and the person given the privilege of helping the learner, and so I have written *Teaching Defiance*. I may have retired from my university post, but the writing bug is difficult to cure.

Australia is the land of my birth and where I live now. And I lived for a good part of my adult life in the UK. But two other countries matter greatly to me. The first is France. It is after all my partner's country of birth, and from 1968 to 1982 when we were living in

England we spent almost every Christmas, most Easters and every single summer in France. My French family had a house in a small village in the south and it is those summers that I most closely associate with our children growing up. We may have lived in London but I see my kids' development marked out in my mind like snapshots in the sun of Provence. And once I was back in Australia and both Joelle and I were working at universities (different ones but both in Sydney) we managed to make our periods of study leave coincide and so spent two periods of six months living in Paris. Since our respective retirements we have spent another five months living there. A lot of my writing has been done in Paris and it has become my second hometown.

The other country is South Africa. I first went there in 1981, invited from England to address a conference in Durban. South Africa was entering its darkest period of apartheid but I was assured the conference would be attended by both blacks and whites and that I could say what I wanted, and I went. In 1996 I went again, this time to spend ten days with the Council of South African Trade Unions in Johannesburg, then a fortnight with the Trade Union Research Project at the University of KwaZulu-Natal in Durban, and finally a fortnight with the Department of Adult Education at the University of Cape Town. I visited South Africa again in 2001, to teach a Master in Adult Education course in Durban and to conduct seminars at both the University of Cape Town and the Trade Union Library in Cape Town. The history of struggle against apartheid, the present struggle against the pandemic of AIDS, the sense of violence and anarchy, the good humour and forgiveness in the black townships, the feeling of despair and hope in the same events, the friends ... South Africa has entered my soul and is present, explicitly and implicitly, in anything I now write.

So what has it all been about? In *Teaching Defiance* I feel a little like a scruffy terrier, growling and snuffling and worrying at the rug of existence. I showed a near-final draft of the book to Joelle. She was pleased that I had turned to three French philosophers and that I had quoted a poem by Louis Aragon. She likes it. Our son is an activist, often using the principles and theatrical processes of Augusto Boal. He likes it and says it has helped him think through issues related to direct action. Our daughter is a circus performer, forever busy either performing or directing. She says she will get round to reading it soon but I am not holding my breath. Which leaves my mum and dad. I think my mother would have liked the bits in the book about using anger and finding positives in the business of hating. She was a lover of life but she was also a hater and there were those wondrous times when she would give full vent to her hatred of cant, hypocrisy, idiocy and injustice. My father was a theologian, shy and undemonstrative. I remember seeing him off at London airport in the mid-1970s. He had come to visit me after my mother had died. We stood looking at each other before he shuffled off through the departure gates. "We don't actually need to say things to let the other know how we feel," he said to me. "No," I said and he smiled at me, those deep blues eyes of his, and he turned and went through the gate. I would not expect him to say too much about what I have done or written, but I think he would smile.

Larry Olds

My last time in the classroom teaching adult students was the last semester of 1999. As I said frequently then and since, "I am not working for money in this new millennium." I ended my job. Twenty-six years earlier I had begun the job at Metropolitan Community College, then Minnesota's only urban community college. It was then that I realized I was an adult educator. Much of my prior experience had been moving me in that direction.

It was a privilege and an honor to have a job in such a place. For more than 25 years it was my job to help adults find out more about the world, and of course, to find out more about themselves as well. It was a job where there were few contradictions between my personal commitments to social change, to "being a little cog on the big wheel of social justice" as I put it in my memoirs, and the contents of the varied curricula for which I was responsible. It was a job with a strong union that both gave me security and protection and won opportunities for "faculty development" that enabled my participation with the global adult education movement, social movements, and the broader mission of peace and justice that I came to see as my work. And finally, it was a job with my own people, the overwhelming majority from working-class and ordinary backgrounds, so many bright and able, so many surprising in their embrace of radical ideas.

My 26 years was divided into three phases: the Chemical Dependency Specialist Training Program, the College for Working Adults Program, and regular political science. In my first five years at the college I facilitated learning about "community agencies and resources" and "personal and career assessment" and oversaw some student-planned learning contracts. In the second phase, after helping to found the College for Working Adults and doing the administrative work of coordination and evaluation for the program's first year, I joined the social science faculty team to teach the interdisciplinary courses that made up the program's curriculum: two twelve-credit blocks – an evening class, a television-based class, and a series of one- or two-day weekend classes – that were on the themes "Work and Society" and "Domestic and International Conflict." The working adults who enrolled brought a rich, rich experience related to the courses. We developed classroom practices that started with that experience and moved to connect, broaden, and deepen it.

The age of the people enrolling in both of the programs on entry was 30 plus. Even in the third phase of my classroom career in the community college, teaching the regular political science and international politics classes, traditional-aged college students 18-20 made up a quarter or less of the students. It was indeed adult education in the college classroom, "popular education in the college classroom" as I have come to understand it. But let me go back to some of the experience that prepared me for this path.

I have been privileged. I often ask how, with my log-cabin-poor-rural-child-of-an-itinerant-worker roots, did I manage to attend a private liberal arts college with an internationalist tradition, Macalester College in St. Paul. My classmates were mostly the sons and daughters of the professional classes – a disconnect that I didn't understand for a long time. But Macalester College opened doors to the world; it gave me the opportunity to begin my teaching career in Africa. Why did I go to Africa? Because of Kofi Annan. Kofi was my classmate at Macalester College. Kofi's chance meeting at the airport with someone he knew from Ghana brought that man back to the Macalester campus to International House, with him the news of the Teachers for East Africa program within days of its creation. I was interested in the world already by that time. I had taken more language than required for a math and physical education major and I attended International House activities on a regular basis. I remember being one of the only jocks to do so.

More than one part of my journey began in Africa; the search for alternatives to traditional education was one of them. I first confronted alternatives in a place one might not expect – in the content of the mathematics curriculum itself. Teaching secondary school mathematics in Uganda schools where the students were preparing for the Cambridge Overseas Examination showed me that things could be done differently than they were done in the USA. This experience raised questions about changing both content and methods. Could education be done a better way? (Later I would understand education to mean for both children and adults.)

Before returning from two years in Uganda I had won a Ford Foundation Fellowship for International Development and chosen Stanford's International Development Education Program to pursue my first graduate study. But I didn't stay at Stanford. The culture shock of re-entry made the adjustment difficult; I left after one quarter. Spring found me enrolled full time in mathematics at the University of Minnesota and searching for a part-time job. I found one as a research assistant working on the development of courses in modern algebra and modern geometry for teachers. The courses used programmed instruction. I was up close and intimate with both this alternative mode of teaching and learning and also with still more alternative content in the field of mathematics – alternatives to the traditional subjects that I had studied in college; they were the New Math with which I was just becoming familiar pushed to higher levels.

We moved on from the courses for teachers to evaluating programmed instruction mathematics materials that had been adopted by the War on Poverty's Rural Job Corps Conservation Centers. I became the evaluation project's coordinator. The Job Corps centers were not only themselves an alternative to regular education – integrating work and job training with academics and often outdoor education in their residential settings – but used programmed instruction as an alternative for the academic teaching and learning. Although I worked with rural Job Corps centers in Minnesota, Wisconsin and North Dakota as the primary sites for data collection for the project, I traveled widely around the country to visit other sites and seeing much of the USA for the first time.

As the Job Corps job was winding down in the summer of 1966 one of my colleagues from the Teachers for East Africa Program recruited me to be Syracuse University's

Contractors Overseas representative to work with Peace Corps teachers in Tanzania. My job would be to provide support and help to make the teachers better by traveling around visiting them in their schools. My job also included being on the staff for the twelve-week training program at Syracuse for the volunteers with whom I would later work, as well as for teachers headed for Malawi and Botswana. I was to do the math education part of their preparation for teaching. Then I would join the volunteers headed for Tanzania the next January for a two-year return to East Africa.

It was an extraordinary time that fall at Syracuse University – intense work that mattered. The work with the rest of the training staff was another rewarding and stimulating part of the experience, the first time I experienced such a high level of collegiality. We had all lived in Africa; we knew what we were doing was important. And central to my own experience was that the volunteers introduced me to the budding counterculture of the late sixties. In the process they reactivated my interest in folk music. I didn't know then but this was laying the groundwork for my later interest in the use of music and the arts in educational work with adults.

But I didn't go to Tanzania. Tanzania decided not to take the 120 upper primary teachers that we were preparing. It was a huge letdown for the Tanzania trainees. As it was in the time of President Nyerere's Education for Self-Reliance speech and the Arusha Declaration, the Tanzanians decided that the Peace Corps, even though modestly paid, modeled a lifestyle not possible for Tanzanians and turned the focus away from people helping themselves. My job disappeared. The letdown was even more dramatic because during the final week of the training program the volunteers and most of the staff had attended a series of inspirational presentations on the ecology of Tanzania that made us all eager to get to Africa. The presentations were also my introduction to ecology and ecological thinking, some of the first threads of my environmental consciousness.

The high idealism of the arguments against having expatriates in the country mitigated my deep disappointment. The Tanzania volunteers were reassigned to other countries, including some to Uganda, where I would soon join them.

The next year I was back in Uganda. I showed up and found jobs that continued my journey through alternative mathematics, a half-time job at Lady Irene Teachers' Training College using United States-inspired modern math materials (and some from an Australian project), and a half-time job at Ndejji Senior Secondary School using British-inspired New Maths materials. This was another big dose of alternative content by the time I left Uganda again at the end of 1967. I didn't know then that the path I had begun in the British-styled Ugandan classrooms would take me away from mathematics and mathematics education altogether just three short years later. I would stay with the alternatives theme, leave the mathematics behind.

I must mention one other activity in Uganda during those two sojourns in the 1960s to do justice to the richness and privilege of my experience: basketball. Along with many of the other American teachers in our program, we started basketball in many of the countries' secondary schools, and gave the club level of the sport a big boost. I coached but I had some great times playing too. We also organized Uganda's first national basketball team. I became the team's coach. I assumed that role again when I was back in Uganda in 1967, this time organizing not only national team tryouts but also a three-week residential training camp that concluded with a weekend of games with the Kenya National Team. We trounced the visitors by a wide margin and won for basketball, for the first time, the attention of the National Minister of Sport. Coaching basketball was my first experience as an adult educator.

From Uganda at the end of 1967 I made one of the great trips of my life. I met an old college friend in Athens and we traveled overland to India. After we parted in Delhi I went on alone to Nepal, Thailand, Malaysia, and Singapore before retracing the overland journey back to Europe and home to the USA. The most searing lessons from the travel were that it reinforced my awareness of my own privilege, showed me many sharp visions of the injustices of poverty (I wrote in my journal about seeing "a million people huddled under one blanket"), and demonstrated the fundamental unfairness of the global economic system.

In the fall after my return from the overland journey I was offered a job with the Work Opportunity Center, a Minneapolis public alternative school for former dropouts. For twelve months I ran a mathematics laboratory classroom for a very diverse group of young adults and that year, by attending a Free University class on alternative schools, began another intense part of the journey. I became an advocate, organizer, and evaluator of alternative schools.

The following year I was weighing a return to Africa when the University of Minnesota Math Department tracked me down in California, where I was visiting returned Peace Corps volunteers I had known in Uganda, to offer me the job of supervising math student teachers. I accepted, returned to Minnesota, and was soon deeply involved with both alternative education and teacher education.

That fall I initiated my own Free University class that would meet once a week in my apartment for the whole year, a class called Alternative Schools and Educational Alternatives. Each week a different guest talked about their school or other educational project. The guest for the first class was a college classmate who had just spent a year at a Danish Folk High School. It was fitting for my evolving future that the course began with adult education.

By winter we began to talk of starting our own school as well as starting an intentional community where we could live together to both support the school and practice an alternative lifestyle. We began to gather the folks who wanted to be part of one or the other. The next fall both the school, The Community School, and our commune, The Laurel House, were operational. We were creating new institutions that would grow as the corrupt establishment institutions crumbled around us. Serious business. In this period I came to realize a core principle of education was that high school students could, and should, be treated similar to adults, could be fully human subjects engaged in making their own world. This common characteristic – that all participants are considered full human subjects – describes better than any other the link between alternative education and popular education.

Spring quarter of 1970 was the last time I had anything to do with math or math education. In the summer I was asked to teach Introduction to Secondary School Teaching, a course on the social and philosophical foundations of education. With this change I took a fork in the road and began the explorations that would sweep me toward social theory and politics. I would take my interest in alternative education inside the teacher education process and the College of Education. Outside we were creating our own new institutions.

Inside the university energies were mobilizing for change. Not only the civil rights and anti-war movements were making themselves felt, but the alternative education movement as well. I was able to offer a class on alternative schools. Later, as my political consciousness grew, the course became Urban Alternatives.

In addition to all that I was learning along with my classes of teachers in training, I got be part of a college-wide committee that advocated remaking the teachers education curriculum by incorporating human relations training into all the courses. (We failed; human relations became a separate course.) Also I had the extraordinary opportunity, for a junior faculty member, to be the lead person in developing an alternative teacher education program. The ideas of that radical milieu were changing the way I thought about teaching and learning. For a time, outside my university life was of one piece with inside – just different and complementary: the Community School; the Laurel House commune; an 18-month-long Paulo Freire study group; the Radical Caucus of the Association for Supervision and Curriculum Development – Marxism, movement music, planning meetings, actions at national conventions of the organization, and an introduction to critical theory; and the Science for Vietnam Collective with its leadership of radical scientists. Inside the university: Experimental College, the Emma Willard Task Force on Sexism in Education, co-teaching with Psychological Foundations that used a social psychology framework, the Trainers of Teacher Trainers (TTT) that used a community organizing model and introduced participatory practices from the training movement, and a summer trying out human relations learning activities with a college-wide committee.

It was a good time to be searching for better ways to educate, but the contradictions became more apparent. When I was asked by the department chair if I could make the alternative teacher education program a "competency-based" program, I knew it was the end. I like to think it was the university's incapacity to change that swallowed all this energy and kept the institution plodding on the same track, not my own inadequacies. When I was discouraged by the lack of support for human relations initiatives and when I realized that the alternative teacher education proposal I was developing was far too radical to get any consideration – it gave too much power to participants, asked too much trust of faculty that their students wanted to learn, and included plans for an analysis of power and oppression in society, in the university, and in the participants – I walked away from my job at the University of Minnesota and a doctoral program that no longer had a focus.

The following 18 months was a time of unemployment, uncertainty, and self-doubt. In spite of a few contracts to do evaluations of alternative schools, a few paying speaking gigs, and a job building a garage for one of my radical scientist friends, I was not sure what would be next. In looking back I can see many of the experiences I had up to that time pointed to work as an adult educator. Further, most of the theoretical elements of a popular education outlook were in place in my thinking. When I got the part-time job at Metro Community College, it was not long before I knew that I had found my place, and I could put into practice the ideas that had been percolating. Popular education ideas and its framework could be applied in the college classroom.

Another of the privileges I have had has been the privilege of meeting and knowing many extraordinary popular and adult educators from across North America and the globe and being part of a global movement.

It was my good fortune to attend an Adult Education Association meeting in St. Louis in November 1980 during the week of Reagan's election. One of the first people I met there was Budd Hall, then General Secretary of the International Council for Adult Education (ICAE). I knew Budd's name from reading ICAE's journal, *Convergence*, to which I had subscribed when I began the Adult Education Master's degree program. It did not take long to make a real connection with Budd. He seemed to know everyone and soon he was introducing me to many others, seeing to it that I went along to all the progressive meetings. For example, he took me to meet with the National Association for Voluntary Learning (NAVL), a subgroup where the progressive folks all seemed to be gathering, a kind of radical caucus of the adult education field.

In early January 1981, as soon as I could arrange it, I went up to Toronto to visit Budd and the International Council for Adult Education (ICAE). At that time the Participatory Research Group (PRG) was in its heyday. PRG was one of the first popular ed-ucation groups in North America, producing a good newsletter and educational materials, translating the experiences of many of the PRG's participants in Latin America and other Third World contexts, and giving energy to building networks of educators and activists interested in popular education. They were just one of the extraordinary group of people and projects that had grown around the Council.

Perhaps I shouldn't really start my story of privilege with that milestone St. Louis meeting. I had already by then made some contacts of my own in this world of radical adult education. When I realized from my work that I was really an adult educator and subse-quently began my graduate program in Adult Education at the University of Minnesota in order to get an official qualification for my job, I immediately looked around the field to see what was happening both internationally and with the radical wing of the field. I had met Myles Horton in 1978 at a meeting friends arranged at my house, had long been familiar with the work of Paulo Freire, and had been introduced to the anti-racism, anti-sexism, class-conscious and participatory parts of the training movement.

It was in 1982 that my contacts in the field of adult and popular education expand-ed beyond North America. Because I was involved in my Twin Cities community with Educators for Social Responsibility and the creation of a local peace education center, my new friend Budd Hall suggested that summer that I attend the Meeting in Finland, then a gathering focusing on adult education and peace. I returned to the Meeting in Finland again the next year after participating with many of the people I met in Finland in the multisession Adult Education and Peace stream of the November 1982 World Assembly of Adult Education in Marly-le-Roi, near Paris. Many wonderful people came to these meet-ings. Many I met again at the World Assemblies in Buenos Aires and Bangkok; a few I had the privilege of working with more closely in the Adult Education and Peace Network at meetings in Venezuela and New Zealand, and a few of the same folks were in the Peace and Conflict Resolution Seminars I cofacilitated at the 6th World Assembly in 2001 in Jamaica.

Part of the work with ICAE has been involvement in building the North American Alliance for Popular and Adult Education (NAAPAE), where we sought to connect North American adult and popular educators with each other, and also through ICAE to connect to the popular education and adult learning networks that existed all over the world.

For 21 years, 1982 to 2003, I was a part of either the efforts to create the alliance or in the alliance itself. NAAPAE was not actually created until 1993, ten years after the first attempt. The 2nd World Assembly of Adult Education near Paris in 1982 inspired John Gaventa of Highlander, Lynda Yanz, then part of the Participatory Research Group in Toronto, and myself to organize a meeting at the Highlander Center in March of 1983. To the meeting we invited representatives from the adult education organizations we knew and the networks that had been meeting as "adult educators for empowerment and social change." We had seen in Paris that the only North Americans represented on ICAE were establishment, not activist education organizations – and we were inspired by the educators and activists from across the globe we encountered in Paris, particularly those from the Global South, many of whom were deeply involved in social movements and popular education.

In spite of developing a process to form this network, it failed to get off the ground. After discussions at the 3rd World Assembly of Adult Education in Buenos Aires in1985 and yet again at the 4th World Assembly in Bangkok in 1990, finally a process was established that led in 1993 to the creation of NAAPAE and the next year, its first General Assembly at Rocky Mountain House, Alberta. In 1994 at the 5th World Assembly in Cairo NAAPAE was accepted by ICAE as its regional member for North America.

I became deeply involved with the fortunes of NAAPAE after I attended the meeting of the NAAPAE Coordinating Committee in Toronto in the fall of 1995 as the representative from Midwest USA. Following that meeting I made several trips to the Toronto office to help with administrative work. Then, after the Renewal Meeting in January 1998 where I became part of the Organizational Development Working Group, I gradually assumed the role of Communications Coordinator by publishing *The NAAPAE Bulletin,* becoming the contact person for NAAPAE in the United States, and, a year or so later, creating a web site for NAAPAE.

There were a number of successful initiatives where I had a major role during the next several years – the Commonfire Conference in Tucson in 1999; the Africa Mural-Making and Popular Environmental Adult EducationWorkshop in Kampala, Uganda, in 2000; and Paulo Wangoola's first North American tour in 2001 among them, but the lack of a coordinating committee and other organizational problems were not solved in spite of the renewal efforts. Several "Leadership Meetings" took place between the Commonfire Conference in early 1999 and the 2001 World Assembly of Adult Education in Ocho Rios, Jamaica, but ultimately failed to get the organization reconstituted. In 2002, in the aftermath of a major failed organizing attempt at the Jamaica World Assembly, I stopped publishing the *NAAPAE Bulletin* and in 2003 closed down the NAAPAE web site.

Often I say, "The job ended but the work continues." What is the work? On the heading of the *Popular Education News,* the free monthly email newsletter (and web site) I have published since January 2003, I define it as "Connecting popular and community-based educators and activists to resources for improving educational work in social movements against oppression and for democracy, sustainability, social justice, and peace."

There have been four parts to this work so far – the newsletter is one of them. The second part of the work is building the collection of popular education and community organizing materials for facilitators and practitioners at the Penny Lernoux Memorial Library at the Resource Center of the Americas in Minneapolis where I have lived since 1974. The collection has had three parts: materials in English, materials in Spanish, and a nearly complete collection of the books by Paulo Freire (with some titles in Spanish, too). The third part of my work is conducting workshops and other sessions introducing popular education ideas, practices, and materials. Since early 2004 the sessions are called Another Kind of Movement Education Is Possible: Popular Education.

Finally there is writing. I had been a classroom teacher not an academic. My only publication had been an essay in a local Minnesota literary journal in 1971. Now I have two manuscripts of memoirs, one of essays with autobiographical elements and the other that I call *A Memoir of My Journey in Adult Education: The Making of a Popular Educator.* The latter has much more about the experiences and ideas mentioned above.

Michael K. Ponton

My story is like most others: financially humble beginnings, first generation to go to college, studied engineering, worked part time while also working in a cooperative education engineering position, saved to get married and then had a son while still in undergraduate school, went broke (babies are expensive!) and dropped out, went to work and saved enough to go back to college, got a degree in physics while working part time, got an engineering job working at NASA, got a part-time job as an instructor to make more money (babies are expensive!—oh, I already wrote that), earned a master's degree part time, got another part-time job as an instructor (little kids are expensive!), began a doctoral program in engineering, dropped out after realizing I never wanted to be an engineer (my father pushed me into engineering), entered a doctoral program in higher education administration after realizing that I truly enjoyed education, got a part-time job teaching (graduate school is expensive!) while still a full-time NASA employee and full-time doctoral student, earned a doctoral degree in less than 3 years (read that as a pat on my back), quit my NASA job and went to the University of Mississippi as a full-time engineer and part-time professor, transitioned to a full-time professor and part-time engineer, quit and became a full-time professor at Regent University. Probably sounds like everyone else's story.

Up to the point of my master's degree, I certainly feel that a great deal of personal initiative (as I now understand the construct) was required to survive; however, it was really the work on my master's thesis in engineering at the George Washington University (GWU) that provided my first major exhibition of personal initiative in self-directed learning. My researcher advisor, Jack Seiner (who also was my NASA lab director as well as an adjunct professor at GWU), provided my research questions. One day, he tore off some paper from the printer (for you younger readers, in the old days printers had a continuous feed of paper in a box underneath them), wrote down about four questions, and said something to the effect "If you can answer these questions you will have a pretty good thesis." That was it. I designed the experiment, designed the hardware, performed the experimental setup, gathered the data, analyzed it, determined the importance of the questions and my results using extant literature, wrote the thesis, and presented it in (virtually) final form to him and my other committee members. One of my committee members was Mike Myers, a full-time GWU professor and my program advisor. I had a difficult time in his courses as they were very demanding (or I'm not very bright, but I prefer the "demanding" argument) and I remember him asking me after reading my thesis, "Does Jack like it?" I replied that he did and Dr. Myers said, "Good, because I don't understand it." In fairness, Dr. Myers did theoretical work while my work was experimental; however, it still made me feel good to know that I was capable of conducting independent research that could stretch the understandings of one of my professors (and particularly one who stretched me!). Not only was my thesis accepted but I later received a NASA award for my scientific discoveries.

After earning my master's degree, I taught developmental algebra part time at Thomas Nelson Community College. The content was not very challenging but the pedagogy was. Dealing with adult learners, many of whom were older than me, taught me that years of less than successful education created psychological impediments to their academic success. Only much later in my doctoral research did I study the construct of self-efficacy, and looking back I can certainly see its role in my community college students' thinking. My NASA colleagues often told me that they would have a hard time teaching a subject that seemed rather "obvious" to them (algebra is not a stretch for engineers and scientists); however, I told them that it was the learners, not the content, that was the challenge. From my perspective, it was the challenge of essentially being able to teach "1 plus 1" six different ways until finally getting an *individual's* light bulb to turn on. While I had a classroom of students, to me successful teaching was based upon one-to-one transactions, as the classroom was filled with individuals, not clones. This planted a seed of curiosity into wondering what the individual differences that affect adult learning are.

Deciding that I would not be satisfied until my formal education was "complete," I entered the doctoral program in engineering at GWU. Unfortunately, my past demons came forth. You see, I never wanted to be an engineer. My older brother was an engineer and my father told me that he would not provide any support for my undergraduate education unless I studied engineering or went to medical school. As I never really wanted to go to college going to medical school seemed to be too much time in college, so I went into engineering. (Interestingly, after a couple of years I began supporting myself without my father's help but continued on in engineering school as my cooperative education position was critical in providing my own family's support.) So I found myself working on a doctoral degree in a field that I never wanted to enter. This bit of self-reflection motivated the beginning of the end of engineering in my life.

I began to reflect on the things that had provided professional enjoyment and my teaching experiences came to the forefront of my thinking; thus, I decided to study education. Fortunately for me, the doctoral program in higher education administration at the George Washington University did not require any previous degrees in education. I anticipated that my employment background combined with this degree would put me in a good position to direct a cooperative education program in engineering at a university and maybe provide an opportunity to enter the professoriate.

My interest in adult learning, as a field of inquiry, began in my doctoral program. My advisor, Gary Confessore, and I discussed several research topics but I was intrigued by the construct of personal initiative, a conative factor suggested by many scholars before me as being an important facet of self-directed learning. The reason for my interest in this construct was my personal identification with this ill-defined factor and my attribution of its role in what few successes I had realized in life. Combined with my interest in adult learning from previous teaching experiences, this research direction seemed to be a perfect match for me.

Interestingly, I enjoyed the discussion (argument?) as to why the study of adult learning is appropriate for a doctoral dissertation in higher education administration, often prompted by other higher ed. faculty. I remember Gary reminding his colleagues that the defining purpose of an educational institution is to promote student learning. Without learning, all other institutional endeavors are unnecessary as the institution itself would be unnecessary. Thus, if we as educators can understand what affects learning then perhaps we can promote better learning and improve the long-term viability of our institutions. My research was accepted by the faculty as appropriate.

But this argument, while sufficiently convincing to the higher ed. faculty, is a bit too simplistic: student learning within the academy is not the sole (or perhaps even the most important) goal of the institution, rather it is the learning that is enabled *after* the students leave. I am very much "learner" centered in my instruction, but this doesn't mean I focus on the *learning* as much as I focus on the *learner* and the development of characteristics that are necessary for lifelong, self-directed learning. Looking back at my own past educational experiences and the present growth and availability of new information, I truly do not believe that any education (even if students could remember all that was covered, which is a huge assumption) is sufficient for lifelong professional or personal satisfaction. In order to get the most out of life (i.e., "suck out all the marrow of life"—Thoreau), a person must self-start learning activities by establishing learning goals, establish plans to achieve such goals, self-generate solutions to any impediments that interfere with desired learning and persist in overcoming such obstacles, and rapidly move from an intention to learn to an action to learn—these actions constitute the construct of personal initiative in autonomous learning as argued in my dissertation. Thus, in my teaching I attempt to instill these habits of action, along with other salient conative factors, to promote autonomous learning skill and tendency. I do not want the influence of the academy limited to the very few years a student is under my charge.

My entire perspective of the importance of education is based upon my view that its real value is to create lifelong, autonomous adult learners. While certainly I do not discount the importance of content transmission for the general purpose of creating an educated citizenry or for the specific purpose of developing a foundation to understand more advanced content, nevertheless I believe that much knowledge acquisition can be done outside of direct instruction and that educators should work to create both the skills and motivation for self-directed learning. I believe that it was this empowerment, first fueled in my master's degree program, which helped me to achieve my personal goals. I wish that this empowerment can be fostered along a continuum beginning with those children who arrive with bright-eyed curiosity but all too often are turned into memorization machines (or at least the "successful" ones are).

For me, the value of my formal education has been what it has prepared me to learn after it was completed. As I wrote in my dissertation front matter, "I have learned that while it may only take three years to get a doctorate, it will take a lifetime to earn it." For me, this "earning" is based upon a self-image as a student rather than as a graduate. Without question, each commencement ceremony I participated in was just that—a recognition of a beginning. My goal is for my own students to get excited about what they are capable of doing after they break loose from the bonds of the curriculum and to realize they don't need me or anyone else to extend their learning in their own satisfying directions. I would like all educators to have this goal as well.

Dr. Robert C. Preziosi

It's the day after Thanksgiving. I'm looking through a box of old baseball caps that I was going to take to the Goodwill truck. There it was. It was the white one imprinted with "Bob's Sports Bar and Grill." A huge smile landed on my face as I instantly remembered where the hat came from. It was a reminder about my commitment to write my autobiography for this book.

*****

There were very early influences on my personal development which would be invaluable to me as an adult educator. My sense of humor came from my grandfather, the funniest person I ever met. I learned unbridled optimism from my grandmother. My mother taught me the importance of education, especially the creative side of it. The importance of combining logic and emotion was something I learned from my father.

My teachers in K-12 were accidental role models. I feel that exposure to them left me with an unconscious list of behaviors worth emulating.

Santo J. Tarantino was my most memorable undergraduate instructor. The course was a senior-level elective in social psychology. I knew it would be a good course after looking at the textbook from Roger Brown. Very intriguing were the chapters on group theory and learning psychology. The real deal, though, was Tarantino.

The very first day began a term of an excellent mix in individual learning and collaborative learning. It was really my first adventure in a learning group. The large classroom discussions didn't compare with the small-group experience. Whenever I develop and design a learning session these days, I plan to follow-up my lecturettes with a small-group learning activity. As my own adult learning experiences continued through master's and Doctoral degrees, I continued to be influenced by the impact of this instructional method.

The other initial exposure provided by Tarantino was the value of an instructor's enthusiasm. More so, it was the excitement for learning among the entire class that I was impressed with. I don't think that the content was the centerpiece. He had managed to get everyone excited about the learning. My own approach in the classroom reflects this. My belief is that the highest priority task for an adult educator is to create excitement about learning. It's also important to make it fun. Steve Jobs reminded me of both as our commencement speaker in June of 2005.

Murray Gellen was my instructor for two master's-level courses. It was clear to me that he appreciated and respected each and every individual student. Whatever a student asked or however a student responded, Gellen worked it into the class discussion. Every sentence uttered by a student had value. There was never a put down, always a lift up. Every time I walk into a classroom I remember how important it is that everything said to students be of positive value.

My instructor for behaviorism was Patsy Livingston. You've never really appreciated behaviorism until you've seen her in action. I learned more about positive reinforcement than I had ever even thought about. Speaking of thinking, it was around this time in my life that I realized that I was mostly a product of my mother's positive reinforcement. There was a lot more to Livingston's course than just positive reinforcement. She was very warm and genuine. The bottom line is that positive reinforcement is so powerful that I can't imagine my own classroom without tons of it and lots of warmth and genuineness.

*****

Sandwiched around my B.A. in Social Science and my M.Ed. in Learning Psychology were 1- to 3-year stints as a high school teacher/football coach, supervisor of training for a fast food company and a youth leadership training administrator for a group of 110 churches in the Archdiocese of Miami, Florida. These experiences all taught me about wanting to learn vs. having to learn, the importance of practical learning and that high school teaching was not for me!

The difference between learners wanting to learn rather than having to learn is a very important distinction for me. I may be in a university business school classroom or conducting a corporate/government leadership training session that is required or is an elective. My perspective is always the same. I must help them want to learn the knowledge, skill or attitude. This makes it a more successful learning experience than it would be if I were having to force it. Thus, I always try to emphasize the personal value of learning the content for each student.

This gets us to the importance of "practical" adult learning. Adults want to know how useful new learnings will be. They want to know what the "take-always" are. I used to think that practical, useful and taking away were really about "hands on." A learner should be able to take something out of a training room or classroom and start doing something different or new. I had an "aha" many years ago which made me realize that "hands on" could also be "mind on" or "heart on." Hand, mind and heart are all practical domains. This significantly altered how I approached learning. I think that this is something that all adult educators need to consider. It will lead to positioning our theories, models and research in different ways. For me it has resulted in framing knowledge, attitudes, and behaviors before and after the theories, models and research. In this case, framing refers to how I make connections in a useful (not necessarily logical) way. Useful means "can be applied" from either a left-brain or right brain perspective. My approach with students tends to be from the right brain because I think they get enough left-brain instructors. I see it as part of my role as an adult educator to develop, as much as possible, the right hemisphere.

*****

My doctoral studies in management exposed me to a variety of instructor personalities and behaviors. I was working full time during my doctoral studies. This taught me two very important lessons. The first was how important it is to use your workplace as a learning laboratory. What an opportunity it was to see learning come alive and to test concepts learned in the classroom. I've always encouraged my students to do exactly that. They are always invited to telephone (or email) me before or after trying something out in the workplace. Learning and workplace application go hand in hand.

The other important lesson came from professors Al Mavrinac and Doug Yoder. Both were excellent at getting students to pause and reflect. The importance of reflection continues to influence my teaching behaviors over 20 years after those two professors emphasized it to me. In turn, I advocate it for my students and create learning conditions for it.

Reflections are essential for value-added learning. Students need to pause from time to time and think about the educational experience they are having. They need to review what they are doing for themselves, their instructors, and their fellow students. Reflection is a time to think about the impact they are having on everyone's learning process. How do they pay value to everyone else in the learning setting?

The other important focus during reflection has to do with the content. Learners need to stop each time a segment of the content is completed. I believe that these pauses are necessary so that learners can integrate their new learning(s) with what they already know. It is equally important that they consider the impact of the new learning on their view of the world and on their own behavior. Building context this way gives increasing achievement opportunities to the learner. Combining world view, behavior and context is a stepping stone for achieving higher levels of performance. My preference for providing these pauses is every 50-60 minutes. I never go past that amount of time in the afternoon; the morning can be 15-20 minutes longer.

*****

The man that I admired most as a role model was Gordon Lippitt. He was a professor at George Washington University when I knew him. He was a consultant, trainer and author extraodinaire. His work and writing in the field of OD was a significant contribution to the field and those who practiced. He was a gracious, considerate and humble man who used knowledge power to its fullest. You knew you were next to greatness whenever you interacted with him. He had a great sense of humor. I still use one of his jokes over twenty years since I first heard it.

Gordon wrote an article that addressed the conditions for peak learning experiences. The article appeared in *Training and Development Journal*. It was entitled "Learning Rhythms" (Lippitt, 1979). I loved that article!

Just the idea of a peak learning experience was remarkably interesting to me! I continue to review that article constantly. I use every ounce of energy I can muster to cause peak learning experiences. Always doing my utmost to create those conditions in a university classroom and in corporate or government training settings is one of my highest goals. Everyone involved in adult education should read and reread this article about the six learning rhythms; learning climate, learner readiness, substance and content, learning facilitator, learning methodologies, and supportive relationships (Lippitt, 1979).

Another article worth reading addresses what's involved in being a world-class facilitator of learning (Preziosi & Preziosi, 2000). I wrote this article with my wife, Kitty, a few years ago. We wrote it together because we share so many of the same perspectives on adult learning. Putting it down on paper was very reinforcing. It validated our cumulative knowledge and experience in classrooms and training rooms as something to share with others. Writing with a partner like her was a peak experience of the variety that Lippitt wrote about.

There are two books every adult educator should take time to read. One is *The Presentation of Self in Everyday Life* by Erving Goffman. The book focuses on exactly what the title says. The author uses the metaphor of acting on a stage as he discusses behavior to help us understand the self and how we behave with others. He writes with great depth and breadth about performance on the stage, teams (players on the stage), and impression management. This book must be read from the perspective of the adult educator as the performer on stage.

The other book that is essential reading is *High Output Management* by Andy Grove. Yes, the book is about management, but the real essence of it is efficient, effective results and how to get them. Adult educators who intellectually flex will be able to take business management principles and apply them to the practice of adult teaching/learning.

There were other sources of learning that helped to shape my philosophies, perspectives and practices. One was a two week program at Harvard's Institute for the Management of Lifelong Education. The world-class faculty that I was exposed to confirmed that I was indeed on the right bus. This was true not only from the content selection frameworks that were quite evident but also from the teaching skills that I witnessed. They were all extremely engaging in a very large classroom. This was a reminder to me that all learners could be included in participative learning. It is simply a matter of choosing various and appropriate instructional methods instead of just choosing a few that had been used to help me learn. Size of the class doesn't need to inhibit participation.

Another very important learning event for me was a three-day consulting skills workshop lead by B.J. Chakiris, an associate of Gordon Lippitt. There were a great number of things that I learned that could be applied in the classroom or corporate training setting. It was information about the roles of a consultant placed on a continuum from expert to facilitator and many things in between. I learned that I had chosen the right role for each classroom learning situation.

The only other learning experience that had a major influence on me was a five-day workshop on techniques for developing curriculum using accelerated learning. I participated in this with a group of corporate trainers from American Express. It was run by Dave Meier of the Center for Accelerated Learning. I took away a great many ideas! I put them to use and conducted research. I used a Solomon 4 research design and found that adult learners learned 250% more when the instructor used accelerated learning techniques than they did when the instructor used traditional instructional methods. Needless to say, I'm a big proponent of accelerated learning techniques.

*****

Writing has been very important to me for nearly three decades now. However, it's only been the last twelve years or so that I have given it a great deal of attention. I mostly write practitioner-oriented pieces because I think that our profession needs that. There is plenty of research, though, in the 70+ publications that I've authored/co-authored since 1999. I love to write with others because I believe so much in collaboration and team in all that I do. Working with others is great fun! One of my most favorite writing experiences was a very recent one. Bauhadin Mujtaba and I wrote a book, *Adult Education in Academia*, already in its second edition. It is for academics as well as those in a corporate setting.

I've also been coeditor of a journal and on numerous editorial boards. This kind of activity is important because it's a chance to give back. Also, you have the opportunity to help others be successful. Isn't that what adult education is all about? Yes, Socrates. And remember to keep asking all those penetrating questions in the classroom.

Another way to make a contribution is through sharing stories of successful teaching/learning experiences. The first time I taught faculty how to teach was nearly twenty years ago. Of course, the methodology included having them share best practices. I've also been training trainers from corporate and government settings for over twenty years.

The importance of writing and helping others to teach/train better is that you are adding value each time you deliver a learning session. You have a richer array of experiences to draw from. You engage learners more and better. You get at the essence of adult education; it is a profession for helpers and givers. When you attain the highest levels of helping people learn and giving your time and resources to others, you will be honored by your profession and your institution for energizing their minds, hearts, and spirits. It feels great when this happens. It's quite a thrill!

*****

I have more to learn. I must learn more about technology and learning even though my own research (and others) finds little differences in learning outcomes when comparing live to electronic learning. I must also continue to stay ahead of the curve on new content and teaching/learning practices. My final current learning need has to do with the multicultural real world (all six continents). I must do better with students across generations so that they learn more and better. I must remember that it is about learning!

I also need to keep reminding myself of something that Malcolm Knowles is supposed to have said. Sometimes our students behave like adult students and sometimes they don't. This means that we must treat them in ways that are not necessarily consistent with principles of adult learning. He believed that a more situational model lends itself to the most appropriate instructor behavior.

*****

Oh yes...the hat. I was one of 16 people who had been given the white baseball cap from Bob's Sports Bar and Grill. It was a restaurant in a hotel where 16 adult educators spent a weekend exchanging best practices in a way I'd never seen up to that point and have never seen since. All weekend the word "we" was used, never the word "I."

References

Goffman E. (1959). *The presentation of self in everyday life*. Garden City, NY: Doubleday & Company, Inc.

Grove, A. (1983). *High output management*. New York: Random House.

Lippitt, G. (1979). Learning rhythms. *Training and Development Journal* (M. Cook, ed.). Alexandria, VA: American Society for Training and Development.

Mujtaba, B. & Preziosi, R.C. (2006). *Adult Education in Academia*. Greenwich, CT: Information Age Publishing.

Preziosi, R.C. & Preziosi, C. (2001). How to be a world-class facilitator of learning. *The 2000 Pfeiffer Annual: Training* (Biech, ed.). San Francisco, CA: Jossey-Bass/Pfeiffer.

Esther Prins

In *Wishful Thinking*, Frederick Buechner writes, "The place God calls you to is the place where your deep gladness and the world's deep hunger meet." For me, that place is adult education. I found my calling in working toward greater justice, wholeness, and well-being with women, immigrants, farmworkers, and others who are invisible and devalued. My six-month internship in El Salvador through the Human Needs and Global Resources program at Wheaton College, then directed by Professor Bob Stickney, introduced me to adult education and sparked my interest in understanding how education can contribute to personal and social transformation. In June 1993, one and one half years after the end of the Salvadoran civil war, I arrived in San Salvador to work with Iglesia Bautista Emmanuel (IBE), a Baptist church that sponsored community development in marginalized urban and rural communities. I began teaching a small Spanish literacy class in La Línea (a squatter settlement where war-displaced families had settled during and after the war), using a Freirean model of discussing problems related to people's lives and using words from the discussion and Bible passages to practice reading and writing. Teaching the class, reading *Pedagogy of the Oppressed*, and observing IBE's community development work provided examples of how adult education could help generate hope and equip people to exercise more control over their lives. Moreover, witnessing Salvadorans' irrepressible hope and receiving their generosity in the midst of these circumstances—crushing poverty, death and raw grief, the horrific effects of war—marked me for life.

Ironically, my education at Wheaton—an institution well known for its evangelical theology and conservative politics—laid the groundwork for the spiritual and political *conscientización* that occurred during the internship and thereafter. Raised with the Reformed theology of the Christian Reformed Church, I believed that Christians should have a redemptive, transformative presence in the world (a perspective that I later realized aligns with radical adult educators' emphasis on social transformation). However, I also grew up believing that Christians were, by definition, Republican, and that liberation theology was heretical because it focused too much on social and economic issues. The IBE internship upset these assumptions. The pastors and parishioners supported orthodox Christian beliefs yet also invited liberation theologians to speak at church, condemned the repression of the Salvadoran and U.S. governments, attended protests organized by the FMLN opposition party, and criticized the neoliberal economic policies imposed by the U.S., IMF

(International Monetary Fund), and World Bank. My experiences with IBE suggested a radical possibility—that I could integrate prophetic Christianity with adult education and community development activities intended to foster social justice.

Many of my Wheaton professors, particularly Dr. Stickney and sociology professors, modeled a concern for social justice and the poor, introducing us to what I now recognize as a "critical perspective," including Freire's approach to literacy, world systems theory, dependency theory and other models of development and social change, the concept of cultural relativity, and so on. I was also shocked to discover from Professor Zondra Lindblade's example and from her teaching on gender inequity and the social construction of gender that "Christian feminist" was not, after all, an oxymoron. These insights, coupled with the internship in El Salvador, precipitated my journey toward a prophetic Christian theology that condemns oppression and the exploitation of the poor, a stance embodied by Monseñor Romero, the martyred Salvadoran Archbishop. This faith grounds my work in adult education and community development.

In graduate school in Adult Education at Cornell—the first nonreligious educational institution I had attended other than kindergarten at a public school in Uruguay, where my parents had been missionaries—I continued to discern how academic theories and my religious faith informed each other. For example, the theological concepts of structural and original sin made me question the assumption in much of the adult education literature that individuals are inherently well-meaning and thus can simply be educated to act justly toward others or to do the right thing. Likewise, my interests in feminism and participatory research led me to scrutinize the hierarchical, sexist practices (as well as the equitable ones) in religious institutions and traditions. Although my evangelical upbringing had taught me to anticipate hostility to any discussion of religion in academe, I found that professors were very open to my examination of the relationship between religious faith and institutions, education, community development, and research. My master's research stemmed from my interest in understanding how community developers and organizers negotiate religious, racial, class, and other kinds of differences in their ecumenical organizations, whereas my dissertation research explored how participation an adult literacy program, sponsored by a progressive Christian NGO in El Salvador, affected women's and men's ability to improve their lives.

A normative vision for adult education is vital, yet scholars often fail to specify, for instance, what people will be liberated *to* or *for* or toward what ends. During graduate school I discovered a concept that presented such a vision. The Jewish concept of *shalom*, meaning peace, justice, wholeness, and harmony among people and with God and nature, has provided a vision to work toward—albeit one that is only partially realized in fragments and glimpses—and has helped me to identify the ultimate purpose or *telos* that guides my work. *Shalom* means that my work should contribute to the creation of communities, policies, and social structures that reflect people's dignity as image bearers of God, meaning they are free of the violence and domination that distort human relationships.

My work in adult education has immersed me in communities where adult learners and other residents experience the brokenness that results from systemic injustice. Seeing how these conditions affected adult learners convinced me that the best way to effect change is not to "make a difference in one person's life," but to change the policies, institutions, and power structures that contribute to poverty and illiteracy in the first place. As the coordinator of the adult education program at Youth Service Project (1994-97), a community-based organization (CBO) in Humboldt Park, a Latino and African-American neighborhood in Chicago, I saw the invisible America. For example, during gang wars it was too dangerous for some GED students, particularly the men, to attend classes. Few of our program participants had ever been downtown, only six miles from Humboldt Park. An ESL student had to flee her husband and leave her daughter with her grandmother in Mexico so she could earn a living in the U.S. In light of these stories, getting a GED or increasing one's reading or math level on the standardized TABE test seemed like grossly inadequate solutions; however, I now recognize the symbolic value and meanings these accomplishments hold for adult learners who have been denied recognition and experienced failure in educational institutions. These experiences led me to enroll in 1997 in the Agricultural, Extension, and Adult Education (AEAE) program at Cornell.

While conducting dissertation research in 2001 on the Alfalit adult literacy program in rural El Salvador—a country still wracked by chronic unemployment, extreme economic inequality, widespread migration, gang warfare, and social violence—I realized anew that adult education cannot radically alter a person's life chances unless social and economic policies also support women's and men's ability to live with dignity. Indeed, several male and female adult learners and my host sister have since risked their lives to migrate to the United States, as their families had no other means of survival. What difference can improving one's literacy abilities possibly make when there is no work—or at least none that pays a living wage? These experiences have informed my adamant opposition to the blaming of "illiterate" people, poor women, immigrants, and other popular scapegoats—rather than social and economic institutions and policies—for economic decline, unemployment, and other social problems.

I learned about the struggles of Latino/a farmworkers and immigrants, including segregated schools, lack of access to health care, and institutional racism, as a postdoctoral researcher in Community Development at the University of California-Davis (2002-04). The reflections of a Latina immigrant on race relations in her town still ring in my ears: "We can't fight them [White residents]. So what can we do? We can never change their way of thinking. If we were to need them, we could never count on them. We have to find a way to survive without them, without needing their help." These perplexing questions and problems lie at the heart of adult education. I believe that my research, teaching, and interpersonal interactions should contribute to explicating and diminishing this kind of fragmentation.

In working with GED, ESL, and literacy students in Chicago and El Salvador, I also discovered that, as Peter Jarvis argues, learning is not a transaction but a moral interaction. I was struck by the importance YSP students placed on the friendships they developed in classes, an observation that led to my scholarly interest in the social dimensions of adult education and my battle against the instrumental rationality that reduces education to the pursuit of skills to support the unjust corporate economy while ignoring the other legitimate purposes women and men bring to adult education. Attending GED and ESL classes, however, was not only about pursuing academic goals; it was about making friends, meeting new people, having fun—or as Jenny Horsman puts it, having "something on my mind besides the everyday."

Likewise, what mattered most to learners in the Alfalit program—especially women who felt lonely and confined because they rarely left the house—was the friendships they developed. The classes provided someone to talk to and a way to *desahogar* (get things off one's chest) and thus helped to reconstruct humane relationships in the midst of postwar distrust and trauma. Salvadoran learners taught me that in focusing exclusively on social change (the radical/critical approach) *or* economic productivity (the dominant, functional approach), we miss something vital: the importance of social interaction. To me, adult education matters because it provides one of the few remaining public spaces where individuals can come together to communicate, to discuss things they care about, and creatively to accomplish their own purposes. Since we are communal beings created for relationship, I view adult education as a place where individuals can satisfy their longing to connect with others—in short, to become more human.

I experienced this myself in graduate school. What I most loved about graduate school was belonging to a community of students and faculty—especially in the AEAE program and CPARN (Cornell Participatory Action Research Network)—who cared deeply about education, community development, and research for social justice. Professors David Deshler and Merrill Ewert in particular recognized the importance of community in education, which they fostered through sailing on Cayuga Lake (David) and group advisee meetings (Merrill) that enabled students to support each other through personal and academic doubts and struggles.

An incident the spring of 1998 during my first year at Cornell represents the culture of creative, passionate, collective action among students in the AEAE program and the university that made Cornell an energizing place to study. A professor leaked to graduate students an email from the dean intimating that the adult education program might be closed. Several of us responded with the "Save AEAE" campaign, asking students, alumni, administrators, and faculty at Cornell and other universities to write, call, or meet with the dean. To accentuate the likely effects of closing the program, we placed black paper X's over the pictures of AEAE students on the bulletin board. I'll never know what ultimately led to a favorable decision, but several faculty suggested that if students had not acted, the program would have been eliminated. This kind of solidarity is what I love about adult education.

The theme of community and relationships is also evident in my efforts to establish reciprocal, equitable relationships with adult learners and research participants. I am still amazed by the *cariño* (affection) with which ESL students in Chicago treated me. They gave me a dozen red roses—my first—and an orchid corsage for *Día del Maestro* (Day of the Teacher), a Mexican holiday. When Carlos, an undocumented student with whom I had developed a great deal of trust, invited me to attend his son's baptism, it forced me to decide what kinds of boundaries to establish with students. YSP discouraged spending time with learners outside of the classroom, yet I felt that attending the baptism would demonstrate that I valued Carlos as a person, not "just" as a student. I felt honored and humbled that he included me in the family baptism photo and the celebration at his home. This incident represents the importance of relating to students as *human beings* whose hopes and worries transcend the classroom.

Teaching ESL classes provided ample opportunities to explore my emergent beliefs about my roles as an educator, as the following journal (6/6/97) excerpt demonstrates:

I struggle with being a facilitator who fields all responses with no reaction… and sharing information which may help students see a subject in a different light. If I know something to be true, what is my obligation as a teacher? Can I facilitate and inculcate at the same time? I don't buy the notion that I must be value-free. If our students think that people are homeless because they are lazy [a view several students expressed in a discussion], I think it's acceptable for me to share views from another perspective. The danger lies in guiding students to the extent that they perceive that mine is the only correct view. I want them to think for themselves.…I see my role as that of a gadfly—to stir up, nudge, and poke, to make others just slightly uncomfortable so that they will explore the discomfort and tension and in doing so, discover the complexity and multi-faceted nature of real problems and issues.

As I later learned in graduate school, the tension between validating and/or challenging learners' beliefs and ideas are inherent in critical approaches to education.

My dissertation research in El Salvador was emotionally exhausting because I was not just a dispassionate researcher but personally invested in the lives of the *campesinos/as* (peasant farmers) who attended literacy classes. I grew very close to the family with whom I lived in Colima (a rural village 45 kilometers north of San Salvador) and was honored when their oldest daughter asked me to be her baby's *madrina* (godmother). Reflecting on these experiences and my tearful farewell with my host family and literacy participants, I wrote:

I think the highest compliment they could give me is their tears, because it means that they hold me close in their hearts, that I've treated them with honor and respect. Our tears mean that I've done at least part of the research well, that I've gotten part of it right—*conviviendo* [sharing one's life with others]—the part that matters most to me.

I concluded that a survey or interviews alone could never have engendered these friendships with my host family and adult learners, nor could they have captured the daily struggles and dreams that mediated villagers' participation in literacy classes.

Several sources have shaped my desire to use responsibly my power as an educator and researcher. In graduate coursework with Professors John Forester, David Deshler, Butch Wilson, Davydd Greenwood, and others, I came to understand how seemingly insignificant actions can crush or expand others' ability to know, to act, and to envision possibilities for their lives and communities. In short, we can use our power to misinform, exclude, or belittle, but also to open up possibilities for action—or as John Forester (citing planner Howie Baum) reminded us, to organize hope. The philosopher Martha Nussbaum's work also shaped my view of practice in education, research, and other fields as moral improvisation, that is, the ability to respond "lucidly and responsibly" to the concrete particularities of a situation rather than rigidly applying an abstract set of rules or principles. My later interactions with school and CBO staff as part of my postdoctoral research compelled me to consider how I, as a university representative, could create equitable personal and institutional relationships with community partners.

Collectively, these experiences and insights have forged my belief that education is ultimately about democratic citizenship. I learned, as Cornell professor Scott Peters often reminded us, that democracy is not about voting, getting everyone to be best friends, or dividing up the

Democracy

"pie" of resources; it's about people coming together as citizens to solve concrete problems, or as planner Lisa Peattie puts it, to make their own world. Drawing on these insights, I have sought to articulate what participation in education, community development, and research means, what it looks like, why it matters, and the predicaments that accompany it. Similarly, teaching courses in the higher education program at Washington State University (2004-05) deepened my conviction that universities and faculty, particularly those at land-grant institutions, have a responsibility to contribute to the public good. As I begin my new faculty position at Penn State, I aspire not only to contribute to scholarly understanding of adult and family literacy, civic engagement, and related issues, but also to assist in solving local problems, particularly those affecting adult learners, immigrants, and poor and working-class families.

Finally, the discovery that education has contradictory potential and consequences has deeply influenced my work. I first realized, for example, that literacy education is not *inherently* liberating when Ira Shor discussed in a presentation at Cornell how English literacy education was used to colonize indigenous peoples. Likewise, Nelly Stromquist and other women's literacy scholars described how Freirean literacy programs often have unintended consequences such as reinforcing traditional gender roles. My exploration of feminisms in graduate school (e.g., Patricia Maguire's work on feminist PAR, *Women's Ways of Knowing*, gender and international development scholars) convinced me that education must identify and challenge gender inequities. In my teaching and research, these insights have led me to highlight contradictions and unintended consequences—that a church might promote women's submission in marriage while providing them with valuable leadership opportunities, the way that Salvadoran women learners complained of social isolation yet restricted their daughters' (but not their sons') recreational activities. In sum, I learned that adult educators must be suspicious of facile categorizations of educational and community development programs or research methodologies as either liberating *or* oppressive and of accounts that depict groups and individuals as victims *or* oppressors.

 What keeps me planted in adult education is the field's tradition of imagining a different world and of working with women and men whom society has discounted to re-imagine their lives, families, and communities. My relationships with adult learners, my religious faith, and my formative educational and professional experiences have shaped how I perceive my calling, the questions that guide my research and teaching, and my efforts to advocate for just social and economic policies and institutions in the U.S. and Latin America. Adult education is the place where I have chosen to pursue my life's work of helping to restore *shalom* in the midst of brokenness and injustice.

B. Allan Quigley, Ed.D.
The Story of a Hopeful Romantic

It has been said that lives are shaped by a mere handful of events. All of our careful planning, our youthful career ambitions, our adult job anxieties, are typically sidelined by the vagaries of circumstance and a handful of events. Now, at age 59, I can look back on my adult education journey and offer this as my story of how my work life was shaped by five such events.

I once might have said my work life was steered by the compass of idealism. Now I would say I began an idealist, but some 35 years as an adult educator convinces me that I now might best be described as a "hopeful romantic." I use this term since those of us who have focused on adult literacy have been accused of being "*hopeless* romantics," but literacy work is never hopeless, even if it is all too easy to become cynical in literacy. By all (allegedly) objective standards, remarkably little has changed in literacy in the past 35 years across North America. The statistical "counts and amounts" surveys reveal remarkably little positive change. Study after study, the total number of adults with low literacy skills remains about the same across North America. Meanwhile, the long decline in funding and infrastructure support for programs has only been matched with an equally frustrating climb in accountability demands. Looking back, such realities leave me but two choices. I can retire an embittered idealist—still an option, but hopefully not an inevitability—or take the view of a "hopeful romantic." Differences such as those between idealism and romanticism become clearer at the end of one's career it seems.

Today, I try to concentrate on individual successes, local victories, and the many positive memories I share with others in literacy. I try to "act globally but think locally," to turn the 90s' mantra on its head. I think Marcuse got it right. Rather than becoming bleakly pessimistic like so many of his colleagues in the Frankfurt School Movement, he chose to hope that the past would not be forgotten—that the future might be better informed because of the struggles, insights, and lived realities of past writers. It is my hope that the small circles I helped create in my time will be widened by future adult educators. Ultimately, hope is the single way forward and our greatest strength as a field.

Events in My 20s: Leaving the World I Knew

My first major life event was to join Canadian Universities Services Overseas, or CUSO as it is internationally known. This is effectively Canada's Peace Corps. I went as a volunteer teacher to India, and it would be fair to say that everything I have come to know about myself—and value—I learned in India. I had completed my Bachelor of Arts degree in English and, at age 19, was not ready to "settle down." Amusing as it may sound, I had become enamored of one of the novels in a modern British literature class, E.M. Forster's *A Passage to India*. That, and a desire to be of some use to people who had less than I made me decide to apply to be a volunteer and leave for India.

It was not as if my family was enthused with this idea, nor had I ever aspired to be a teacher. In fact I did not want to be a teacher. I had been raised on a farm on the flat prairie of southern Saskatchewan and attended a small town school. My mother had hoped I might become a lawyer like my family-famous uncle. I began university with that goal in mind. But, in 1967, with every Canadian town and citizen patriotically organizing a centennial project to celebrate our 100th birthday, my project was to leave Canada. However, to apply, I first needed to have some skills on my resume. I had majored in English literature with a minor in philosophy. What skills could I possibly put on my resume? I imagined that teaching might be something I could do. Interestingly, I later would learn that thousands of adults have similar imaginings in this field. In fact, imagining that teaching adults is a simple task anyone can do appears to be our best recruiting strategy since the vast majority of adult educators simply fall into the field—often as teachers—then stay because they value the work.

In India, I taught at a higher secondary school for boys. These schools are supported by the state and the few rupees of tuition that the boys' families can afford. However, many of my students' families could afford nothing. The students came on their bicycles from my "small town" of about 100,000 and the surrounding villages. Summer and winter, they made their way wearing only thin cotton pajama-type pants, thread-bare shirts and sandals. Like most of the other teachers, I taught outside with students sitting cross-legged on long hemp mats. My students would come and find me, then run around to the other classes to try and find, or "borrow," one of the scarce tin blackboards used for teaching, then prop it up against the teacher's chair. Unlike blackboards, chairs were always available since the teachers used them to doze off on. I once used a brick wall as a blackboard. I would not recommend, it as it is very hard on the chalk supplies.

It made no small impression on me to be approached by lepers and beggars, to see starvation and squalor stretching out for miles in cities like Calcutta. I will forever be thankful that my fiancé came to India with CUSO in 1968. We were married in the former British capital of Simla in the Himalayas—the second major event that changed my life. Together we learned to see beyond the squalor; we saw the people beyond the surface—and this is vital to education, if not to life. The kindness of strangers was a large part of our survival and I have often wondered why we North Americans are typically less considerate of the needs of immigrants who come to our countries.

We learned that people can be astonishingly resilient. We learned that appearances of poverty are often illusory and have little to do with personal or family happiness. We learned that appearances of illiteracy, of inadequate coping skills, and the illusion of ignorance are often just that—appearances. More accurately, they are often mirror reflections of our own ignorance. Above all, I learned that I could make a difference in the lives of a few and that education could make that difference. I could provide a voice where there is none. My life's philosophy became quite simple during those years. We are here for a short while. If we seek to be of some value to others, there is no better way than by fostering learning. And there is no more powerful force for change than literacy.

Events in My 30s: Coming Home

Back in Canada, I pursued a master's degree in English. Having completed the coursework, I needed a job that would allow me to finish my thesis. I took a job with Saskatchewan's provincial Department of Adult Education, but I was still not ready to take on literacy as my life's ambition. My wife and I went to northern Saskatchewan. It was there that I learned how much adult students could teach the teacher. Using fictitious names here, I remember Dale, who finished the basic education program and went on to work as a heavy equipment driver in the high Arctic. He ended up confident and happy, earning far more than I ever will. I remember Albert, a 20 year old First Nations man with a chronic drinking problem, a wife with four children and another child on the way. During the program, he stopped drinking and later became a Band Council leader on his reserve. Most of all, I remember Bob and his wife Doris. "Big Bob" came to the program with Doris only because, as he said, "She is always nagging me to learn to read." But, with anger in his voice, added, "I'll quit in a few days because I hate reading." Big Bob was twice my size, loved hunting, and wore a cap with moose blood on it.

He had quit school at age 12 in grade 3 after being told once too often, "You're stupid." He had been quitting jobs ever since—often after punching the boss in the nose. The only thing I could think of with Bob was to bet him $20.00 that he would read within a week. If he couldn't, I would pay him $20.00 and he could leave. But if he could read, he had to stay and pay me the $20.00. He took the bet. He remained behind day after day when the other students had gone. And we struggled together. With no real training, I was trying to teach a man of my age as he hunkered down and sweated in a school desk. He was struggling to overcome his fear and loathing of the printed word and of teachers like me. At the end of the week he could make out simple words. For instance, I wrote "MEN" on the blackboard and he slowly read it. I asked him how he found the bathroom. He said if there wasn't a symbol on the door, he just waited until a male or female went in one door or the other. I then escorted him to the men's bathroom, he read the sign on the door for the first time, and we celebrated the victory of literacy together at the urinals.

We regularly went on our "walkabouts" by leaving the class and walking the main street as I encouraged him to read what he saw in shop windows. During those months we talked about many things, including his parenting and marital concerns. When they graduated from the program, Doris took me aside and said, "Thank you for saving our marriage." They went on to better lives, as did all of the others. I was hooked on literacy.

Still trying to finish that thesis, the third event was a teaching position at a vocational institute in northern Alberta. Again, I did not want to go to Northern Alberta but the job was there. And it was there I realized I had a "character flaw." I succeeded in the classroom but failed "staff rooming." This was my first experience with a large adult education institution. I soon realized that most of the basic education teachers held their adult students in contempt. For instance, when I invited my students into the staff room—the place where teachers went to "escape them"—if my students needed me, the other teachers said: "Keep them out! We see enough of them in classes!" Here was my first real introduction to the deficit perspective. In their eyes, our literacy adult learners were not just deficient in their academic skills, they were deficient of every social, cultural, economic and moral value. It was largely for this reason I moved into the management of the college, the fourth major event in this story.

"Managing Learning, Managing People"

In 1973 I became the first coordinator of the Further Education Program at that vocational institute. This involved developing and managing all of the evening and noncredit programs, including the university transfer program. Two of my most successful evening courses were taught by a husband and wife team. The husband taught gourmet cooking; a few doors away his wife was teaching the Ladies' Dieting Workshop. I had the perfect formula for student-recycling and participation problems.

These were exciting years as our management team succeeded in bringing the institute into community college status. For my part, I learned that I could succeed as a manager in a higher education setting. However, failing once more to earn a moose-blood hat, we left the North and returned to our home in Saskatchewan where I was involved in perhaps the most productive period of my life.

In 1977, a group of five of us envisioned and created the community college in the capital city of our province. Initially I was the community developer for the college and went to the surrounding towns and rural villages to establish local advisory committees. Those committees decided what types of learning events would take place in their communities. It was the job of programmers such as me to help make anything from general-interest hobby courses, to university-transfer courses, to technical skills programs happen in the town halls, schools, skating rinks, and farm yards of our college region.

It was at this time that I learned how vital women are to adult education. Women comprised the local advisory groups, women decided the courses and women, mainly, attended the learning activities. Dying rural communities were re-vitalized, community centers were refurbished, families learned together. The men typically asked for farm-based courses. If the content was immediately relevant, the men came out in the hundreds. Relevance was everything to the men but women were the college's mainstay.

After two years, I took over the Adult Basic Education Program for the college and established decentralized ABE centers around the city. I hired and supervised some 35 part- and full-time literacy, ABE and ESL teachers and counselors. The college became the largest of the 17 colleges established across the province, but, following two strikes—one 7 months in length—I was dramatically reminded that my life's work lay in improving lives, not in attempting to manage them. In 1978, I moved to the province's Department of Continuing Education. For the next five years I was in charge of the province's GED program, most of the ABE program, all of the ESL policies, and I helped train the new trustees in the colleges across the province. It was a great college system.

Tragically, a new right-wing government was elected and they eliminated the college system we had created. They closed the very college I had been part of establishing. In fact, I was actually called upon within the government to advise on how to do this. I decided it was a good time to pursue doctoral studies. Through my government years, I learned how political policies and political decisions could be vitally important, or destructive, to the lives of adults. I also learned how unappreciated government workers can be and how so many strive to ensure that good policies are arrived at and implemented. I came to realize the value of good social policies.

Events in My 40s: Returning to University

I entered the doctoral program at Northern Illinois University in 1984, completed my coursework in one year and, less than a year later, my dissertation won the Adult Education Research Conference Outstanding Student Award. This was the fifth major event in my life. I was fortunate to study under Ron Cervero, John Niemi, Sharan Merriam, Bob Smith, and Phyllis Cunningham. Once again I did not plan to go to the U.S. to study. It came about when Ron Cervero replied to my NIU letter of inquiry saying I could finish most of my coursework in a year, could be considered for an assistantship, and would be very welcome. No other graduate school did this.

For the first time in my life, critical reflection and informed dissent were encouraged and valued. After two more years back home with the government of Saskatchewan as Director of the University Affairs branch responsible for all of the funding and policy support to the province's universities and university colleges, my wife, son and I moved back to the U.S. I was now in the role of Assistant Professor of Adult Education at Penn State University. In keeping with my story's theme of the nonplanning and circumstance, Ron Cervero had sent me a Penn State job ad and asked if I was interested. He had been my dissertation advisor earlier and had suggested I submit for the dissertation award mentioned earlier. I owe him more than I can ever say.

At Penn State I worked to establish both the Master of Adult Education program and create the Center for Graduate Studies in Monroeville, Pennsylvania, a suburb in east Pittsburgh. This Graduate Center served southwestern Pennsylvania and was effectively created by six of us: the Center's administrator, the amazing front office staff, and me. But, beyond the Center, I found I had joined an entirely untenured faculty of five faculty. Therefore, I was working to establish the program, the Center, and gain tenure; our decentralized group of faculty was creating one of the most innovative outreach programs in America. Students were often linked between the Monroeville Center and the campus in Harrisburg by audio conference, or by audio between Erie and the University Park campus, or all four were connected by a combination of audio or video using team teaching and cross-campus travel. It was exciting, but I relearned nothing is permanent.

Despite my personal objections and the struggle to keep it open, the Graduate Center was ultimately closed by the Penn State Continuing Education administrators in 1997. It was time to go home. We returned to Canada ten years to the day that we left.

Looking Back, Looking Ahead: Events in My 50s

If there is any doubt about the vagaries of circumstance, I found the position for professor at St. Francis Xavier University in Nova Scotia, where I now am, on a bulletin board when teaching a summer class at the University of British Columbia. We traveled to Antigonish, liked the town, the program, and the colleagues I now have who are among the best I have ever worked with. And I have stayed with adult literacy as my area of study.

Over the course of some 18 years of academic life, my book, *Rethinking Literacy*, won the Houle Award for Outstanding Literature in 1997, I have been awarded the Kenneth Mattran Award for literacy leadership, the Award of Academic Excellence from Penn State, and the Award for Adult Educator of the Year from Pennsylvania's Association of Adult and Continuing Education. I have published in a range of national and international journals and given presentations in many states and provinces. I have worked with practitioner professional development across the U.S. and Canada helping build a capacity for practitioner-research using action research. My own research has taken me from student retention to health literacy, from the history of literacy to authenticity in teaching. I have been helping establish a new Health and Learning Knowledge Centre out of the University of Victoria as well as a new Adult Learning Knowledge Center out of the University of New Brunswick. I am advising on the rebuilding of New Orleans following Hurricane Katrina with the Mayor's Committee on Adult Literacy. I have a new book in press entitled, *Building Professional Pride in Literacy*. And, at St. Francis Xavier, I advise some 35 master's students in different parts of the world using distance education.

But it is adult literacy that continues to hold me. A hopeful romantic to the end. Recently, a man who works with the university physical plant staff on our campus came to my office and wanted to shake my hand. He said it was because I had helped get a literacy course on our campus for the service staff. Then he told me that yesterday he had been mopping the floor of the Music Building—as he has done countless times before. He said, "Then I looked up at a poster. And realized, 'Hey, I can read that!" Here is a field of hope. It changes lives, including my own.

John R. Rachal

I came into adult education in the usual way—dumb, blind luck. In 1976 I was nearing the end of a four-year stint as instructor of English at East Carolina University, and I was professionally betwixt and between. Thus it was that I found myself in the office of the Chair of the English Department at North Carolina State University, where I had completed a master's degree, asking advice as to whether he might recommend pursuit of a doctoral degree in English. My skepticism concerning that path, given the depressing buyer's market in the liberal arts at that time, I must have articulated, for he then uttered the words that were likely little more than throw-away lines in a routine professor–former student conference to him, but which set in motion the course of the rest of my professional life: "I understand that the adult education program is placing its graduates." Having competed with about 140 applicants for the modestly remunerated, nontenure-track, four-year (tops) instructor position at East Carolina, and suspecting that a Ph.D. in English would yield more of the same, I trimmed sails and concluded that a new course on unexplored seas might be just the thing. Larry Champion's words changed my life—and left me forever after to marvel at the chance words or events that lead to decisions that change everything.

But *education*? Oh my goodness. I was a classic liberal arts snob, nor have I even now purged all the vestiges of that. And I had loved the liberal arts. In high school, sports, girls, and motorcycles had been my occupations (my ranking in the bottom half of my graduating class gives brute testimony to this), but then a certain girl came along—a reader—and I acquired my first naïve glimpse into the house of intellect. A couple of teachers watered that pitiful little seed, and I continued to read, though not very discriminatingly—from Pearl Buck to Kierkegaard. By college, I knew that philosophy was for me, and while my comprehension of all those heavy thinkers rarely could have exceeded five percent, my professors were indulgent and kindly towards true believers, however callow and wayward. As a sophomore I even had the foolhardiness to present "a paper" at the Philosophy Club, only to suffer the inevitable deconstruction such youthful forays into verbal combat entail. I licked my wounds, but loved *philo sophia* even more, and when the philosophy major was done, English beckoned as I began for the very first time to have some vague glimmering of the questionable potential of philosophy to feed the body part of body and soul.

Thus armed with majors in philosophy and English, I offered myself in 1970 to the tender mercies of eighth-grade language arts students for a year, then moved on to a graduate assistantship in NC State's master's in English program, then the English instructorship at ECU, and finally to Larry Champion's office. It would be so nice to say that I had come to adult education through some Paul-on-the-road-to Damascus experience in which I recognized adult education's role in ameliorating social inequity, but it would not be so. Sure, as a teenager I had had warm arguments over the fairness of the White and colored drinking fountains on the capitol grounds, and even warmer ones over the hypocrisy of churches with white-only congregations. I had wondered why James Meredith shouldn't be able to attend Ol' Miss, and later I had even worn that Klansman's roundhouse punch to my seventeen-year-old left jaw for heckling at a Klan march with an ambivalent, youthful pride. But antipathy for such assaults to fundamental fairness was not what brought me to adult education, especially since I did not even know that adult education could have such a role. What I did know was that, in a job market flooded with liberal arts majors, State's adult ed. program was "placing its graduates."

So in 1977 I enrolled in a class through extension, and the next term I was on campus taking courses with Edgar Boone, Conrad Glass, and Malcolm Knowles. I learned from all three: Boone's class (endearingly known as Booneology) influenced my own teaching of program planning in coming years; Glass's course was so interesting and solid that I chose him for my doctoral committee chair; and Knowles's course introduced me to his concept of andragogy and provoked a good bit of reflection on the process-content question—reflection that has endured. What *is* the proper balance between teaching methodology and content? For Knowles it was all process, since the andragogical process was the universal medium to any particular end, and since, through this process, the facilitator would engender self-direction in students, the content would ineluctably follow. But for me, the balance is about 30:70 process-content. I am a little less sanguine about the andragogical process inevitably leading to acquisition of content, precisely because I am less sanguine about the assumptions Knowles makes about the adult learner that led him to andragogy. I find that learning contracts in the Knowles mold—the high-water mark of the Knowlesian andragogical method—may be appropriate when there is not a prescribed content to be conveyed and acquired, when learner motivation and ability are already high, when external or institutional constraints are low, and when time constraints are low. For me, contracts are especially applicable to special problems courses, internship experiences, and readings courses. They could also fit a course like Controversies in Adult Education, but they do not quite so neatly fit, say, program planning, where the learner really needs to acquire some proficiency in the *whole* process, not deep proficiency in one aspect but highly superficial knowledge in others. It is for that reason that I would argue for the application of andragogy—or any other method—to be situational, requiring adaptability of the educator. Professors of education, whether K-12 or adult ed., are right to stress method and process; we have all experienced the content expert who could not teach his way out of the proverbial wet paper bag. But an excess of concern for process can also imply a diminished *need* for content and thus a diminished provision of it and acquisition of it, as if it is a kind of lagniappe, or the mere frosting on the cake of *process*—we have experienced those professors, the content-lite ones, as well. If teaching method and process were vastly more important than the content to be taught, then education professors, as presumptive masters of process, should be the best professors in the university—yet I have never heard anyone make that claim.

The teaching of the professional discipline of adult education, such as a graduate course on the adult learner, is not the same as the every day practice of adult education in daily life, however. Lindeman was the first to distinguish between the practice of adult education and the teaching of collegiate academic subjects, including adult education, in universities. This little dilemma was one of the very first that I confronted as a professor: isn't it hypocritical to proclaim the necessity of such a learner-focused practice for my adult education graduate students when I myself still gave tests and pre-determined the course content? This was Knowles's dilemma also, and he addressed it with the implementation of the learning contract, which was a kind of compromise between the institutional needs for accountability and his philosophical need for significant learner input, if not outright control. Lindeman addressed it by simply saying that higher education (degree-seeking, entrance requirements, exams) is by definition not adult education, thus eliminating adult education's moral imperative to relinquish professorial control. I have tried to address the dilemma by combining those two approaches—arguing that degree seeking is simply *and appropriately* not compatible with the fully learner-centered tenets of the ideal of adult education while at the same time trying (though not always succeeding) to provide learner freedom within instructor-defined parameters. Though not a perfectly comfortable philosophical stance, it seems justifiable in view of the ethical imperative to provide safe practice based on the discipline's collective wisdom concerning what its credentialed practitioners *should* know, rather than just what that soon-to-be-credentialed practitioner *thinks* she should know or *chooses* to know. Thus as an adult education professor teaching prospective practitioners, I have obligations to the profession and to the public to assure that those practitioners acquire a body of knowledge; by contrast, I did not have those obligations when I was teaching adults recreational tennis and could afford to work on serving the ball with those who wanted more help there and backhands with those who told me they needed that.

But I have gotten a little ahead of myself. I graduated with my doctorate in Adult and Community College Education and a minor in English in 1979; soon after I was dabbling in administration at a technical college in North Carolina. I loved my boss—we still exchange Christmas cards 26 years later—but found administration less appealing than the classroom and the rush associated with seeing my name in a professional journal. So in 1980 when I was offered an assistant professorship at the University of Southern Mississippi, my former wife and I pulled up stakes and headed south (a debt I will always owe her). My bumpy transition from liberal arts to adult education was not yet resolved, however, and I spent two years wondering if adult education was really what I wanted to do, even in the allegedly exalted role of professor. But slowly I acquired my sea legs, becoming more comfortable with my courses and my students (many of whom were older than my 32 years), and I began to settle in for a career. It would be a career in which I have tried to mesh my interests in philosophy, history, and literature with learning and education for adults.

As if on cue, Elias and Merriam published a book which helpfully filled what I considered a philosophical vacuum in the field, namely a typology of adult education philosophies. Knowles had given us andragogy, both a philosophy and a method, focusing on the notion of learner control. But Elias and Merriam's typology (later modified by Darkenwald and Merriam) laid out different philosophical stances one could take to adult education based essentially on adult education's various purposes. What, then, was my purpose as an adult educator? As I tell my Foundations class students (after our debate in which teams argue for each of the five philosophies), if allowed to choose only one position, I would choose Personal and Social Improvement. This is the somewhat generic position that splits the difference between adult education to change the individual vs. adult education to change society. But if I could choose *two* positions, I would choose Cultivation of the Intellect (learning for intellectual growth, which is essentially the liberal education position, and I absolutely include science in this—in fact, the whole spectrum of human intellectual and artistic endeavor) and Social Transformation (the rectification of social injustice through empowering the dispossessed position), and in that order.

These two may seem a strange marriage, especially in view of the common perception of Cultivation of the Intellect as conservative, politically and socially neutral, and pedantic—in short, the "OK, so you've memorized two tons of Shakespeare" caricature. I prefer to see Cultivation of the Intellect not merely as an antiquarian collection of intellectual history's artifacts, handsomely displayed on one's mental shelves. Rather, it is an exploration of and a critical engagement with the greatest of human culture's ideas, past and present, *and* the development of the critical thinking skills that such engagement demands. I do not, however, have an objection to stocking the shelves of one's mind with a little art, literature, science, history, and philosophy just for the pleasure and satisfaction of it. That is adult education as well. To suggest otherwise is to argue that education must have instrumental value, that is, it must serve as a means to some purely practical end. I have no objections to practical ends either, whether they be vocational training or combating social ills. But I do object to the notion that all education *necessarily* has to be the conduit to some utilitarian purpose in order to have value and without such purpose it is at best a frivolous thing. One might as well say that poetry and art are frivolous, or join Henry Ford in saying that "history is more or less bunk." Right there is the birthplace of anti-intellectualism. So liberal adult education is not, then, instrumental, nor is it mere expertise—though on a more transcendental scale, one might argue that it is the ultimate utilitarian philosophy, as it teaches us to think, reason, appreciate, and discriminate. I believe that it is in this sense that Mortimer Adler believed that *only* adults can be educated; children and youth, he says, are *schooled*. Such an education broadens us, moves us beyond the provincial, and teaches us something about both human folly and human possibility.

Dissenting from Darkenwald and Merriam's summary of the Cultivation of the Intellect position (especially as exemplified by Lawson and Paterson), I disagree that it is a values-neutral position. No education is value-free. Thus I can also embrace social amelioration and, where necessary, Social Transformation as a compelling adult education philosophy. The world is filled with tears, and an empowering education is potentially the most effective tool in addressing egregious oppression and exploitation. It is in this context that my research on Freedom Summer is the scholarly work of which I am most proud. If the slippery terrain from education to propaganda is often in the eye of the beholder, and if all education is value-laden, whose values should prevail? I do not know. But I believe that a sound liberal education wedded to a social consciousness, both furthered by the self-directed learning that all good education should inspire, can arm us with Lyman Bryson's "rational skepticism." And it is precisely that skepticism which teaches us, and allows us to teach others to be wary of and to deconstruct the narcissism, piety, intolerance, mendacity, propaganda, and especially the fundamentalism afflicting both the extreme right and the extreme left. In the space between those extremes, good people will differ as to which values education should embrace and advance. I believe that one of those values of education—as opposed to propaganda—is that contrarian views have an equal right to be heard, just as they have an equal obligation to submit to critical scrutiny. In education, there should be no heresies, for the very reason that there should be no dogmas.

One of the beauties of adult education for me has been that it has allowed me to try to blend my interests in history (my primary area of recreational reading), literature, philosophy, and adult education into a career that is, despite all probability, still coherent, I hope. For all of my 26 years at the University of Southern Mississippi, my colleague Lee Pierce ("Willie" to me) has been a friend who, among other informal teachings, has modeled a fine equanimity that has on more than one occasion quelled, or at least tempered, my somewhat more tempestuous or apocalyptic instincts. Whatever I may have taught my students in these 26 years, they have nicely reciprocated in teaching me: softening a few edges, perhaps hardening a few others, and sometimes shaping my thinking and teaching in ways unknown to them. One long-ago student influenced me so much that I eventually asked her to marry me, and her counsel—invariably reasoned and wise and often challenging—is still the first I seek.

One might quip that autobiographies are the supreme examples of fiction. And even where deception is not the intent, memory is the best of liars. So, *caveat lector.* I began with the fairly commonplace fact that my entry into adult education was the result of an unexpected, though not entirely fortuitous, observation from a respected teacher, and that much, at least, is true. Other roads, not taken, might have led me to careers in carpentry or photography—had not talent deficits and bookishness dictated otherwise. Despite an uncertain start, adult education long ago became home to me. I recommend it.

Dr. Kathleen B. Rager

My career in adult education began somewhat typically in that I was an adult education practitioner before I knew there was such a field. I entered adult education in the early 1980s quite by accident and have stayed for more than twenty years because the diversity and breadth of the field have satisfied my recurrent desire for challenge and change. My career is characterized by a passion for learning and personal growth. Feminism, transformative learning theory, and self-directed learning have remained consistent themes in a personal journey filled with surprising twists and turns.

I shifted my career from teaching children and having a home-based educational sales business to adult education when I answered a classified ad. Our local community college was seeking someone to teach adults to give business presentations. I had liked the presentation part of my home-based business but did not like being responsible for the product part of my enterprise. This opportunity sounded like a better fit for me. It was part time and was compatible with my first priority, raising my daughters.

The community college offered me the chance to develop and deliver a 12-hour business presentations workshop for IBM employees. I look back on that experience as a life-changing leap of faith. I can still vividly recall how petrified I was waiting to begin my first session and how, to my amazement, I completely calmed down by the end of my opening sentence. I started with a quote from Pericles that is dated 400 BC: "A man who can think and does not know how to express what he thinks is on the level of the man who cannot think." I added, "A woman who can think and does not know how to express what she thinks is on the level of the woman who cannot think."

Pericles' message is still as powerful for me today as it was on that morning. I treasure the opportunities I have had through the years to help thousands of people learn to "express what they think" through my work as a trainer. It remains a central part of what I do even today as a faculty member at the University of Oklahoma. I teach students to become trainers with both a strong theoretical and practical background. Most importantly, I facilitate their ability to think critically and then to "express what they think."

What contributed to the success of that first training course was my ability as a self-directed learner. Years later I would learn that self-directed learning or self-teaching is the most common type of adult learning and that it has been of central importance in defining the field of adult education. At that point in time, however, I simply went about the business of locating the best resources I could find on business presentations, networked with IBM managers to find out what was expected of their employees, and learned about designing and delivering training.

A significant portion of my personal training ground was the five years I spent in the elementary classroom working hard to motivate my students to match my excitement about learning. When I switched to an adult audience, I brought with me many of the lessons I had learned in the classroom. I made sure that my adult students knew how the course would benefit them and I kept my workshops relevant and interesting. They responded very positively, as did IBM, who insisted that from then on my course become the standard for business presentations training in that program.

With that success, my career was launched as an independent training consultant. For the next five years I made more money than I thought I deserved, designing and delivering training programs in the Hudson River Valley of New York. IBM was my major client and I benefited from entering the field under the influence of such a sophisticated training consumer. My learning curve was incredibly steep at that time and all of that learning was self-directed.

To add more stability to my work, I took a position at Marist College in Poughkeepsie, New York, as the Director of Corporate and Professional Education. I liked the sound of that title as well as the opportunity it afforded me to work as part of a team. I continued to conduct training programs myself, but most of my time and energy was now focused on program planning and management. I designed a slate of noncredit workshops for the general public each semester. However, most of the revenue I generated came from successfully competing for education and training contracts with area businesses. I found myself in the position of intermediary between the sometimes conflicting cultures of academia and business. It was not without its interesting challenges.

While at Marist I began to formalize my background in training and adult education. I took graduate courses, attended conferences, and participated in relevant workshops. I began to learn the terminology and theories underpinning what I had been doing in my practice. I also became heavily involved in the quality improvement movement that was gaining popularity in the late 1980s. Process management entered my professional life when IBM selected me to adapt an existing workshop on the topic for use with its Data Systems Division in Poughkeepsie. This turned out to be a significant experience for me as process management became another cornerstone of my career and practice. It involved applying techniques that were successful in the manufacturing environment to white-collar processes. I was impressed by the fact that most defects or mistakes are not the result of human error but are rather due to process problems. I embraced the advice that it was important to "fix the process, not the blame." In addition to conducting training sessions on process management, I applied it to my own practice. In my role as manager, I worked with my staff to flowchart the processes we used in delivering contract training services with an eye toward improving their efficiency and effectiveness. As a result we were able to reduce the time it took to respond to a request for proposal, streamline the workshop evaluation process, and reduce the time it took to pay instructors.

After five years at Marist, I was personally and professionally ready to make another leap of faith. This one landed my youngest daughter and me halfway across the country in

Wichita, Kansas. I was now divorced and two of my daughters were working professionals. Answering another classified ad, this one in the *Chronicle of Higher Education*, I successfully competed for a position at Wichita State University. While there, I added the development and management of an extension center to my skill set. With ten classrooms and a computer lab in downtown Wichita, I concentrated on making good use of the space by offering credit courses, developing credit certificate programs, providing contract training services, and presenting public sessions. I also stayed active as a trainer myself.

My entrance into a doctoral program at Kansas State University occurred because a number of factors came together at just the right time in my life. These included the convenience of courses being offered in Wichita, wonderful support in my personal life, enthusiasm from my employer, and my last child preparing to leave for college. I am a case in point for the chain of response model proposed by Cross (1981) to explain participation in adult education.

My ambition to complete a doctorate had been dormant since finishing my master's degree as a nontraditional student more that twenty years prior. That was when I learned that education was not just about memorizing information and giving it back verbatim on the final exam. As an adult student in my master's program at the State University of New York at New Paltz, I became a true participant in my learning. I was encouraged to find my own voice and to speak my own truth.

A pivotal experience for me at that time involved the publication of a paper I had written for one of my master's courses. It reflected my interest in women and education at all levels. This focus is obviously influenced by my own gender, but even more profoundly from being the mother of Betsy, Sharon, and Kristen. They have always inspired me at a personal level. That inspiration translated into my professional practice as well. Additionally, both my high school and undergraduate education took place at all-female institutions. That feminist thread was also exhibited in the programming specifically designed for women that I initiated both at Marist College and at Wichita State University as well as in my research agenda.

My paper, entitled "Little Girls and Picture Books: Problem and Solution," addressed the absence of active roles for women and girls in children's literature at that time. I developed a suggested reading list that was useful with my young daughters. Through publication the list reached other mothers as well as nursery and elementary school teachers. This was my first publication. With it, the idea that I could produce something worthy of dissemination germinated and years later helped to foster the belief that I could succeed in a doctoral program.

My confidence grew as I progressed through my coursework at Kansas State in their Ph.D. program. The faculty skillfully practiced andragogy, "the art and science of helping adults learn" (Knowles, 1980, p. 43). When it came time to pick my dissertation topic, I was drawn to self-directed learning both because of my own experience and also because of its importance to the field of adult education. Ultimately, the topic I selected was the self-directed learning of women with breast cancer. I was motivated by the comments of Rosemary Caffarella (1993), who wrote of her experiences in this context. The potential to contribute in a meaningful way to a topic affecting women also played a significant role in my decision.

I expected the dissertation process to be challenging but was unprepared for the "compassion stress" that I experienced during the 14 months it took to complete. My qualitative study on the self-directed learning of women with breast cancer was published as well as articles related to issues that sprung unexpectedly from that investigation. One article concerns my experience as the researcher in this context. I have called attention to the need for self-care when a qualitative researcher engages in a study that is likely to elicit powerful emotional responses. I assert that strategies should be implemented that facilitate dealing with those emotions as they come up. I also suggest that the self-care of researchers in similar circumstances needs to be addressed in courses designed to prepare novice qualitative researchers.

In the acknowledgment section of my final document I wrote, "This dissertation has been a wonderful but difficult experience." In particular, I thanked the breast cancer patients who had participated in the study, and I acknowledged, "They have made this an extraordinary journey." What I didn't anticipate was that this "extraordinary journey" would change the direction of my career once again. As a result of the process of completing my doctorate, I became passionate about research. It was natural therefore that I shifted my career to the professoriate. I have been at the University of Oklahoma for five years where I teach in graduate programs offered through the College of Education. I am responsible for the emphasis in training and development for the master's and Ph.D. degrees in Adult and Higher Education. I see this new endeavor as a chance to give back to the profession that has so enhanced my life. I am excited about the opportunity it provides to prepare the next generation of trainers and to pass along many of the lessons that I have learned both formally and informally over the past twenty years.

On campus, I spend quite a bit of time in the Bizzell Library. For me, libraries have always been powerful symbols of boundless opportunity and change. That sense of optimism and potential is at the heart of my philosophy of education. From an academic perspective, Mezirow's (1994) theory of transformational learning is probably most compatible with my own experience and with my core beliefs about adult education. In my view, changes in organizations, communities, and societies are manifestations of changes in individuals. My own career has taken many unanticipated twists and turns over the years. However, there are consistent threads that are at the heart of my educational philosophy. At that core is a passionate love of learning and an appreciation for the potential that learning has for changing lives—including mine. I am grateful to all the teachers in my life, both the official ones and the ones who played a role in my self-directed learning. I am also indebted to the field of adult education for the many and varied opportunities it has afforded me. I continue to be excited to be a part of this dynamic field.

References

Caffarella, R. B. (1993). Self-directed learning. *New Directions for Adult and Continuing Education*, (57), 25-34.

Cross, K. P. (1981). *Adults as learners: Increasing participation and facilitating learning.* San Francisco: Jossey-Bass.

DeFilippo, K. B. (1976). Little girls and picture books: Problem and solution. *The Reading Teacher (29)* 7, pp 671-674.

Knowles, M. S. (1975). *Self-directed learning.* Chicago: Follett Publishing Company.

Knowles, M. S. (1980). *The modern practice of adult education: From pedagogy to andragogy.* (2nd ed.) New York: Cambridge Books.

Mezirow, J. (1994). Understanding transformational theory. *Adult Education Quarterly (44)*, 4, 222-232.

Jost Reischmann
Becoming a Professor in Andragogy—Lived History

Should I really be a part of this book? I know of at least two arguments against it: First, I am not an American adult educator; I live and work in Germany. However, for more than 25 years I have regularly visited conferences and colleagues at their universities in the USA and have them as guests and friends at my university and home. Phyllis Cunningham commented about me at the annual conference of AAACE (American Association for Adult and Continuing Education) 2002 in St. Louis: "Perhaps Jost is more American than some other professors!" (Still I hesitate – Was this a compliment?).

Second, I have an identity problem: Am I an adult educator? For a number of years I clearly would have said, "Yes." Still today I sometimes work in adult education institutions (companies, churches, adult education centers) for some extra money or fun or because I cannot say no, but in my main profession I am and I feel like a professor of adult education (officially, "Chair of Andragogy"), educating students in an academic discipline. We teach, learn, research about the education of adults, but I see my university work not as adult education.

Nevertheless, both anti-arguments also offer opportunities. Sometimes things can be seen clearer from a distance. The international-comparative perspective from outside provokes to overcome ethnocentrism. Occasionally I had the feeling this provocation was my role in the collegial interchanges. I have to confess: Now and then I enjoy playing this provocation role! Moreover, the professor's perspective has the advantage that (because I do not have not to represent one specific direction of adult education) I have the academic freedom to think beyond the different institutions, traditions, and movements where adult educators in the practical field are sheltered. (Are you aware that I do what I described one sentence above?) I hope that helps to justify my inclusion in this book.

How I Came (Not) into Adult Education

I started fairly early to "work" in adult education. As I could operate a slide projector and a 16mm film projector I was asked in my late teenage years to become the technique guy of our local adult education center (*Volkshochschule*) - $1 for showing slides, $2 for films. Especially I liked the presenters that brought slides and film ($3). Beside the money being momentous for me, I could listen to lectures without paying. "Beautiful flowers of the Alps,"

"Great Philosophers," "The New Movie-Culture," "Traveling to Wheresoever," that bouquet of enriching and entertaining themes plus a number of language courses represented the majority of public adult education one or two evenings a week in the 1960s in Germany.

Adult education? That was in the 1960s no option for a vocation. In adult education I met slide-showing or book-selling travelers or humanists with a firm income otherwise. There were the spouses having an earning husband, so they could offer a mixture of social and educational work. There were the school teachers, teaching a foreign language or another school subject to make some extra money and/or to escape for some hours from their child-oriented schoolwork. This all provided no prospect for making a living wage. Adult education was volunteer work, part time, no training was available, so it had to be done "by the heart," with conviction and often with pride. Adult education was neither a vocation nor a profession.

This situation lies in many countries not very far back in history. No wonder that this image of adult education—volunteer work with full heart, empty pockets, done with content expertise and teaching intuition, and sometimes with a lot of vulnerable pride— still can be found widely.

Today, only(!) 40 years later, I am Chair of Andragogy at Bamberg University, Germany. About 100 students study andragogy as their main subject, 150 more as a side subject. This number doubled in the last ten years. They all will work in adult education and make their living as andragogical professionals. This is not an optimistic hope, but reality, as we know from our own as well as others' research about graduates in andragogy/adult education.

Adult education within one generation within my life, developed from "volunteer moonlighting" to academic study and profession. No wonder there are tensions and confusions in the field of adult education; they result from the rapid changes that happened in the years between 1970 and 2000 and started a new chapter in the theory and practice of adult education.

Was It a Detour?

It was clear from the beginning that I wanted to work in education (at least I knew nothing else). As a teenager I was in several boy groups and often found myself in leadership-functions, i.e., a boy of 14 taking care of the 10-year-olds in summer camps.

Consequently, after finishing high school I started to study at a teachers training college. I am still thankful that this introduced me in a systematic and profound way into pedagogical thinking and acting. There I learned—and that still is part of my understanding today—that educational situations have to be rationally planned and designed, that "knowing content" is not enough, but that "designing seminars,", "activating methods," or "didactic and methodic" are necessary; these all are contents today in our curriculum at Bamberg university. Andragogs must have the competency to teach didactically as a professional.

There I also learned a more hidden lesson still important for me today. I found there two different groups of professors. One group was the "experienced practitioner," having missions and visions, telling us about their successful years of practical experiences. This group I loved; it was convincing to listen to them, learn their tricks, and follow their understanding of successful education. They knew the answers. There was the other group I liked much less: the young "academic" professors that made us read scientific (= difficult) books. In addition, they made us reflect critically and not to just believe, they made us doubt, compare, and test hypotheses and theories. They knew the questions (and I very much doubted the teaching competencies of these "theoreticians"). In my first years of being a school teacher I tried to imitate the practitioner-professors and to forget the theory-professors. However, the longer I stayed in education the more often recollections came to me about the theories and books. Today I know that this knowledge of pedagogical theories helped me for a longer period of time and more than the practical tricks or visions which in the beginning were a survival toolkit but became either outdated or did not help in complex and difficult situations. I discovered theory is not theoretical, but a help to understand practice. Some theory-texts of that time I still teach to my students today. "Theories," "history," and "foundations" are of course today contents of our andragogy curriculum. Andragogs (and I limit this title to academically educated persons) must be able to perceive, describe, analyze, reflect, and criticize andragogical situations, now as well as in twenty years, when they will face new institutions, tasks, movements, and problems we don't even know today.

I do not want to be remembered by the following specific experience. Being a young school teacher I was asked to teach a class of adults in the local adult education center. I did exactly what I found later criticized in adult education books: I treated the adults at night the same way I treated children during the day. Please, participants from then, forgive me! What else had I learned?

I taught a couple of years in public schools; then I went to a "real" university (the University of Tuebingen, Germany) where I studied, now being 23 years old, pedagogy, psychology, and sociology for another nine semesters.

After graduation (1970) I stepped into academia again as a technique guy. As I could handle punch-cards and do some basic programming I was hired by the university in educational psychology and did my dissertation about effects of testing in school classes. What remained from this: academic professionals (= our graduates) must be able to ask questions open-mindedly, research them with methodological rigor, and add new knowledge to themselves and the field. No doubt, like in other academic studies, research classes and a research thesis are part of the andragogy curriculum.

Then I was hired by the Department of Media and Distance Education and still was focused on children and student learning. But what I did not know at that time, by studying pedagogy I had learned basic lectures for my work in andragogy today.

A Whole New World

During the 1970s a hurricane-like storm of developments triggered a transformation. First: The three professors of our chair, headed by Guenther Dohmen, a truly international person and later (1999) in the first group of Germans inducted into the International Adult and Continuing Hall of Fame, team-taught a class called "How Do Adults Learn?" The literature and research at that time in Germany filled one or two bookshelves. However, I had the clear feeling this is not only a field of application and practice, but it has and deserves a firm and genuine anthropology and theory, going beyond particular convictions and movements. The institutions, the practice, the various "missions and visions" existed, but was an academic (sub-) discipline "above" these fields of practice conceivable? In spite of the scholarly work done since the 1920s in Germany, at that juncture the answer was "No." Nevertheless, the fact that university faculty asked this question and started to include topics dealing with adult education in their curricula (and not only exchanged it at outside institutions or within interest groups) helped to change perspectives and awareness.

Second: From the international contacts of Guenther Dohmen we learned about a project Courses by Newspaper, at University of California–San Diego. Nationwide newspapers published a series of weekly articles for 12 to 16 weeks, covering a specific topic (i.e., "Oceans," "Death and Dying"), additional textbooks were available, and colleges offered courses. I transformed this idea into the German system and for five years was director of Zeitungskolleg at the German Institute for Distance Studies (DIFF). In this practical work grew the awareness that general theoretical concepts were blended into the practical project, worthy of being researched and developed: "open learning," including "nontraditional learning," "self-directed learning," and "life-related (meaningful) learning." All together I focused on two questions, one of practical application and the other of theoretical reflection. The practical-application-oriented question was, "How can adults be supported in lifelong and—as I called it later—in 'lifewide' learning?" The theoretical-reflection-oriented question was, "What sort of 'learning' is that, and how does this experience help us to better understand the learning of adults in their life?" I currently require my students at Bamberg University to answer these two standard questions in their diploma thesis.

Third: In the mid- and late 1970s a new movement sprang up, the encounter movement. The term "encounter groups" originated from a book by Carl Rogers, but besides his "person-centered approach," many other concepts added to that movement: Fritz Perls's Gestalt therapy, Alexander Lowen's bioenergetic, the T-Group movement and others. Some were more reflection oriented, some focused more on feelings, others on sensory awareness and body work. My pilgrimages included to Carl Rogers's Center for Studies of the Person in La Jolla, CA, and the Esalen Institute, Big Sur, CA. "Touch me, feel me, heal me" was a great message. Moreover, as I saw it, all these were oriented toward learning and education. Adults were learning in a powerful and personal way, sometimes painful, sometimes joyful, in learning settings far from school formats. Here I learned about "freedom to learn" (Rogers) and the personal power of meaningful learning. Even more, I learned methods how to support this type of learning, not by teaching but by counseling. This opened the access to listen carefully to adults on their journey "on becoming a person" and to facilitate and accompany their personal learning in a professional way, another professional method andragogs must have at their disposal. Classes and trainings about "Communicative Skills for Andragogs," "Strategies of Counseling," and "Coaching" represent these competencies now in our curriculum.

Fourth: "Schools do not solve educational problems, they produce them!" was the provoking statement of authors like Ivan Illich and Paulo Freire, claiming to "de-school society." "More organized and institutionalized learning, or less?" seemed to me a difficult question for children learning, but for adult education it made sense. Alan Tough had empirically proven that adults spend about two hours every day in learning projects, most of them self-directed, using a wide variety of outside resources. This confirmed self-directed adult learning was not a romantic myth. Moreover, for institutionalized learning Malcolm

Knowles offered methodic and didactical arrangements for "modern practice of adult education." This taught me the next new lesson: Adult education is only a part of the education of adults. The learning of adults happens not only lifelong but also *lifewide* in a multitude of traditional and nontraditional, formal and informal settings (workplaces, families, churches, marketplaces, television, "the life" …). Consequently internships, classes about "institutions of adult education," research and workplaces today exceed the traditional institutions and fields of what was perceived to be adult education four decades ago.

Looking back on these hurricanes of adult learning and education ideas in the 1970s and later, the challenges in understanding adult learning that my age group went through seems to me nearly incredible. In this formative decade of the 1970s the face and understanding of adult learning changed for me as a person as well as for the field as a whole. This may be a common experience my age group can report in Germany as well as in the USA.

In this stream of experiences my adult education baptism experience took place: I had to teach a credit course, Educational Psychology, at an adult education center in a little city in the Black Forest. I did everything new: arranging the chairs in a circle, welcoming the 15 participants, and letting them close their eyes to meditate about their goals for which they came. Then I asked them to hold their neighbors' hands for two minutes to come in contact with the group. After that they had time to interview one other person in the room and to introduce this person to the group. I felt very innovative. Nevertheless, after all of what I thought were beautiful beginnings, the group clearly told me: No gimmicks any longer! You are the professor—teach us! At that critical point I was able to beg them for trust to try this new way of referring to their own experiences for three sessions,- then we would make a decision to go on with the new way or change back to the old way. This course became a very enriching experience for the group and me. It clearly felt totally different from my prior teaching experience. After three sessions it was clear; we went on the new way. I had that flash-like insight: Now I am an adult educator!

However, my activity as an adult educator always remained like in the old tradition a side activity, at public adult education centers, with churches, with companies. In my main profession I made my living at Tuebingen University and the new "Chair of Adult and Continuing Education." There I was an associate professor, until I got a call to Bamberg University as full professor and chair. As I described about Tuebingen University in the beginning, here at Bamberg I have three professors working with me, and we have twenty to thirty graduates every year (http://web.uni-bamberg.de/ppp/Andragogik). Most of my life I had the privilege to work in a university context that allowed me to research, read, analyze, theorize, and I had the pressure to publish or perish and the opportunity to reflect on the practice I had at various institutions. There was a clear difference between my activities and my identity as "adult educator/trainer" and as "researcher/scholar."

The Chance of International Exchange and Learning

I love to travel. This brought me in the last 30 years about 30 times to the USA and other countries, in the beginning mostly to conferences, in the last years more and more for vacation (a snowbird in Arizona).

An important role in starting these international contacts was in the 1980s an active exchange between AAACE and the Deutscher Volkshochschul-Verband DVV. Representatives from AAACE and DVV visited for a couple of weeks the other country in organized tours. In 1982 the German group experienced Texas hospitality in adult education centers and at the AAACE conference in San Antonio. I was not prominent enough to be invited into the German travel group, but I travelled on my own and got to know not only American colleagues but, to their surprise, also German adult education representatives. This made me "visible" not only to the American colleagues but also to the German. The visibility became very rewarding: At most conferences in the USA I was the only German, so I was individually named, welcomed, and had to get up and smile around (which never happened to me at German conferences). This visibility opened many doors and allowed me to meet respected colleagues and dear friends. Just to name some: Tom Damon, Alan Knox, John A. Henschke, Roger Axford, Alexander Charters, Malcolm Knowles, Douglas Smith, Trenton Ferro, Huey B. Long, Lorillee Sandmann, Sharan Merriam, Judy Koloski—many who today have been inducted into the International Adult and Continuing Education Hall of Fame. A personal and professional enriching network of "internationals" came into being. Contacts and friendships between institutions and persons from that time until today still exist. The problem I fear today and am uncomfortable about is that the persons being active at that time are now 20 years older and retiring. Consequently, these contacts and networks soon will be outgrown, and no young people are following in the footsteps of these pioneers. It seems time to start again such an organized exchange.

In general I found adult education in theory as well as in practice not more developed in either Germany or the USA, only different. Main topics of American adult education, like adult basic education, ESL, or GED preparation, are marginal in Germany. Historical, institutional, and even theoretical themes in the USA are different. We do not know much about the other country. When I published the book *Adult Education in West Germany in Case Studies* (Reischmann, 1988), I discovered with surprise that this was indeed the first English-language book about adult education in Germany. Americans seldom show up at German conferences and have a language barrier. So my role on one side became a "bridge-builder," informing about foreign experiences, and my role on the other side a provoker, asking confusing questions, offering alternative explanations. Perhaps this was the "exceptional and innovative leadership" mentioned in the AAACE President's Award which I received in 1998.

After conferences in Montreal, Quebec, Ljubljana (Slovenia), Prague, and Berlin, the network of internationals became more formal in the International Society for Comparative Adult Education (ISCAE). In 1992 at the AAACE conference in Anaheim, CA, Alexander Charters nominated me president of this society. About 140 colleagues working in international and comparative adult education in 34 countries are members today. We organized conferences in Bamberg (1995), Ljubljana (1998), St. Louis (2002), and again Bamberg (2006). The upcoming e-mail and internet—becoming a hobby of mine—(http://www. ISCAE.org) opened immediate access to persons, institutions, and information in many countries. Need information about adult education in Alaska? No problem, send an e-mail to Gretchen Bersch, University of Alaska at Anchorage. Making a visit to Ljubljana, Slovenia? Just call Ana Krajnc or Zoran Jelenc, who will be glad to present their work. One of my students was recovering from graduation stress by travelling in Australia. I gave her the address of Roger Morris. "Yesterday he invited me to attend his class," she tells me on a postcard.

Some of these international activities led to my induction into the International Adult and Continuing Education Hall of Fame in 1999 (http://www.occe.ou.edu/hallof-fame/). "Jost Reischmann has been a dynamic force in the field of adult education, building vital bridges between theory and practice" is written there. However, knowing that some of those who recommended me to this honour had been guests in my house, I believe that a big reason for my induction was the good German breakfast that my wife presented to those friends when they visited in our home.

Enriching value through the international contacts helped reduce some personal blindness and ethnocentrism. Better understanding of adult education in other countries helped me develop a broader and deeper understanding of adult education in my own country. The personal benefits of being a more "international" person include understanding, open mindedness, tolerance, and humility—and good times with good friends in many places in the world (for example, in a *Biergarten* during the summer in Bamberg, Germany). Moreover, there is also a global perspective. The UNESCO Hamburg Declaration on Adult Education (1997) put this in words: "One of the foremost challenges of our age is ... to construct a culture of peace based on justice and tolerance within which dialogue, mutual recognition and negotiation will replace violence, in homes and countries, within nations and between countries." That is the reason why I try to include my students in international meetings (i.e., Cincinnati, Phoenix, Prague, St. Louis).

Towards a Scientific Discipline: "Andragogy"

The term "andragogy" in the USA is mostly attached to the specific concept of the American author Malcolm Knowles. In Europe this is different. "Andragogy" became connected to academic and professional institutions, publications, and programs, as for example the Yugoslavian Society for Andragogy, the Andragoski Center Republike Slovenije, the Katedra Andragogiky of Prague University (Czechia). Similarly, Venezuela has the Instituto Internacional de Andragogia; Korea publishes the journal *Andragogy Today*.

An academic discipline with university programs, professors, students, and graduation is a rather young element in the history and division of labor of adult education. I experienced its development firsthand. It exists today in many countries, perhaps not for very long, but it exists. Furthermore, this new element (in most parts of the world) confusingly still labels itself with the old name used for the field of practice. So we are not clear in what we talk about when we discuss "the future of adult education," "methods in adult education," "the history of adult education." Do we talk about places where adult education is practically carried out or about universities? Teaching an ESL class or writing a thesis about ESL classes—should both be named "working in adult education"?! It confuses the clarity of thinking and acting when we cannot discriminate between the field of organized practice ("adult education") and of academic reflection ("andragogy") because we use the same label for both. We need a separate word for the newly grown field of scholarly work at universities.

That is the reason why I aggressively promote the term "andragogy" to brand the scientific discipline dealing with the lifelong and lifewide education of adults (http://www.andragogy.

net). This discussion is not a mere matter of definition. I want to influence the coming reality: to challenge "outside" (demanding a respected discipline in the university context) to confront "inside" (challenging my colleagues to clarify their understanding and consensus of their function and science), overall to stand as a self-confident academic identity.

We are already far into the professionalized times with a division of labor. The "romantic times" of adult education are over; those were the times of Grundtvig, Miles Horton, Paulo Freire, Alfred Mannsbridge. Convincing in life-practice and enlightening in theory-writings they set an example to many followers. Nevertheless, now and in the future more and more people will have an academic andragogical education, producing theories, knowledge, research, critical thinking. The inspirational amateurs who played a role in the field decades ago will more and more be replaced by academic specialists and their knowledge – both a loss and a gain.

Summary

When I read what I have written here I am surprised myself. It seems I am a living document about beginnings in adult education (don't call me a fossil!). Of course the history of adult education dates back for centuries. However, within one or two generations the volume, the scope, the necessity, the finances, the institutions, and the theoretical reflections have grown into new dimensions. It was and is fun to be in the midst of this, together with good friends here and there on various sides of the oceans. I hope a lot of younger people will take over in this field of practice and theory. They are our future.

Jennifer A. Sandlin

"It is our inward journey that leads us through time—forward or back, seldom in a straight line, most often spiraling. Each of us is moving, changing, with respect to others. As we discover, we remember; remembering, we discover; and most intensely do we experience this when our separate journeys converge." (Eudora Welty, *One Writer's Beginnings* (1983), p. 112, Warner Books Edition)

The summer before I started college, the school I was about to attend sent each freshman a copy of Eudora Welty's autobiography *One Writer's Beginnings*. We were asked to read it before we arrived because Welty would be coming to campus to read us excerpts. Like Welty, I had from my very earliest years loved books, reading, and learning. I was headed to college in Jackson, Mississippi, where Welty had been born and raised. I planned to study literature and couldn't wait to start. Having studied her work in high school, I was thrilled at the prospect of seeing, hearing, and possibly meeting Ms. Welty, and she did not disappoint. I'll never forget listening as she read from her autobiography with such great passion.

Also like Welty, I am a White, middle-class woman who was born and raised in the South—in Georgia, Louisiana, and Mississippi. While I have lived outside of the South—in New Mexico and Illinois—my life journey seems to keep spiraling me back there. I have struggled with this Southern aspect of myself because I am deeply rooted in the South yet am incredibly troubled by the racism, sexism, and economic inequality that continue to plague the South. At the same time, growing up immersed in the cultures of the South has given me an emic perspective on many of these issues of inequality and has led to a deep commitment to social justice, specifically around issues of gender, race, class, and sexual orientation. I believe my Southern roots are intimately tied to my becoming an adult educator and have shaped the kinds of issues I investigate and embrace in my research and practice as an adult educator. I also believe, like Welty, that the encounters I have had with other people—many of whom were educators working for social justice—have helped to shape who I am and what I care deeply about. There is a great deal of social justice work to be done in the South, and many of the mentors who have touched me deepest, given me the most insight into issues of justice, and have inspired me most along my journey have been educators, including those from the South and those from all over the world who have been transplanted to the South.

My journey towards becoming an adult educator committed to issues of social justice began in high school, although I didn't realize it at the time. I spent my high school years at a public, residential boarding school that hosted students from all over the state of Louisiana. This was my first real exposure to points of view that were radically different than those accepted as given in the conservative community I grew up in. It was during those years that I began reflecting on the privilege I had grown up with and became increasingly aware of and concerned about the social problems that go along with an unjustly hierarchical social system. This reflection and exploration continued in college. Through everyday encounters with friends, classmates, and professors from a variety of different backgrounds and political leanings; through involvement with political groups like Amnesty International, Food Not Bombs, and a student anti-apartheid task force; and through classes in history, anthropology, sociology and ecology, I began to encounter discourses and ideas that contradicted or problematized the taken-for-granted ideas about the world that I had grown up with.

I began college studying English Literature and ended up receiving my bachelor's degree with a major in Literature and a minor in Classics. However, during my last two years of college I became more focused on the social sciences classes I was also taking. I found myself increasingly wanting to learn about the suffering that took place around the world and to understand why it existed. I became involved in the student anti-apartheid organization at my college and was a leader in a student organization working to create the political will to end global hunger. I began to see past my individual actions to see how racism, sexism, and other forms of oppression are socially constructed and systemic. I saw that decisions we make can negatively (or positively) impact people half a world away. This caused me to think more about the implications of my everyday actions and to feel more responsibility for the inequalities and injustices in the world. I came to see that I occupy a privileged position in a privileged nation. It was this thinking that led me to pursue postgraduate work in archeology and anthropology. I thought that by understanding the human past and how people had dealt with problems in the past, we could gain insight into solving the problems we encountered in the present. After three years in an archaeology doctoral program, I had become frustrated with what I perceived at the time to be its lack of connection to present-day social problems and began to see that for me, the theoretical study of the human past was not the best way to address contemporary social justice issues. I wanted to find a career path that would give me more direct involvement in solving these problems. I was also beginning to focus more on social problems and disparities in privilege within the United States and less on global environmental and hunger problems.

I hadn't considered pursuing study or work in the field of education up until that point, but during this time period when I was struggling to find a new path, I heard Johnathan Kozol speak. His descriptions of the educational systems he had studied in East St. Louis greatly moved me and made me begin thinking about education and its role in both creating and resisting oppression. This was one of the major turning points in my life, and I began trying to figure out how to pursue a career in education. During my final year of archaeology graduate school, I began exploring options within the world of education. That year I got five part-time jobs in various educational systems and programs, working with a variety of learners in grade school, junior high, and high school. In addition, a friend had begun tutoring a woman in adult literacy and introduced me to the local adult literacy program in Albuquerque. In retrospect I can see that at that time I had what Quigley (1997) calls the maternal view of adult literacy. Basically, this view portrays the adult literacy student as lost and naïve like a child in need of the help of a parent. But in this case the parent is the literacy volunteer who will help the adult student learn to read. I knew how important reading was in my life, and I imagined that people who could not read had big voids in their lives. I also believed, however, in the power of human agency (especially collective agency) to bring about social change. I thought that education was a powerful tool and hoped that teaching people to read would help them to be able to change the social situations around them.

At the adult literacy training program in Albuquerque, through the help of one of the tutor trainers, I came into contact with the philosophy and pedagogy of Paulo Freire. The trainer who taught the program I went through talked about literacy as a social problem rather than an individual deficit and taught us to use the life experiences of our learners as curriculum material. After attending this program I began tutoring three Latina women in reading and writing. I grew close to these women and enjoyed this work because it seemed to make a true difference in their lives. Throughout the time that I tutored, the women seemed invigorated as they learned. Together we created curriculum materials and discussed issues of class, ethnicity, and gender affecting them and their communities. The women addressed problems they faced in their own lives, and one woman ultimately concluded that she could no longer live with her abusive husband and began to build a new life for her and her children.

Because I found this work so meaningful, and because I resonated much more with the adults I was working with than I did with the younger learners I was working with through all of my part-time jobs, I decided to pursue a doctoral degree in adult education. My knowledge of the field of adult education was incredibly limited – in fact, I really didn't know that the field of adult education existed. I remember sitting down at the library with those huge reference books that describe graduate programs throughout the United States, trying to find a doctoral program where I could study "something that combined social foundations of education and adult literacy and social justice issues" (which was how I was not very articulately articulating my interests at the time). Fortunately, I stumbled across the adult education program at the University of Georgia and started my doctoral studies in the fall of 1996.

While pursuing my doctoral degree at UGA I worked on the Adult Literacy Staff Development Project, funded by a grant from the Georgia Department of Technical and Adult Education. As part of this project I worked with Dr. Tom Valentine as co-editor of *Beyond Basic Skills*, a curriculum guide published every four months aiming to foster critical group discussion around social issues in adult basic skills classrooms. During this project I interacted with a wide range of teachers operating in diverse programs throughout the state of Georgia and began investigating adult literacy and welfare-to-work educational programs, through which I began asking tough questions about the social contexts of adult literacy and welfare-to-work education. I began to realize that the empowering experiences I had been a part of in New Mexico were not the norm in literacy education. Although many learners who attended literacy programs throughout the state struggled with racism, poverty, domestic abuse, violence, and other forms of oppression in their daily lives, the publicly sponsored literacy system not only often failed to address these issues directly, but often actively avoided them in order to stay on the "safer ground" of academic skills divorced from their social contexts. The programs I saw focused almost exclusively on individual workbook instruction, skill development, and standardized testing while few teachers employed discussion and critical thinking activities designed to help students understand and critique the world around them. Writing this curriculum allowed me to combine my theoretical interests in critical education with my desire to do something practical that would affect adult education teachers and learners. Critical pedagogy and adult learning theory informed the curriculum, and Tom and I created a product teachers could use immediately in their classrooms. This process was a great learning experience about how to combine research, theory, and practice.

My life experiences and my educational experiences up to and including my graduate work at UGA have led to the research interests I have pursued both in graduate school and in the three years I have been an assistant professor at Texas A&M University. This research agenda consists of three interrelated strands. First, I have been exploring welfare-to-work education, specifically its ideological assumptions concerning work, women, workers, and the assumed connections between education and work. This research is focused on issues of power, gender, race, politics, and curriculum in welfare-to-work policy and educational programs, in particular basic skills programs and workforce-related programs geared towards welfare recipients. The basic assumption underlying all of this research is that education is a political enterprise. Given this, adult educators and researchers need to ask, following Cervero and Wilson (1994), "In whose interests is this education operating?" I approach these topics as a critical feminist, seeing workforce education as a gendered and classed site of practice. I have investigated the ways in which dominant discourses about work, welfare, welfare recipients, and workforce education play out in textbooks, classroom practices, and policy. Through this research I hope to alter public discourse about women on welfare and hope to affect public policy and educational practice.

My dissertation research was located within this general area of inquiry, focusing on political issues surrounding workforce education, specifically welfare-to-work education. I became interested in exploring education's connection to economic and work issues and began researching the assumptions that welfare-to-work policy and popular rhetoric make about women on welfare and about the representation of workforce education as a panacea for macro-economic problems. The purpose of my research was to explore how ideologies about work and workers contained within welfare policy rhetoric were enacted in educational programs for welfare recipients. I conducted a qualitative case study of two welfare-to-work programs, finding that official program discourses upheld common stereotypes about the welfare system and welfare recipients, and stressed mainstream views regarding the ability of education to solve problems such as unemployment and welfare "dependency." Since my dissertation, I have continued to explore subsections of this overarching theme, concentrating my research and publications on topics such as 1) the construction of welfare recipients in welfare-to-work policy and practice, 2) the gendered nature of welfare policy and practice, 3) the construction of success in welfare-to-work programs and adult literacy education programs, and 4) public and program rhetoric concerning the connection between education and work, specifically regarding getting the GED and being successful in work and life.

My second strand of research centers on consumer education for adults. Several years ago I conducted research examining the hidden curriculum of consumer education texts used in adult literacy classrooms and found that these texts make unwarranted negative assumptions about the adult learners they are purporting to help. Subsequently I conducted interviews with women on welfare to learn how they construct themselves as consumers and found they defied many of the negative stereotypes the consumer education texts made about them. I have recently begun renewing this area of interest for research and publication. I am especially interested in nonformal sites of consumer education for adults, especially those sites that question the norms of consumption and create resistance to consumer culture. Using the framework of cultural studies, where consumption is viewed as inherently cultural and culture is viewed as inherently political, consumer education can be reframed as a political site where adults learn particular ways of relating to consumer culture and consumer capitalism – a site where consumers are constructed to have particular reactions to consumption and consumerism. This line of research fits very nicely with research into social movements that is gaining momentum in adult education, and also brings into adult education relatively unexplored theoretical frameworks such as cultural studies. I am very excited about this line of research and plan to pursue it for the foreseeable future. One of the main subtopics within my interest in consumer education for adults concerns how to create a more critical consumer education, when consumer education has traditionally been very technical and apolitical. This interest falls within my third research strand, which is a more general interest in critical perspectives in adult education and critical pedagogy and critical curriculum studies in adult education. In fact, this interest in critical adult education underlies most of my other research and is foundational to the way I view adult education and the way I construct and conduct my research.

I was initially drawn to and subsequently have remained in the field of adult education because of the social justice issues it addresses. This social justice commitment is embodied in so many of the adult educators I have encountered along my journey in adult education—at the University of Georgia and Texas A&M University; through my participation in conferences such as AERC, SCUTREA, and AAACE; and through the Commission of Professors of Adult Education and the Women Professors of Adult Education. I feel lucky to have found the field of adult education and feel fortunate to have had such great support from so many mentors in the field. For me, the best learning has occurred when our separate journeys have converged, as Welty puts it.

References

Cervero, R., & Wilson, A. (1994). *Planning responsibly for adult education: A guide to negotiating power and interests*. San Francisco: Jossey-Bass.

Quigley, B. A. (1997). *Rethinking literacy education*. San Francisco: Jossey-Bass.

Vanessa Sheared

I have been in adult education for 19 years—first as a student and later as a faculty member and administrator. As many others have said, and now I add to the chorus, my entrance into the field came through the back door. Initially, I did not plan on going into adult education, per se. I just thought that I wanted to work in higher education and make a difference within it for students in general, but African American students in particular. I wanted to make sure that other potential African American scholars might see me and by seeing me, they would begin to see themselves. Moreover, they might begin to dream about seeing themselves in higher education and ultimately join me and those other African American educators who had joined the ranks of professor in the academy of higher education within our history.

So my journey, as you might guess, has evolved out of a renewed sense of understanding and reflection about who I am and how I might contribute to increasing and enhancing my understanding about myself as well as others. I believe that moving into the field of Adult Education has allowed me to do this on multiple levels. Before moving forward with where I am, let me just share briefly what I have done and where I have been and how I arrived where I am today.

I received a B.A. from Wheaton College (Sociology, 1977), an M.A. from Louisiana State University (Counselor Education, 1980), and an Ed.D. from Northern Illinois University (Adult Education, 1992). I have held positions as an administrator and counselor in universities, community and vocational colleges, and nonprofit agencies; given presentations at international, national, state, and local conferences; and conducted research and taught in the areas of race, class, language and gender, policy and leadership, instructional and funding strategies, and Africentric and womanist perspectives. I have been invited by several campuses to either teach or co-teach courses related to "giving voice." I was invited to teach as a Distinguished Professor at the University of Alaska (1998) and a Visiting Professor at National Louis University (1999). In 1999 I was awarded a Cyril Houle Emerging Scholars research grant and was a member of the first cohort of nine scholars in the United to States to have been granted funding. I co-authored an article with two students that worked with me on this project, entitled "Literacy and Welfare Reform: Marginalization, Voice and Control."

For the last 12 years I have served in multiple capacities and as a result of my reflections about who I am and what my role is as an educator, teacher and now administrator, I have learned how to operate from and within the margin and the center, and along with this, I have gained a consciousness that extends from the fact that I am a womanist and Africentrist. As a womanist and Africentrist, I believe in the importance of centering oneself within one's history, beliefs, values and motifs with respect to race and gender. Furthermore, I believe that our lived experiences as humans are grounded in our ability to reflect upon and gain an appreciation for our own as well as others' multiple and varied realities—we are polyrhythmic. For instance, I am a teacher, writer and administrator, mother, daughter, colleague, friend, one who operates from an Africentric and womanist perspective. I believe that the aforementioned factors intersect with who one is with respect to one's race, gender, class, sexual orientation, religion, language and other factors that affect how we see ourselves, as well as how others view us.

I am currently one of two associate deans in the College of Education at San Francisco State University. I am the author of *Welfare Reform, Race, Class, and Gender: The Elusive Quest for Self-Determination* (Fall 1998); co-editor with Donna Amstutz of *Adult Basic Education in the Urban Community,* an issue of the *Education and Urban Society Journal* (2000); co-editor with Dr. Peggy Sissel of *Making Space: Merging Theory to Practice;* and I have authored several chapters on the importance of understanding and giving voice to one's polyrhythmic realities in formal and informal learning contexts.

Although I began my career in higher education with only one intention, to teach and write, I find myself now serving in an administrative role. As an associate dean for Academic Affairs in the College of Education and a professor in the Center for Adult Education at San Francisco State University, I am responsible for coordinating, supervising, and managing people, things, time, and resources. While I find this stimulating, I guess, as a womanist and Africentrist, it's ironic that the very institutional and hierarchical structures that I as a faculty member once theoretically challenged, I now find myself a participant in.

Throughout this journey, one thing has remained constant, and yes, in spite of the fact that I am an administrator now, I still promote the idea that within higher education we must continue to question and challenge ideas and actions as they affect people based on their race, language, gender, culture, religion, sexual orientation and any other distinguishing (whether visible or invisible) characteristics that might cause one to be marginalized or oppressed.

My Journey

Prior to joining the faculty at SFSU, I served as an assistant professor and co-ordinator of the Community College Doctoral Cohort (1991-1992) at Northern Illinois University. While at Northern, one of the senior faculty members asked me if I would be willing to allow him to nominate me to serve on the Board of Directors for the American Association of Adult Continuing Education (AAACE). I was humbled by the fact that I, a recently graduated doctoral student, was asked to serve in this capacity. I said yes, never once thinking that I would actually receive enough votes to be elected to serve in this ca-pacity. I was elected and served two terms on the AAACE Board of Directors. In addition to serving on this board, I also was elected to serve on the steering committee of the Adult

Education Research Conference (AERC). This came about as a result of my involvement as co-coordinator and organizer of the first African Diaspora Pre-Conference, which was held at Penn State University in 1993 in conjunction with AERC. I coordinated the first two conferences.

The pre-conference is an outgrowth of the vision of several graduate students at Northern Illinois University, and with encouragement from Phylllis Cunningham, it was born in 1993. The purpose of the pre-conference is to provide a forum for masters and doctoral-level students to present their research – research primarily aimed at increasing our knowledge about the history, culture, philosophy, and motifs of the African Diaspora. Throughout the last 12 years, this conference has served to increase the number of those within the African Diaspora presenting research on or about members of the African Diaspora, as well as increasing the number of individuals from the African Diaspora who attend the Adult Education Research Conference. Moreover, a significant number of those individuals are now faculty members in various universities and colleges across the United States. Currently this conference is coordinated by Juanita Johnson-Bailey, one of the first presenters of the conference in 1993, who is now a professor at the University of Georgia.

In 1993, I joined the faculty in Adult Education at San Francisco State University. I moved through the ranks, from assistant to full professor, from faculty member to chair of the Department of Administration and Interdisciplinary Studies, and then into my current position. As Associate Dean of Faculty Affairs in the College of Education, I am now responsible for supervising and coordinating the College of Education's Credential Services and Data Management Office, Cahill Media Resource Learning Laboratory, and Teacher Preparation Center. I serve on the College of Education's administrative cabinet, review student appeals, and serve on various administrative and community committees and subcommittees throughout the college and local school districts. I am also responsible for assisting and working with faculty in evaluating and conducting program and course reviews for submission to the California Commission on Teacher Credentials (CCTC) and the National Council for Accreditation on Teacher Education (NCATE).

As you can see, over the course of the last 12 years, I have been actively engaged in the field of adult education as an educator, writer and administrator. While the intent of this task was to provide you with a glimpse into who I am and where I have been as an adult educator and person, I think that it is also important to note that several individuals have played a significant role in my journey.

First, my mother, who plays and has played a significant role in how I write and what I write for publication. The question I ask myself, given that I am a first-generation college graduate, and moreover, I have a doctorate in adult education and I am a professor, is, Will my mother understand what I am talking about and will she say, yes your words made a difference in my perspective—not only about you, but about what you are writing about? Second, I believe that my family, my faith, and my son have challenged me on many occasions to stay on the path and to pursue my dreams. Third, my sistah-friends and colleagues, whom I have asked to review my writings and to help me stay on the path of exploring my polyrhythmic realities: Drs. Doris Flowers, Donna Amstutz, Scipio A. J. Colin, III, Juanita Johnson-Bailey, Ming-yeh Lee, Marilyn Stepney, and Barbara Ford, just to name a few. Fourth, I believe that had it not been for Dr. Ronald A. Cervero saying in my interview (I am told) for a position as a lecturer in Adult Education and consultant for the Northern Area Adult Education Center in 1986, "Hire her, she's a sleeper," and Dr. Phyllis Cunningham's willingness to take me on as a novice and challenging me to question theories, perspectives and practices with respect to their import to one's race, gender and class; and to pursue a career in the field, I might not have begun this journey. Finally, I believe that as a student and practitioner within the field of adult education that researchers/theorists and philosophers like Alice Walker, bell hooks, Patricia Hill-Collins, Carter G. Woodson, M.K. Asante, Wade Nobles, Phyllis Cunningham, Scipio A.J. Colin, III, Cyril Houle, Paulo Friere, Malcolm Knowles, Eduard Lindeman, Carl Rogers, Jack Mezirow, B.F. Skinner, Robert A. Gagne, faculty members at Northern Illinois University in Adult Education, as well as many others, have challenged me—directly and indirectly—to think about my own practice as well as my perspectives about what it means to be an adult educator. I must say thanks to all of you for helping me on this journey. As a student I was often challenged by faculty and now as a faculty member and administrator I am challenged by my colleagues and those in the African Diaspora who preceded me—to critically reflect upon who I am and how I might make a contribution within my community and society. Hopefully, I have.

Dr. Joyce Stalker

It find it rather hilarious to think that I might be in a book of "American adult educators." After all, for the last 14 years I have lived and worked in none of Canada, the USA or Mexico. Mind you, I live at the edge of the world, in New Zealand/Aotearoa, and sometimes it feels like I am more a citizen of international airports than any particular country. It also seems impossible that in the years which have whizzed by since I graduated in 1989 with my doctorate that I could be selected as a "notable" for this book. It is amusing, it is flattering and it is awkward. In Maoridom there is a saying that the *tui*[1] does not sing its own praises, but I am sufficiently egotistical to want to be part of the publication. Thus, below I present a mix of personal and professional information which I hope will help those interested in my academic work to better understand it.

I was born in 1948 in Kingston, Ontario, Canada. It was the year in which 14 members of the Scots Guard, as part of the British operation to contain and defeat Communism in post-World War II, massacred 24 unarmed Malaysian civilians and then set fire to their village. Israel declared its independence and Mahatma Gandhi, leader of the independence movement and champion of nonviolent protest in India was assassinated. In Canada, Mackenzie King retired and was succeeded by Louis St. Laurent, who extended the welfare state. In New Zealand/Aotearoa, the Maori housing scheme was established and the General Assembly of the United Nations passed the Universal Declaration on Human Rights.

I was born into a farming family in a conservative, rural area of eastern Ontario, Canada on the edge of the Bay of Quinte. I have always been acutely aware of that conservative background. Canadians are, after all, rumoured to apologize to a telephone pole if we bump into it. Andrea Dworkin might call me a "shameless hussy" who struggles to escape herself and others' imposed boundaries of restraint. Sometimes, I succeed. I remember as an undergraduate student being told that my seminar presentation was "too forceful" and as a graduate student that I was "nicer" before I started that "feminist stuff." In retrospect, those seem moments to celebrate, yet I know that there were other times when I silenced myself because of my inherent conservatism and self-doubts.

I was the third child in a family of two halves: my two older sisters and I were born in the early years of the marriage; my younger sister and two younger brothers reflected the

---

[1] An indigenous bird with a bobbling little white-feather priest's collar and a delightful song.

more affluent years of the late 1950s. I was shaped by the charitable underpinnings of my parents' involvement with the United Church (a liberal Protestant/Methodist hybrid), their unflagging belief in hard work, their interest in all things political and their involvement in the community. It was not until after they had both died in the mid-1990s that I realized how much I missed the shared laughter. Huge family gatherings around the barbeque, freshly made Chelsea buns, the race with full stomachs against aunts and uncles for the kitchen couch, waterskiing on the lake—all were done with that peculiar brand of rural Ontario humour which is both understated and quick.

I followed my two older sisters through primary and secondary schools. It was a hopeless situation as they carved out a path as bright and able. I found my niche as a usually uninterested student who was still capable of being editor of the school annual publication. My university undergraduate preferences wavered between journalism and home economics and I settled on the latter with much encouragement from my parents. For the most part, and despite my election as a student rep. to the University Senate in my final year, the Civil Rights movement, Vietnam and student unrest swirled around me. After I completed four years of science and a few exciting design courses I "went West." to British Columbia. Three years later I was married to an Australian whom I had met at the first of three UBC (University of British Columbia) summer schools. They qualified me to teach in secondary schools during the years between.

John became a physical education teacher, and together we learned to ski, take overnight hikes, snowshoe and explore the peaks and valleys of British Columbia. He had the typical Aussie desire to travel and after he graduated from UBC, we followed the sun from Vancouver to Alaska, to Central America and back again. Our approach was to work, make good money, travel until our money ran out, and then do it all again. Travel provided me with formative experiences at two levels. First, during our travels, I felt the joy and freedom of not living a 9-5 existence nor of having to tolerate the repetitive drudgery of lives which seemed to revolve around mortgages and the acquisition of furniture. I began to develop a deep cynicism for the ideology which promoted the importance of paid work and the trustworthiness of the bosses and I saw our travel as an act of resistance to those ideas.

Second, upon my return to Canada from travels, I recognized that the experiences of some Canadians paralleled the poverty and oppression within so-called "Third World" countries in Central America. I was amazed that my fellow Canadians were as proud as ever of our system, for I felt a deep shame.

Upon our return from one trip, we taught in Fort St. John, in northern BC. I taught an upgrading adult basic education course—a remedial programme designed in modularized, competency-based, individualistic units. Mostly First Nations women took the programme, which was based in White middle-class values and experiences. Their experiences of culture, tradition and language were not incorporated into the programmed units. I enthusiastically encouraged my students to complete the course and discussed with the counselor ways in which I could maintain and improve their motivation, attitudes and social skills. We inserted career counselling and resume writing sessions. There was a high completion rate among the students and we established a warm and supportive environment which we all enjoyed.

Slowly, I began to seriously question this way of working with students. I read statistical information that my First Nations' students were less likely to find work than my White students, and then I saw those statistics lived out in the experiences of my students. Simultaneously I enrolled in a life skills course. It stressed the importance of one-to-one communication and listening skills and we shared our experiences and feelings with each other endlessly, the better to facilitate it among our students when we returned to our classrooms. Somehow, it did not make sense to me. I knew these students' lives and I knew that improved communication skills were unlikely to stop their abuse and harassment by some of the local police. Basically, however, I remained pretty naïve and it wasn't until many years later that I realized that a woman student's bruised face was not from a visit to the dentist as she explained but much more likely from domestic violence.

Eventually John and I did the traditional trip to Europe via a camping trip across Canada and after 11 months of skiing, exploring and soaking up our histories, we flew to his hometown of Sydney, Australia. There I landed a job with the YWCA (Young Women's Christian Association) as director of Women's Affairs and shortly after with the State Public Service in an area devoted to EEO (Equal Employment Opportunity) and women's advancement.

In the government job, I watched bureaucrats slow EEO policy and senior administrators in various ministries and departments sabotage the implementation of EEO legislation. I unearthed statistics about women's employment relative to men and watched the newly appointed Aboriginal equity officer sit in solitary isolation at his desk. My best friends were long-time unionists who had much more astute structural analyses than I did. We ran, hiked, swam, drank good Aussie wines, laughed and talked politics together for about two years. In an era without email and cheap international phone calls, I was homesick and John, not being a typical Aussie "bloke" was comfortable to return to Canada.

In Vancouver, I began the Master in Adult Education programme at the University of British Columbia. My master's was on equal educational opportunity and when it was suggested that I go on to the doctoral programme I decided that if I lived to 80 and looked back on my life I would regret not giving it a go. However, just as I enrolled in the programme, Kjell Rubenson, my preferred supervisor, was offered the first chair of adult education in Sweden and decided to return there. Newly out of my marriage, I asked to follow him and his family to study with him there. He was immensely helpful and with the aid of a scholarship, I spent about four months in Sweden, basically at the University of Linkoping. With his help, I attended many other adult education events around the country. When I returned to UBC, I was a much stronger, more forthright student, my voice fostered by the collegial relationships with top-flight Swedish academics. When Kjell and his family returned to Vancouver, I was able to continue with him as my chief supervisor.

The UBC adult education programme at the time had its pluses and minuses. On the plus side, there were three key elements. First, there was a fantastic group of women like Shauna Butterwick, Jane Munro, Jane Dawson, Sue Collard—all much stronger and wiser feminists than I was. Second, there was an assumption that students would attend AERC, the annual adult education research conference—and many of us did. This gave us an excellent start to our academic careers and a good understanding of how to play the game.

On the minus side, the programme had two main flaws. First, it was located geographically on the margins of the UBC campus. This meant that the possibilities of taking women's studies or sociology courses were distant both in real terms and intellectually. Maybe it wasn't even possible to take them within the regulations—I just know I didn't consider it. Second, the programme of those years was dominated by male academics and feminist analysis was lacking. This is difficult territory, for certainly I benefited from those men's support and encouragement—and who knows, maybe I became a better feminist for having to find my own way in the literature. However, I think it is fair to say that the programme at that time was not gender sensitive.

In 1989, I took my fresh doctorate across the mountains to the University of Calgary to a job with the Faculty of Continuing Education. The backcountry was wonderful: skiing at Sunshine Village, hiking into new valleys, listening to sorrowful country and western songs as I drove across the foothills. Catherine Warren, a good feminist with a great sense of humour and strong sociological analysis, became a supportive colleague and playmate. Professionally it was not so comfortable. There was a sexual harassment case in process, complete with stories with which I was already too familiar; the job was part academic and part programme planning, and the mix had little appeal to me. I jumped at the chance to apply for a fully academic position at the University of Waikato in the North Island of New Zealand/Aotearoa.

In February 1991, my dad and I drove from Calgary to Vancouver on black ice, I farewelled my Mom and twenty-plus hours later arrived in Auckland. Within 24 hours I was swimming in pristine waters at a white-shell beach on a sunny day.

My life in New Zealand/Aotearoa has been shaped primarily by two things: a relationship and the unique nature of the country. My relationship with Michael Law has had a profound effect on me. It has, of course, kept me in New Zealand/Aotearoa as he shared in the raising of his three boys, but the particular nature of the man has also been important to me. I first knew Michael as a student at UBC and we reconnected when I came down to New Zealand/Aotearoa. He had been deeply involved with the anti-apartheid movement, anti-Vietnam movement, workers' rights, unions, Communism and student movements – often in leadership positions. My parents never knew all of that but accepted him for his gentle ways, hearty appetite and ability to make a cup of tea properly. For me, he has been the only person in my life who has told me that I should be MORE stroppy, MORE opinionated, and MORE angry. As a new immigrant, I had the opportunity to reinvent myself and his encouragement/chastisement dovetailed nicely with the vision I had of who I wanted to become. In addition, he had a clever, fast wit and was fun to be with.

Because Michael was a respected adult educator of many years standing in New Zealand/Aotearoa, and also worked at the University of Waikato, I sometimes stood in his shadow in those early years. Gradually, however, through our deliberate decisions to have overlapping but separate, noncompeting, academic careers, he shifted his focus to unions and adult education and I focused on feminism and adult education.

Recently I said to Michael that when I got him, I didn't just get a man, I got a lifestyle. New Zealand/Aotearoa is a unique country and it has given me a particularly rich environment within which to establish myself as an academic. It has three elements which are particularly relevant here: marginality and bicultural and political contexts.

First, the marginality of this country has presented both barriers and freedoms I could never have anticipated. In the first instance, it has been difficult to keep up with the trends, literature and new ideas at the centre. This was particularly so in the early years. It is less so now with Google and library e-collections, but the major publishers are still located in the USA and UK. I realized early on that if I wanted to get back to a job in Canada, then I had to be very, very visible. Thus, I began a habit of presenting at one, and sometimes two, conferences a year in the Northern Hemisphere. Often those papers were developed into journal articles.

Most of these academic forays included some annual leave and a visit to Vancouver where my parents had relocated. As they became more ill, the visits became rushed emergencies. I learned that it was possible to cry all the way from Auckland to Los Angeles only to find out that modern medicine in Canada had saved a parent once again. After Mom and Dad both died in 1994, the impetus to go back to Canada did not lessen. Reunions with sisters and brothers were equally important. Attending conferences continued as a way of life and Michael and I selected ones which suited us both, so we could go to them together. It paid off. I was invited onto the boards of journals, I was asked to contribute to books, and we made and sustained warm friendships with academics who visited our home and slept on the living room foldout couch.

Marginality in a small country like New Zealand/Aotearoa also has meant an academic career without the energy and stimulation that comes from a large number of colleagues in your backyard in the same area of research. On the other hand, it meant that I became involved with the grassroots and community organizations in New Zealand/Aotearoa.

Marginality also has some clear benefits. Since I have been marginal to the discourses in the field, I have been able to choose to opt in and out of them. I have developed an outsider's view of issues and feel like I do not fit either in the Northern academic world or in the Down Under world. As a result, my work has tended to have a global, international and more abstract approach—and thus was publishable in both worlds.

My marginality has also connected me to others in special ways. I think that partly as a result of my location I have had opportunities to work with UNESCO, UNESCO Institute of Education, the Gender Education Office of ICAE (International Council for Adult Education) and ASPBAE (Asia South Pacific Bureau of Adult Education) in Thailand, India, and Brazil.

The second characteristic of this country which has influenced me and my work is its unique context. In the first instance, it is bicultural. From the first day, I have had to learn what partnership with Maori means. I have struggled with protocols which prevent women from carving or speaking on most *marae*.[2] I have tried to include relevant materials for my students yet not presume to know about their experiences, or indeed about much at all in New Zealand/Aotearoa. I have enjoyed the special moments of song and spirituality which seem to be a part of this land's *wairua*.[3] I treasure our slower pace of life, sustained in the

---

[2] focal point of settlement.

[3] spirit.

face of pressures from consumerism imported via cable TV channels, American fast food outlets and offshore investments.

In the second instance, New Zealand/Aotearoa has a distinctive and highly visible political system and this heightened my socio-political analysis. When I arrived in New Zealand/Aotearoa, it was in the grasp of the New Right agenda. It resulted in funding cutbacks to education, the vocationalization of education, an increased competition for jobs and the privatization of many state assets and responsibilities. The impact of that political stance was absolutely clear and had a particularly devastating effect on women. Eventually, in 1996, the people had had enough of the devastation of the foundations of "God's own country" and brought in a center-left government. Led by Helen Clarke, that government attempts to balance social-democratic and new-right ideals.

The past 15 years in New Zealand/Aotearoa have sharpened my feminism. I've watched as others shifted to postmodern analysis and wondered why I still sound like a socialist/Marxist/reductionist feminist. I can identify three peak experiences which drove me into that kind of analysis. First, I have lived the last 15 years surrounded by a Kiwi male culture of sport (particularly rugby), endless swearing, boy racers and binge drinking. Canadian hockey, lacrosse and drug use sound like they would have given me a similar context, but it is the intensity and normalization of this Kiwi male culture which sets it apart.

Second, I have had the good fortune to participate in workshops, fora and seminars with women from many of the countries in Africa, Asia and South America. I also have spent three months teaching at the University of Botswana. From the women in those places, I heard their stories of working with women who were raped as the army went north and then again as they retreated south, with women who were trafficked between countries as "nannies," of women struggling against multinationals who wanted to dam their valley. I was humbled by the courage and determination of the adult educators and the women with whom they worked. A conversation about complexities wasn't really helpful—the issue was really pretty simple—how to stop, immediately, all forms of violence against women.

The third element which sharpened by feminism was the continuing publication of articles about barriers to women in tertiary education—many of which seemed like the same old, same old to me. Given my experiences, misogyny (hatred of women) made a lot more sense to me. Many of the women I interviewed for the misogyny article told stories which had me angry and in tears after we parted. I sometimes phoned Michael to de-fuse —often with, "How can you men be such bastards?" I was furious that all men, regardless of their gentleness and sensitivity are oppressors. I was angry that hours of my intellectual and personal struggle to have such issues heard were reduced to a few moments at a conference, in a tea room, in which men, and sometimes women, listened and showed their understanding, yet it all seemed to stop there.

I was, of course, struck by the irony of my situation—living with, loving and seeking support from a man while I wrote about men's hatred of women. Finally, I knew that I needed a break from the anger and frustration. I wanted a new research project but I knew that I couldn't make an intellectual decision and leap into it. I knew it had to come to me. I made head space for it and continued to sew, run, tramp and boogie board in the surf.

Eventually, the penny dropped into place. We were in a pleasant Greek restaurant in the middle of the mile-long strip of restaurants which fill Melbourne's Lygon Street. The four of us were good mates—two couples with a fondness for good meals and lively political discussions whenever Michael and I travel "across the ditch" to Aussie. Somewhere between the moussaka and the karidopita, the conversation turned to the Pinochet 1980s regime in Chile and somehow I made casual reference to the arpilleras created during those years. Small woven and quilted pieces, they told graphically of the atrocities practiced by Pinochet's army. When they were smuggled through borders under the very noses of the oppressors, these pieces of "ladies' work" generated no suspicion yet alerted the 'more developed' world media to the horrors of the citizens' day to day lives.

To my amazement, our friends were not familiar with *arpilleras*. I knew that if these politically aware and well-read activists did not know of them that many others also would have overlooked them. Thus began my search for how women use fabric art/craft work to make political messages.

The area is a wonderful convergence of my undergraduate degree in textiles science and design, my commitment to social justice and my feminist stance. My work has been enhanced by a funded joint research project on community arts/crafts with Darlene Clover at the University of Victoria, BC, Canada. That relationship has resulted in papers, a quilt show in Auckland of Canadian and New Zealand/Aotearoa political quilts, a special issue of *Convergence* (in press), visits back to Canada and lots of laughter. As one might expect, of course, the project has come full circle to misogyny; women often use fabric arts/crafts to say things which are unsafe to articulate with their voices; political quilts often deal with the violences against women, and so on and so on.

Now 58, I am a Kiwi associate professor,[4] and retirement is within sight. That prospect has made me pause and re-think my research. The creativity which surrounds my research has encouraged me to play with ways to and present my work. I am planning exhibits in lieu of publications. I'm working with the New Zealand/Aotearoa Human Rights Commission to establish an HRC Challenge for political quilts at the 2007 Biannual New Zealand/Aotearoa Quilt Symposium. I have a dream that it will become a permanent event.

I've also realized that I have become a role model for some younger women academics who know me. I'm encouraged by the vibrancy, enthusiasm and outspoken-ness of many of them. I'm impressed by their ability to stand their ground and challenge sexism when they experience it, by their willingness to interact collegially with both men and women, by their concern for racism, the environment and homophobia as well as for women. I want to encourage them to push the boundaries of what and how they research and to claim the academy in their own terms.

Most importantly, I want to encourage them to do a better job of being a "responsible academic" than I did. Too much of my life since entering the academy has been dominated by my paid work. Some time ago I wrote a poem which captured my frustration with the way I was living my life and the difficulty I was having controlling my overwork:

---

[4] Professor in the North American system.

Death of an Academic
Or
They Don't Put It on Your Tombstone

Dr. Alma Joyce Stalker (1948-TBA)

BHSC (University of Guelph)
Med (University of British Columbia)
EdD (University of British Columbia)

BELOVED CONTRIBUTOR
(to refereed journals, books, newletters and reports)

FAITHUL MEMBER
(of editorial boards of national and international journals)

DEVOTED PARTICIPANT
(of regional, national and international conferences)

CHERISHED LEADER
(of University, School, Department and professional committees)

SHE WILL BE MUCH MISSED.

The poem tried to capture how I was living my life as if all the things I did in my paid work life would go on my tombstone. I know that is not true. I know that in the end, it will say only something like: "Beloved partner of…," "Dear sister and daughter." Currently, I'm trying to restructure my life and model for new academics a more sane, healthy and joyful way to reflect that reality. A Maori proverb captures the essence of it:

Ha aha te mea nui o te ao?
He tangata, he tangata, he tangata.

What is the most important thing in the world?
It is people, it is people, it is people.

In conclusion, I need to point out that I never intended to be "notable." I simply wanted to make a difference. I hope that my work, both as a published scholar and as a teacher, provokes thought and legitimizes those who are frustrated at the continuing reality of most women's situations. I hope that it stimulates readers to speak out against those situations, to awaken others to them, and to act to create a better world.

Kia ora.

Alan Thomas

I had lunch with Roby Kidd in the autumn of 1952. He offered me a position at the Canadian Association for Adult Education (CAAE) in Toronto. I never looked back from that meeting.

I knew nothing about Adult education in Canada, or really anywhere else, though I had a glimpse of Adult education at Teachers' College at Columbia (1951). But only a glimpse. Adult Education was a new world for me. Canadians I met there were labour educators, businessmen, professionals, academics, and all varieties of competent women. In Canada, as in other countries, adult education in Canada was a "cause" and the CAAE was its heart and mind, and a life for me.

I met my wife, JoAnne at the CAAE; we married in 1955, just before we went back to Teachers' College, where I had fellowship from the Fund for Adult Education. I was an old hand as a student, and I was able to teach the Social Foundations course with Sloan Wayland in the summer of 1955.

University of British Columbia, Vancouver

In the next year we went to Vancouver to the University of British Columbia(UBC). In the next few years we had four children: Alan, the firefighter; Matthew, the opera singer; Rachel, the trombonist; and Martha, the chartered accountant. JoAnne died in 2004, just before our fiftieth anniversary.

I was determined to replace Roby Kidd when he retired. I knew that you couldn't lead a national, voluntary organization before you lived in some other part of Canada other than Toronto. JoAnne and I moved to Vancouver in 1956 to take a divided position with the new College of Education and the Department of Extension. I liked the adult educators at UBC. I liked my job. I lived essentially in the Department of Extension, which was more exciting, and where I could do the job of adult education, that I had learned in a short time, at the CAAE. UBC was a young university, recovering from the Second World War, anticipating the enormous boom in education that lasted through the fifties and sixties. The "establishment" was concerned with the education of the young, and there were a lot of them. The "baby-boom" generation, with its numerate power, marched behind me all my life. But the veterans, who had learned so much about the "martial arts" during the war, and likely to be forgotten as in World War I, were not to be denied their "continuing education" through their lives. UBC was an original "land-grant" college and continued supporting the Department of Extension until the seventies. Then, in Canada, the bloom was off for the financing of formal education. I was involved with many projects during my six years at UBC, including programs for private broadcasters in British Columbia. But the program which had lasting effect was the creation of the first, full-time program for adult educators in Canada. The support of Neville Scarfe, the Dean of Education, and John Friesen, the Director of the Extension Department, made the project easy to accomplish.

The Canadian Association of Adult Education

The call came from the CAAE in 1960. Roby Kidd knew, as I learned also, you can stay too long as director of a voluntary organization. I thought that I should go home from a self-imposed exile. But because of my earlier manifestation at CAAE, the executive committee didn't completely trust me, and I was teamed with a co-director, until half-way through the first year, when the CAAE had financial difficulties. The co-director resigned, and I was the captain of my own ship with eight staff members. I learned quickly that the CAAE was always in financial difficulties, and that, as director, more than half of my time was raising money-mostly from the federal government. Because it was "project money" and Canada was without a national educational body until the 1970s, my imagination was free to imagine anything.

The sixties lay before me. They were restive, turbulent, and exciting. Canada was awakening; the "quiet revolution" in Quebec was beginning, the women's movement was emerging; and there were two chickens in every pot.

The CAAE was founded in 1935 from a meeting in Toronto of the relatively few adult educators in Canada. It was founded as a "clearinghouse" for adult education. The first director was Ned Corbett, the second Roby Kidd; I became the third director in 1962. Ned Corbett was impatient with the idea of a clearinghouse and created several "national" programs: Farm Radio Forum, Citizens Forum, involving in both projects a liaison with the Canadian Broadcasting Corporation with regular radio broadcasts, discussions, pamphlets, and feedback. The third staple organization was the Joint Planning Commission (1947-1968). Born out of the Wartime Information Board, it involved three annual meetings, in Toronto, Ottawa, and Montreal, for the representatives of national voluntary organizations. It was a purely Canadian organization; it never had a formal membership, it never passed a motion, it never had a constitution, it just existed for 21 years. But Ned Corbett and Roby Kidd saw the JPC as a citizenship-building dynamo for all of Canada, except for the Province of Quebec.

I was determined to make the CAAE a voice of adult education in Canada and a radical member of the establishment, not only the educational establishment. In 1961, I was a key speaker of the first National Conference of Adult Education, in Ottawa. I spoke about the "learning society" and its implications for Canadian society. I had been distinguishing "education," which had been the mantra since 1945, from "learning."

There were lots of national conferences and Royal Commissions in the sixties. The former included two on education, labour educators, the environment, health, the family, and youth, among others. The latter included the status of women, health, taxation, and the Commission on Bilingualism and Biculturalism. National conferences were relatively new in Canada; Royal Commissions were relatively common whenever the national government had a big problem to solve. The interesting fact about commissions and national conferences was they set national agendas for thirty years. We made briefs for all the Royal Commissions, sometimes participated in them, and finally published shorter versions of the text and distributed them nationally. The Royal Commission on Health, establishing the health system in Canada, was 1,100 pages. When we published a shorter version, by our principal précis writer, Elizabeth Wilson, the chairman read it and said, "I didn't discover anything you left out."

The profession of adult educators was growing and proliferating. When I was at CAAE, I knew almost all the adult educators in Canada. In the eighties I didn't know half of them. CAAE tried to keep pace with all of them, as we had in the forties and fifties, but we never became a professional organization like the AEA. They tended to cling to their parent organization, like the Universities, the Colleges, the School Boards, and Health, which was largest growth of numbers of adult educators in the nineties.

I tried to create a new organization for the CAAE. Originally, it was a loose organization with a membership that started in 1960-61 at 676 and went to 1,266 and 112 organizations in 1968-69. Any individual or organization could join. The new plan was to organize the provinces into divisions and try to make sense of the finances where all the money flowed to the Toronto office and the divisions got a fixed amount. It didn't work because each province had a separate amount they could raise in the good years. The CAAE abandoned the division model in 1970. I was good at project-money raising, but I was not good at the maintenance of such complicated structure.

The last project was establishing a new organization for the community colleges. in Canada. The community colleges were called different names in different provinces, like the Colleges of Applied Arts and Technology (CAAT) in Ontario. I liked the model because it was a different route to a postsecondary education from the universities. The colleges promised to attract adults as students. The colleges in Canada grew in the 1960s, and by the end there was at least one in every province. The colleges created a new generation of students. In 1967, students of a new college in Toronto marched four miles to celebrate the Minister of Education. Given the student revolt in that decade, I expect the Minister was very surprised.

I raised $202,800 from the Kellogg Foundation for a three-year grant, the largest grant that CAAE ever received. We created the National Commission for the Community Colleges and gave rise, three years later, to the Association of Canadian Community Colleges which still exists. The difficult part was creating a new, independent organization, but I had done it before for the University Extension group and for the Guidance and Counseling Association.

In 1996, there were lots of "white papers" from the federal government. Thinking about a new thrust, I wrote and published, with CAAE colleagues, a new white paper, on "learning." We planned the release of it with all the professional media-like craft. We assigned all the education system, level by level, to concentrate on learning rather than teaching. It didn't create the revolution we wanted, but in the eighties and nineties "learning" was the mantra.

The Province of Quebec was assigned, in the fifties, to a committee of CAAE because it was a "distinct" province; the Quebecoise centrally used the French language rather the English language. When the Quiet Revolution broke out in Quebec in the sixties, the province began a new "national" organization for adult education, the Institute Canadien d'Education des Adultes (ICEA). They were determined to be independent. We tried joint conferences. Some of them worked. We tried to be equal with ICEA and approached them with a plan to persuade the federal government to give an annual grant. That was successful and worked until 1991, when the federal government, struggling with a deficit, cut most subsidies to voluntary organizations. The greatest success was for the Centennial (1967), when the CAAE and the ICAE created a North American Conference for Adult Education, including Mexico and the United States. The Quebecoise wanted some other language, Spanish, to be present at the North American Conference, and it worked. I and the director of ICAE went to Mexico City several times to persuade the Mexicans, who weren't sure they were part of North America. The recent trade agreement between Canada, the USA, and Mexico suggests that they, indeed, are part of North America, and the conference was ahead of its time.

Before I left the CAAE I was invited by the Commonwealth Foundation to go to East Africa to help adult educators. I had never been to Africa. I decided to take my family, JoAnne, Alan (7), Matthew (5), and Rachel (Under 2). We left in 1967, Centennial Year, to spend three months in Uganda, Kenya, Zambia, Malawi, and Tanzania. We got home in April, after a week surveying "community colleges" in England and Scotland for the Commission. The children were a passport to meeting communities and other children everywhere we went. I met many groups of potential adult educators. There were a group of sergeants that had to train their troops in Zambia; a number of elementary teachers who were seconded to the secondary schools in Malawi; I taught at many teacher training institutes throughout East Africa which had been a kind of federation, though they were at that time splitting apart. I don't know whether we did much good, but we learned a lot about East Africa. We left with a very optimistic view of the countries of East Africa. Then the "oil monopoly" raised prices continually over the next many years and the countries of East Africa were devastated.

The Federal Government

In 1969 I had an invitation to be an executive assistant to a Minister in the first Trudeau government. I went from a small poverty-stricken national education organization to a big, wealthy organization: the Federal Government, where you "couldn't see the edge of it." The Minister was the Assistant Secretary-of-State, and the next year, the Minister of Communications. There I was not the "captain of my ship" (I was never that again in my professional life). There was a lot of "voluntariness" at the top of government. Ministers' change inadvertently, and the minister's staff change at the same rate. I had eight staff with two offices, one on Parliament Hill and the other in downtown Ottawa. Other ministers had a much bigger staff. I was the supervisor of the staff anywhere they were. The minister's secretary was in the parliament office, the constituency man was in Toronto, most of the time, where the minister's riding was.

There was power, which I got used to, and secrecy. Actually, I didn't know what was secret in the Minister's office and what was not, so the result was I didn't say anything in public. I liked the Minister, I think I was older than him. You didn't know whether, when you were standing in for him, you were representing the power he had or being your own self, a "flunky." I learned about large organizations and the ubiquity of political power. I didn't do a lot for adult education because, on the surface of it, education was a provincial responsibility at that time jealously guarded. When the federal government learned about "learning" in the eighties and nineties, they were much freer to speak about education. I stayed about two years, helping the Minister through two portfolios, and then went to Toronto, to the Ontario Institute for Studies in Education (OISE). An executive assistant to a Minister was paid only what the member of parliament was, about $18,000. When I went to OISE I was paid twice that amount, benefiting from the inflation in professors' salaries and in formal education in Canada.

The Ontario Institute for Studies in Education

I went to OISE as chairman of the Department of Adult Education. OISE was founded in 1965, and the Department of Adult Education was founded the next year. It was the smallest department at the OISE; 25 years later it was the biggest. I stayed as chairman of the department nine years and then reverted to a faculty member for the next 22 years. A future faculty member of OISE named the new institute Ontario Institute for Studies in Education. He wanted to avoid any acronym. Knowing what students do to full titles, "OYSIE" was inevitable.

I loved the work at OISE: administration, teaching, and research. It was a new organization with new people learning about each other and a splendid open atmosphere. It grew very quickly and had a new pristine building with all the electronic appurtenances, like central film projection to each classroom. They were rarely used.

The organizing of the administration of OISE was a rigorous democracy. There were regular plenaries which faculty, administration, and staff attended. There were endless committees; democracy takes a lot of time. When we became part of the University of Toronto, a small part of a big university, the democracy declined and it became like a standard graduate department.

In the Department of Adult Education we had open offices, divided by movable partitions, and no doors. It was far from the government and its "padded baise doors." It was hard to have secrets, so we went to lunch privately. I guess most people don't like an open décor. In twenty years it was all private offices with doors.

The two rituals, annually, were admitting new students and looking for faculty. We had four programs, M.Ed., M.A., Ed.D. and Ph.D. Adult education was new in a graduate faculty. We had to design all the courses. There was a great growth of adult education graduate departments in the USA and Canada in the sixties and seventies. Some of them disappeared in the nineties. Why adult education should be at the graduate level I never knew! Now there are two undergraduate programs in Adult Education in Canada, and the community colleges have diplomas and certificates in Adult Education which are shorter and more practical.

In teaching, I thought that as chairman of Adult Education I should teach the introductory course. That way I could be in touch with the entering students, with all their knowledge of practical adult education. I did that for thirty years, until I discovered that my references were too distant even for graduate students.

In research I decided that adult education in Canada was only faintly described. I set out to describe it more fully with more clarity. Some of my colleagues joined me. I was interested in large programs that had grown during the sixties and seventies, like adult education in the military, labour unions, industry, and later the enormous growth in health. The first project was describing the in-house programs of adult education in some representative industries. I chose Bell Telephone, Ward Air (defunct), the Canadian Broadcasting Corporation and Marks & Spenser. I discovered that among our existing students that we had a vice-president of training for Bell Canada, a head stewardess of Ward Air, and an existing board member of Marks & Spenser. There is lot that you can do with adult graduate students. Those results were privately published.

The Canadian government had started to support adult education in the labour movement in Canada. I was asked to evaluate the program twice. There were several labour federations in Canada. I decided that I couldn't do the Quebec unions because I wasn't satisfactorily fluent in French, but I evaluated the two federations in English Canada.

I was interested in law and adult education. Fortunately I had a graduate from the Law Faculty at the University of Toronto pursuing his M.Ed. degree. Between the two of us, we published a pamphlet, "Accidents Will Happen," about teachers and accidents which became a "best-seller" for an educational book.

In later years we were asked by the federal officer to evaluate the educational program of the Canadian Correctional System. We used a model developed by the OECD to evaluate the education in member countries. I had a familiarity with that model because I was invited by the OECD to evaluate Finland's education system. The model involved a first explanation from the host who described and evaluated the prison educational system. Second, a committee of us, including adult educators from OISE and from other universities, visited a dozen federal prisons in Canada and wrote a report. Third, the prison system replied in writing. It is a good system of evaluation when dealing with independent countries who are always sensitive about their own education. I learned a lot about the federal prison system in Canada, and I learned particularly that prisons are communities that ordinary citizens are basically ignorant of.

In 1991 I published a book called *Beyond Education: A New Perspective on Society's Management of Learning,* published by Jossey-Bass, adult education's publisher in the United States. It was drawn from all the research I had done in the previous 20 years.

Lastly, I became interested in prior learning assessment (PLA). I learned about it in the sixties, when a pamphlet was published about Brooklyn College's introduction of PLA. I never forgot the anecdote that Brooklyn College published in the pamphlet, about a woman who left high school before she graduated but was traveled, mature, and had taken part in America's highest endeavours. The author said that if we had denied her entrance to Brooklyn College, we had denied Eleanor Roosevelt. I taught about PLA, wrote about PLA and its stellar method of developing "portfolios," but I had never written a portfolio until last year. It was an extraordinary experience, especially for me.

Conclusion

When I encountered adult education in my twenties, one of the tasks we had to accomplish was to persuade adult people that they could learn. Unfortunately, one of the "I.Q. tests" in the twenties or thirties spread the word that adults couldn't learn, at least they couldn't learn anything important. Now, the research results tell us that adults can learn anything they wish, with appropriate time, entering education at any time they wish to or need to. I had a marvelous life in pursuing adult education and convinced myself that "education floats on a turbulent sea of learning."

Susan Ann Timm, Ed.D.

Roots

"What does that sign mean?" I remember asking while staring at the words over the department store's water fountain. Although I can't recall exactly how old I was, I know that I was mature enough to read the words. Why were these two words so confusing? They just didn't seem to make any sense. I read the sign out loud, stretching my mind, thinking of all the possibilities. The words remain vivid in my mind in spite of all the years—Whites Only!

My older sister recalls crying as our mom entered a laundromat with all six of us children in tow. "Whatever is the problem?" my mom wanted to know. Through sobs, Jenny expressed her grief over not being able to wash her new green pants. "Why would you think that?" my mom asked her. As our gazes followed the little girl's outstretched finger, we saw she was pointing to a sign—"No Coloreds."

As I grew up in the Deep South, these and other such dominating signs confronted me often. Their words served as my first lessons in social inequalities, even though I never came to know the true depth of their insinuation until I was an adult, if indeed one can ever fully grasp their true meaning without having been on the losing end of the oppression. Adult education opened my eyes to more of these signs as well as to concerns for social justice and equality—too many more than most people would ever want to know. Indeed, ignorance can be bliss. Or as John Lennon wrote, "Living is easy with eyes closed." Once confronted, however, we must choose how we will react. And now a new sign has become etched in my heart: If you aren't enraged, you aren't informed!

Even at a young age, my awareness of discrimination was being heightened both by the environment in which I was living and because of my mom's insistence. All six of us, my siblings and me, were born in Texas. My dad was also a Texan. My mom, on the other hand, was a Yankee, a damn New England one at that, and people just wouldn't let her forget that fact. Although others were being derogatory, Theresa would often brag about that label, as if it were some badge of courage. As I look back on that day and time, I do believe it was.

My mom was quite feisty, especially considering she wasn't even quite five feet tall; I can remember her telling us children how stupid all those signs were, and she would make special efforts to strike up conversations with Black women when we were out in public. She never discouraged us from playing with the Mexican children who seemed to always be at the farm next door to where we lived at one point. Only after her death did I learn of my mother's own Hispanic roots. Did that make her more sensitive to others? Did that ancestry touch me in the same special way? I can only guess that they indeed did.

When John Howard Griffith published his real-life experiences of becoming "Black" in the Deep South, I was about six years old. Although I didn't read the book myself until many years later, I began to realize what my mom was telling us all along—something was very wrong with the signs of our time.

When I think back on my life and reflect on why and how I became involved in advocating what I call the e-philosophies of adult education—equality, education, emancipation—many of these images come back to my mind. We must keep them at the forefront in hopes of stopping history from repeating itself and in an effort of trying to alter the course of the future.

Enduring Traveler

Growing up, we didn't seem to live in one place for too long. At first, we moved around quite a bit because of the lack of funds. My dad said that he never rented from anyone who required a lease. So if he could find a place that was less expensive, we would go there, even if we had just moved the month before. Through it all, my dad managed to stay in college, eventually graduating with two bachelor's degrees while working full time and feeding six children. Later, the pull of a steady income and housing and food allowances brought my dad back into the military, where he had once served. So now we began moving when my dad would get stationed at a new base, which for a while was just about every two years.

When I was young, we moved to Spain. I remember that everyone had a maid. In that way, we were helping the Spanish economy, or so we were told. Since then, my heart has been opened to the plight of many domestic workers around the world and in the U.S.—forced to be adults at an all-too-young age—who are, in reality, part of the new slave trade.

In Spain, we hired Maria, an older teenager, who was born into that vocation and who could never leave her lot in life, or so she and her family believed. We befriended Maria, who became just like one of the family. I recall one day, we all piled in an old station wagon and drove for several hours to take Maria to see her parents, whom she hadn't seen in many years. They lived in something that looked like a cave, with dirt floors. The adults all stooped to go inside. We heard the story of how Maria's father had once worked in a university, until someone who had come into power threw all the "intellectuals" out of the cities.

When the time came for us to head back to the States, my parents pleaded with Maria to come with us. They assured her that she could go to school and learn a new trade. They would support her as if she were one of their own children. But Maria could not imagine breaking free of the bonds that held her to the lower social class to which she was cast. She simply accepted her fate. I can't help but think that many others in bondage feel the same way, those controlled by those in authority through abusive work and personal relationships, drugs, etc.

When I was in middle school, we moved to Happy Valley–Goose Bay, Labrador, south of the Arctic Circle. As we arrived in July, snow was falling. Two distinct populations lived that far north—those living on the U.S. and Canadian bases and the inhabitants of an

Indian village, referred to by those of us in uniform, including the U.S. government, who used the label in the 2000 Census, as "Eskimos." Sure makes you wonder why groups of people are not free to choose their own labels even today in the "Land of the Free."

Two years later, we moved to Upper State New York, way up north in the Adirondack Mountains, just south of the Canadian border. I later learned that this area is one of the major economically depressed areas of the U.S. The scenery was spectacular; the poverty, sickening.

My Formation as an Educator

My father valued education and constantly told us children that we would all go to college one day. My mother, on the other hand, didn't believe that education was a priority; for us women, getting married was the goal. Keep in mind that we didn't even have girls' sports in high school until my senior year when, finally, Title IX was passed. My mother had gone to dress designer school before she married. As we grew, she made all of our clothes and prepared homemade meals every day. She even baked all of our bread. She was the model housewife.

Even so, I always remember my mom working outside the home to help supplement my dad's meager income. When we lived in Texas, she was a cosmetic dealer. When we moved to New York, she owned a small ceramic shop, and her business grew to the point that she became a distributor of supplies. Since she was a "working" woman, I thought she would appreciate my desire to continue my education past high school. When I expressed an interest in going to college, however, my mother simply said that if I were to go, I should take courses that would make me a good wife—"You should major in home economics," she said.

In addition, none of my older siblings went or stayed in college. I'm the fifth of six children—three brothers and one sister were born before me. My older sister did start college, but she didn't finish. Instead, she married, and they moved to an area where no colleges were conveniently located. So for a while, she stopped going to college. All three of my brothers went into the military right out of high school. So I was the first in my immediate family to graduate from college. Since then, all of us have graduated with at least an associate's degree!

My father served in Vietnam during my junior year in high school, an important year for college preparation. My mom didn't even talk about college, although my older sister was a senior in high school at that time. She checked out colleges with her friends.

In the meantime, almost all of the girls in my high school had "getting married" as their goals. Many were married right out of high school, if they even graduated, and they usually had children immediately, if not before getting married.

At the time I was growing up, the overarching view of society was that women should concentrate on getting married and having children. Going to college was viewed as a luxury, not a necessity, especially for women who most likely wouldn't be working outside the home anyway. And if you had to work, you couldn't afford to be in college.

Even so, some of my female classmates only had getting an MRS. degree in mind. They thought that college was a great place to find a good husband. As soon as they could, they'd drop out and get married. Thus, the new sign in front of me—No Women—was prevalent in many educational and career opportunities.

When trying to decide about pursuing college, I couldn't help but think life had to have more—so much to learn and experience—and I thought college would help me to discover these new things, and indeed, it has exposed me to so many more things than most people can imagine. Some of the things that I have learned are far from pleasant—the realities and horrors of discrimination, for instance. Even now, I strongly believe that adult education can be a great equalizer.

State University of New York at Plattsburgh

Since junior high, I became involved in communication-related areas of study. I quickly learned that although challenging, the ability to speak to others with perceived confidence is powerful and that words impact people dramatically. At first, I wasn't sure what I should study in college. Eventually, I earned both my bachelor's and master's degrees in communication studies from the State University of New York (SUNY) at Plattsburgh. My dad was concerned about what I could do with this degree. Although I wasn't certain myself, I felt determined that if I were pursuing something that I enjoyed doing, a job would come along eventually. In eighth grade, I had become involved in forensics, competitive speech and debate, and I continued that involvement all the way through my master's degree when I served as an assistant coach in individual events.

Because we were at a remote base in Happy Valley–Goose Bay and then lived in the isolated North Country whose economy was boosted by the local Air Force base, I was not affected by student riots and protests against the Vietnam War that were otherwise happening across the country. The local media was conservative as well. I only saw hippies once, other than on television, when in 1968 we traveled through the San Francisco neighborhood of Haight Ashbury when in California for one of my brother's wedding. Consequently, other than issues related to the dire poverty of some of the residents of Upper State New York, the larger, more controversial political issues of the country evaded me at this time.

Northern Illinois University

My academic pursuits at Northern Illinois University (NIU) started in the Department of Management in the prestigious College of Business, where I began doctoral studies. For years, I had been conducting communication seminars in business and industry, so the doctorate in education for business seemed to be a perfect fit. My area of focus within the department was training and development. Since we had to select a cognate outside of the College of Business, I chose adult education in the College of Education because I viewed it as being similar to training and development. Ironically, in many ways, these two areas proved to be the opposite of each other, yet in some ways they were very much the same. For example, I noticed that faculty within the Business Education and Adult Education departments were more down to earth and caring than some of their academic counterparts in other areas across the campus. Neither one of these two groups of educators was elitist, which was quite refreshing for me.

Adult education put my thoughts and words into theories and resurrected my concerns for social justice and equality. I was introduced to social theory and educational reform through the classic writings of the great adult educators, Paulo Freire (1973) and bell hooks (1994). I really couldn't seem to get enough from my adult education classes, which always left me wanting more. One NIU adult education professor, Paul Ilsley, stressed that to truly grow and learn, we had to stretch ourselves beyond our comfort zones. He really challenged me to look at a more liberal view, and my learning escalated substantially because of his insistence. The learning guru Bob Smith challenged us to learn how we learn and to facilitate others through the process so that they, in turn, could be empowered. The concepts were invigorating,

In my business classes, I brought forth some of the ideas from adult education, which resulted in some lively discussions from those focused more on management's perspective than on the workers'. My business education professors, Jolene Scriven and Betty Schroeder, especially, pushed me to continue to advocate on behalf of the working class, many of whom we would eventually be teaching through vocational education programs in the schools. Interestingly, both departments taught about the value of experiential learning as opposed to the outdated lecture model. I was able to share with my business education counterparts many of the learning theories and empowering methodologies that I gathered in the adult education camp.

In one of my first adult education classes, I teamed up with Keith Armstrong to engage in some independent learning activities related to diversity, the topic that I had felt compelled to study since I could remember. Between his prolific ideas and my more extroverted persona, we worked well together; we eventually pursued several divergent projects, the findings of which we began to present at conferences and in publications.

My husband is a retired, blue-collar worker. Chuck's association with the Teamsters provided me with a unique insight into the unions about which both colleges taught. The College of Business tended to focus on management's perspective, whereas adult education strived to put forth the struggles of the working class. Ironically, Chuck is the one who urged me to earn a doctorate degree. He offered me encouragement and financial support if I wanted to pursue this educational opportunity. Because Chuck was the adult learner whom so many of us wanted to reach, he served as a sounding board for many of our ideas, and he became a partner in research with me on various different projects, including my dissertation.

I knew the moment I began my doctoral studies that I wanted to continue my research in communication. As I began more detailed research in both communication and multicultural sensitivity, I found direct links between these two areas. The opportunity to expand on previous research in communication and in issues of human diversity through my dissertation study was inspiring. Thus, I seized the opportunity to develop a practical approach aimed at expanding individuals' levels of multicultural sensitivity and communication knowledge. For all these reasons, I am drawn to continually researching methods for advancing intercultural relationships.

Life as an Adult Educator

Just as I started work on my master's degree, an opportunity came along for me to teach at the local community college (Clinton Community College) for one year while the regular speech instructor went on sabbatical. In that one year, I studied more than I did for my entire bachelor's degree. And I fell in love with teaching. I had found my career. I appreciated the opportunity to let others know how empowering education can be. I witnessed first-hand the growth in individuals' self-esteem and confidence.

For many years, while raising a family, I taught part time at various colleges throughout the Northeast and the Midwest. The community colleges afforded me a greater opportunity to interact with students more my age, some who were adults struggling to balance the demands of work, family, and schooling. And when I became a single mom to my two daughters, Amanda and Kristin, teaching at the community college gave me some acquaintances my own age who could relate to my frustrations and fears. Later, when I remarried, the flexibility of teaching allowed for a better blending of two families.

Northern Illinois University

Since one way to pay for a college degree is to work at the institution at which you are studying, I found myself working in various capacities at NIU, including as an educator, support staff, and as an administrator. Throughout my 15 years at NIU, I have taught in three different colleges: Business, Education, and Liberal Arts and Sciences. Perhaps the early experiences of feeling frustrated by being a woman in a man's world led me to continue my efforts in advancing women, especially in relation to education. As a faculty associate for women's studies at Northern Illinois University, I took advantage of the chance to further help other women. To this day, I am becoming even more focused on gender issues and reaching out more to assist other women in their own pursuits.

Needless to say, I met some more amazing individuals at NIU who helped me continue in my own transformation as an adult educator: Phyllis Cunningham, Jorge Jeria, John Neimi, Rick Orem, Gene Roth, and Glenn Smith, Adult Education; LaVerne Gyant and Derrick Smith in the Center for Black Studies; Jean Mausehund, Management; Wilma Miranda and Lucy Townsend, Foundations of Education; Aquanette Simpson, Human Resources/Affirmative Action; Dan House, Institutional Research; and Charles Tucker, Speech C ommunication. Many of my fellow graduate students also influenced my life in various ways—too many people to mention them all here. Plus, one of the dangers of naming a few is that you are certain to forget someone of importance. I'm certain that some of them have already become great adult educators whose research is greatly impacting the field. Their work will become the classics for future generations of adult educators.

University Resources for Latinos

In another one of my adult education classes, I met fellow graduate student George Gutierrez, director of the Office of University Resources for Latinos (URL), who opened my world to the cultural realities of Latinas/os both in academia and in the U.S. at large. I started working at the URL as an academic counselor and eventually became assistant director. By the time I left that position seven and one-half years later, I had learned about my own Hispanic roots from my mother's heritage.

The issues of social justice and equality came to the forefront again as I made great efforts under the mentorship of Gutierrez to help Latinas/os navigate through a system that had roadblocks and obstacles strewn along the path—some inadvertently institutionalized racism, others intentional cases of discrimination and prejudice.

Before long, the students openly accepted me as one of their own. They knew that my concern for them and their educational attainment was sincere and long-suffering. Student-organized activist groups like El Fuego de Pueblo taught me a lot about the importance of working within a system to influence change. The Latina sorority, Sigma Lambda Gamma, and its brother fraternity, Sigma Lambda Beta, allowed me into their worlds so that I could understand, yes, even experience, some of the struggles and frustrations along with their victories and accomplishments. My life became intertwined with theirs. To this day, I have maintained friendships with some of the young adults with whom I worked.

Consequently, I am proud to think that I was part of some landmark studies dealing with retention of Latina/o students that will ultimately help to empower more Latinas/os through education. My involvement at the local, state, and even national levels was fulfilling while at the same time frustrating. For as much as we would talk, little was actually done to make the great strides that are needed. Latinas/os remain the least educated group in the U.S. ("Educational attainment," 2005; O'Connor, 2004).

Although I had started this job primarily as a cultural learning experience while working my way through my doctoral degree, I learned just as much if not more about myself in the process. Indeed, leaving this position was one of the more difficult decisions of my life. Ironically, if not for retention studies that verify the utmost importance of the instructor in the classroom, I would most likely be working there or in a similar capacity even now. In spite of all of my sacrificial efforts to assist through student support services, research points to the educator as the single most influential factor in a students' success. Since my goal is to help to empower others through education, I felt that my sphere of influence would be much greater back in the classroom. Even so, I continue my efforts to impact all students, especially those of color, whenever possible.

School for New Learning

Because of my background in adult education, I was given an opportunity to teach at DePaul University's School for New Learning (SNL). This innovative program introduced me to some outstanding adult learners and educators. Many of the adults whom I met through this program touched my heart in ways that are mostly unexplainable. My philosophy that all are simultaneously learners and facilitators of that learning saw direct application in this arena as my students taught me as much if not more than I could possibly teach them. Watching learners grow in self-confidence and transform into more critical citizens can be empowering for oneself.

While at SNL, I became involved in the formation of a publishing house aimed at getting work into the mainstream that might otherwise go unnoticed. Its creation was adult education at its finest—true experiential learning. Some of the administrators and staff from SNL never believed that students could pull off such a demanding task. Indeed, others with more education and money have tried to start publishing firms and have failed. Yet, from the very beginning, SNL students, under the leadership of Keith Armstrong, took control of their own project, which today stands as a testimony to the true value of knowledge. Again, the transforming power of true learning cannot be overestimated.

Elgin Community College

After earning my doctorate, I yearned for a position in an area community college so that I could get back to an educational environment that focused on its learners more specifically than the university as a whole. A community college is one of the best platforms for reaching out to adults who, at some level, understand the importance of education. Indeed, this arena makes doing so relatively uncomplicated as many adults, partly because of the lower cost and more accommodating schedules and to a certain extent because of fears associated with the academic rigors of a university, seek to advance their education by starting at a local community college. I have found that home at Elgin Community College (ECC).

One of the more exciting things about ECC is that many of the instructors come from adult education backgrounds. Thus, they speak my language and understand some of the issues facing adult learners in a more traditional educational institution. They constantly challenge me to validate the learning that is occurring within my own sphere of influence, both in and out of the classrooms.

Although obstacles exist even within faculty philosophies, many of my colleagues are open to experiential learning models and willing to allow the learners to accept some of the responsibility in the knowledge process in an empowering as opposed to a shaming way. Unfortunately, however, even the latter still occurs in some circles.

At times, confronting the system that is in place can be frustrating. As with all institutions, racism occurs at different levels, in both perceived and invisible ways. Talking with students, faculty, staff, and administrators of color reminds me that the struggle is far from over. In some ways, we've only just begun. The challenge can be invigorating at times, exhausting at others. Sometimes I wonder if a place in administration would help me make more of an impact as a change agent.

Summary

As I have continued through my journey in life, I have tried to pay particular attention to the signs that are erected before me and to those symbols that I, in turn, put up, both knowingly and unknowingly. My strong Christian faith has helped to sustain me and to cause me to continually reflect on making society a better place than what I have found it to be.

As a result of living in and traveling to various countries, including Canada, Colombia, Mexico, Japan, Spain, and Taiwan, my global perspective has been enhanced. I ascribe much of my exuberance to these travels where I was afforded the opportunity to meet new people and to adjust to unique environments. Throughout my travels, education, work, and personal experiences, I have interacted with people from a wide range of diverse cultures. I find that most people are sincere in their desire to relate peacefully with others. In spite of this fact, learning to be more understanding and tolerant of diverse cultural groups continues to be a major problem for many of us.

At this point in my life, I am saddened by the lack of compassion and the blatant racism that remains prevalent in society as a whole and that is found even within my own extended family. For as many steps as we have moved forward in the fight for equality, the U.S. appears to have entered a time of escalating hatred. Today, tensions extend not only from the general public but also from university communities where intellect was once thought to eliminate such biases.

I have been involved in institutions of higher learning either as a student, instructor, counselor, or administrator since 1973. Throughout these years of experience, I have observed discrimination in educational environments from the East Coast to the Midwest. I've become frustrated and sickened; however, through it all, I remain hopeful. I hold onto a faith like that of Dr. Martin Luther King, Jr., who believed that we shall overcome. Yet, unlike my sisters and brothers of color, I have the luxury of stepping back from the fight whenever I desire to do so. My lighter skin and relatively privileged background provide me just such an opportunity. I pray that is never the case, however, as much more work remains; many people are needed to keep tearing down old signs of discrimination and hate and erecting new ones of tolerance and understanding.

Although I have yet to be a part of any large, organized effort to combat the many issues facing our country, in my own way I will continue to impact the lives of those adults whose paths have crossed mine for one reason or another, no matter the time frame or purpose. Thankfully, through adult education, I have found a platform that works for this purpose. As with all of us, I can look back on my life with some regrets yet thankfully more successes. My hope is to continue to erect the signs of peace for all so that one day I will hear, "Well done, my good and faithful servant."

References

Educational attainment of the U.S. population by racial and ethnic group, 2004. (2005, Aug 26). *The Chronicle of Higher Education*, p. 16.

Freire, P. (1973). *Pedagogy of the oppressed*. New York: The Seabury Press.

Griffith, J. H. (1961). *Black like me*. Boston: Houghton Mifflin.

hooks, b. (1994). *Teaching to transgress: Education as the practice of freedom*. New York: Routledge.

King, M. L., Jr. (1964, Dec 10). "Nobel Prize Acceptance Speech" [Electronic version]. Oslo, Norway. Retrieved 12/28/2005 from http://www.nobelprizes.com/nobel/peace/MLK-nobel.html

Lennon, J., & McCartney, P. (1967). "Strawberry fields forever." On *Magical Mystery Tour* [Record]. Hollywood, CA: Capitol Records. Retrieved 12/27/2005 from http://www.stevesbeatles.com/songs/strawberry_fields_forever.asp.

O'Connor, Tom. (2004, May 15). *Understanding discrimination against Hispanic/Latino Americans.* Retrieved 7/17/2005 from http://faculty.ncwc.edu/toconnor/soc/355lect13.htm.

Kristopher Wells

"We make the road by walking." – Myles Horton and Paulo Freire

For me, this famous quote and the book by the same title represent key goals of critical adult education in the 21st century. How might we as adult educators respond to globalization and a complex world that is increasingly shaped by techno-rationalism, instrumental educational agendas, the suppression of diversity, and the deskilling of educational professionals? To answer this question, I ask myself what the purposes of adult education should be. Do we stay with tradition and educate to replicate the status quo? Do we work in communities to facilitate the development and training of neoliberal subjects focused on individualism, competition, and economic gain? Or do we work to help smuggle hope and possibility through the cracks in the walls of oppression and injustice?

In my teaching, research, and community service work I frequently draw upon my own lived and learned experiences as a queer person using autobiographical narrative inquiry to inform inclusive public pedagogy. In this narrative inquiry space, I use critical and poststructural theorizing to explore how the personal, political, and pedagogical intersect in the study and practice of adult education. Thus, I share a brief narrative account of how I first entered the field of adult education, and I share the early influences that have shaped my own ethical, critical, and transgressive approach to adult education.

In 1999 I walked away from my job as a public school teacher in Edmonton, Alberta. I left feeling tired, beaten, and broken as I had spent the better part of my teaching career living a life in the closet. I silently watched as students under my care struggled to come to terms with their own sex, sexual, and gender differences. I felt as though I could do nothing to help them without casting the ever-present gaze of suspicion onto myself. I'd heard the words in the hallways and staffrooms – "faggot," "queer," "freak." Those same teachers who were my nine-to-five colleagues were also my silent tormentors. None of their hateful comments were ever directed at me, but the scars still remain from the symbolic violence of their words.

I was at a crossroads in my life. Do I stay as a classroom teacher and continue to put up with the homophobia and heterosexism that permeates our schools? Or do I attempt to find a way to challenge the hegemonic structures that regulate heteronormativity in our schools and society? Ultimately, I chose to step away from the classroom for a year as my health and happiness had been deeply affected by the insidious nature of homophobia and heterosexism. By fortuitous circumstances during my teaching leave, I had the opportunity to become a volunteer facilitator with Youth Understanding Youth, which is a social/support group for lesbian, gay, bisexual, trans-identified, and queer (LGBTQ) youth and young adults in Edmonton. After working with this group for a year, I felt empowered to pursue graduate studies with the hope that I could find the support to develop theoretical and conceptual tools that would enable me to help challenge the structures of oppression that so deeply affected my life and the lives of so many LGBTQ students and teachers.

In 2000, I made appointments with various department chairs in the Faculty of Education at the University of Alberta to discuss my proposed goals for graduate studies. I went to the meetings prepared. I had a list of questions that I asked each department chair, and I clearly articulated that my graduate work would be focused on creating safe and caring schools and communities for LGBTQ teachers and students of all ages. Some of the professors were taken aback by my direct approach and told me that it would not be possible to do this kind of educative work in their department. It seemed that door after door was closing in front of me, until one professor who heard about my queries contacted me and suggested that I talk to a new professor who had just arrived in the Faculty of Education. That new professor's name was André P. Grace.

I arrived at André's office door with my list of questions in hand. André greeted me with a warm smile, a hot cup of tea, and proceeded to answer all of my questions patiently. Then he posed a few questions of his own. When our conversation was over, André said to me, "The work you want to do is heart-and-soul education for youth and young adults, and I'd like to be your supervisor." I left that meeting feeling exuberant and energized. I walked down the hallway corridor thinking to myself that a new road had opened in my life's journey. Now all I had to do was take the first steps and begin walking down the road.

Today, as I sit in my office at the University of Alberta reflecting on these experiences, I can still taste the fear, anger, and sorrow that I experienced as a closeted teacher. Through my graduate studies, I've learned to channel that anger and hurt into a burning rage that fuels and focuses my personal and professional ambitions to counter institutional and political efforts to privatize queer reality by keeping it hidden, invisible, silent, and unannounced in education, culture, and religion. I use the tenets of critical adult education and queer theory to challenge the (hetero)normative status quo. I continue to work in the community with Youth Understanding Youth, and I also work closely with the Alberta Teachers' Association (ATA) to develop educational resources and professional development opportunities to help preservice and practicing teachers engage in building understanding of their professional, ethical, and legal responsibilities to create safe, caring, and inclusive classrooms and schools for *all* students and *all* teachers.

I've been fortunate to have this work strongly supported by my new colleagues, the ATA, and my Faculty of Education. My LGBTQ research has been recognized with provincial and national awards, which tell me and others that this work is indeed valuable and necessary. Sometimes amid the successes I still need to remember that much hard work remains to be done. Luckily, things are slowly changing for the better. As Canadian society becomes increasingly accepting of LGBTQ persons, more and more teachers are finding support and coming out in their schools. A whole new generation of young teachers – "Generation Queer," as some have called it – have spent most of their young adulthood out of the closet, and they are not willing to go back in when they re-enter the classroom as beginning teachers. What new challenges will this generation face? Will they still hear homophobic slurs in the staffroom? I'm hopeful that it will be easier for Generation Queer, but even though these young adults are coming out at younger and younger ages, with their visibility also comes the increased risk of violence and victimization. Queer students and teachers still need to remain vigilant as they wonder if the next person they come out to will be a source of support or a specter of fear.

In conceptualizing my personal and professional study and practice of adult education, I draw upon the scholarly work of André P. Grace, my master's and doctoral supervisor, to demonstrate how all forms of education intersect with adult learning and the ways in which they influence teacher professional development. When working with teachers, I try to engage them in a public pedagogy of resistance and resilience that helps them to build knowledge and understanding of the needs, desires, issues, and concerns of LGBTQ persons. To help conceptualize the theoretical underpinnings for this public pedagogy, I draw upon Paulo Freire's notion of conscientization and Paula Allman's call for radical adult education to help me develop an ethical framework comprised of seven guiding virtues or principles. These virtues are intended to help teacher-educators acknowledge the rights and privileges of full citizenship for LGBTQ students, teachers, and same-gender-parented families. They are grounded in educational values aimed at critical transformation and include commitment, vigilance and shared responsibility, honesty and truth, passion and desire, critical and hopeful thinking, willingness to transform the self, and honoring democratic classrooms and schools, all of which are situated within critical and queer theoretical ideological constructs.

Commitment: I believe that critical social transformation takes time and open dialogue. We will not build queer-friendly educational environments overnight. Societal and cultural change has to be built upon a foundation based on advancing human rights and encouraging social responsibility. By helping to construct dialogic coalitions and support across multiple differences, we can begin to open the dialogue towards full inclusion, meaningful access, and unrestricted accommodation.

Vigilance and Shared Responsibility: I believe that challenging homophobia, transphobia, heterosexism, and sexism requires constant reflection and evaluation. How are the structures of oppression connected? For example, how is homophobia utilized as a weapon of sexism? How does it intersect with white supremacy and privilege? Vigilance and shared responsibility are embedded in the belief that we need to look more critically at our schools and communities as we ask: Who is included and who is excluded? Why?

Building queer-friendly schools and communities is not the sole responsibility of LGBTQ teachers and students. Everyone has a part to play in creating safe, inclusive, and welcoming schools and communities. In some cases heterosexual allies may be in the safer position to advocate for change.

Honesty and Truth: I believe that we need to ask ourselves: What are the realities and resistances in engaging in this counternormative pedagogical work? By sharing our personal stories we invite an openness and vulnerability that encourages others to share their own stories and experiences of difference. We all live storied lives. Stories are the way in which we relate and make sense of our shared experiences. By sharing our stories in an open and honest way we can begin to open the hearts and minds of others.

The virtues of honesty and truth are also embedded in the difficult work of challenging the status quo. This work can be understood as a part of what Griff Foley describes as "learning in the struggle" as we strive to dismantle the structures of oppression.

Passion and Desire: I believe that ultimately we need to be able to internalize social justice and compassion in order to live them out in our everyday practice. The construction of knowledge is not separate from our lived experience. There can be no false dichotomies, rather there is a dialectical unity that is not linear but dynamic and reciprocal where theory and practice mutually work together to help develop a critical consciousness.

This desire for critical knowledge begins in groundlessness that affirms that destiny is not pregiven or predetermined. Instead we need to envision and become the change that we seek in the world. We should work to overcome our own inherent biases and learn to dwell in the radical possibility of sharing life with the "Other." This Other exists in the space of hope and possibility that stems from our commitment to social justice, freedom, and democracy.

Paulo Freire reminds us that we can have two basic types of encounters with people. It is our choice as to whether those interactions will be humanizing or dehumanizing. Which one will we choose? Will we continue to demonize the Other, or will we open our hearts and minds to accept and learn from them?

Critical and Hopeful Thinking: I believe that critical and hopeful thinking not only involve asking "why" and "how," but also "why not," "what if," and "what about" questions. We need to believe that we can change society for the better. We can start to establish the foundation for this hope by creating glimpses of the social transformation that we seek in our schools and communities. This begins by smuggling in hope through the cracks in the walls of oppression. For example, this can occur by intervening when homophobic language is used, incorporating LGBTQ educational topics in the curriculum, and establishing gay–straight student alliances and other counternormative programs that seek to open up rather than close down spaces and conversations.

Willingness to Transform the Self: Noam Chomsky has passionately stated, "If we believe there is no hope, there will be no hope." Ultimately, I believe that we as ethical beings choose how we live and interact in the world. Before we ask others to change, we need to begin with ourselves and ask if our own values and beliefs are inclusive. We should question: "What makes us uncomfortable? Why?"

We must first start any process of transformation by learning to love and forgive ourselves. We need to overcome a legacy of external and internalized homophobia, transphobia, and heterosexism. We must also recognize that we will make mistakes in this journey. However, these practices of failure can become sites of success if we interrogate and attempt to learn from them.

Honoring Democratic Classrooms and Schools: I believe that at the heart of any critical praxis is the understanding that classrooms are communities of learners. When one member feels excluded from this community, everyone loses access to that person's knowledge, insights, and contributions. In this heartfelt community there is no learning *for* students, only learning *with* students. In this way the teachers and the students both become the co-educators.

Democratic classrooms and schools ought to attempt to move away from a simple process of transmitting knowledge to a more complex understanding of transforming relationships to knowledge. In these schools, classrooms become sites for critical democracy where students and teachers learn to embrace rather than fear diversity and its challenges.

As an educator and community activist who works within the academy, I believe that I have an ethical and professional responsibility to move beyond the sole production of theoretical models in an attempt to liaison and work with community members to help counter normativity and open up the horizons of possibility for individuals to construct a more just world. My teaching, research, and community service work stems from these seven guiding virtues.

Returning to my commitment to community development and the roles and responsibilities of adult educators in this process, I try to live out these seven virtues in my everyday cultural work for social transformation. One recent community-based project that André P. Grace and I have developed is Camp fYrefly, which is a summer leadership retreat for LGBTQ youth and young adults. Camp fYrefly was designed to help counter the educational silences and pedagogical absences that mark the lived experiences of younger members of sexual minorities in their schools, families, and communities. For four days each year, we bring together over 50 youth from across Canada to help them learn how to become change agents for social justice. To our knowledge Camp fYrefly is the only LGBTQ youth leadership program of its kind in Canada. The camp programming is guided by a youth advisory panel and facilitated by trained adult educators and youth workers in collaboration with a team of artists, dramatists, and community and youth leaders who offer a wide range of powerful youth-focused workshops and creative skill-building and self-esteem-enhancing activities. The camp is peer driven and jam-packed with drama, music, writing, visual art, empowerment and reflection exercises, anti-oppression work, personal growth opportunities, healthy socialization, and in-depth learning activities about specific youth topics and social issues.

Many camp participants have stated that Camp fYrefly is a unique and powerful experience that assists them in developing important friendships and leadership qualities through activities that challenge them to explore their identities, build resilience, and enhance self-esteem. Overall, Camp fYrefly focuses on building and nurturing the leadership potential of participants in an effort to help them learn how to become social change agents.

Much like Myles Horton's Highlander School, I believe that Camp fYrefly reflects and helps participants to live out our fundamental belief in the role of citizenship education as a transgressive and transformational method to develop leadership capacity in marginalized communities. Participants come together in a safe and supportive space where they can learn from their individual and collective experiences in the struggle against oppression. They create the lived curriculum of the camp from the daily experiences of their lives. At camp, various workshops have been developed and presented by participants on a variety of topics, which include facilitation and skill building; confronting bias and dealing with diversity; coming out and coming to terms with sex, sexual, and gender differences; negotiating relationships with parents and care givers; healthy dating and relationship skills; fighting oppression through art; health and safety; participatory drama; networking and self-esteem building; and nurturing ourselves and our knowledge.

Through these formal and informal workshops and discussions the camp partici-pants become the educators. Just as Rosa Parks was empowered through her participation at Highlander to refuse to give up her seat on the bus that fateful day, we hope to create the conditions that will help to empower LGBTQ youth and young adults to be, become, and belong as full citizens in their schools, families, and communities. As the camp participants tell us, fYrefly stands for fostering, Youth, resiliency, energy, fun, leadership, yeah!

In conclusion, in keeping with the constant call throughout Paulo Freire's work "to create a world in which it will be easier to love," I try to reflect these values and beliefs in my own inclusive project for LGBTQ citizenship. This precept speaks to a world in which human dignity is protected and respected, diversity and difference are embraced, and ev-eryone's individual destiny can be achieved. Creating this world is our ethical obligation. It is a project of hope, humanity, and possibility that exists within the hands of all educators if the goals of critical and transgressive adult education are to be realized.

Dr. Stephen R. White

As a professor at Appalachian State University in Boone, North Carolina, I teach in post-secondary and adult education graduate programs. I hold the Doctor of Arts degree (D.A.) from Idaho State University in intradisciplinary studies in political science and interdisciplinary social sciences and was a Doctoral Fellow for the Advancement of College Teaching. The Doctor of Arts degree was developed by the Carnegie Foundation for the Advancement of College Teaching, PEW Charitable Trust and the National Council of Graduate Schools with the specific objective to educate interdisciplinary scholar-teachers with expertise in postsecondary education pedagogy (White, 1993, 1994; White & McBeth, 2003). My doctoral research was on the politics and educational socialization into globalization within the context of global education theory and constructivist pedagogy (White, 1997).

In preparation for my doctoral studies, a Bachelor of Science degree in political science was achieved from Utah State University as well as a degree in philosophy from the University of Utah. Both degree programs were completed with academic honors. Likewise, a Master of Public Administration degree (M.P.A.), with an emphasis in higher education administration, and the Graduate Certificate in Teacher Education (Ed.C.), with a concentration in instructional and curriculum theory, were completed at Idaho State University. My teaching experience has been educating diverse adult learners in community college, undergraduate, graduate and doctoral degree programs.

My scholarly interests are extensive: politics of higher education, history of higher education, foundations of adult education, interdisciplinary theory, global education, educational organization, degree program design, teaching as scholarship, and constructivist theory. Specific interests include the theoretical infusion of French philosopher Pierre Teilhard de Chardin and Indian scholar Sri Ghose Aurobindo's evolutionary theories of collective consciousness and Swiss psychologist Carl G. Jung's theory of collective unconscious into educational musings.

Scholarly papers have been presented before various international, national, and regional academic associations: British Educational Research Association, American Research Association in Education, American Association of Community Colleges, National Doctor of Arts Association, National Conference on Adult Developmental Education, International Society for Technology in Education, National Council of Graduate Schools, North Carolina Association of Educational Research, International Alliance of Teacher Scholars (The Lilly

Conference), Hawaii-Asian International Conference on Education, and as the keynote speaker before the North Carolina Association of Adult Educators.

My research has been published in various international and national forums: Educational Foundations, Journal of Educational Thought, Journal of Instructional *Psychology, Journal on Excellence in College Teaching, International Education Quarterly, Journal of Thought in Education, American Secondary Education, American Education, Journal of National School-Development, New Horizons in Adult Education, New Directions in Higher Education, The International Society for Instructional Technology in Education, Reform in Education* and the *Journal of Thought in Education.*

The Reich College of Education conferred upon me the Scholar of Distinction Award and recognized me as a Distinguished Graduate Faculty member. Idaho State's School of Graduate Studies has acknowledged me as a doctoral alumnus of distinction in recognition of the advancement of interdisciplinary scholarship and the art and science of postsecondary education pedagogy.

Albert Einstein stated, "It is the supreme art of the teacher to awaken joy in creative expression and knowledge." Karl Jaspers, American philosopher, states:

> Teaching as a scholarly activity… like research, must never become routine. It is the opportunity for the teacher to present in dramatic fashion, augmented by their unique insight and zeal for knowledge and the dissemination of it, material that cannot be conveyed with the same effectiveness in print. Through a scholarly lecture the learner can see enacted the power, excitement, and transformative force of ideas. The postures, gestures and intonations of the teacher carry as much force as the words themselves. Conversely, these same ideas when reduced to print often rest passive on the page and do not animate the mind nor nourish intelligence. (Smith, 1991, p. 212)

Within our academic culture we strive for objectivity and a strict adherence to rationality. Congruent with these cultural values, my teaching is grounded upon scientific principles and my approach to learning is founded upon logically sound theories.

Teaching is a scholarly activity. My theoretical foundation to teaching and learning is from the constructivist approach. The scholarship of constructivist teaching can be metaphorically conceptualized as follows: The learner's mind is the laboratory, the content is the elements, the context is the learning framework, and pedagogy is the methodology.

The essence of teaching is a highly emotive act. Teaching and mentoring adult learners for me is an intimate relationship. Teaching energizes my spirit and facilitating learners through the process of knowledge discovery and self-development is a poignant experience that fans the fire of my very soul. Being a teacher is being a learner.

My position is that one effective way to augment the interconnected intellectual space between the teacher and adult learners is through the construction of a learning community. It is my desire to make the learning community a comfort zone for intellectual exploration and self-development while fostering critical analysis and deep reflection. The question(s) of how to construct learning experiences that will provide significant intellectual engagement on the part of me and the adult learner and how to balance the subject content to a learner-centered context resulting in mindful learning is continuously pondered. This requires me to stay engaged with the research on college teaching such as active

learning, taxonomy of adult cognitive development and planning scholarly teaching strategies in an effort to empower me as a teacher to creatively enhance the learner's educational
experiences. I truly enjoy working with diverse learners. Collectively, learner diversity makes
the learning community more dynamic, resulting in the learning process being richer in
meaning construction. It is my position that outstanding teaching results in learning that
empowers the individual, advances society and promotes social justice.

As a constructivist, my position on learning is based upon the fundamental premise
that acquisition of knowledge is connected to a deep search for meaning. Meaning requires
understanding the interconnectedness and interrelatedness between knowledge sources. To
nurture learning well requires understanding the mental models learners use to understand
the knowledge. There is not one best way to teach. Teaching is an expressive art that is also
grounded on scientific principles of cognition.

Within a constructivist perspective, knowledge is discovered or constructed in a
new context every time interaction between the teacher and learner occurs. Constructivist
teaching is an act of knowledge discovery, integration, and application of knowledge
through stimulating learners to become intellectually engaged in active learning. Sound
teaching stimulates in learners the desire to inquire and to construct new knowledge that is
meaningful. Each act of knowledge construction is in itself the discovery of new and novel
knowledge that makes a valuable contribution to the foundation body of knowledge and to
the learning community.

Today some adult developmental educators are exploring alternative assessments regarding the affective, noncognitive characteristics of at-risk students. These affective characteristics include motivation, self-efficacy, and meaning construction. The objective of my
research in this area is to improve our understanding of the teaching and learning dynamic
in adult intellectual developmental and enhance at-risk student retention in postsecondary
education.

Most recently I've been exploring the relationship between spiritual intelligence
(SQ) theory in regards to adult learners' affective intellectual development as well as educational organization and leadership disposition. The notion of spirituality has no linkage to
a religious ideology or an endorsement of a religious orientation or theological disposition.
Spirituality is the soul of intellectuality that moves us toward increasing levels of selfhood.
The synthesis between spirituality and intelligence is rooted in our need for understanding
the world and our place in it. My assertion is that this spiritual intelligence theory is consistent with constructivist teaching and learning.

Richard Wolman, who has developed the Psycho Spiritual Intelligence (PSI) instru-
ment, terms spiritual intelligence as "thinking with our soul." Wolman writes (2001):

> By spiritual I mean the ancient and biding human quest for connectedness
> with something larger and more trustworthy than our egos – with our own
> souls, with one another, with the world of history and nature, with the invis-
> ible winds of the spirit, with the mystery of being alive….Spiritual intelligence
> can best be seen as a capacity for a particular kind of experience we humans
> possess, and one for which we also demonstrate certain related abilities. Our
> task now is to understand how this intelligence can and does influence our

lives, how its energy can be harnessed, and how we can come to know ourselves better through spiritual self-direction. (pp. 26, 119)

I surveyed a group of North Carolina Community College students currently enrolled in developmental classes to explore the possibility of constructing a linkage between SQ affective assessment as a means to improve developmental education practices and enhance at-risk student retention. The students' PSI scores are ranked by gender and a high, moderate, or low score in the following categories, the working hypothesis being that if there are identifiable trends between adult and at-risk students PSI scores then we can conclude that a strong relationship might exist and pursue further research. The research did show a positive correlation and the findings were presented before colleagues at the 3rd National Conference on Developmental Education in Charlotte (White, 2001b). The response was very positive and the findings are now being developed for a manuscript.

I presented "Community College Teaching and Transformative Learning: Contextualizing Spiritual Intelligence" at the International Alliance of Teacher Scholars Conference (The Lilly Conference) at California Polytech University, Pomona, California (White, 2005c). Transformative learning is a unique theory of adult teaching and learning. Transformative learning is a shift of consciousness that dramatically and irreversibly alters our way of being in the world, our understanding of ourselves, our relationships with the learners, other humans and with the natural world, and our sense of possibilities for social justice and self-fulfillment. Transformation is usually triggered by a problem or new challenge. As we enter this period of tribulation, people will naturally reflect critically on the issue through deep thinking or dialogue with others in search of an intellectual resolution. During the thinking phase, we typically find that they can no longer maintain previous ways of thinking and being. As a result, we are compelled to change, to become transformed.

Jack Mezirow distinguishes among three kinds of critical reflection that occur during the transformation process: (1) *Content reflection* is when the person critically reflects on the content or description of the problem or issue. (2) *Process reflection* is when the person critically thinks about strategies that can be used to solve the problem rather than the problem itself. Process reflection is rational reflection that does not incorporate intuition or affective cognitive processes. (3) *Premise reflection* is the process of logically questioning the relevance of the problem or issue. The person questions the basic assumptions, beliefs, or values that are underlying the problem. This process is distinct from problem solving and has the potential to lead to transformative learning (Cranton, 1994).

However, it is my position that another form of reflection occurs that is inclusive of the subjective and affective cognitive development during the learning process. I term this aspect of transformative learning *transcendental reflection*. Transcendental reflection includes affective motivation, self-efficacy, and meaning construction.

Furthermore, my works "Reconstructionism and Interdisciplinary Global Education: Curricula Construction in a Teilhardian Context" (White, 2001a) "Educating Toward the Future: A New Societal Myth and Pedagogic Motif" (White, 2004b), and "Adult Education and Global Education: Contextualizing Socialization into Globalization" (White, 2004a), explore social reconstructionism as a philosophical movement that conceptualizes education as an institution for social engineering and to develop innovative curricula and pedagogical strategies to construct a new consciousness of collective social cooperation. Thus global education is an area of intense interest to reconstructionists. The central thesis of this article is that avant-garde French intellectual Pierre Teilhard de Chardin's (1881-1955) theories of psychosocial evolution can be effectively utilized as the theoretical foundation for contextualizing interdisciplinary global education curricula and serve as a theoretical template for social reconstructionist global educators.

Political Education and Social Reconstructionism: Contextualizing the Philosophy of Sri Aurobindo (White, 2005b) and *Aurobindo's Thought and Global Education* (White, 2005c) are multicultural approaches to global education. Globalization is an emerging political, social and economic phenomenon. Sociological research of empirical global issues has influenced educators' disposition toward the problem. The thesis of these works is that educators need to explore novel ideas that provide a meaningful metanarrative of globalization.

Indian philosopher Sri Ghose Aurobindo (1872-1950) constructed a meaningful meta-narrative of social evolution and the conscious transformation. Aurobindoian thought is a relevant meta-narrative for educators to explore political and social evolutionary notions of global solidarity and the ultimate meaning of globalization. Aurobindoian thought is described within the context of an educational motif for advancing our socialization into globalization.

My manuscript, "Organization of a Constructivist Learning Community: A Teilhardian Metaphor" (White, 2002), advances constructivist learning and educational organizations as learning communities—a constructivist learning community model. The article provides an organizational metaphor of a constructivist learning community. The metaphor, grounded on French scientist and philosopher Pierre Teilhard de Chardin's (1881-1955) evolutionary theories of socialization and personalization, is beneficial for conceptualizing a constructivist learning community. Uniquely, extracted Teilhardian concepts are congruent with many notions of constructivism and learning community organization. Thus Teilhardianism is an intellectually fertile platform for the development of a constructivist learning community metaphor.

"Developmental and Remedial Education in Postsecondary Education" (Boylan, Bonham, & White, 1999); "Experiential Learning Theory, Field-based Internship, and Technology: Augmenting the Learning Process" (White, 2004c); and "Information Technology and Visualizing Future Education: A Teilhardian Metaphor of a Global Learning Community" (White, 2004d) explore the notion of teachable moments as a teaching and learning phenomenon. Teachable moments are defined from the conventional perspective that the teacher designs the subject content, and learning context is creatived in such a way as to enhance the knowledge acquisition and learning. This definition is grounded upon rationally predetermined cause and effect pedagogy.

The second is an intuitive appreciation of the teacher's and learners' consciousness and the learning space it enigmatically fills. Teachable moments like these are also part of the craft of teaching where information is transmuted into knowledge and knowledge is transformed into wisdom. My hypothesis is that Swiss psychologist Carl Jung's *theory of synchronicity* can shed new light on teachable moments and the life-world of teaching and learning. The theory of synchronicity states that meaningful coincidence of a psychic or physical state or event which has "no causal relationships to one another do happen. When moments of synchronicity occur, the teacher is often presented with a teachable moment of intense, insightful, and meaningful learning experience that was not planned but just happened. I think all conscious teachers can relate to such moments of synchronicity that have empowered their teaching and illuminated the subject being learned.

Finally, it is my position that in adult education the teacher and mentor roles are so interconnected and interrelated that they cannot be separated. There are two principles that guide me as a mentor of adult learners: *trusting relationship* and *personal empowerment (fulfillment)*. Thus inherently, unlike scholarship or teaching, mentoring is not as tangible to judge or measure. The best when can do, perhaps, is to listen to the voices of the learners who are on their educational journey or have just completed that journey. They are the ones who can express the sense of safety that comes from a trusting relationship with the adult educator or feel a sense of deep fulfillment within themselves and a passionate intellectual voice that has emerged by providing the space for personal empowerment. But to be a small part of adult learners' intellectual and personal transformation through education as their mentor is a daunting honor, a delicate balance between leadership and stewardship. The mentor in adult education is entrusted with an awesome power and responsibility.

References

Boylan, H.R., Bonham, B.S. & White, S.R. (1999, Winter). Developmental and remedial education in postsecondary education. *Promising Practices in Recruitment, Remediation, and Retention*. New Directions in Higher Education, Vol. 1, No. 108.

Cranton, P. (1994). *Understanding and promoting transformative learning: A guide for educators of adults.* San Francisco: Jossey-Bass, Inc.

Smith, P. (1991). *Killing the spirit in higher education.* New York: Viking Press.

White, S. R. (1993). The Doctor of Arts: A candidate's view of the teaching doctorate. Paper presented at the Council of Graduate Schools (CGS), Washington, D.C.

White, S. R. (Ed.). (1994). The *D.A. and the 21st century: Proceedings of the second national conference of the Doctor of Arts.* Pocatello, ID: Idaho State University Publications, Vol. 2.

White, S.R. (1997). *Global education and social reconstructionism:Constructivist pedagogy in an era of global change.* Unpublished dissertation, Idaho State University, Pocatello.

White, S.R. (2001a). Reconstructionism and interdisciplinary global education: Curricula construction in a teilhardian context. *International Education, 31* (1).

White, S.R. (2001b). Spiritual intelligence (SQ) and developmental education: Exploring affective assessment system of at-risk adult learners. Presentation at the 3rd National Conference on Developmental Education, Charlotte, North Carolina.

White, S.R. (2002). Organization of a constructivist learning community: A teilhardian metaphor. *Journal of Educational Thought.*

White, S.R., & McBeth, M.K. (2003). The Doctor of Arts in American higher education: A history of interdisciplinarity and pedagogical scholarship. *American Education, 123, (4).*

White, S.R. (2004a). Adult education and global education: Contextualizing socialization into globalization. *New Horizons in Adult Education, 18(1)*.

White, S.R. (2004b). Educating toward the future: A new societal myth and pedagogic motif. *Educational Foundations, 21(2)*.

White, S.R. (2004c). Experiential learning theory, field-based internship, and technology: Augmenting the learning process. *Society for Instructional Technology in Education Annual*.

White, S.R. (2004d) Information technology and visualizing future education: A teilhardian metaphor of a global learning community. Presented at the Society for Instructional Technology in Education International Conference, Atlanta, Georgia.

White, S.R. (2005b). Community college teaching and transformative learning: Contextualizing spiritual intelligence. Paper presented at the International Alliance of Teacher-Scholars Conference (The Lilly Conference), California Polytech University, Pomona, California, March.

White, S.R. (2005c). Political education and social reconstructionism: Contextualizing the philosophy of Sri Aurobindo. *International Education Journal*.

White, S.R. (2005a). Aurobindo's thought and global education. *Journal of Thought in Education*.

Wolman, R. W. (2001*). Thinking with your soul: Spiritual intelligence and why it matters*. New York: Harmony Books.

Miriam Zukas

Belonging? A (Non-American) Adult Educator's Story

When I received an invitation from the editors of this book to contribute my autobiography to a collection about American adult educators, my immediate reaction was, on the one hand, to be flattered to be asked, and on the other, to be puzzled as to why I had been included as an American. I felt a certain hesitancy—to call this sensation "resistance to colonisation" would be putting it too strongly—but certainly I felt appropriated. And then I remembered my experience of travelling through Northern California and Oregon in the summer of 2004, being asked repeatedly by those trying to register voters if I wanted to get Bush out of the White House; I most certainly did—but alas, I was not American and could not vote. Yet how I wished to be able to play my part in what was bound to be one of the closest elections ever; how I wished to support my friends and colleagues in changing this dangerous, right-wing and xenophobic government. Perhaps then I should take up the invitation to have a voice? Perhaps I should read this invitation as one which tries to create a less nationalistic, more inclusive "America"; to understand the invitation as a tribute from my colleagues and to stop being so sensitive to issues of nationality.

I am on my fourth nationality at the moment. Like so many people of Jewish origin, my family story is one of migration and complexity. My father, a Lithuanian, came to what was then Northern Rhodesia (Zambia, after independence in 1964) just before the Second World War; my mother, born of French and Polish parents, moved from France to Israel just after the war. When she met my father in 1954, they did not share a language in common. My mother, who spoke German as well as French and Hebrew, learned Yiddish from my father. My parents married in 1955 and my mother moved to join my father in his home in Northern Rhodesia (a British colony which was then part of the Federation of Rhodesia and Nyasaland) where she learned English, although she and my father spoke Yiddish when they did not want us to understand. I was born in 1956 and I understand that I spoke with a French accent until I went to school. My first passport was a British Colonial one (that is, British, but not really); I became Zambian after independence, French in my twenties (so that I could work in the UK) and British in 1997 (partly because of my commitment to the UK and partly because I wanted to be able to vote). I have now lived in Britain longer than I have lived anywhere else, and I feel British – except when I am mistaken for Spanish, Greek or Italian.

During the early 1950s, my father's older brother, Simon, had been a leading radical in the fight for independence. My father played his own somewhat less visible part, so that when my uncle was deported from Northern Rhodesia in 1952, my father stayed behind and kept in contact with many of those who were later to form the government of the newly created Zambia. Some of those individuals, including Kenneth Kaunda, the first president of Zambia, came to stay with us when I was a little girl. Despite being brought up in a community of Jews and educated in a school which was initially White, by the time I was eight or so, I had some sense of both Black people's changing status and a vague notion that important things were happening – the political slogans "One Zambia, one nation" and "one man, one vote" still ring in my mind. My uncle's return to Zambia in 1964 was a momentous occasion – he was hoisted high on the shoulders of his long-standing political friends and the iconic picture in the paper the next day still fills me with a childish thrill (Zukas, 2002). To this day, I am asked by those who have had any connection at all with Zambia if I am Simon's daughter.

Simon's political activities affected us all. We were declared prohibited immigrants from South Africa and later Mozambique, leaving me with a strong sense that I had no place in such countries. Later, in my teens, I realised that this was a badge of honour rather than shame. But my uncle's return to Zambia was also highly significant for me in another respect. As a young man, Simon had won a scholarship to university in Cape Town in South Africa where his political activism had taken shape. On learning this, I asked my father what university was, and he told me that clever people went there. With the ruthless logic of a cocky nine-year old, I decided that, since I was clever, this was to be my future, and my parents never questioned my right to do this – they believed strongly that children should choose their own futures. I am the only member of my immediate family to have gone to university.

A parallel strand for me was an awareness of my Jewish identity. There was a large Jewish population in the country at that time for complex historical, political and economic reasons (Macmillan & Shapiro, 1999), and we were part of a well-established community. Although my parents were not at all religious, my father's parents were, and it was expected that we would learn the basics – enough to see us through the main festivities. We made weekly visits to learn Hebrew with other Jewish children, and we were tested regularly. I remember one occasion (I must have been about seven) when we were told that the winner of the test would carry one of the children's scrolls round the synagogue on a particular festival. I came in first by quite a long way and I still remember the shock of being told that the prize didn't apply to me because I was a girl and girls were not allowed to carry the Torah; until that point, I had never consciously encountered anything I wasn't able to do because of my sex. I made such a fuss about it that I was given a special dispensation by the rabbi, and I proudly paraded the baby scroll round and round the synagogue. I regard this as the first radicalising experience of my life.

I went to school in what was then Southern Rhodesia (now Zimbabwe) because my grandparents lived in Salisbury (now Harare). Despite the regime of Ian Smith, my school was relatively "liberal'" with girls from other than White backgrounds, provided their parents could afford it. Another radicalising moment for me was when the Debating Society was setting off for a debate with a government-run (as opposed to private) boys' school, and we were told that one of the students would have to get off the bus because she was "coloured" and wouldn't be allowed into the school. I had of course observed the contrasts between Zambia and Rhodesia – in Zambia, Black people were in government; they were on television; they were in the newspapers; they stayed in our home. In Rhodesia, they were absent except as servants and workers. But I had not realised until that moment that these arrangements were intentionally racist and that they applied to my school friends. I was ashamed.

Race aside, the values in my school were bizarre – on the whole, worth was measured in terms of sporting success or number of boyfriends; I had no interest in either and was therefore technically a failure. I had already decided that I wanted to go to university in England because South Africa was both unappealing and, as a Zukas, I was banned. I did not want to stay in Zambia – I wanted a bigger field to play in, so that I could find others with similar interests. The atmosphere at school was stifling and I wanted to get away.

My decision to study psychology came out of a set of so-called "aptitude tests" by one of our teachers, which I now recognise as IQ tests. I was told that, according to my profile, I should do psychology – I scored highly on abstract reasoning and had the right kind of linguistic skills and scientific understanding. I sent off to the British Psychological Society to find out what psychology was and thought it was probably an interesting thing to do. Now all I had to do was decide where to go, with few cues to work with except size, gender split and the nature of the degree.

After a brief spell in Switzerland learning French and clearing my asthmatic lungs in the mountains (my school year finished in December and university didn't start until October), in 1974, I came to England to start at Exeter University. Within three months, my Rhodesian accent had vanished because, at that time, anyone with something like a South African accent was assumed to be racist. However, I was alerted to Britain's covert racism in a number of ways. Those giving out rooms in my hall of residence had assumed I would be Black, and I was therefore one of very few first years to have my own room because "some people might not have wanted to share with a Black person." I had to visit the doctor because I came from "the Tropics," and he recommended that I take a course of treatment which he recommended to all "tropical" (i.e., not White) students; when it came back from the chemist, it was a course of worming tablets. Both these experiences alerted me to the contradiction between the overt anti-apartheid stance which many in the university appeared to take and the covert racism that operated throughout the country.

I enjoyed my degree and learned a lot, but I was increasingly concerned about my fate afterwards because I had a Zambian passport and was not entitled to work in the UK. My only option appeared to be to study for a doctorate, but I knew nothing about how to find out about opportunities. So I responded to an ad in a newspaper for a scholarship; although I was not eligible, they were happy to take me on as a paying student, and I was very fortunate as my parents were willing to continue to support my studies. I spent three years at another university where I began to teach undergraduates and then adult education classes in order to earn money, but the doctorate itself was a disaster. First, I struggled to overcome the necessity to carry out experiments under controlled conditions (a sine qua non of psychology at that time) in my study of nonverbal communication; how could I know about conversations if I took the life out of them? Now I can talk about paradigms of research, the construction of the subject within psychology, the problems with discourses of measurement, prediction and control, and so on, but at that time, I thought it was me. Second, as was frequently the case in British universities at that time, my supervision was neglible so that I ended up further and further down the track of a thesis I did not believe in. Simultaneously, I began to get involved in feminism – I started to read *Spare Rib* and to buy all the Virago Press books that appeared in the late 1970s – although it was several years before I was able to make the link between feminism and the difficulties I'd had with psychology as a subject.

On the back of my experience teaching adults, I arrived in Leeds in September 1980 to take up a post as lecturer in psychology in what was then the Department of Adult Education and Extramural Studies. I had no idea, as I moved into my new house at the beginning of November, that two weeks later the Yorkshire Ripper was to murder his last of many victims round the corner from where I lived. From then on, like most other women in Leeds, I lived in fear. I taught adult classes in the evening and had to return home on the bus, and I was frightened. The university advised its women staff not to go out after dark – but how was I supposed to carry out my job when I did not drive? Eventually I realised that Leeds was a hotbed of revolutionary and radical feminism (in no small part, I think, because of the Ripper) and I began to get involved politically. When the Ripper was caught a few months later, I was already edging my way into the scene.

I spent years with other women trying (and failing) to set up a women's centre in the city, although we succeeded with other campaigns such as the First Feminist Book Fair. My political activities and my work began to come together; we started the first women's studies course in the university; I began to teach undergraduates about women and psychology; I became involved in New Opportunities for Women courses with community adult education. Despite (or even because of) the Thatcher government, this was a vibrant and exciting time for radical adult education. We won money to set up technology courses for women in the community in the mid-1980s, and we later generalised the courses to other disadvantaged communities. We ran Access courses which challenged the university's assumptions about who should attend university and what they should study. My department was internationally renowned for its pioneering work with disadvantaged communities and I was fortunate to be involved at that time.

In 1991, we were approached by a consortium of further education (community) colleges in Leeds to set up a partnership to provide training for teachers in the further education sector, and this was to become a rich new focus for my work, as community and liberal adult education were slowly choked to death by new regulations that insisted that all courses be accredited. If we couldn't radicalise the students, perhaps we could work with teachers who worked with those students? Together with a new university colleague, Janice Malcolm, and colleagues from further education, we tried to offer teachers support at a time when colleges were turned into businesses through a process called "incorporation." These were difficult and often hostile times, with long-running battles between unions and managers and a blatant undermining of professional terms and conditions of employment. My work in this area continues.

In 1997 I became the chair of my school, which more than occupied me for five and a half years. On reflection, much of our time was spent trying to maintain a space for adult students in an increasingly regulated and commodified system. I was fortunate to be in a department which had a rich history of trying (if not always succeeding) to be collegial, democratic, consultative. I had a range of talented people to work with, and I was able to work within a community with a strong sense of its democratic tradition, so I felt well supported by most of my colleagues.

However, as a senior woman, the university was an odd place to be—at one stage, I was the only woman at my level, despite a strong will on behalf of the university to change this. I am still on Senate, not least because I want women to be visible, but I am one of only a handful of women in a sea of a hundred men. However, times are changing—I am no longer looked at to raise and respond to all gender issues. Men will sometimes deal with these without prompting, although on the whole, they seem less prepared to raise class and race issues.

Invisible Colleges

While all these developments were happening back at base, another part of my life was developing nationally. In 1982, it was suggested that I go to my first SCUTREA (Standing Conference on University Teaching and Research in the Education of Adults) conference. This was an uncomfortable but interesting experience in which the women's group rebelled against the structure and ethos of the conference. Nod Miller (an interesting person with blue stars stuck around her eyes) and I were nominated to launch the attack at the final plenary. The organisation responded badly at first, but by 1984, I had been asked to become Honorary Secretary. In the same year, the Kellogg Foundation very kindly funded the first of a series of transatlantic exchanges in which those new to the profession of adult education were to visit each other (thanks to the efforts of people like Phyllis Cunningham and Gerald Normie). I made my first trip to the USA along with eight other British colleagues and encountered my first North American conference – AAACE at Louisville Kentucky; the impressions of that conference and that experience could form the basis for entirely another paper but I have two lasting impressions: every time anyone mentioned Marx, a sharp intake of breath could be heard, and Reagan won the election to the misery of some – but only some – of those attending the conference.

I was fortunate enough to be placed for a week with Ron Cervero (one of the original exchange participants) and Phyllis Cunningham at Northern Illinois University. I was given a range of anthropological experiences including the opportunity to sit in on a women's studies course at one of the universities in Chicago and it was here that I became aware of a particular form of political correctness (I do not think the term was in use at that time) which shocked me: the class spoke of "spousal abuse," by which they meant abuse of women. This confirmed an ongoing discomfort I'd had on my visit—on the one hand, a clear and overt acknowledgement of gender issues and, on the other, a strange depoliticisation that seemed to go with this.

I returned again to the U.S. the following year with another six colleagues in the second round of visits, only this time as an officer of SCUTREA. The result of those two exchanges was to transform a number of people's lives in the UK, at least (Miller & Zukas, 1995). The two dozen or so people involved over the two years in the Kellogg Exchanges decided that a joint SCUTREA/AERC conference was the way to go, and in 1988, together with CASAE, we held our first joint conference in Leeds – the Transatlantic Dialogue. Some 200 people from all over the world (many supported by the Kellogg Foundation) came together to talk about adult education research; the so-called "telephone directory" or proceedings still sit proudly on my shelf at work (Zukas, 1988). Through the conference planning group in the UK, I formed some of my closest collegial relationships both here and in North America. Another joint conference will be held in Leeds this year, nearly twenty years later, with some (but by no means all) of the original group.

In terms of my own work, over the years I have shifted more and more away from psychology. During the 1990s, together with Janice Malcolm, my research began to focus on teachers' identities (Malcolm & Zukas, 2001). In 2003, I became the director of the Lifelong Learning Institute at the University of Leeds, which focuses on bringing together practitioners, policy makers and researchers concerned with lifelong learning across the university and the region. But it has also been a time of great pain. My school was reviewed by the university for more than three years and finally abolished in 2005, like so many other units of adult education. Together with some of my colleagues and with the Institute, I was transferred to the School of Education where I am learning that history and culture cannot be changed overnight. Although I had spent the last eight years or so working with Janice to bring together ideas from adult education with further and higher education, and drawing increasingly on theoretical ideas which had their origins in initial education, my practice (except for occasional forays into psychology) has always focused on those who teach adults and/or who are themselves adults, so I find the school focus of my current department bemusing and culturally sometimes unintelligible. But I am learning.

I still have many connections with my invisible college. For example, I was fortunate enough to become editor of the journal *Studies in the Education of Adults* in 2004, a challenging and invigorating role which keeps me in touch with a wide range of colleagues across the world. Our challenge at the moment is how to break what some of the Europeans call the Anglo-axis (the domination of North America, Britain and Australia) within the journal.

As I review this brief autobiography, I see the same themes emerge: identity (recent events have confirmed me in my decision to become British), feminism, a commitment to adults and their entitlement to a challenging and critical higher education, collegiality, and an ongoing struggle – as so many of us have – to have a meaningful life outside work (which I do, thanks to my partner) and to keep work in perspective.

References

Malcolm, J., & Zukas, M. (2001). From here to pedagogic identity: A tale of two journeys. In L. West, N. Miller, D. O'Reilly, R. Allen (eds.), *Travellers' tales: from adult education to lifelong learning ... and beyond.* (pp. 253-256). University of East London: SCUTREA.

Miller, N., & Zukas, M. (1995). Exchanging places, trading learning: The impact of cross-cultural visiting in personal and professional development. In I. Bryant, (ed.), *Vision, invention, intervention: Celebrating adult education.* (pp. 135-139). Proceedings of the 25th Annual SCUTREA Conference. Winchester: University of Southampton.

Macmillan, H. & F. Shapiro. (1999). *Zion in Africa: The Jews of Zambia.* London: I. B. Taurus.

Zukas, M., ed. (1998). Transatlantic dialogue: A research exchange. *Proceedings of the joint SCUTREA/AERC/CASAE conference.* (p. 514). Leeds: University of Leeds.

Zukas, S. (2002). Into exile and back. Lusaka: Bookworld.

Postscript
Lee W. Nabb

Giving an account of how one comes to a life's service in adult education in such a limited space is a tough assignment. Everyone has at least one book to write, and all of the educators included in this compilation could undoubtedly write lengthy autobiographies to flesh out and expand upon what they have shared here. Our dedicatee, Dr. Phyllis M. Cunningham, is an appropriate example to illustrate this point. After reading her piece for this experiment, the editors couldn't help but take advantage of our relationship with her to talk with her over lunch about some of the many questions raised in our minds.

We asked Phyllis what drove her, what gave her hope and purpose as she went about the business of effecting social change. She answered:

> I have always believed that universities should be open to communities. I think that there should be the idea that communities should be part of the university, and...the idea that everybody has the capacity to make knowledge, and that knowledge production is not simply a university function. ...[T]he kind of knowledge [universities] produce is oftentimes knowledge that is...rarified and perhaps out of touch. ...[I]t's very important to keep in touch with your people. ...there is an everyday reality and you need to be in touch with that reality. So...it's important for people in the university to be in touch with the community because if you forget that you also limit yourself.

We asked whether she fully understood what her work for social change meant at the time it was taking place, a question which led Phyllis into a discussion about her time with the International Council for Adult Education (ICAE) and its effects that covered different, more personal ground than that in her autobiography. She explained:

> I was probably not as aware there [at ICAE]...until I got into it a little bit more, and I think my own consciousness was beginning to become more critical. ...So my time at International Council was a chance at becoming more aware. When you go to places like Africa or...Thailand or India...you get pretty aware of what's going on outside the United States. ...When I got back from places like that, I really started saying to students, "You should go abroad...basically to the south...to places where they don't speak English

and where you would feel more of a disconnect from your culture than [you would going to] someplace like…Canada or England. …" So I really encourage faculty and students…[to travel abroad] because it really jolts you, gets you to see the differences of what it's like…not to experience all the privileges one has of being in America.

Phyllis also explained in more detail the "less conscious…religious experience" mentioned in her autobiography that prompted her to choose a tour with the Pioneer Girls (at a significantly lower salary) over a job directing a hospital:

> At the time…I became a Christian. So being a Christian, I started doing a lot of different kinds of things that I hadn't been doing before and Pioneer Girls was a part of that. …[I]t's a matter of developing a certain service mentality…the choice that I was making was this: do you go on with a career, or do you stop out for a couple of years and do some service? So I made the choice to stop out for a couple years and do some service. …I maybe was about 26 at the time…you weren't doing it for the money. That wasn't the point…money wasn't the issue at all.

As a final piece of evidence that the personal stories in this collection are mere sketches or skeletal outlines of incredibly rich lives of service and accomplishment, Phyllis added more color and texture to her account of the Urban Life Center:

> [T]he Urban Life Center was a very significant engagement…a place for college kids to come and develop their own life view of the world. …That was a very exciting experiment. ….Kids on campus who were not getting along because…of their political views or…lifestyles…would come into the Urban Life Center and then suddenly their views were really quite conservative. … They were with people who didn't think that they were that odd at all…and so now they had space and they had to really think through their views…what their Christianity's all about. …[N]obody told them, "This is what you have to think." [Instead they had to ask,] "What is it I think?" and they're at a formative period. …[I]t's very exciting what happens to kids at that age…and they're in a situation where they have to think for themselves and…get along with each other.

In her autobiography, Phyllis mentions learning the "difficulty of establishing a nongovernmental organization . . . that would create permanent space in civil society." This brief comment, made almost in passing, severely understates the investments of time, energy, and sacrifice she made to develop the program and make it successful. The following description sheds some light on this point:

> [The Urban Life Center] was put together by five of us who were graduate students and some people in Chicago. As I say, it's very hard to put a [nongovernmental organization] together and make it work. That one is still operating and that was dedicated in 1970. It's in its 36th year now. I think it's a little more career oriented now than when we were in it. …What we knew was this: we knew that White people were the problem…not Blacks. So we decided to work on the White people. So that's how we did it. As I say, there were about

six or seven of us, and none of us had any money. I bought the house [after running the program in a rented church]. I was the one who had the most money, and as I said, I had just been turned down for a credit card from Sears. But I was also graduating, so as soon as I graduated Sears gave me the credit card and I was able to buy the house. …Hyde Park Bank was trying to get religion and sell to women…that was at a time when a woman couldn't have a credit card if she was married to a man…you have to remember these times. …I had to borrow the money from my father to put for the down payment.

When asked if this transaction was scary, Phyllis emphatically indicated it was not: "I was still young and foolish at 40," she said. "Anyway…I had just started working for City Colleges, I was making $18,000 a year then."

As one can see by Phyllis's example, the autobiographies contained in this book are only the beginning, the tip of the iceberg, the hint of greater things. We hope this experiment will spark new conversations and new perspectives on research and history, at least in the field of adult education. As these things take hold, we expect that more adult educators will be encouraged to share the tips of their icebergs in future editions of this collection, thus keeping the great personal conversations alive. We thank all who have contributed to this book and encourage their further introspection on how their lives have affected, and continue to affect, adult education and vice versa. As for Phyllis Cunningham, the person who was gracious enough to lend this project her name, we understand that her full autobiography is forthcoming. We await it anxiously.